Rewilding

A compilation of writing from the journal
ECOS on wildland issues, projects and
species re-introductions

Edited by
Peter Taylor

for
The British Association of
Nature Conservationists

published by
Ethos

First published by Ethos in the UK in 2011.

This book was sponsored by the Wildland Network an informal group of individuals dedicated to communicating the issues and practice of rewilding in the UK. Proceeds from sales will go toward the work of BANC and Ethos.

ISBN: 0-9547064-2-0

Ethos Publications
Windmill Farm
Walton Hill
Somerset
BA16 9RD

Cover design by Ethos.
Front cover image: Mark Hamblin/Northshots
Back cover images: Hunter with Lynx, Peter Cairns/Northshots; Glen Affric, Peter Taylor/Ethos
A catalogue record of this book is available from the British Library.

Printed on demand in Milton Keynes by Lightning Source. This company has received Chain of Custody (CoC) certification from: the Forest Stewardship Council (FSC); Programme for the Endorsement of Forest Certification (PEFC) and the Sustainable Forest Initiative (FSI).

The Wildland Network has sponsored this compilation in association with:

BANC

The British Association of Nature Conservationists whose members have pioneered *rewilding* through networking and the publication of articles in their journal ECOS.
www.banc.org.uk

&

ethos

a communications and publishing consultancy specialising in sustainable landscapes, community and biodiversity.

CONTENTS

Introduction and history of the Wildland Network

Part 1: Issues

Part 11: Projects

Part III: Species

PART I

Issues and definitions

Towards a wildland strategy

Connectivity and networks

Scary or what?

Rewilding the human

PART II

Projects

Scotland

Wales

Holland

PART III

Species

Beaver

Boar

Wolf

Lynx

Bear

Feral Big Cats

Water Vole

Big Birds

Authors and Contacts

*Editor's Notes: As in all ECOS articles, the views expressed by the authors do not necessarily represent the views of their organisations. I have updated addresses and affiliations but an * marks contacts that may be out-of-date.*

Philip Ashmole is volunteer Co-ordinator of the Carrifran Wildwood project. Philip.myrtle@ashmole.org.uk

Troy Bennett has studied wolves in France, Romania, Poland and Portugal, including tracking, radio telemetry, prey and scat analysis, kill-site analysis, and territory mapping. He gives seminars and on the wolf and its prey species. loopdeloup@hotmail.co.uk

David Blake is the Project Development Officer for the Cranborne Chase and West Wiltshire Downs AONB. dave.blake22@btinternet.com

Urs Breitenmoser is project leader at the KORA carnivore project based in Switzerland see: www.kora.ch

Gareth Browning is an Area Forester and Wild Ennerdale Partner based with the Forestry Commission gareth.browning@forestry.gsi.gov.uk

Peter Cairns is a freelance nature photographer based in northern Scotland specialising in human-wildlife interactions and land-use issues. He is also the founder of several conservation media projects such as Tooth & Claw and more recently, 2020VISION. info@northshots.com

Steve Carver lectures at the Department of Geography, Unversity of Leeds, is a founder member of the wildland-netowrk and is director of the Wildland Research Institute www.wildlandresearch.org s.j.carver@leeds.ac.uk

Hugh Chalmers is Carrifran Wildwood Project Officer and Site Manager for Borders Forest Trust. www.carrifran.org.uk

Ciro Castellucci is president of the Gruppo Ecologico Apennino Centrale. He has been studying and promoting the conservation of the Apennine brown bear for more than 20 years. He is a founder and honorary member of the Italian Wilderness Association. *see* http://www.geacitalia.it/chisono.asp

Alister Clunas is property manager at National Trust for Scotland's Mar Lodge estate   marlodgeestate@nts.org.uk

Adrian Colston is now general manager for the The National Trust on Dartmoor adrian.colston@nationaltrust.org.uk &   www.wicken.org.uk

Luke Comins is director of the Tweed Forum. luke@tweedforum.org

Howard Cooper is the Wicken Fen press officer, www.wicken.org.uk

Alasdair Dawes is Project Officer for the Great Bustard Group, see www.greatbustard.org

Samantha Ellis is a playwright. Her play about wolves, now retitled *The Last Wolf in Scotland,* had an amateur premiere at Stage@Leeds, and will premiere professionally at the Edinburgh Fringe in 2012. She blogs at http://samanthaellisblog.blogspot.com/

James Fenton was formerly the National Trust for Scotland's nature conservation advisor for the Highlands and worked for Scottish Natural Heritage. He is now a freelance consultant at info@james-hc-fenton.eu

Alan Watson Featherstone is Executive Director of Trees for Life. www.treesforlife.org.uk

Mark Fisher runs *Self Willed Land* mark.fisher@self-willed-land.org.uk

Martin Goulding is an independent wild boar consultant (www.wildboarconsultancy.org.uk) who has been involved with Britain's free-living wild boar since they became established in the 1990s.. Martin authors the website: www.britishwildboar.org.uk

Derek Gow is a consultant ecologist. He specialises in mammal reintroductions, water voles, and beavers. DerekJGow@aol.com

Adam Griffin is co-founder and trustee of Moor Trees, www.moortrees.org and is now a consultant at www.adamgriffinconsultancy.co.uk

John Hall is Director of the Essex Wildlife Trust.

Neil Harris is Land Management and Conservation Advisor with Natural England's South West Region. neil.harris@naturalengland.gov.uk

David Hetherington completed a PhD at the University of Aberdeen on the feasibility of reintroducing the Eurasian lynx to Scotland. He now works as Ecology Advisor for the Cairngorms National Park Authority. davidhetherington@cairngorms.co.uk

Peter Holden is senior ranger at the National Trust's Mar Lodge estate marlodgeestate@nts.org.uk

Rebecca Isted is now policy and programmes officer - biodiversity, with the Forestry Commission in Bristol. Rebecca.isted@forestry.gsi.gov.uk

Michael Jeeves is Head of Conservation with the Leicestershire and Rutland Wildlife Trust. mjeeves@lrwt.org.uk

Keith Kirby is Forestry and Woodlands Officer (Evidence Team) with Natural England. keith.kirby@naturalengland.gov.uk

Gersa Kluth * is a member of *Lupus Wildlife Consultancy* http://www.lcie.org/Docs/Regions/GermanyBohem/WolvesOnOurDoorsteps_en .pdf

Andy May is Conservation Manager at Essex Wildlife Trust. AndyM@essexwt.org.uk

Jonathan McGowan runs the zoological section at the Bournemouth Natural History Society and is a freelance naturalist, taxidermist and author *jrmczoo@tiscali.co.uk*

Richard Neale is the National Trust's Property Manager covering Snowdonia and Llyn in North West Wales. richard.neale@nationaltrust.org.uk

Matthew Oates is Advisor on Nature Conservation at the National Trust. He is a founder member of both the Grazing Animals Project and VINE - Values in Nature and the Environment matthew.oates@nationaltrust.org.uk

Roger Panaman * promotes wolf reintroduction in the Highlands. Read more about reintroducing wolves at www.wolftrust.org.uk

Alison Parfitt is a freelance consultant on landscape and community and a founder member of the wildland-network.

Hannah Pearce is a freelance journalist and communications consultant who has written extensively on the environmental policy and news agenda. zintl@gn.apc.org

Dan Puplett worked for Trees for Life for over 10 years. He now works as a freelance outdoor educator, teaching a range of skills including animal tracking, natural history and bushcraft. dan.puplett@gmail.com

Jules Pretty OBE is Pro Vice Chancellor (Sustainability and Resources) and Professor of Environment and Society, University of Essex. jpretty@essex.ac.uk and www.julespretty.com

Geog Rauer * is with the, World Wide Fund for Nature Austria, Ottakringerstraße 114-116, A-1160 Wien, Austria

Ilka Reinhardt * is a member of *Lupus Wildlife Consultancy*

Heather Robertson recently retired from Natural England and now works in orchard conservation.

Peter Samson is with the North Pennines AONB, Co. Durham, DL13 2FJ

Gavin Saunders is project manager for the Neroche Scheme and a freelance conservation policy and project advisor.   gavin.saunders@forestry.gsi.gov.uk

Roger Sidaway is an independent consultant and lecturer. His book Resolving Environmental Disputes was published by Earthscan in 2005. roger@rogersidaway.plus.com

Chris Soans is now the Property Manager at Wicken Fen - he can be contacted on   chris.soans@nationaltrust.org.uk

Peter Taylor heads the environmental consultancy Ethos. He is a founder member of the wildland-network and author of *Beyond Conservation* (Earthscan)   peter.taylor@ethos-uk.com

Manuela von Aux is with the KORA project, based in Switzerland. www.kora.ch

Victoria Ward * was formerly at the Department of Geography, University of Leeds, where she helped produce the wildland-network.org data base.

Stuart Warrington is Regional Wildlife and Countryside Advisor at the National Trust, East of England Region stuart.warrington@nationaltrust.org.uk

Tony Whitbread is chief executive of Sussex Wildlife Trust tony.whitbread@sussexwt.org.uk

Charles Wilson * was Senior Wildlife Management Adviser in the Rural Development Service (later incorporated into Natural England) dealing with wildlife legislation and the resolution of human-wildlife conflicts.

Derek Yalden is President of the Mammal Society, and has recently retired after 40 years as Reader in Vertebrate Zoology from Manchester University.

Rachel Yanik (now Oakley) is the Wild Ennerdale Project Officer based with the National Trust. rachel.oakley@nationaltrust.org.uk

Additional contacts mentioned in the text: **Simon Ayres** is director of the Wales Wild Land Foundation and a founding member of the Wildland Network, simon@forestmoor.com; **Toby Aykroyd** organises the Wild Europe initiative -www.wildeurope.org and see also www.rewildingeurope.com; **Rick Minter** edits ECOS, is a freelance facilitator and is also a founding member of the Wildland Network; **Robert McMorran** edits the newsletter of the Scottish Wildland Group http://www.swlg.org.uk/

Special thanks for photographic material are due because ECOS does not keep the original illustrations and we have had to ask for authors and organisations to help with originals or other suitable photos: to Keith Kirby of Natural England; Chris Robbins and Carl McKie of Derek Gow Consultancy ; and Peter Cairns and Mark Hamblin of Northshots; Charlie Burrell at Knepp; Adrian Colston and Stuart Warrington for the National Trust at Wicken Fen; Adam Griffin for Dartmoor tree planting; Gavin Saunders for Neroche; John Wright of Leicester & Rutland Wildlife Trust; Luke Comins for the Tweed Forum; Gareth Browning for Ennerdale; Andy May at Essex Wildlife Trust for Abbott's Farm; Rich Howorth at Sussex Wildlife Trust for the Weald projects; Joe Cornish for Snowdon; Alan Featherstone of Trees for Life; Hans Kampf for Dutch photos of Heck cattle; Fridolin Zimmermann of KORA and www.luchsprojekt-harz.de for lynx photos; Lupus Consultancy for wolf tracks; the Great Bustard Project for bustard photos; the Great Crane project for Somerset's cranes; and the RSPB for images of goshawk and kite.

Introduction

There is a wealth of information and experience among wildland projects. much of which is recorded but dispersed in ECOS articles and in the notes and proceedings of Wildland Network meetings. This volume meets the growing need for a single source for this and related rewilding material for students, journalists and writers. WN felt it important to have a source book that reflects the very special work in Britain compared to the large scale projects and planning in the US and the special circumstances of continental Europe.

There has been a 'rewilding' movement in Britain since at least the mid-1980s (thinking in particular of the Trees for Life project in Glen Affric) but it has received far less publicity than American schemes. This rewilding has emerged from our own roots and circumstances, with a philosophy appropriate to a crowded island, rather than on a continental scale. The US dictum, 'cores, corridors and carnivores' has relevance, but we are some way from bringing back large carnivores - at least deliberately, whereas cores and corridors have been central to conservation thinking in Britain for several decades.

As this text has come together, one thing has struck me forcibly – the great range of topics and individuals, organisations and strategies involved, representing a formidable amount of work – truly a 'new wave' in nature conservation thinking. But perhaps *most* impressive of all is the range of on-the-ground projects with their histories. This is not a revolution of thinking alone, but a quiet practical unfolding of new and more creative ways of extending reserves and managing land

In this, the role of WN has been simply to network thinking and practical experience. Since its inception in May 2005, we have brought a very large array of people together from every major conservation organisation in Britain. I can recall a time when ecologists within government agencies in England knew very little of the pioneering work of Trees for Life in Scotland, or the significance of the Ennerdale project and its cooperative model engagement between major land-owning bodies such as the National Trust and Forestry Commission.

At the outset, a small number of people meeting as the 'wildland group' decided that a network structure would best facilitate what was effectively already under way. Our task would be to facilitate dialogue, mutual learning and opportunities to see things from other points of view in a 'neutral' space. Such a non-membership structure has the limitation that it cannot so readily lobby or campaign and this concerned some of us, but that limitation more readily supported a wider participation, with no one organisation or individual needing to fear being compromised by campaigns and press statements – whether calling for the re-introduction of carnivores or opposing wind turbines in wild and beautiful places.

We also did not get embroiled in academic issues of definitions – it was wilder to have none! Though the pages of ECOS did rehearse the issues, there was a wide church and we accepted that any practice that made things 'wilder' was relevant, and thus although there was always a core interest concerned with large-scale land management and restoration of ecosystems. our interests stretched to smaller scale rewilding of river systems and urban areas.

As editor of this volume, I have focused on issues, projects, and candidate species for re-introduction. The book is therefore in three parts, with an introductory history of the Network itself. This latter brief review covers eleven meetings and issue-based seminars in England, Scotland and Wales between 2004 and 2009 – the first being preparation for the launch of the Network in 2005 and the last being the launch of the Wildland Research Institute (WRi) in October 2009, after which the Network felt that its primary work was done. This historical section constitutes, among other things, a guide to activism that I hope students of conservation will study in itself, because conservation – much as I would personally like to replace a term that embodies conservatism, if it is to advance, *requires* active engagement in policy. Such engagement takes many forms: it requires hours of dedicated and dull work setting up meetings, booking venues, organising speakers, food and accommodation, controlling expenses and then writing it all up and disseminating the results. In this, I have been fortunate to work with some extra-ordinary individuals in the core-group who do not feature large in the writing of articles – the ECOS editor Rick Minter, alongside Alison Parfitt, have been stalwart organisers and facilitators, with Alison taking on a huge amount of work in the write-ups; Mark Fisher has held the website together; on a regional level, Simon Ayres and Mick Green have networked in Wales and Dan Puplett and Alan Watson Featherstone in Scotland; Toby Aykroyd has taken the message into the upper echelons of European bureaucracy under the Wild Europe initiative; and in the later years, Steve Carver with the help of Mark Fisher brought together the academic element as the Wildland Research Institute at Leeds University, just four years after we had our launch there.

In any appraisal of the schemes over the past twenty years, students should note above all that change has come through the actions of key individuals – champions *on the ground* and in their own community. David Russell, head forester with the National Trust, was hugely influential in pioneering a more 'hands off' approach to large areas under the Trust's management; Gareth Browning, beat forester in the western Lake District, took on the task of maintaining the Ennerdale vision. Keith Kirby at Natural England (and all its predecessors!) engaged with the many facets of this growing public desire for rewilding. Respected academics such as Jules Pretty at Essex University and

Adrian Phillips at Cardiff University have chaired meetings that have helped raise an ill-defined movement toward respectability in the corridors of government. Simon Ayres, a forestry consultant, organised meetings in Wales and latterly founded the Wales Wild Land Foundation and the Cambrian Wildwood Project. Progress in Wales has been slow and as with any shift in an old paradigm, movers and shakers face a lot of inertia.

At the start of 2011, members of the WN founding and coordinating group still network. However, they have realised that their earlier aspirations to raise awareness, bring people together to share and develop learning and experience have in large measure been achieved. Therefore a new phase of wilding and developing wildland is now needed. At this stage it is worthwhile to reflect on things that are missing from the picture or early aims that have not manifested. We had hoped to have had more detailed maps of potential wildland, 'opportunity mapping' of landscape scale projects and habitat restoration, corridors, barriers and conflicts (such as renewable energy developments). There are at present several such maps 'on paper' within organisations such as the Wildlife Trusts and the RSPB, but still no overall national picture or point of contact. This is work that WRi would be able to co-ordinate.

We had hoped to have seen greater levels of cooperation between the larger voluntary bodies such as the National Trust, Forestry Commission, the Woodland Trust, Wildlife Trusts and RSPB in creating core-areas and corridors – in particular through the strategic purchase of land. However, none of these organisations is entirely free to embrace the wildland ethos even as a subset of its broader strategic aims. Some of us would like to see a new organisation that would take on this task – of mapping the potential and then marshalling resources for strategic purchase. Just 10% of the income stream from the major voluntary bodies would exceed £20million/annum and there would be a good chance that government or lottery funds would match that investment.

In the immediate somewhat austere future, the Heritage Lottery Fund has an undiminished amount available and an enthusiasm for landscape scale projects - witness Neroche and the Great Fen project, but with that source also comes the need for access, interpretation and maintenance of a cultural heritage that does not readily embrace rewilding. I would still argue as I did in the book *Beyond Conservation* for three flagship core-area rewilding schemes in England, Scotland and Wales. And I note, that, as then, we know very little of developments in Northern Ireland and the Irish Republic.

There is also still much to be learned about European and US projects. In this volume we have pulled together a good few articles on the Dutch experience, which has great relevance for crowded, largely urban environments, and also on species re-introductions in Europe that may have lessons for Britain, but there is much more to document. Given the pace of development unleashed by the EU's intended remedies for climate change – turbines, barrages, biofuel plantations and hydro-schemes, with their attendant roads and pylons and all in wild places, we need to know much more about what is happening in Eastern Europe, Greece, Spain and Portugal.

We also need to know more about prospective changes to the EU's agricultural support schemes. They are currently being revamped and although many organisations are involved in lobbying, including Toby Aykroyd's 'Wild Europe' initiative, it is difficult to get any sense of how successful this process may be. There is an excellent website - www.rewildingeurope.com which features regional initiatives in Spain, the Carpathians, Croatia, and the Danube delta, all of which aim to bring wild grazers to open landscapes threatened by abandonment (see also www.largeherbivore.org).

Finally, there is a sense – expressed recently among BANC council, that with the 'new austerity' and the shifts in consciousness that go with it, that the constituency of conservation is also likely to shift. We are seeing a growing involvement of the health and education sector in wildland issues as well as in 'nature' generally. There is a public hunger for closer contact with wild nature – contact that has spiritual and therapeutic motives that are not necessarily met by the strictly scientific criteria and targets applied to key habitats (see the articles by David Russell, Samantha Ellis and Hannah Pearce).

The 'issues' we have covered in Part 1 are diverse: the nature and role of 'aliens' such as grand old Douglas Fir, Norway and Sitka Spruce...which the public have grown to love; grey squirrels; feral boar and big cats; preparing for climate change; the 'common' and popular (such as elder/blackthorn scrub) versus the rare and largely unknown (such as Large Blue butterflies). Indeed, love itself is gradually daring to speak its name as conservationists come out from behind their analyses of ecosystem benefits and EU Habitats Directives, and start to celebrate this broader world of public perception and desire. Wild nature still offers succour to the jaded souls of a crowded land and a competitive world and in this, the future constituency for rewilding is very large.

ECOS has always encouraged writing at the interface of conservation science, public policy and public perception, without necessarily elevating science above the world of appreciation and feeling. However, the more clearly poetic and artistic does not feature large and rewilding has a lot more to offer than traditional conservation practice in this respect. I would personally like to see more of a marriage in our work between the left and right hemispheres of the brain as evident in our gathering at Findhorn and in the *Forest Schools* approach at Neroche.

In Part II we present an amazing variety of projects. One of the great services that BANC and in particular Rick Minter has performed is the pulling together and presentation of this work in ECOS and in the commissioning of *Beyond Conservation*. I never fail to be impressed by the diversity of approaches – from private landowners such as Charlie Burrell at Knepp, who has little interest in a commercial project, compared with Paul Lister in Alladale, who envisions a touristic safari-park; to collaboration of large organisations like the Forestry Commission, National Trust and United Utilities in Ennerdale – all land-owners, some with tenant farmers, or the collective purchase by subscription of marginal grazing land in the Southern Uplands, by the Carrifran initiative and the Borders Forest Trust. Organisations such as the RSPB are engaged in large scale habitat restoration – such as reedbed and fenland as well as coastal marshes, and we could have liaised more in the past to pull this together and showcase it here, as also with the Wildlife Trusts' regional initiatives. The role of government agencies and funders in relation to all of these projects would also make an interesting research topic as it is clear that Natural England and the Forestry Commission have worked to bend the rules that presently favour the old paradigm of domestic grazing. The Heritage Lottery Fund is becoming a key funding source and we should know more of it values and modes of decision making.

On species reintroductions, reviewed in Part III, there are more problematic issues to report. At the time of writing, Scottish Natural Heritage look to have actioned a capture and eradication scheme for escaped beaver on the Tay, whilst supporting a pilot but well-contained release project in Knapdale. We document the mixed reception that escaped wild boar have had and the dilemma that Whitehall faces. Government is still in (public) denial about the existence and possible breeding of feral big cats in Britain, despite mounting evidence and an admission from the Forestry Commission in the Forest of Dean that they have monitored panthers as well as wild boar in their woods. Several police forces accept the presence of the cats. I am still waiting for my first personal sighting (an impressive video of a distant running black panther was taken only a week ago in Westernzoyland, only a few miles away!), but donning my zoologist's hat, I have examined undoubted big cat kills in Wales – and many trusted friends have seen both black 'panther' and puma. There are many reports of lynx in mainland Britain.

We are thus faced with ongoing 'rewilding' as much by accident as design and a rather confused government response. Much is made by scientists of provenance and genetics – which a public admiring charismatic animals cares little about, and this surfaced with 'escaped' eagle owls breeding in Northumberland. Even the RSPB were unenthusiastic about this powerful predator. That ultimate symbol of the wild – the wolf, would be well received by large sections of the public, but governments respond to entrenched and often ignorant and irrational attitudes from both the farming and game-shooting communities, despite evidence that wolves in Europe and the US do not compromise the economic well-being of rural communities and may bring much-needed visitor revenue. If we ever get to an introduction of bears in Scotland, we will know not only that attitudes have fully revolved, but also that habitats have been extensively restored to support them.

And finally, from a privileged position of having either worked with or met many of the people engaged in this movement and featured in this book, I know that the rewilding process is very much a matter of the heart. In this, science takes its rightful place as a tool-kit. We are not here just to study or conserve nature, but to transform it! We are thus working as co-creators. Yet, nature reserves were set up very largely as laboratories for scientific study – representatives of ecosystems and habitats and assemblages of species in areas of *special scientific interest*. Only later, with the large scale transformation of agriculture and road transport, did they become islands besieged. They were not designed for this purpose. There is a need for larger scale reserves, corridors, core areas and re-introductions of species that in themselves transform and sustain habitats – such as beaver, wild grazers and their predators. We are perhaps one-fifth of the way forward on the ground, and perhaps as much as half-way in the shifting of paradigms.

Peter Taylor
May 2011

Development of a Wildland Strategy: a short history.

The concepts and practices of rewilding did not start with the Wildland Network, of course, but antecedents are not well traced. Certainly, the full rewilding ethos was articulated in the mid-1980s by Alan Watson Featherstone and the Trees For Life group which he founded at Findhorn. They pioneered the long process of looking for potential large areas, talking to landowners and managers, and getting volunteers on the ground – in this case to restore tree cover to the Scottish glens. TfL also mastered outreach and communication and was rewarded after more than twenty years of hard work in the field, by donations sufficient to buy their own land and build toward a core area.

By the turn of the Millennium there were many initiatives seeking funding for large area schemes – the Borders Forest Trust being notable, with a strategy for direct fund-raising and shares in the scheme at Carrifran. The National Trust and Forestry Commission were already mapping out the Wild Ennerdale Project. This work had built upon several initiatives of the 1990s – the National Trust Centennial Conference in 1995 at which 'wildland and wilderness' ethos was first discussed; BANC's Wilderness Britain conference at the Open University in that same year; a major conference at Newcastle University in 1999 on rewilding the National Parks; and the ESRC funded Seminar Series 1999-2001 on *Wilderness Britain: social and environmental perspectives on recreation and conservation* which were attended by government and NGO practitioners.

Thus, as the first meetings of the 'wildland group' began to form a network - finalised in the autumn of 2004, for a launch in May 2005 at Leeds, there was already plenty to network. In September 2004, the core-group met at Alison Parfitt's home in Hatherley Road, Cheltenham:

- Adam Griffin and Chris Layton travelled up from Dartmoor and introduced Moor Trees – the project inspired by Trees for Life and active on Dartmoor since 1997, with a major conference in 1999. It was a small start with tree nurseries, educational outreach and mobilisation of volunteers in what was a huge challenge to prevail against current land-use interests that kept the moor entirely barren and prevented the National Park from investing in wider restoration.

- Toby Aykroyd presented plans for a Wild Britain initiative that focused on economic benefits and outlined his busy schedule of meetings with directors of government and voluntary bodies in seeking a coalition – something that precipitated much discussion of the value of such top-down approaches compared to the grass roots initiatives. He also outlined plans to create coalitions in Europe.

- We had a student – Peter Parkes, join us, who was engaged upon writing a thesis on wilding projects at Nottingham University – a sure sign that the new thinking had penetrated academia and a good example for us of the value of the network, in that we could direct him to practical projects that otherwise he may have missed.

- Simon Ayres had come over from West Wales where he was championing the involvement of Wildlife Trusts and (hopefully then) the John Muir Trust in a rewilding of the North Cambrians – an area faced with massive expansion of wind turbines.

- David Russell, then chief forestry advisor to the National Trust, led a discussion on issues of intervention, public relatedness to and growing commodification of nature, targets and over-management based on species action plans – and how we can negotiate through this mindset.

Alison Parfitt, Rick Minter and myself, with Steve Carver at Leeds, then formed a core group to organise a launch at Leeds in the following year – when we also would launch *Beyond Conservation* – a compilation of issues and projects that I had worked on with a commission from BANC over the previous two years. We realised from the diversity of views and values within our own group, that diversity itself was a strength! There was still some unease that we would focus on networking rather than campaigning – against for example, quarries, turbines, roads, pylons, or CAP reform, but my own argument was that networking did not rule out any individual or participating organisation from campaigning and that the network would in that respect support and facilitate such political work. Our main focus would be the restoration of landscape and habitat, species re-introduction and the human value of nature and wildness – we would network 'best practice' through regional seminars, national conferences and special editions of ECOS. I was to work on a Wildland Manifesto that would be published on the Ethos website.

Our focus for 2005 was to be a North West regional meeting in the Lake District as a follow-up to the launch at Leeds. Toby Aykroyd would organise a gathering at the Royal Geographical Society to host the Dutch specialists in rewilding the polders and a trip would be organised to Holland in the autumn.

The launch of the Wildland Network at Leeds University, May 2005.

Forty two people attended the launch, with participants from English Nature, The Grazing Animals Project, the Wildlife Trusts, the Countryside Agency,

BANC, John Muir Trust and National Trust. Steve Carver led the proceedings in which I introduced the book and its list of projects; Toby Aykroyd led a workshop on economics and land use; Steve Carver and Simon Bates (of Natural England) on the value of mapping, Rachel Yanik of the National Trust at Ennerdale took on an overview of projects and Derek Gow on re-introductions.

The publication of *Beyond Conservation: a wildland strategy* was delayed and copies were not available for the launch, but the book was published a month later. I was able to outline is contents – the first wider publication of the large range of projects as well as discussions of the major issues.

Visit to Oostvaadersplassen in the Netherlands

The Network organised a study-tour to the Dutch project on the polder of Oostvaadersplassen during May 2006. This 5000 ha reserve has been managed as wildland with the instigation of more natural grazing regimes using red deer, wild cattle (Heck – reconstituted Aurochsen) and wild horses (Konik from Poland). This was an opportunity to discuss issues arising in relation to natural processes of death, disease, and intervention policies with wild herbivores, vegetation dynamics, biodiversity indices, absence of predators, connectivity, etc., and the site visit and lessons are reviewed by Alison Parfitt and Steve Carver in Part II.

Regional seminar in the North-West: Newton Rigg, Cumbria, October 2005

Over fifty people attended this fist regional seminar with a wide range on involvement from government agencies, community groups, individuals and voluntary organisations.

There was a small Scottish contingent and Robert MacMorran an advisor to Scottish Natural Heritage outlined the *Wild Scotland* initiative (he was later to found the Scottish Wildland Group and newsletter). Peter Samson of the North Pennines Area of Outstanding Natural Beauty, outlined a range of projects in the north and with Gareth Browning of the Forestry Commission, led a discussion on flexibility within government grant schemes for supporting wilder grazing (at this stage, not Aurochsen, wild horses and more deer, but more cattle on the fells and in the woods!). James Fenton of the National Trust and Martin Lester from NT's Wicken Fen project outlined the problems of welfare and fencing of livestock – NT was using Polish *Konik* ponies at Wicken Fen.

We asked Charlie Burrell, a farmer and landowner in Sussex, to speak about his pioneering project to return cropland to wild grazing with Exmoor ponies, semi-wild breeds of pig and long-horn cattle. Thus, participants from the wilds of the Lake District and Scotland could hear of the successes in adapting single farm payments and the economics of farming on boulder clay. Toby Aykroyd, who had joined the management group at the Alladale wilderness-park project, was able to discuss fencing, access, welfare and attitudes to danger. Adam Griffin came up from Dartmoor and contributed to discussions with Hugh Chalmers of the Borders Forest Trust on community initiatives, fund raising and purchase of land.

In all, eight small working groups -facilitated (and later documented) by Rick Minter and Alison Parfitt, discussed the practical challenges of wilder grazing regimes, animal welfare, land acquisition, revenue, species re-introductions, show-casing benefits, landscape quality and resilience. After the seminar, there was a BANC AGM hosted by Wild Ennerdale and a guided tour of the Lakeland project the following day.

The *ECOS* volume 25 (3/4) *Wilder Landscapes, wilder lives?* was published in the autumn – which provided an update on the projects outlined in *Beyond Conservation* as well bringing more projects into a data base that was being built for a WN website to be hosted by Mark Fisher and Steve Carver in Leeds.

Rachel Oakley of Wild Ennerdale briefing the group, September 2005.

Wild herbivores at the Royal Geographic Society

Under an initiative of Toby Aykroyd, specialists from the Dutch ministries and the Large Herbivore Foundation (LHF) were invited to present their projects and experience at the RGS on October 26th, and this gave an opportunity for a wider public to appreciate the cooperation between Dutch ministries and voluntary bodies such as the Lottery Heritage Fund in advancing large scale rewilding.

'Wilder landscapes, wilder lives?'

This was the title of an issue of ECOS (Vol. 25. 3/4) in 2005 in which members of the Network outlined their projects to the general conservation community.

Wild Boar – welcome back? National Seminar on DEFRA consultation, December 2005.

The network organised a national seminar on the issue of feral wild boar, hosted jointly with BANC and held at *Nature in Art*, Wallsworth Hall, Gloucester. Rick Minter and Alison Parfitt facilitated discussions with Charlie Wilson, Senior Wildlife Advisor at DEFRA, which had put out a consultation document on the issue.

Briefings on issues of biology, provenance, behaviour, diseases, farming conflicts, access and safety as well as impacts on woodland management were made by Martin Goulding – author of *Wild Boar in Britain*, Derek Gow – consultant ecologists, Derek Booth and Ian Horrell of the British Wild Boar Association and Jenney Farrant, a farmer with regular experience of boar on her family farm.

Over fifty participants came from Wildlife Trusts and AONBs, farmers, landowners and marketers. The day was organised into three groups dealing with the diverse issues such as intrinsic value of the species to Britain and the complex costs and benefits of their impacts. (These issues are reviewed in detail under the Wild Boar section of Part III dealing with re-introduced species).

Wildland in Wales: regional seminar held April 7th, 2006, Plas Dolguog, Machynlleth.

This seminar was organised by Simon Ayres and followed two morning presentations by Steve Carver on mapping wildland and criteria for wildness, and Derek Gow on the issues of beaver re-introduction. It was a relatively small gathering that was not well supported by the Welsh government agencies – who had felt that 'rewilding' might be too forceful an approach in an area of strong tensions between the farming community and conservation organisations.

There was much discussion of what was 'wild' and 'natural' and how perceptions varied in the locality. Scale was a key factor in wildness – along with the absence of roads and light pollution. On beavers, various myths were laid to rest on precisely what beavers needed and what impacts they could have – for example, that in Europe they seldom built dams. The experience at Ham Fen, Kent was rehearsed, where prolonged DEFRA licensing requirements had caused beavers to die in quarantine and at the Lower Mill estate at the Cotswold Water Park, where containment by sophisticated electric fences had been a requirement for release. (Editor's note: the Welsh Wild Land Foundation has just received a lottery grant of £5000 to prepare a beaver introduction site in Cwm Einion, close to their planting project).

There followed discussions led by Jeremy Wright of Powys County Council, on the value of branding and 'gateway' species such as the red kite, that could aid in eco-tourism. He pointed out that local people were more globalised than might be expected from the indigenous stereotype and that many hill farms wer facing a bleak future of an ageing population, falling incomes and financial indebtedness. Wildland could offer a range of ecosystem services as well as more direct uses for health and educational programmes. There was an issue of how to conserve wildland values and at the same time promote their use – and the need for sensitive developments, such as bothies in barns, was emphasised. Wilder grazing regimes and organic meat production were earmarked as ways to integrate wildland values and support a faltering upland economy.

We heard that the Countryside Council for Wales was planning for large-scale landscape restoration projects – but sadly at the same time, the Welsh Assembly was planning to open the Forestry Commission holdings to wind farm development – the North Cambrians had been selected as a major search area. We decided to make a review of the wind issue with respect to the Nant y Moch search area (on Plymlimon) and to lobby against its inclusion in the turbine search areas (I was commissioned by WN to prepare the background on wind turbines for a submission to have Nat-y-Moch excluded from the search zone). The over-arching message of the seminar was that the tranquility and beauty of the Cambrians needed to be positively promoted and marketed as the best defence against invasive development.

We all felt that the agencies were behind the times and a later invitation for me to give a presentation at a gathering of the Welsh section of the Grazing Animals Project – which was proving a successful partnership between the agencies, Wildlife Trusts and farmers, showed that many had realised rewilding was an advancing practice and should not be ignored.

25

Bringing back the Beaver: a joint conference with the Cotswold Water Park Society and Derek Gow Consultancy, May, 2006.

The purpose of this Network meeting was to further the cause of beaver re-introduction in England. I recall that Alan Featherstone, Rick Minter and I had travelled to France in 1991 to explore r-introduction issues, and yet, fifteen years on, only the Scottish government was making moves toward introduction. Simon Pickering at the Water Park organised a register of interests (he has since moved but maintains his involvement - simon.pickering@ecotricity.co.uk).

During the meeting, a range of issues were addressed: such as, do beavers' activities at sites with public access present a health and safety issue? What are viable populations for beavers and what distances will beavers travel to access nearby cropland?

It was noted that the Environment Agency was interested in catchment scale re-introduction for England, as a trial, but it remained a challenge to get awareness and interest in beavers into mainstream professional thinking and practice. A recently launched Wetland Vision (a joint initiative with DEFRA and NGOs) was discussed as a vehicle for focusing a commitment on re-introduction – in particular whether a beaver trial would be able to illustrate the benefits for water management as well as any problems.

There was already ample evidence from overseas and beaver's role in water retention needed clarifying and promoting to policy makers and politicians. A key reference on this aspect is Frank Rosell, et. al. 'Ecological impacts of beavers and their ability to modify ecosystems'. *Mammal Review* 35 (3-4) July 2005.

Scottish Natural Heritage already had much information on the benefits and the effects of beavers which could be used by practitioners elsewhere in UK and it was agreed there was no point in duplicating the information and research already produced. Duncan Halley offered to show people beaver habitat and management issues in Trondheim, Norway:

The situation in Scotland was indicated as open for partnerships of relevant bodies to propose demonstration projects which would show the consequences of beaver activity in different situations. In the Cairngorms written and e-mail support for beaver reintroduction would help back the case for including this in the Cairngorms Management Plan.

In Wales, Toby Aykroyd reported there was ongoing consultation amongst all stakeholders in relation to beaver reintroduction and his 'Beavers Mean Business' initiative was trying to catalyse action and interest in relation to the benefits, including for tourism. There were varying views about timescales for action with a feeling among some 'we now need to get on with it', whereas others felt there should be more time to persuade and involve bodies so that they have a chance to be on board.

Scary or what? September 2006, Cirencester.

A meeting to discuss the re-introduction of species generally was held at an organic farm's small conference centre near Cirencester. It was a joint initiative of WN and BANC and chaired by Adrian Phillips of the University of Cardiff – who is also an IUCN commissioner. Seventy six people attended with wide representation from English nature, the National Trust, the Wildlife Trusts, DEFRA, the RSPB, the Countryside Council for Wales, the Welsh Assembly and the Council for the Protection of Rural England. Troy Bennet traveled from France to contribute to wolf discussions and Robin Rigg from Slovakia. Dan Puplett and Alan Featherstone came down from Scotland to contribute their perspectives on the potential at Glen Affric.

Presentations were made by Roy Dennis on the experience of 40 years of bird re-introductions, especially of sea eagles and kites; Derek Gow on the issues of beavers; David Hetherington on lynx; Martin Goulding on boar; Peter Taylor reviewed bear and wolf introduction programmes in Europe and the USA; and Matthew Oates and David Bullock of the National Trust reviewed experiences and opportunities with wild herbivores. Group discussions were facilitated by Rick Minter and Alison Parfitt.

Big cats in Britain.

Following the Cirencester meeting, a seminar to specifically address the issue of feral big cats in Britain was convened at Oak Hall, Keynes Country Park at the Cotswold Water Park on 10th September. Thirty seven people attended with Rick Minter convening what had become, for him, after his own personal sighting of a black panther in Cumbria, a special area of interest.

Rick Minter introduced Jonathan McGowan, of the Bournemouth Natural History Museum, who had spent over ten years tracking animals in Dorset and Wiltshire. He presented the mounting forensic evidence for breeding populations of melanistic leopard and puma. Chris Moiser, a zoo keeper and Frank Tunbridge, who had tracked and encountered animals in and near the Forest of Dean, gave presentations. Discussion groups then fed back to the plenary.

Jules Pretty OBE, Professor of Environment and Society at University of Essex, chaired the meeting and summed up proceedings. Evidence had mounted that viable populations of big cats existed and this was accepted by numerous police forces (and confirmed by a spokesperson for the Forestry Commission in 2009. ed.). If damage mounted and in particular, anyone were injured, there would likely be calls for an eradication programme. There was clear evidence of melanistic leopard (or jaguar), puma (possibly also melanistic forms) and lynx. WN should be prepared for the eventual 'outing' of the cats and present information of their potential benefits to the ecosystem – in particular upon deer numbers. Jonathan MacGowan had been convinced that predation on deer and badger had altered behaviour and browsing patterns. His work was published in ECOS and there is a section under species re-introductions.

Rewilding Middle England, 22 November, 2006 at Cropston Visitor Centre, Leicester Wildlife Trust.

This meeting was organised by Micheal Jeeves of Leicester Wildlife Trust and chaired by Jules Pretty. Sixty six people attended with discussions ranging across the nature of the 'black hole' for wildlife in the Midlands, to habitat restoration projects, with Chris Gerrard of the Great Fen Project reporting on this large scale reedbed and grazing marsh initiative. Sam Lathaway reported on the progress of the new National Forest and Ruth Needham on the Trent Project of rewilding the river. Kieth Kirby of Natural England, Andrew Halston of the Environment Agency and Jonathan Spencer of the Forestry Commission presented the outlook of government agencies. There was representation from managers of the Wildlife Trusts, the Grazing Animals Project, the National Forest and National Trust's Wicken fen.

Rick Minter and Alison Parfitt facilitated discussion groups and feedback on reintroductions, wild herbivores, Biodiversity Action Plans and 'ecosystem services', with Michael Jeeves and Peter Taylor summing up the day. An article by Michael Jeeves was published in ECOS and is represented in Part II.

Making wildland pay – a review of markets and enterprises from wild land and rewilding. A one-day workshop hosted by the Knepp Estate and WN in Sussex, 12 April 2007.

This event brought together practitioners with examples of markets and enterprises based upon wildland. Thirty five people attended with representation across the government agencies, wildlife trusts and individual projects.

Jason Emrich, project manager at Knepp, outlined the estate's programme and experience to date – with the main purpose being to return several thousand acres of former farmland to wildland and use near-natural grazers such as Tamworth pigs and English Long Horn cattle, which would also provide an income from organic meat production. Exmoor ponies and fallow deer added diversity to the grazing regime.

Frans Vera of the Dutch Forestry Service and author of the seminal 'Grazing Ecology and Forest History', presented 'Fascination will Pay', an appraisal of the economic benefits from wild cattle, deer and horses grazing the Dutch river floodplains and the polder at Ooostvaadersplassen. Views from the UK Forestry Commission (Alison Field) and Environment Agency (Bill Watts) were also presented, discussing the FC's experience of managing visitors and rewilding its forestry practices, as well as the more general economic benefits of wildland ecosystem services in flood control and water quality.

Discussions facilitated by Rick Minter and Alison Parfitt centred on key questions: such as the economic drivers for wild land: what are the priorities and how can they be sustained? In what ways can wild land add value and offer a brand to farms, estates, nature reserves, forests and related ventures ? How can Government bodies assist enterprises linked to wild land? e.g. through payments, advice, training, etc

I was commissioned by WN to write a review of the UK experience of relevant economic ventures – such as income and jobs created by visitor centres or branded marketing of wildland products, health and educational usage etc.. A report 'Wildland Benefits' is available for download on the Ethos website.

Wild, free and coming back? The return of key species to Scotland....what, where and how? 16-17th September, 2008. Followed by optional visits to Alladale's large mammal project, 18 Sept; Glen Affric 19 Sept - Caledonian ecosystem restoration, & wild boar experiment; Carrifran wildwood, 20 Sept - whole ecosystem restoration in the Moffat Hills.

This conference was hosted jointly by the Wildland Network and Trees for Life at Findhorn, Forres. The meeting was held in the Universal Hall at the Findhorn Foundation and field visits were made to Alladale, Glen Affric and the Carrifran project. Alan Watson Featherstone of Trees for Life and Steve Carver introduced proceedings and Rick Minter and Alison Parfitt facilitated discussions and working groups. Sixty eight people attended, with many traveling from England and some from the continent. There was a wide representation of interests, with many students, individuals and managers from voluntary bodies such as the John Muir Trust – though fewer from the government agencies than WN would normally expect. The field trips were well attended with staff of the Alladale project hosting a day of briefing and walking into the glen; staff of the Forestry Commission and Alan Featherstone of Trees for Life hosted the tour of Glen Affric and Philp Ashmole and Hugh Chalmers took us round Carrifran.

Hugh Fullerton-Smith briefs the group at Alladale, October 2008.

On the first morning, Roy Dennis of the Highland Foundation for Wildlife gave a presentation on the history of bird introductions – with Scotland's extensive experience of sea eagles in particular. Iain Valentine, head of animals, education and conservation at the Royal Zoological Society of Scotland, relayed progress and prospects on beaver re-introductions in Scotland. Peter Cairns spoke about 'facing the predator – are we ready?' and his organisation 'Tooth and Claw' also organised an exhibition of high quality photographs on this issue. Alan Featherstone covered targets and visions for the return of Scotland's missing mammals and there was then a discussion on targets and time-lines. The afternoon was then split into discussion groups on species issues: beaver, lynx, wolf, herbivores and birds. In the evening, the conference was treated to a performance of 'Where the Wild Things Were' by the storyteller Margot Henderson.

On the second day of what was WN's first residential conference, Hugh Fullerton Smith, manager of the Alladale Wilderness Reserve, Philip Ashmole and High Chalmers of the Carrifran Wildwood project and Alan Watson Featherstone with Liz Balharry of Trees for Life, gave presentations on the theme of restoring whole ecosystems – 'what's happening in Scotland'. There then followed a presentation by Kenny Taylor on the 'Lore of Fauna Celtica'.

The gathering thus wove a thread between the science, public perception and folklore of animals and the issue of re-introduction, particularly of predators. David Hetherington, Britain's leading expert on lynx, chaired discussions on perceptions of predators, in particular the barriers created by myths as well as apparent economic interests. Simon Ayres chaired discussions on the potential livelihoods in the tourist or educational potential of introduction schemes; Chris Marsh chaired a session on farming issues and David Blake presented issues related to game shooting; I chaired a session on community-based re-introduction projects led by Roy Dennis, and Tony Whitbread chaired a session on ecosystem restoration and how it might be driven by key re-introductions.

A number of key questions arose:

- Is it best to promote reinstatement of iconic species in their own right, or to promote restoration of entire ecosystems, with reinstatement of keystone species as a necessary component?

- Can we identify specific parts of Scotland where large-scale habitat restoration could create conditions for reinstating particular iconic species?

- How can we mobilise support from politicians, agencies, NGOs, and private individuals to establish rewilding as the primary management objective in particular large areas?

The general feeling from the workshops was that species reintroductions and ecosystem restoration needed to be pursued in tandem – and that key species could drive restoration, for example, of wetlands by beaver or open forest by wild grazers. There was already a well-developed appreciation of habitat networks and opportunities, and although there was a rising level of awareness of wildlife generally, there was little public appreciation of the missing species or the scale of ecosystem restoration required. It was agreed there was a need for concerted action with regard to public perceptions and also a need to seek common ground among the conservation organisations. There was still a need for more detailed mapping of opportunities and more integration of objectives among disparate organisations with regard to wildness and the need for ecosystem restoration.

On the question of how to mobilise support from politicians, agencies, NGOs and private individuals, the general feeling was that more could be done to establish rewilding as a primary management objective in some large area schemes. Thoughts on target audiences ranged from a rewilding 'task force', for example through Scottish Environment Link or the RSPB, and that a rewilding NGO needed to be created that could channel funding.

On the issue of farming it was evident that communication lines were not well advanced and that this community and perhaps also the game and fishing community, were far less aware of the potential balance of positive with negative impacts than was the case with forestry. There was clearly a need for economic support (subsidy) to include wildland objectives, such as payments for wild grazing regimes. Detailed examples of impacts in European communities that managed beaver, boar and predators in particular, should be communicated.

With regard to livelihoods from reintroductions, group discussions identified the following key issues:

- there would be a need for infrastructure to gain revenue, for example as happened in Yellowstone National Park, USA, with regard to wolf watching;
- land managers should be involved at a very early stage, for example, learning lessons from sea eagles on Mull;
- There are numerous indirect spin-offs from tourism and a need for a Farming and Wildlife Advisory Group form of service on rewilding – particularly with regard to keepering and the game community.

However, there were questions regarding the sustainability of car-based tourism and the dangers of 'commoditisation' of nature. A long term strategy would need to be in place for sustainable tourism, with better prospects if overseas travel became more expensive.

There was detailed feedback from the groups discussing perception of predators and general agreement that lack of public knowledge and education was a key issue and should be addressed well in advance of any plans for reintroductions. The role of the media is likely to be crucial – with a tendency to polarise views where there could readily be common agreement. It was important to establish common ground amongst all stakeholders. Experience-base education would be invaluable – for example, at wildlife centres where people can see wolves and lynx. Lessons needed to be learned from European experience – for example of opposition to reintroduction of bears in the Pyrenees or the positive approach in Sweden where government rewards landowners for the presence of wolves, lynx or bear (in contract to more negative government responses in Norway).

Often, predators had an 'image' that was far from the reality, with a tendency to be 'demonised' – these polarities could be offset by a strong programme of public education, starting in schools. The work of 'Tooth and Claw' in this respect was highlighted – and it was agreed that TfL with a contribution from WN would co-fund a DVD production for educational use.

The conference discussions raised many more questions than could be answered, and it is useful to re-iterate some points here as they show a certain level of critical self-reflection and realism, rather than an ungrounded enthusiasm: for example -

- The restoration work at Carrifran is taking place in a policy vacuum: the project has its own targets but these do not relate to any formal conservation policy context;

- Biodiversity Action Plans (BAPs) are about setting objectives for conservation policy and targets. But, rewilding points to further products beyond those within a conservation policy context. Rewilding could thus inform an evolving BAP policy.

- Conservation policy is wedded to a species-specific mindset. It needs to be shifted to embrace a wider awareness of what matters in nature and become more flexible.

- In their early stages, Trees for Life struggled to have any influence in conservation policy related to their interests. Thus they decided to get on and do it, as a way of actively demonstrating their philosophy. The practical results of TfL's work have served to influence both policy and practice.

- Are we humans and policy makers willing to give up control of nature? Rewilding challenges us to explore this.

- Beavers are a hybrid in policy and organisational terms. How can we learn lessons from the success of lobbying for birds and bird habitats?

- Can we achieve a mammal-based message about the worth of reintroductions, which matches the relative success of bird conservation?

- Who is 'we' in these discussions? When making recommendations and when taking things forward, it will help to be clear who 'we' is (this re-iterates the point about a rewilding advisory group)

- European legislation dictates many of these conservation-related issues and can take 10 years to take effect. Need to recognise this when planning ahead on these issues.

- What about setting up a large lobbying group to push for the return of key species, especially as a follow-up to this event?

A number of points arose after Kenny Taylor's presentation that do not often get addressed within the conservation community – for example, that we need a closer relationship with nature (eg. as when solo in the wild) and to reconnect with ancestral knowledge and feeling for nature that would have been more right-brain than left. There was a need for *new* stories about the creatures we want to bring back that would re-create the *power* of the old stories which existed within a shamanic consciousness – as in the power of totem animals in tribal cultures such as the American Indians. There was an argument that we have lost the knowledge of how shamanic journeys and the power and presence of animals can help us get round obstacles - including the limitations of old style conservation thinking! A signpost example is Jerome Bernstein's book *Living in the Borderlands, The Evolution of Consciousness and the Challenge of Healing Trauma* www.borderlanders.com/index.html about the cultural issue and loss of experience - a work that underlines the need to understand that eco-restoration sites can be healing for us as well as healing for the earth and for a cross over between the 'felt experience' and science/facts – this should be what environmental education does and for this there was a need for the right images and cultural engagement, especially with children and it is we (grown ups) who don't realize this connection. The idea arose of creating a prize for a children's story which explores a positive / mysterious / respectful / magic relationship with nature – the Good Wolf Prize (i.e. not the big bad wolf again)

Four workshops discussed and reported upon reintroduction of beaver, lynx, wolf and wild herbivores. Each group heard an outline of context, and questioned and commented on that, before discussing three questions. 'Visitors' from other groups then had time to review and contribute before key points were chosen.

The beaver group concluded that most large river systems in Scotland would be suitable and that reintroductions should be on a catchment scale. There was a need for openness and honesty with the public and education was crucial in avoiding misinformation and lobbying by uninformed special interests. The issue of sub-species and the 'right' kind of beaver was less important than establishing genetic diversity and adaptability to modern conditions – thus mixing populations from Norway, eastern Europe or Bavaria should not be seen in a negative light.

On the question of lynx, uppermost was the simple fact that the public does not know lynx - we are working with a blank slate and need education to win hearts and minds. Habitat is already suitable and available but there would need to be an ecobridge/connectivity across the Central Lowlands to link up with border forests and Northumberland. There was a need to target landowning organisations & advisers, prepare the ground for creating incentive payments – rather than compensation/profit and foregone payments. There would also be an issue of hunting versus protected status issues eg. at what stage to control. There was a general feeling that following an educational programme lynx was very feasible – habitat and prey animals were available, Eurasian populations could provide animals and there was practical experience in Europe of relocating animals. the key requirement would be to get a group or landowner and the Forestry Commission of Scotland on board to champion a project. The first such site might become iconic and would provide a potential 'branding' for local lynx-friendly produce, as occurs in parts of Europe. Political support would be essential and in this respect, learning from previous release projects would provide better understanding. A schools' education pack could provide the background.

On wolf reintroductions there was a clear need for an advocacy group for all large carnivores. Advocacy and education is more important than more information and an education & demonstration centre would be invaluable in this regard. But there was also a realistic sense that a paradigm shift would be necessary –a change in ourselves and attitudes with a need to rethink the whole question of risk.

On the issue of source population and viability, whilst there is general agreement on the availability of habitat and prey, the most appropriate source population might be from those habituated to red deer (perhaps in Scandinavia). There would need to be a robust management policy of dealing with individuals wandering from core areas of wildland, such as in the Cairngorms National Park.

There was an obvious marriage possible between conservation & ecosystem issues and the charisma of an animal with considerable tourist potential. We needed a European 'map' of experience with wolf; to study socio-economic, psychological & cultural as well as ecological issues, particularly with regard to conflict areas such as traditional hill farming – although current framing trends could create an economic opportunity. What was needed was imaginative communication with initial stakeholders in forestry, tourism interests and heritage and an incentive rather than a compensation approach.

On the question of herbivore reintroductions there was a feeling that Scotland had too many wild herbivores and among conservationists that domestic breeds would better deliver management objectives – with less complications for management! There was a pressing need to reduce deer populations and little understanding of the complex interactions between different wild herbivores – for example, wild cattle, moose, wild horses and wild boar. Feral goats were also an issue – as non-natives, should they be encouraged or eradicated? In certain areas there would be conflicts of interest – for example, for ground-nesting birds. It was not clear where specific sites existed or where there might be interest in a broad spectrum of grazers – Trees for Life has experimental pens for wild boar, as did Alladale, where moose were also kep in an enclosure to begin a breeding programme. There was a clear potential for economic benefits from eco-tourism, hunting and marketing of wild meat.

Participants were asked what they would like to see within ten years – here are some post-it notes from the conference discussion board:

"The first Lynx from Slovenia or Norway brought over by SNH/Forestry Commission/Tress for Life!"

"Cranes displaying near beaver ponds beside forests with Lynx roaming free"
"That reintroductions as a common talking point – schools, newspapers and acceptance!"

'White tailed eagle around all Scotland's coast. Red kite everywhere. Beaver pilot successful and spreading widely. Lynx reinstatement well underway"

"Common Cranes breeding up Scottish straths"

"Scottish Gov recognition through laws protecting all reintroduced species"

"Wildcat population stabilised & expanding. Beavers a success. Boar & Lynx started"

"Beavers properly established in the wild"

"Beavers fully reintroduced. Licence for Lynx trial"

"Beavers & Lynxes living widespread in a habitat that can support them indefinitely"

"Wild cat, Pine Marten & Polecat returned to the Southern Uplands"

"Wolves West of the Great Glen"

"Field study week an integral part of every school year through to the top year. A wilderness week to feature at least twice in every pupil's education"

"A public receptive to ecological restoration and hungry to see it happen"

"A Species Action Plan for Lynx"

"Beavers, wild boar, and Moose established. Realistic proposals for Lynx and serious discussion about Wolf"

"Political will & resources to meet EU obligations re reintroductions"

"A fresh perspective with our lost fauna and each other & a more Biodiverse UK"

"Beavers successfully reintroduced. Lynx reintroduced. Current species doing well eg Wildcats"

"More productive and integrated ecosystems with prolific runs of salmon feeding other animals along streams in Scotland. Greater awareness, understanding & examples of people living together with wildlife"

I was asked to make a summary reflection on the proceedings. Perhaps the key aspect was the need to avoid polarisation through advance planning, participation and above all education. There was work to be done showcasing the experience from projects in Europe and the USA and there was a cultural shift required in the general public's relationship and appreciation of wild nature, predators and risk – as well as a paradigm shift in management practices of control and focus upon specific objectives. The role of science, though essential, should not take precedence over the cultural elements of a closer relationship to nature – and in particular, there was a need for an understanding of nature as healer and educator, with each species having a certain 'medicine' or meaning, as they formerly had in shamanic cultures. It was clear that there was enough habitat and perhaps also enough goodwill in the conservation and forestry communities – it was less clear where the game conservationists would stand, and it would seem farming interests were implacably opposed, though largely out of ignorance and fear of economic losses. Education was the most important 'next phase' and in particular making use of pilot schemes and examples from Europe.

In this respect, there was an agreement to set up species working groups and begin production of educational materials {ed. note: we did not manage to follow up the species working groups in a productive way but Peter Cairns and 'Tooth and Claw' did produce the DVD and their work with photography and the book 'Wild Europe' has carried through the first phase of the public education). Rob MacMorran has set up a Scottish Wildlands Group with a newsletter.

Wildland Research Institute (Wri) launch, Leeds University, 21st Oct 2009

The WRi launch was the culmination of a 'wild' week of celebration in Leeds. The first day saw the opening of a stunning exhibition by the wildlife photographers who are Tooth & Claw and the week ended with a first staged performances of Samantha Ellis's play *The Last Wolf in Scotland*. In between, primary and secondary school children came into the University to do workshops as well as see the exhibition. And both Roy Dennis and Jay Griffiths gave thought provoking talks as part of an evening debate with an audience young and old who had come from both sides of the Pennines.

The launch day itself was a seminar for nature agencies, national parks & conservation NGOs as well academic representatives and activists to set some early research priorities. About 50 people worked through an agenda including:

- sketching out trends and drivers for wildland
- 3 presentations about national and European context & agendas
- detailing wildland issues
- imagining good and bad futures for wildland 50 years on
- back-casting what could, should happen to get us from here to 50 years on
- and then thinking of what we want and need to know to enable those changes.

The three presentations enlarged the context for the day, which were summarised as:

1. Working towards better protection of Europe's wilderness.

Zoltan Kun, Executive Director, Pan Parks Foundation, gave a briefing about wilderness/wildland in Europe, e.g. the EU Prague conference resolution (Apr 2009) and the Wilderness Think Tank and Pan Parks network.

2. Wild Europe, Turning Ideas into Policy.

Toby Ackroyd, who has developed the Wild Europe Initiative, sketched the formative steps and detailed an action plan for the Wild Europe Initiative as well as finishing with next steps for more wildland in the UK

3. Current projects, Intent and Implication.

Keith Kirby, Chief Woodland Conservation Officer for Natural England, talked about wildland as a continuum and what it might look like. Then he offered a framework which relates degrees of wildness and scale. This very helpfully allowed us to see notions about wildland past and present and position current projects, e.g. Knepp, or species reintroductions, e.g. Red Kite, in relation to each other. It provides a helpful overview for what can be a confusing diversity of projects and intent which are broadly more wild.

Delegates suggested that 'heaven', for those of us alive in 2060 and wanting more wildland, would mean that there is green space in every neighbourhood and wildland in every region. Other aspirations gave us 30% of all land will be near natural and that the National Wildland Network would be complete, connecting uplands and lowlands, urban and rural. Sketching out steps in decades between then and now revealed a range of thinking or prophesy which included:

2040 - 2050
- Large scale Government buy-out of non viable farms to allow landscape scale wildland project
- Network of IUCN II sites designated
- Education provides courses for 'new' land stewards

2030 – 2040
- Culture of 'wild nature' as normal and is universally accepted
- Individual landowners cooperate & create core areas
- Changes of attitude after official reintroductions of species (lynx especially)

2020 – 2030
- Flagship report proposes PAN Park network & identifies sites
- Tourist Boards accept value of re-introductions

The Key research questions that emerged were:

- How do we deal with the switch from human control to natural process?
- What does this cost – in economic and cultural terms? Currently any cost benefit analysis is skewed by what we do not know.
- Would economic interests loose competitive edge by doing this? And how?
- What is the cost benefit of ecosystems?
- Need to look at the climate change effects on ecosystem delivery.

I personally argued against a standard academic research agenda and for greater focus upon *ways and means analysis* - i.e. What do we need to know, for instance, to achieve 10,000 sq kms of wildland in England, in Wales and in Scotland? This would involve weighing costs against benefits to arrive at cost efficiencies and current experience is too short a time to evaluate e.g. six years of Wild Ennerdale cannot tell us enough, yet, about benefits. So how do we value? How do we use numbers to value? But a ways-and-means approach could also be complimentary to a cost benefits approach: What areas do we have now that could be wildland ? What can we learn from schemes to date and can we identify gaps and assess transferability of overseas examples. What is determining how rewilding is taking place in different countries across Europe? How is this happening? Who is making this happen?

The issue of monitoring arose, as it always does in a research environment – what are the successes and failures? What data do we need – as there is little data about protected landscapes and reserves efficiency.

From these discussions the meeting moved to considering what are the best tools, strategies, and methodologies to influence and campaign for more wildland and how can we achieve core wildland areas in England, Wales and Scotland? We also need to identify what could prevent this, ie. talk to all stakeholders (social science research) to identify potential conflicts along any route we take to achieve this goal

A complete record of the seminar and the presentations is available on www.wildlandresearch.org<http://www.wildlandresearch.org/>

Gathering at the entrance to Carrifran, October 2008.

Since then!

In December of 2009 the coordinating group of WN met to review progress and consider its future work. It was agreed that the 'network' phase had delivered on its key objectives – to further communication among practitioners and to raise awareness on rewilding issues. In that year, 'rewilidng' as a term had been heard on the lips of an environment minister giving a keynote speech, yet there were significant areas of work that still needed addressing. Prime among these was reform of the EU Common Agricultural Policy that supported domestic grazing regimes for conservation purposes, but had no payment scheme that would properly support 'wild grazing'. Although there was evidence that UK agencies would bend the rules in this respect, the situation needed improving at a European level.

We can feel happy that there is a beaver 'reintroduction' pilot project, but not at the limited scale, nor the negative response of the Scottish government to the discovery of a free-living population of beaver on the river Tay. There is only a limited enthusiasm for the Dutch model of combining free-living 'wild' horse, red deer and wild cattle. On the other hand, there appears growing acceptance of wild boar and growing realisation that Britain has a population of feral big cats that appear to be breeding. We are likely to see more small beaver projects – for example, with the Wales Wild Land Foundation in the Cambrian mountains.

The 'new austerity' has already seen the abandonment of a sea eagle project in East Anglia, but moves are continuing to repopulate the east coast of Scotland.

The 'species group' idea has seen little activity, but there is an overall agreement that the lynx should be the main target species. In this regard the work of 'Tooth and Claw' and the WN-sponsored DVD is a step in this direction.

There is still a need for more coordinated thinking and planning between the main players on large scale management schemes – for example, the RSPB, the Wildlife Trusts, the National Trust, Woodland Trust and the Forestry Commission, and we have yet to see a government initiative in the form of a 'challenge fund'. Political developments may not favour government participation and it is to be hoped that whatever happens to the public land resource, key elements of forward thinking in the Forestry Commission and Natural England will be retained in the 'public service'. The voluntary organisations who might be expected to take up the cause – if government disposes of its forestry and conservation responsibilities to the private sector, are not yet well-practised and disposed toward cooperative schemes. The major public-private initiative in Ennerdale has depended a great deal upon the foresight and sensitivity of public servants within the Forestry Commission and it would be a great risk to have to fund this entirely from the private or voluntary sector.

The Wildland Network may have completed this phase but there is still a need for conferences and sharing of experience, and BANC will take up that role – an autumn conference is planned for 2011 at the Neroche project, led by the Forestry Commission, at which many of these themes will be discussed and networking can continue.

PART 1: ISSUES AND DEFINITIONS

Towards a wildland strategy

ECOS editorial 25 (3/4) 1-3. (2004)

PETER TAYLOR

It has taken almost two decades, but conservation is finally moving beyond protectionism and towards the strategic creation of wildlife habitat. We may be a far cry from the US Wildlands Project strategy of 'cores, corridors and carnivores' linking protected areas and restoring natural predator-prey relationships, but we do have some candidate core areas, and fledgling corridors – with our necessary British priority of restoring enough vegetation for natural herbivores to be sustainable.

Alan Featherstone's vision of a large core area in the western Highlands is demonstrating the practical reality of ecological restoration, with its mix of planting programmes, fencing out deer, and natural regeneration. It is also demonstrates the power of example and persistence of a dream – spawning Moor Trees on Dartmoor. It is part of an expanding wave of purchases by voluntary bodies and private initiatives aimed at large scale restoration of native vegetation, such as Carrifran, Mar Lodge, and Snowdon in the uplands, and the Cambridgeshire fenland project – all of which are featured in this issue.

This process of strategic purchase and enlargement is wider than these examples – we could have included the Woodland Trust's work at Glen Finglas (3,000ha), the Royal Scottish Forestry Society at Cashel (3,000ha), the RSPB in Abernethy, and its strategic creation of reedbed and heathland in southern England; the work of Scottish Natural Heritage in the regeneration of natural vegetation patterns on some of their larger reserves, such as Ben Eighe; and the recent moves toward 'coastal retreat' in Essex and East Anglia. There is a long list of projects, and we shall feature these in future wildland pages of ECOS. There are no collated statistics on this progress towards larger areas and natural processes – and to this end, BANC has sponsored a book, available from Earthscan in April 2005, Beyond Conservation - a Wildland Strategy. The book attempts such a review, and addresses the obstacles to further progress. It recommends three major core area initiatives to be taken up by government, and it outlines a strategy of habitat networks making use of river catchments, river re-wilding and riparian woodland regeneration. The latter is much like the experience of the Tweed Forum, described in this issue by Luke Comins.

Some of the practitioners and thinkers involved in these projects have recently formed a network for swapping experience: The Wildland Group - hosted at www.ethos-uk.com (ed. in 2005 the network created its own website www.wildland-network.org.uk) The group is building upon Steve Carver's 'wilderness' quality mapping and assessing the potential social and economic dimension to large scale conversion of marginal agricultural land, explained here in Toby Aykroyd's 'Wild Britain' proposal. It will develop an open forum in 2005.

Within the Wildlife Trusts, there is a move toward landscape-scale networks, such as the Sussex Wildwoods described by Tony Whitbread who first drew attention to the Dutch experience of re-introducing large wild herbivores to nature reserves as management tools (much as the smaller scale beaver project does in Kent – see ECOS 23 (2) 23-26). Adrian Colston reports on the National Trust's plans to do something similar with large but tame herbivores in the Cambridge fens, and Simon Bates argues for the Dutch 'nature map' approach across our own landscapes. English Nature has followed these developments closely, as Keith Kirby reports on its wild grazing projects. Links have been made with the Large Herbivore Foundation in the Netherlands, and there is now a steady flow of Konik horses to English projects, although Joep van Vlassaker of the Large Herbivore Foundation is puzzled at this choice, considering the presence in England of Europe's most primitive wild pony, the Exmoor. Perhaps the charismatic reconstituted aurochsen will follow!

Will we ever be able to move to that ultimate wildland experience – the presence of large carnivores and the re-establishment of natural predation? As we have seen in ECOS, lynx and puma are already at work in the English countryside, but Manuela von Arx of Switzerland's successful lynx re-introduction project, urges caution – any deliberate re-introductions need to be carefully planned, and much attention given to education. Ilka Reinhardt describes the problems of the re-appearance of a large carnivore such as the wolf in a pocket of wildland on the border of Germany and Poland, and Geog Rauer demonstrates how difficult a bear re-introduction programme can be. In this case, the problem was guarding the honey, but recent reports of three mushroom pickers fatally attacked by a bear on the outskirts of the large city of Brasov, highlights the risk that this top predator would pose.

Whether voluntary groups will be able to follow the outstanding example of restoration of natural vegetation at Carrifran given by Philip Ashmole and Hugh Chalmers, and purchase whole valleys by subscription, may depend on a more strategic direction in support from major funds such as the Lottery.The immediate future will doubtless involve small steps toward natural processes operating over larger areas, and particularly cooperative projects between major landholders embracing a wilder land ethos – as demonstrated with Wild Ennerdale, a project of the National Trust, the Forestry Commission and United

Utilities. This may prove a model for development of the English and Welsh uplands, with some areas under domestic grazing regimes and small scale local-use forest products, and other areas left to be reworked by natural processes. Such projects prompt a philosophical quest as to the true nature of human activity, natural or not? At the tamer end of the spectrum, these areas may involve hardy breeds such as Highland cattle and Exmoor ponies, rather than fighting aurochsen and the return of red deer herds, wild boar, and beaver, with their challenges for current agriculture and forestry.

We are a little further than the beginning – but much work has to be done to both explain and promote wildland values. Gareth Browning and Rachel Yanik explain the philosophy at Ennerdale, where the natural forces of the river mean that geological action is not being held back. Meanwhile, the experience of the National Trust at Mar Lodge and in Snowdonia shows the difficulty of making radical moves beyond traditional land uses that provide some local employment. There is, as yet, no full social and economic assessment of what wider scale wildland would entail, although Steve Carver and Peter Samson report that wildland cannot compete with subsidised upland grazing – unless, of course, it is also subsidised as an integrated land-use. We need a study that looks not at how wildland might currently compare – when there are no support systems for wild grazing, nor credits for carbon sequestration, water quality or flood control, but at what support systems would be necessary to foster wildland with such benefits as well as a role for those currently employed in traditional uses.

As government moves toward a joined up land management agency for England and the CAP is reformed to create a safety net for rural communities on the margins of agricultural production, there is potential for such support systems to emerge. To this end, we might begin to draw some lines on a map of the projects outlined in this edition – of where future forests, river restoration and other habitat initiatives might be more strategically located.

A wildland strategy will not be a people-less agenda – the Moelyci initiative (see *ECOS* 24 (2) 51-56) demonstrates what can be achieved by people wanting livelihoods from wilder land, perhaps servicing the health, education and activity sectors advocated here by Toby Aykroyd. The National Trust's fenland wild corridor, outlined by Adrian Colston, will reach right to the edge of Cambridge, providing recreational and educational outlets. The 'Future Nature' of Bill Adams' book for BANC is beginning to take shape. We have moved beyond conservation and can look to a time when near-natural areas expand across the uplands, snake out across lowlands, and even penetrate towns and cities.

Affric &
Ben Eighe

Cairngorm

Trossachs
& Ben
Lomond

Tweed catchment &
Borders region

Northumberland NP
Great North Forest
Tees Forest

North York Moors NP

Ennerdale &
Lake District NP

Yorkshire Dales NP and North
Pennines

Mersey Forest

Peak District NP & Rockingham Forest

Snowdonia NP &
North Cambrians

Forest of Mercia

Wicken & Cambridge Fens

Forest of Dean

Epping & Thames Chase
Community Forests

Brecon Beacon NP

Gt Western Forest

Exmoor NP

New Forest

Sussex Weald

Dartmoor NP
& Tamar catchment

Cores and connectivity - the potential in Britain.

45

By 2050, if it is a land wild enough in the heart as well as in wildlife, with extensive herds of deer, wild horses, aurochsen, boar, and beaver in the core areas, we may then find a welcome for our competing but unquestionably more charismatic predators.

Wild thoughts...

What are the meanings of wildness, wild and wilderness, and what are the implications for land management, or non land management, for conservation groups? ECOS asked three practitioners to argue it out... Each contributor read each other's essay and produced a follow up note in turn. Whether you side with any of them or not, their debate helps focus on this slippery subject...

A new paradigm for the uplands
ECOS 25 (1) p 2-5 (2004)

JAMES FENTON

The Oostvarrdersplassen in Holland, where large herbivores are left to roam free, is widely accepted as visionary conservation thinking, and we in Britain are actively discussing how to create our own ' Oostvarrdersplassens'. But maybe, without realising it, we have them already in the uplands – and are now losing them owing to 'conservation action' arising from the mindset that grazing is a bad thing and the climax vegetation should be woodland.

'Wild' - the Dutch or English models?

As part of a recent conservation conference at Lancaster University, we went on a field trip to the Pennines where staff of English Nature proudly showed us an experiment in the 'wilding' of the eastern flanks of Ingleborough. To them being 'wild' meant removing all grazing and planting some trees. The next day we were back at the University to hear inspirational thinking from Frans Vera about returning wild nature to Holland – at the Oostvarrdersplassen,[1] – and we heard even grander plans to create large-scale wildlife corridors from there to Germany and France.

The essence of these Dutch schemes is the reintroduction of wild herbivores. Being 'wild' in Holland does not mean excluding grazing, but the introduction of a range of large herbivores, in this case wild cattle, horses and red deer, and seeing what happens. These animals, of course, have a major impact on the vegetation pattern, the only constraint on their numbers being the amount of forage available in winter.

Is woodland the climax vegetation of the UK uplands?

Frans Vera argues convincingly in his book *Grazing Ecology and Forest History*[2] that large herbivores have always been part of the natural ecosystems of Europe, with the result that the natural vegetation of temperate lowland Europe would not have been closed high forest but a mosaic of forest, parkland, scrub and grassland: grazing prevents woodland from regenerating under its own canopy, which thereafter cycles to grassland and thence to thorny scrub. Trees can only regenerate in this thorny scrub, which subsequently reverts to woodland. This theory is fine for fertile, lowland Europe, but what happens if you apply the same principles to the infertile uplands of north and west Britain, where the thorny scrub species of hawthorn and sloe are rare or absent? What is there to protect the trees from grazing?

Another recent book *A Highland Deer Herd and its Habitat*[3], which looks at the impact of deer on the Letterewe Estate in Wester Ross, argues that there is no such thing as 'overgrazing' where wild herbivores such as red deer are concerned, because grazing levels are naturally constrained by the winter availability of forage. Likewise, on St Kilda, where there have been feral Soay sheep for centuries, if not millennia, sheep populations go through a four-year cycle, with high mortality when numbers exceed winter food supply.

Although there are pockets of native woodland, upland Britain is largely treeless, and the general mindset to date has been that, as woodland is the climax vegetation, the uplands must have become treeless through human activity, and remain largely treeless through 'overgrazing'. Hence a lot of current conservation effort in the uplands is devoted to reducing grazing levels and planting trees. In the Scottish Highlands, for example, it is argued that a grazing level of four red deer per square kilometre is needed in order to achieve natural regeneration of woodland, although this low figure is considerably less than that which the vegetation can support.

Is moorland the climax vegetation?

If, on the other hand, it is a general principle that the number of herbivores is limited to what the vegetation can support, then perhaps, in upland Britain, we need to remodel our whole mental landscape: we need to get away from the 'woodland as climax' model. Maybe our upland landscape is relatively natural in terms of vegetation pattern, albeit natural grazing by red deer having been replaced by domestic sheep in many places?[4] And lack of winter feed will still have limited the number of domestic stock on the hill (as did the presence of wolves in the past).

Hence there is a possibility that the current vegetation pattern of the unenclosed areas of upland Britain is within the range of possible natural variation.[5] Pollen analysis indicates that there were more trees in upland Britain in the distant past, but natural soil deterioration over the past few thousand years (leaching, iron pans, lack of worms, mor soils, etc.) has perhaps made conditions less suitable for tree regeneration, so that even a relatively low grazing pressure will keep the landscape open.

Woodland can still be a component of upland vegetation, particularly on crags and in gullies where soils are better and grazing less. Likewise, Wistman's Wood on Dartmoor and Keskadale Wood in the Lake District, and a much greater range of examples in Scotland, indicate that woodland can regenerate in the presence of grazing; and, in any complex upland landscape, grazing will vary temporally and spatially, giving some opportunities for localised woodland. For example, in some areas of the Lake District oak can be seen regenerating in bracken, and, in Scotland, rowan and birch can be seen regenerating in gorse and oak and birch on slopes of deep heather. Hence, even with heavy grazing, trees will persist in at least some upland landscapes, but perhaps our mistake is to expect lots of them!

If there has been anthropogenic woodland loss, it is most likely to have taken place on the steeper, well-drained valley sides, but even here can we be certain that any anthropogenic loss has changed the natural endpoint of a mostly treeless landscape? As peatland and mor soils spread over much of the flatter ground, herbivores tend to become restricted to the remaining better soils, resulting in a direct competition between woodland and animals. In other words, if, instead of a 'woodland as the climatic climax model', the 'natural decline' model fits the facts better, humans may only have locally accelerated an existing trend.[4]

Are the uplands our ' Oostvarrdersplassens'?

At the conference referred to above, there was much talk of how to create our own Oostvarrdersplassens in Britain. But maybe in much of upland Scotland at least, we have had our Oostvarrdersplassens all along – large tracts of land with significant numbers of indigenous herbivores, resulting in a relatively natural vegetation pattern. Maybe, we have them *throughout* upland Britain, the only difference being that sheep have replaced red deer. It is a common observation in Scotland, that, if sheep are taken off a hill, red deer come in – perhaps confirming the perfectly reasonable theory that forage availability determines grazing levels.

However, if we already have our upland Oostvarrdersplassens, we're also in very real danger of losing them, as the demand from conservationists is to reduce grazing to very low levels, and large-scale native woodland planting schemes have been created that fragment the predominantly open landscape.

At the Oostvarrdersplassen there are wild cattle and horses in addition to deer. However, what is not certain is the range of natural herbivores upland Britain would naturally support, for the Oostvarrdersplassen has very fertile soil whereas much of upland Britain is infertile and may not be able to hold such a range of species. Likewise, it is hard to say whether, in general, carnivores keep herbivore numbers down to below the vegetation's carrying capacity. In Yellowstone Park, for example, both wolf and red deer numbers are going up simultaneously![6] There were wolves in upland Scotland until 300 years ago, and the landscape has been largely treeless since way before then, which suggests that the presence predators has not kept the grazing to a low enough level to allow woodland to be the dominant vegetation.

Norway is often given as a model of what the UK uplands 'should be', but that country has a complex landscape and a different ecology; for example, unlike oceanic climates, the presence of winter snow-cover both protects vegetation from grazing and keeps herbivore numbers down.

A new paradigm for the UK uplands?

Moving away from the idea that woodland is necessarily the climax vegetation on our unenclosed hills opens up whole avenues of new thinking. It also means we would have to rethink our conservation action: if the vegetation pattern of our hills is relatively natural, then maybe there is little short-term conservation action that is needed – other than ensuring that grazing continues and burning is within the bounds of natural variation; long-term there are possibilities of reintroductions of native large mammals, although we need to be careful that the ecological conditions are right.

There may be some areas where grazing is obviously way above the natural ecological carrying capacity (eg. parts of Wales or western Ireland), but on the whole perhaps we should let our uplands be wild, and let the vegetation pattern develop under the influence of grazing, and concentrate our action on areas that really need more wildlife and are fertile enough to take it – the lowlands. And the current large-scale plans for Wicken Fen and Epping Forest give us cause to hope that the lowlands of Britain can be made wild.

For the uplands, though, we need to stand back and rethink their whole ecology, so as to ensure that well-intentioned 'restoration' does not end up making them less wild and turn them into designed landscapes. Letting our hills be wild means having no predefined outcomes, but letting nature decide the vegetation pattern – under the influence of grazing which is ideally from indigenous herbivores, but in their absence maybe sheep are as good a species as any.

Britain's wild horses on Exmoor's heathland. (Toby Hickman)

1. See, for example, *Special issue "Grazing and Grazing Animals". Vakblad NATUURBEHEER*, 41 jarrgang, May 2002.

2. Milner, JM, Alexander, JS, Griffin, AM (2002). *A Highland Deer Herd and its Habitat.* Red Lion House, 2002.

3. Vera, FWM (2000). *Grazing Ecology and Forest History.* CABI Publishing.
4. See, for example, Fenton,J (1997). Native Woods in the Highland: Thoughts and Observations. *Scottish Forestry* Vol. 51. And Fenton, J (2001). Native Woods in the Highlands: Doubts and Certainties. *Scottish Woodland History Discussion Group: Notes VI,* 2001.

5. Fenton, J (2003). Deciding on the Balance Between Moorland and Woodland in the Scottish Uplands: an overview at the landscape Scale. *La Cañada* No17.

6. Levy, S (2002). Top Dogs. *New Scientist* 2 Nov 2002.

Self-willed land: Can nature ever be free?

ECOS 25 (1) p 6-11 (2004)

MARK FISHER

Lessons from the natural world

I like wildflowers and so I seek out landscapes that contain the distinct habitats in which those wildflowers can exhibit themselves in their natural communities. I encourage my garden design class to observe wildflowers *in habitat*, hoping that they will recognise that many of the wildflowers that they see locally have cousins in garden use. This has two lessons: that garden plants grow best within the cultural conditions of soil, moisture and light availability that their wild form enjoys (right plant in the right place); and a transfer of aesthetic through observing how wildflowers grow in self-supporting communities and adopting this pattern in their plans for garden planting.

Plantlife[1] recently promoted a book that is a celebration of the wild flowers of Britain and Ireland. It's a book of superlatives, but it deserves careful analysis if it is to be used as a measure of the natural state and abundance of our wildflower populations. Where these are magnificent in the book, the habitat shown is distinctive and has a common property – it is outside the margins of our productive or settled land. Where examples are given from productive land, the habitat characteristics have been smoothed out over the centuries by tree clearance (more of which later), ploughing, land drainage and mineralisation. Thus the flush of meadow flowers shown is dependent on the influences of historical management, and on its contemporary management by livestock grazing to keep it free of scrub. In what has become the modern paradox, the sheer brilliance of this meadow display is obscured unless livestock are removed before flowering time, and we now compensate the landowner through stewardship schemes for this privilege.

I have been less content in recent years with the wildflower experience of Britain, seeking instead landscapes that show less influence from humans and their livestock, and more so from wild nature. It's a sad reflection that there is little part of Britain that is considered to have been untransformed by people and their activities[2], and it is our systemised productive use of the land – agriculture in the main - that is to blame. The western and north-western extremes of Ireland are lightly used and thus offer some solace, but it is in America that I have observed the better state of nature, its reverence for its own sake by its people and its abundance of distinctive habitat and wild flora. A corollary to this

51

abundance of wild flora is the presence of all the other components of wild nature in the wild animals, birds, predators and other forces of nature that go together in shaping a natural landscape. To the Americans, this is the land of wilderness, a self-willed land where they have chosen to remove their influence and allow nature its own dominion.

Learning from the wilderness experience

Wilderness[3] in America is defined in the Wilderness Act (1964) by a simple requirement:

> "A wilderness, in contrast with those areas where man and his own works dominate the landscape, is hereby recognised as an area where the earth and its community of life are untrammelled by man, where man himself is a visitor who does not remain."

The Act enabled the American Congress to set aside nine million acres of publicly owned land in their national forests, parks, wildlife refuges, and other federal lands to be kept permanently unchanged by humans. More bills have followed and there are now 105 million acres in the National Wilderness Preservation System. It is worth noting the characteristics of wilderness defined in the Act:

> "Wilderness is an area of undeveloped Federal land retaining its primeval character and influence, without permanent improvements or human habitation, which is protected and managed so as to preserve its natural conditions and which:
>
> (1)   generally appears to have been affected primarily by the forces of nature, with the imprint of man's work substantially unnoticeable;
> (2)   has outstanding opportunities for solitude or a primitive and unconfined type of recreation;
> (3)   has at least five thousand acres of land or is of sufficient size as to make practicable its preservation and use in an unimpaired condition; and
> (4)   may also contain ecological, geological, or other features of scientific, educational, scenic, or historical value."

I am struck by the term primeval character as it speaks to what I believe is the difference between America and Britain. The history of our landscape in Britain is contested. One view, from Oliver Rackham[4], is that a massive transformation began after the arrival of agriculture from the Middle East. Our aboriginal ancestors drew their existence from forest, river and sea, but the early farmers living side by side some 6000 years ago progressively reduced an abundant tree coverage either through uprooting, or through grazing pressure from concentrating livestock. We lost half of our natural woodland by the early Iron Age (500BC) with the clearance continuing so that there is no real wildwood left today (i.e. self-sown, self-regenerating and unmanaged) and actual woodland coverage is sparse. Along the way, we extirpated our larger indigenous animals, including predators, and made it impossible for a primeval approach to life to continue. Thus a post-aboriginal culture, with its methods of systemised production, has been around in Britain for some 5-6000 years and it has reshaped everything in its path. In North America, by contrast, the pressure on their landscape was imported with its *discovery* by Europeans as recently as 500 years ago. North America still has some landscape that bears testimony to its original state[2]. We, however, have to be satisfied with our inheritance of entirely human-made landscapes.

With no true wilderness left to preserve, it is unsurprising that we have no Wilderness Act nor any ethos that gives wilderness its value. We do have legislation that provides for National Parks, inspired originally by the American example, but we did not follow their ethos of removing human influence. England and Wales's National Parks (save for the recent hybrids of the Broads and the New Forest) are in upland areas: all of them are populated and subject to agricultural activity. The Parks are distinguished by their restrictive planning laws, but many commentators regard the biggest threat to be overgrazing by livestock, something for which there is no legal constraint. The *woolly mower* thus reaches every part of our island, holding back natural succession and successfully maintaining it as an artificial landscape.

Peter Marren[5] has well described the history and effectiveness of our National Nature Reserves and Sites of Special Scientific Interest. He points out the obvious – these land protections rely on co-operation between the conservation agency and owner/occupier. He accepts the reality of the land being populated and under systemised productive use, and he makes the case that our wildlife is dependent on this for its survival. Thus isn't it true that our appreciation of wildlife is predicated on species that are maintained in these almost-certainly-artificial landscapes? The fact that these landscapes need managing (i.e. external intervention by grazing animals) indicates that they are not self-willed, and that we may have become entranced with plant and bird species that will not have such a key presence if our land was allowed to rewild. Marren again notes this, predicting a significant drop in diversity if land is left to manage itself, but is he basing this on observation of a few poorly featured nature reserves (how could they now be otherwise in Britain) and over a relatively short period?

Further proof of our skewed appreciation is that nature conservation is rarely about wild mammals. Where re-introductions are contemplated, the hue and cry from landowners is utterly predictable. It was ever so because wild mammals pose a greater threat to agricultural productivity than wildflowers and birds. The pilot program to re-introduce beaver into Scotland[5] is hedged with cautions that could see it halted if reaction from land users becomes too heated. Will we have to compensate landowners to tolerate the planned re-introduction of beavers?

Long horizons

Can we exclude the influence of people and embrace rewilding?

I believe that a desire for self-willed land will only gain acceptance if it is universally appreciated that it has to be without human influence and that there are opportunities to experience it (as a visitor only) within the reach of most people. With no extant wilderness, the task will be to rewild a significant area of farmed landscape (removing livestock would be a start) but the result is unlikely to be true wilderness. Sadly there is no guarantee in present circumstances that the land will regain a full complement of nature's species.

Should we need inspiration, we can look to the Wildlands Project[6], set up in America some 10 years ago. The Project aims to build on the 662 wilderness areas of the National Wilderness Preservation System by restoring more of the natural heritage of North America through the establishment of a connected system of wildlands. Their approach is simple - to allow the natural recovery (rewilding) of whole landscapes in every region of North America and to link them into a continuous wildlife corridor. They believe that recovery on that scale will take a 100 years or more, but the Project has a clear idea of what it seeks: a wild home for unfettered (self-willed) life.

There is a concern for self-willed land in Britain. The John Muir Trust[7] was founded with the object of conservation and protection of wild places. The Trust interprets wild to mean places: "where the presence of people and the influence of human actions is not predominant, ... and where other non-human influences such as weather, landscape and wildlife prevail." One aim of the Trust is to "renew wild places, where they have been damaged, by encouraging natural processes." The Trust believes ownership is the only way to protect wild land and so it has bought parcels in seven areas in the Highlands and Islands of Scotland, totalling 20,000 hectares. These are not unpopulated or unused areas, but they are some of the least populated and by degree the least managed.

The National Trust for Scotland and Scottish Natural Heritage have both issued policy statements on wild places, but perhaps the most significant event is the recognition of wild land by the Scottish planning system[8] (NPPG 14): - it is defined as "uninhabited and often relatively inaccessible countryside where the influence of human activity on the character and quality of the environment has been minimal."

I consider that the habitat least affected by people in England is the coastline between low and high water mark. It is a short distance from there to the sand dunes and the coastal cliffs, both of which have no use in agriculture, but which exhibit some of our best wildflower displays. I am encouraged that coastal areas in England are also providing a test bed for one form of rewilding of our landscape. The Environment Agency[9] proposes to restore the natural landscape around the estuarine outlet of the Cuckmere River on the East Sussex coast. The banks of the canalised river are now in poor repair. By deliberately breaking a bank on one side, it is envisaged that a salt marsh of around 113 acres will develop, forming a haven for waterfowl and protecting the valley against future flooding. DEFRA[10] has also recently put out a proposal on wetland creation to compensate for areas of saltmarsh and mudflat destroyed by port developments on the East Coast in the 1990s. Low-lying farmland on Wallasea Island is thought to be suitable for creating new wetland through managed coastal realignment.

Facing a future in the wilderness

In the future, the quality of our landscapes will depend on whether we can trust ourselves to live in rural areas without imposing our will on every square foot of it. Aldo Leopold[11], a founding member of the Wilderness Society in America, foresaw this problem when he wrote: "Ability to see the cultural value of wilderness boils down, in the last analysis, to a question of intellectual humility. The shallow-minded modern who has lost his rootage in the land assumes that he has already discovered what is important." Leopold's concern led him to propose a Land Ethic in which people become an integral member of the wider community of plants, animals and the land, rather than have dominion over it.

I am a professionally qualified Permaculture designer[12], and I learnt from this earth science that wilderness has value in providing lessons on how we can design enduring self-regulating processes based on natural systems. Permaculture embodies a land ethic in similar vein to that espoused by Aldo Leopold. Land-use design using Permaculture principles will allocate areas of decreasing influence and affect (i.e. decreasing intensity of use) and will seek to include some regenerating self-willed land where observation is the only activity.[13] We can then advance from the self-willed land on individual holdings – where nature is gifted back part of the land to non-productive use - towards a collective will to gift land back to nature in larger publicly owned preserves.

There is an internal consistency within the Permaculture approach that is important - we may be able to regenerate and conserve self-willed areas, but they will become merely museum pieces always under threat if they are surrounded by overworked and degraded landscapes. Moreover, whilst at first sight the advocacy of self-willed land could be dismissed as another 'highland clearance', there is the recognition that the Permaculture approach to land use can sustain a greater rural population than there is at present.[14]

Self-willed land becomes a greater prospect every day that we see the profitability of farming in marginal areas unravel and that there is a growing public will to have a collective view about future landscapes.

References

1. Bob Gibbons and David Woodfall (2002) Flowers at my Feet HarperCollins.

2. American Association for the Advancement of Science (2001) Atlas of Population and Environment www.aaas.org/international/atlas/about.htm

3. See the wealth of information on www.wilderness.net

4. **Oliver Rackham (1986)** *The History of the Countryside* **Dent.**

5. Peter Marren (2002) *Nature Conservation: A Review of the Conservation of Wildlife in Britain 1950-2001* HarperCollins

6. Wildlands Project www.wildlandsproject.org

7. John Muir Trust www.jmt.org

8 NPPG 14 Natural Heritage www.scotland.gov.uk/library/nppg/nppg14-00.htm

9. Environment Agency News Release 60/03 (2003) *Permission sought for Cuckmere Estuary restoration project.*

10. DEFRA (2003) *Possible wetlands creation at Wallasea Island.* Public consultation.

11. Aldo Leopold (1949) *A Sand County Almanac* OUP

12. Permaculture Association (Britain) www.permaculture.org.uk

13. An example of regeneration using the principles of Permaculture can be seen at Tir Penrhos Isaf. www.konsk.co.uk/index.htm

14. Chapter 7 and the PPG7 Reform Group (2003) *Sustainable Homes and Livelihoods in the Countryside – Suggestions for the Forthcoming Revision or Replacement of Planning Policy Guidance 7* Chapter 7 www.thelandisours.org/chapter7/PPG7.html

To wild or not to wild: the perils of 'either-or'

ECOS 25.1 p12-17 (2004)

PETER TAYLOR

In so much of the debate about wilderness, wild land, conservation priorities, management and intervention, a certain aspect of the rational scientific mind inevitably surfaces – I do not have a fine word for it, other than 'either-or-thinking'. It affects policy as well as scientific research and conclusions. In the latter it leads to an inability to consider multiple causative factors. Its opposite can be summed by the even less erudite term 'both'. Perhaps some sociologist will provide a suitably long word, and the phenomenon will get the recognition it deserves.

In this debate it would mean that any statement regarding removal of management, use of wild or domestic herbivores, climax vegetation versus managed grazing regimes, and any new theory or paradigm, would not be generalised across all our nature reserves. Thus, we could argue for a *spectrum* of regimes, from core areas dominated by 'natural' processes, buffer zones of suitable economic activity (e.g. multi-purpose forestry, low-intensity grazing) corridors of less-intensive agricultural regimes, wild-river corridors, urban corridors, wild estuaries, headlands, and so on.

Degrees of natural

This principle also applies to the dodgy term *natural.* Despite being central to what we as nature conservationists are attempting to conserve, it is fraught with confused meaning. Mark Fisher strikes a chord when he finds fault with Peter Marren for a supine acceptance of domestic grazing regimes in our national 'nature' reserves. James Fenton, on the other hand, citing Franz Vera, offers us a paradigm of acceptance where domestic stock help us maintain open landscapes in the uplands in the absence of the natural grazers that would have kept them almost as open in pre-agricultural times.

As domestic stock are agents of human intervention (and benefit), this is perhaps a polarity based ultimately upon the way we see ourselves. *Either* humans as interveners in the landscape are natural *or* not, when we could be *both*, depending upon our definition. The work of paleontologist Tim Flannery[1] (see for example *ECOS* 24 (2), pages 85-88), suggests that even more natural humans have been exerting major landscape scale influence for the past 60,000 years at least, largely through the extinction of mega-herbivores in the last glaciation (and see next point about 'deep time' perspectives). Thus, no landscape, not even in the Americas, is now without past human influence, and a thick European forest devoid of elephant and rhino, riverine hippo and beaver, is clearly not in its natural dynamic. Nor are the National Parks of the USA, now devoid of mastodon, giant sloth, and their sabre-toothed predators.

Would we define that great mega-faunal extinction as 'natural'? Or were those paleo-Indians with their flints and bone tools in some sense unnatural? And further back, the aboriginal colonisation of Australia some 60,000 years ago, not only caused the extinction of a celebrated marsupial Serengeti, but wrought enormous changes in Australia's forests which became more prone to fire and favoured fire-resistant species. At what point in human history did humans cease to be natural?

At the other extreme – few would want to categorise the megafaunal depletion of the oceans, where 500,000 great whales were taken, causing widespread ecosystem changes, and driven by profit and a market for whale-oils, as part of the natural scheme of things, but as with all spectrums, where you draw the line is a matter of what exactly you wish to separate.

Perhaps the answer lies therefore in the degree to which humans, being apparently dominant, *surrender* that dominance to *natural processes*. Clearly, if we remove keystone species, prevent migrations, eliminate dangerous animals, or otherwise deter major natural processes for our own benefit, we have not surrendered that dominance.

In a forthcoming BANC book on rewilding, I propose *Areas of Natural Sanctuary* where nature, in the sense of that process which gave birth to us, is honoured by as little intervention as possible. Permaculturalists do this by devoting 10% of any holding to nature's wild processes, partly for observation and learning, and sometimes, partly as a sacrament. I have very largely dropped ideas based upon the ethos of ecosystem restoration which I started with, after becoming aware of a deeper time perspective.

Deep time perspectives

A deep-time perspective, such as Flannery's, gives us two conclusions that have yet to be factored into modern conservation thinking. Firstly, few ecologists realise just how severe human impact has been upon the temperate forest fauna. This fauna evolved over two million years, during which the current genera of herbivores and their predators and their inter-relations with each other and the plant kingdom were constituted. This evolution of form has been determined very largely by the processes of *climate change* inherent in periodic glaciations. In those fluctuations, huge swathes of European forest periodically contracted to glacial refuges, accompanied by massive fluctuations in numbers of forest and open country herbivores. There were also significant changes elsewhere in the amount of tropical rainforest and savannah. I recommend Derek Yalden's recent *History of British Mammals* for the local scene[2], and Turner and Anton's *The Big Cats and their relatives*, especially the chapter on climate changes, for insights into herbivore and predator guilds.[3]

The complex grazing regimes that emerged at the end of the last ice-age, and to which many refer to as a 'natural' pre-agricultural base-line, varied across Europe, according to latitude, altitude, and soil-type (the main determinants of tree species). However, this base-line was already massively compromised by the extinction of mammoth, forest elephant, forest rhino, and the decimation of horse and bison, which had both open country and forest eco-types, and would have profoundly affected forest dynamics. Thus, no European forest, however large it was and however minimal the human intervention, could today be regarded as 'without human influence' or 'true wilderness' with a potential for the 'full complement of nature's species' as Mark Fisher might hope. What then of the forest being 'self-willed'?

Franz Vera's 'new theory' has been a long time in the coming – conservation professionals are just waking up to what paleo-ecology has suspected for several decades. Referring to this new thinking, James Fenton now proposes, in the absence of the original herbivores guild, that sheep and cattle can do a decent job of mimicking natural processes, and further suggests that the current British uplands – virtually our only remaining 'wild' land, and for which rewilding conservationists have been urging a retreat from economic use - might *already* sufficiently represent the *natural* balance of vegetation. Again, this does not acknowledge the potential for several solutions, each appropriate to different landscapes. It also skates over the detail of 'natural' processes and over-simplifies the ecological elements of the landscape. The post-glacial herbivore guild (i.e. already denuded of European elephant, rhino and hippo) had a particular structure – one species of cattle, one large deer or moose, one or two medium sized and one small deer, one forest pig, one beaver, one bison and one horse (the last two with various ecotypes). Each member of this guild grazed and browsed in different forest niches (the terrain-altering hippo grazed as far north as the Yorkshire Ouse in the previous only slightly warmer interglacial). Moreover, the presence of predators, whilst not necessarily affecting total population size, would determine spatial density and hence grazing and browsing pressure. The ecological consequences for shrubs, berry crops, field layers, germination patterns, insect pollinators, avian diversity, dung recyclers etc, would have been great and complex.

Either grazing on the left, or no grazing on the right - Snowdonia (Peter Taylor)

Thus, whilst it is not now possible to re-create or restore a full-spectrum 'natural' ecosystem in Europe, it can be done by degrees of naturalness that will depend both on the restoration of natural processes and the presence of keystone species or their substitutes. A British moorland of low-intensity Cheviots and Welsh Blacks, a balance of heather and grassland, a scattering of rowan on the slopes, oak and ash in the valley hangs, will have much to satisfy urban wanderers, and will clearly contain some natural processes and support an abundance of birds and insects. Much as this may be an appropriate management choice as a 'nature reserve' under many circumstances, it is a far cry from wildland proposals that would restore a broader herbivore guild, predators, and natural processes of disturbance and succession.

Furthermore, the current spate of tree planting, while hardly a natural process at its outset, is but the beginning of a restoration process for denuded soils. Once established, new forests would mature into a habitat network, aided by both human intervention in the early stages, and the re-introduction of wild herbivores or their rare breed equivalent. In some places, ancient British cattle and Soay-type sheep may be appropriate, and they would be accorded normal veterinary protection, in other larger areas protected by buffer zones, wild Heck 'auochsen' and primitive ponies, (the Large Herbivore Initiative thinks Exmoor ponies are more primitive than Poland's Konic) could be left to fend for themselves.

Cultural elements of a wild heart

We have seen little discussion of the cultural reasons for doing the things we might do at each end of the spectrum, and these are the real drivers of policy. Our current nature reserves exist, as both James Fenton and Mark Fisher point out, courtesy of agreements with landowners who need to make a living from their land. Furthermore, these largely unconnected semi-natural lands are isolated agricultural lands, and are not viable in the long term for reasons of genetic vulnerability and climate change.

I would agree with Mark Fisher, that there is no scientific derivation for an ethic of action. We might suppose that our own species' ecological stability depended upon a fully functional ecosystem, but at a prospective 10 billion people in the next decade or so, that planetary ecosystem is not going to resemble anything that went before! Self-interest might just conserve sufficient forest for tigers and gorillas, but it will not bring elephant and lion back to European temperate ecosystems! We might ascribe a 'right to survive' to re-constituted aurochs and tarpan, but we still have to find them enough genetic and migratory room for that survival, and then agree they have a right to slow death by natural diseases, death by combat, or predation by big cats. Even the laudable effort of the Dutch at Oostvarrdersplassen failed to get the first of these, despite getting the second, and is a far cry from bringing back the northern European lion!

Choosing our risks

In my view, it comes down to how wild we want the world to be. I value the presence of dangerous animals and the element of risk. I am happy to walk in forests where an encounter with a bear is a possibility. I am not so brave (or foolish?) as to do the same in a lion or tiger reserve, though I am quite happy in leopard or puma country. Bears, leopards and puma regularly kill people, as do cattle, horses, and even sheep, even in England, but the humble wasp is England's biggest wildlife threat. We accept some risks and not others. Different people accept different risks. There is a huge amount of hypocrisy too. Hunters and fishermen over-hype the effects of predators. Farmers play up sheep losses. Neither refer to the natural losses of disease, or to deaths from cars, renegade sheep dogs etc.

Where we go with this will be a matter of culture and, ultimately, not just of eco-spirituality, but also of its translation into market realities. A great deal of debate and education needs to take place about risk, as well as the economics of subsidised farming, and from this we can perhaps derive a better perspective on the benefits of a spectrum of wild land, core and corridors.

On the nature of that spectrum we might conclude that:

- natural processes occur at all levels in all ecosystems and that how far they predominate is a matter of degree and ultimately, a human decision.
- some natural processes cannot be replicated at all because essential species are extinct, or only in large areas, and even then, with some level of human-induced substitution; for example, the myriads of ecological processes created by forest elephants and rhino, river hippos and beavers.

Thus, a corn field with no hedges and no margins, no weeds, and genetically modified strains enabling broad spectrum herbicides, is very far from natural; whereas one with a hedgerow, unploughed marginal strips, farmed with natural strains, harvested with rotations to build up soil structure and fertility and under organic standards with no pesticides is a lot more natural in its use of nature's processes, and will have a greater diversity of the creatures we care about, such as butterflies and birds. Even so, it would present a barrier to migrating herbivores, but not an insurmountable obstacle if a river corridor of un-farmed land existed nearby.

Sanctuary in Britain

With regard to core-areas that could be connected by corridors, we could single out one large area of moorland (my book proposes one each for England, Scotland and Wales), with its current 1-2% of relic native woodland, no through roads, no other major human artefacts, where we could create something at the wildest end of the spectrum. In Scotland, Alan Featherstone has suggested an area of some 1500 km^2 west of the Great Glen, where natural processes would predominate. Studies in this area have already shown that deer numbers do suppress the vegetation and prevent regeneration. The forest is already out-of-balance. However, reducing deer numbers currently depends upon culling, that is, human intervention. Ideally, deer would compete with the larger spectrum of herbivores – and here, wild cattle, 'tarpan' like ponies, re-introduced moose, boar and beaver would restore something approaching the natural grazing and browsing regime. Predators such as bear (largely vegetarian but a regular predator of fawns and foals), wolf (deer and moose) and lynx (roe deer and hare), would, if not affecting numbers, at least affect spatial density sufficient to influence tree regeneration. The presence of predators can prevent deer remaining in one place, and herbivores avoid wolf-denning areas – all elements of the natural forest dynamic. We could add beaver to that picture, with their coppiced willow water meadows and luxuriant emergent vegetation.

In the smaller areas of England (North Pennines or Dartmoor) we might find 200-400 km^2, and a similar area in Snowdonia (the Rhinogydd) in which a more diverse herbivore guild could operate, but with perhaps only lynx and the hint of a naturalised panther to represent the carnivores.

The establishment of several large *Areas of Natural Sanctuary* could certainly be achieved by cooperation of a few landowners and organisations within current conservation thinking. A recent inter-agency Land Use Policy Group initiative to develop *New Wildwoods* proposes 'forest habitat networks', with National Trust and Forestry Commission holdings providing the starting points.[4] The main focus of the initiative is to kick-start a failing forest recovery plan by broadening the rationale of tree cover to encompass rewilding objectives. The proposals include conversion of plantations to native species but have yet to seriously address mammalian re-introduuctions. There are problems with wild herbivores that can harbour commercially damaging diseases, and prospering carnivores will export their progeny to areas where domestic stock graze.

Finally, as the Europeans are discovering, none of these 'core areas' makes much sense unless the animals can move between them, and thus rather extensive corridors are required and all that implies for the infrastructure of industrial areas, intensive agriculture, energy, water management and transport. Without such corridors, genetic isolation would threaten the large mammal populations, and in the longer term, where would they go when the ice comes back?

References and notes

[1] Tim Flannery (2000) *The Future Eaters* on Australian ecology and (2002) *The Eternal Frontier* on the past faunal history of North America.
[2] Derek Yalden (2000) *The history of Britsh mammals.*
[3] Turner and Anton (2000) *The Big Cats and their relatives.*
[4] Land Use Policy Group (2003) *New Wildwoods*
see also *www.caemabon.co.uk*

Wild thoughts followed up…

ECOS 25 (1) 18-20 (2004)

JAMES FENTON

I agree with Peter Taylor that palaeocological studies are essential in understanding the nature we have today: Jared Diamond in *The Rise and Fall of the Third Chimpanzee* argues that there never was a Golden Age when humans were 'in balance' with nature, citing the extinctions of large animals that took place when humans colonised new areas. Thus, as Peter argues, we can never return to a pre-human complement of species, or distribution of vegetation.

The ancient guild of herbivores in the pre-glacial forests of Britain - Straight tusked forest elephant, moose, forest rhino, aurochs, tarpan, and wild boar - with red deer, roe deer and hare still present. (Peter Taylor)

The argument of what is 'natural' is basically a semantic one: humans have coined the word 'natural' as a contradistinction to 'artificial' - it is a useful way of looking at the world to separate that which is given *a priori* and of which humans are not in charge (i.e. nature), and artefacts. If the world 'natural' is used to include humans, then everything we do is, by definition, natural - even making species extinct - and no consistent rationale for conservation will be possible (this is not to deny that we have not evolved from nature, and there will have to an arbitrary cut-off point as to when humans became a species). I find it a very useful word, as it helps us make sense of the world: before humans existed, everything was natural - now there is a mix! And, of course, it is rarely black or white: I might create a pond, for example, i.e. an artefact, but its ecosystem could be natural (i.e. is identical to a natural analogue). If the word 'nature' is dodgy, as Peter states, then all of us involved in nature conservation might as well give up and go home!

Additionally, one needs to be very careful with the word 'natural processes': nutrient cycling and chemical pathways, for example, are natural processes, although the origins of the chemicals can be anthropogenic; eg. loss of species by adding fertiliser (eutrophication) is a 'natural process', as is global warming from increased anthropogenic CO_2 emission. On analysis, what is meant by 'natural processes' becomes synonymous with 'processes with no human involvement', which, in my view, becomes synonymous with 'wild' - 'letting nature be in charge'.

If we are to let nature be in charge in certain areas, i.e. be wild, we have to mean what we say, and get rid of our preconceptions of how the system should operate: we must have 'undefined outcomes' with respect to habitat and species composition. As indicated above, we cannot return to an earlier 'natural pattern'. This is not to say, though, that we should not be seeking an understanding of natural systems, so we can get an idea of how natural systems operate: I was arguing that such an understanding leads to the perfectly reasonable hypothesis that, in the infertile uplands, natural successional trends (in the presence of grazing) lend greater credence to 'the natural decline' woodland model, than the alternative models of 'woodland as climax' or Frans Vera's 'cyclical model' (although all will have validity at a given location). Lee Klinger, for example, has argued that peat bogs are often the endpoint of succession as they are more self-buffered against environmental change (although there is evidence that blanket peat itself has a limited life time).

I would thus argue, in contradiction to Mark and Peter, that much of upland Britain, particularly in the far north and west, *are the 'wildernesses' that they say we do not have in this country* (albeit lacking some of the mammals, although this has not affected the vegetation pattern): it is just that their preconception, or mental image, of the 'wilderness as woodland' is incorrect - at least in infertile upland Britain. And such infertile areas (low potential biological productivity) will not support such a range of species, including large mammals, as in lowland Britain. Hence one must be very wary of generalising across the UK. My fundamental point for upland Britain is that, even if humans have modified the natural processes of grazing and burning, the uplands would look much the same even if they had not: i.e. the current vegetation pattern lies within the range of natural variation.

Likewise, in Scotland, and naturally (through chance) their natural species complement would vary: some may have had large herbivores, some predators, some none, etc, so we cannot say "the system should have this or that complement". *Perhaps letting things go wild means getting rid of the word "should"?* However, the fact that Scottish moorland vegetation appears pretty uniform, regardless of its history, implies that the general successional trend has been towards open moorland. Also, I do not think size is always relevant, as Mark suggests: some of our most perfect 'wildernesses' could be very small off-shore islands that have never experienced human impact (other than global warming and input of air-transported anthropogenic chemicals). Likewise, I have created pond in my garden, but I am not in charge of the underwater ecosystem: the balance of amphibians, invertebrates, plants, etc in it is probably indistinguishable from a nearby natural pond, and is, in effect, a wilderness! (I have been watching pond skaters on my pond, and their social system appears to be a more liberal democracy than, say, ants or bees. However, the great diving beetle appears to have eaten them or chased them away, which shows how liberal democracies can be upset by bigger, violent bullies!)

I do not think either Peter or Mark are willing to fully let go, or 'let nature be in charge': they assume that 'having nature be in charge' will automatically mean more species and diversity: this may or may not be the case at a given locality. Allowing nature to be in charge may well result in bracken invading a species-rich sward, or foxes and crows being more common than other species: *we have to get rid of value judgements - accepting things we do not like as much as things we do like*. This, though, is where size does become important: the bigger the geographical area, the more scope for conserving the full range of species.

Peter states that "deer numbers suppress vegetation and eat regeneration." I would argue strongly that different grazing pressures result in different vegetation patterns, and generally, in upland Scotland, evidence suggests that the greater the grazing level the greater the number of *vascular* plants (which is not to say they will all be flowering as, for, example in a Yorkshire hay-meadow, which is perhaps a cultural artefact and the wrong model to hold in one's mind!). Deer have been around for millions of years, and have always been eating trees, and trees just have to put up with it! If they cannot, they become rare! It is a difficult to answer the question "what is the natural grazing level", as people argue either way that predators affect herbivore numbers. I prefer the theory that grazing is limited by forage availability in the limiting season (e.g. cold or dry).

Perhaps the only way to find out is to stop managing and see what happens, adding missing species where possible: culling deer because we perceive there are too many to me appears the opposite of letting nature be wild!

In upland Britain, my fear is that we already have a (relatively) natural, wild network of moorland core areas, that we are replacing with woodland corridors - based on a dubious reading of the ecological history. Woodland corridors are also ideal conduits for the spread of introduced species like grey squirrel and sika deer: our approach to alien species, though, deserves a whole new debate, but in my view, conserving biodiversity means conserving the full range of species and habitats indigenous to an area.

I have been arguing for a long time that nature conservation is a broad church, and that different approaches are necessary in different places (see, for example, my article in *La Canada* No17, spring 2003):

1. wild areas are those with no predetermined ecological outcomes;
2. nature reserves are prescriptive, with defined outcomes;
3. in the rest of the countryside, nature has to fit in.

I believe that in wild areas or wildernesses, we have to let go our preconceptions, as well as nature!

ECOS 25 (1) 21-22 (2003)
MARK FISHER

Perhaps another two words can be joined together to convey a meaning for Peter Taylor's 'either-or-thinking': I would choose the similar sounding, but with opposite meaning AUTARCHY-AUTARKY. Autarchy means absolute sovereignty, and is what I think characterises our approach to land management in Britain. The recent observation of the Herpetological Conservation Trust that pheasants released for gaming purposes may be driving down snake and lizard populations is yet another manifestation of the range of our intervention. On the other hand, autarky means self-reliance, something we deny wild nature and that which I seek to return to it. While Peter may juggle with our pre-history, I'm not sure I want to set myself up to be the judge of whether my species has intervened past the point of return. I do, however, accept responsibility to act in good faith in restoring species where they still exist in European refuge, and accept willingly any risk that is posed.

The causative factors that Peter speaks of are either happenstance or they are contrived. I cannot deny a role for the human species when the part we played in the extinction of mega-herbivores would certainly have exerted an influence on planetary flora. But would we have foreseen that at the time, and would it have been our conscious intention? My time perspective for our species must therefore date from the point of removal of happenstance, when our drive for survival saw a merit in maintaining the existence of those we depended on. As a mark of our increasing sophistication in reasoning, we contrived a landscape to suit our purposes and chose which species to exterminate when they posed a threat to it. Are we not also the only species that harvests the lactation of others?

It is this analysis that tells me that the American approach to self-willed land, of excluding the influence of people and their productive activities, is the best hope for giving that self-reliance back to wild nature. It is a necessary counter to the incorrigible weakness of compromise that infests our modern day approach to conservation. If it will help, I think of it as an atonement to wild nature, to the species we have extirpated and to our autochthonous ancestors. For those who revolt at the agricultural improvements and enclosures of more recent history that led to landless labour in rural England (and a clearance of the populace in Scotland) then the removal of some of that land from agriculture into publicly owned wild nature will at least sever it from that tainted inheritance.

Culture and metaphysics aside, Peter's proposals for *Areas of Natural Sanctuary* at least have an element of reforestation about them. On the other hand, James' new paradigm for the uplands is a maintenance of the status quo and would perpetuate the enforced coexistence of wild nature with agriculture. On the nature of this agriculture, Peter gives us idealised visions of two different farming systems. The current trend is for us to consider that it is more acceptable for a co-existence of wild nature with the superficial attractions of organic farming, while overlooking such inherent drawbacks as loss of soil carbon from tillage and mineral depletion, neither of which coincidentally would affect his other farming example. These contested approaches to farming are the 'either-or' of the moment, missing the leavening of Peter's *spectrum* of regime, and reaffirming to me the need for a separation between wild nature and agriculture. I would, however, put in plea that we now look seriously at other no problem with Vera's challenge to a primeval blanket of climax wildwood approaches, such as integrated farming systems, agroforestry and Permaculture.

It was only a matter of time before the theories of Frans Vera in his *Metaphors for the Wilderness* would end up in a justification of agriculture in nature conservation, though James does only apply it to upland areas. I have across Europe because instinct suggests that it is too simple an explanation, and it belies evidence from other continents showing a variety of grassland, scrub, and open and closed woodland. But if we go with Vera's theory, we have to examine the range of weather and soil conditions, the dynamism (turnover) in tree population, the stage at which wild herbivores exerted their influence, and their population size (would it have been equivalent to the 10 million cattle, 30-40 million sheep and untold rabbits and horses that we have now?). We would then try to predict what the situation would have been at steady state.

There are co-dependent and independent variables in there that stretch my capability for modelling. Thus in the absence of such proofs, I have to rely on the observations I make every time I walk the millstone grit and limestone landscapes of Yorkshire. In a natural system that has co-species plants, herbivores and carnivores, the balance for our temperate climate and soil conditions would be more area of woodland of various types compared to the area of open grassed spaces, even in most of our upland areas. It then becomes a circular argument as to whether the herding and concentration of livestock by a post aboriginal population is the driver that led - through grazing pressure - to a reverse in the ratio of woodland to open space, or if it was assisted by farmers clearing the woodland themselves to provide carrying capacity for livestock and for growing crops. Either way, the diminutive woodland coverage of today is the end result, along with a landscape wholly fashioned by people. I think wild nature can do better and I am willing to give it a chance.

ECOS 25 (1) 23-24 (2004)
PETER TAYLOR

I will take some convincing that 'upland Britain is within the range of natural variation'. I would like to tackle that issue first, because James' view, if accepted, would be at serious loggerheads with the whole 'wildwoods' strategy of Forest Habitat Networks, corridors, and core areas. There are, however, some misunderstandings regarding that strategy:

i.) we are not talking about continuous canopy woodland as a 'climax' vegetation, but of a *mosaic of habitat* where woodland might occupy about 40%, with open heath, blanket bog, wet flushes, rocky ground, and glades the rest (and that very much building upon and respecting the current conservation value of key upland areas), and I feel, intuitively, this would be closer to the habitat we would now have had human not interfered so much. That is nowhere near the case for large areas of the current British uplands. We should also take care not to generalise - the 'uplands' vary enormously, from almost treeless areas of blanket bog, to equally treeless areas of bracken and heather or acid grassland, all of which would respond differently to being left alone, or afforested with an added complement of indigenous grazers and browsers.

ii.) there is a problem with infertile upland soils having probably had less tree cover under natural herbivores - even poor soils and exposed conditions will support woodland, - Wistman's Wood being a good example, and if the soils *were* originally impoverished, they would have attracted fewer herbivores and thus have been less open. Given the propensity of rowan, birch, juniper and willow to hang on it the most exposed places, and colonise ungrazed sites close to seed sources, I cannot see that the current pattern is likely to reflect past patterns.

iii) the problem with letting nature take over and thereby *losing* biodiversity may be an artefect of size and time scale - small reserves of species rich grassland would become less diverse in flowering plants - though who counts the beetles and thrips? And even if the insect fauna of twenty hectares of woodland that replaced downland *were* more diverse - on a national scale, the country might lose diversity (though not the continent!). But if nature reserves were larger, then natural processes of disturbance and grazing might safeguard that diversity. Initial losses might be time-dependent, being made up as the ecosystem matures.

iv) culling deer is not necessary, of course, if the endpoint is the current open moorland and limited natural regeneration of forest - they will find their unnatural limit, sans predators, sans competitors, but it is clearly necessary if the aim is to re-establish a more forested landscape (from 1% ancient woodland to 40%, for example, over a large area such as Snowdonia, Dartmoor or Caledon); with regard to aliens, such as grey squirrel, sika, muntjac and the like - these are likely to prosper, but they are also a fact of the globalised present (and not dissimilar in *process* to invasions caused by land-bridges on an evolutionary timescale).

Ultimately, these issues *do* challenge what we have called *nature conservation!* Nature, as natural, as not artificial, no longer exists. But rather than pack our bags and go home, we could be honest about that - the emperor of nature conservation science may have a few clothes left, but they are decidedly ragged. Better to admit that, and develop a new ethos - that we will conserve what we like for no other reason than we like it. That liking might include a purely economic motive - such as deer for trophy hunters, or even an economy based upon visitors to the scenery. There are utilitarian and aesthetic values in nature conservation, but curiously, supposedly scientific values of biodiversity, ecosystem stability, and even naturalness, currently hold sway. It is rather like a reverse of the demise of religion - the old paradigm was flawed, a result of special interests, and as the flaws become more widely understood, new values are emerging. The challenge for conservationists is to adapt to these changes. One crucial adaptation will be a pluralistic process, with different management models, involving many interest groups, with the mix varying from place to place, and where participation in the setting of values is paramount. The kind of changes that the National Trust and Forest Enterprise are working in re-wilding Ennerdale, for example, where plantations are being made more natural, grazing reduced, river and lakeshore rewilded, but economic activity maintained, would complement another wilder core-area in the eastern Lakes or Northen Pennines, where sheep were removed, woodland regenerated, deer allowed back, and a few lynx re-introduced.

Likewise, Alan Featherstone's proposals for Caledon, would contrast with other areas, such as Knoydart, where crofters would have a presence in the relatively wild landscape; and in Snowdonia, the National Trust are extending the treeline on the flanks of Snowdon with reduced grazing, and this will always be a high recreation area of open landscape, whereas the Rhinog lends itself to core-area status, few visitors, and the re-creation of a large oak forest.

Connectivity and networks

Thinking big – a better deal for connecting nature

ECOS 31 (3/4) 18-24 (2010)

The Lawton Report, Making Space for Nature, *offers a more bold and creative approach to wildlife conservation. Conservation groups must press for its endorsement in the coming White Paper.*

TONY WHITBREAD

Nature conservation has traditionally focused on conserving the most important parts of our natural environment. Find the best areas, protect them and then look after them through some form of conservation management – this has generally appeared to be our conservation strategy. However, even right from the start this has not really been the case. Different generations may have had different words, but these special places have often been seen as reservoirs, or hot-spots, or centres of colonisation, or core areas. The picture is not one of isolated living museums; it is more one of important parts within a much wider ecological network.

Gains but net losses

The environment of tomorrow can only evolve out of what remains today, so there must be no question of any new approach sweeping away the hard-won levels of protection for our most important nature conservation assets. Special areas (Nature Reserves, Sites of Special Scientific Interest, and Local Wildlife Sites etc) are important in their own right. But they become far more effective if they are part of a much wider system of functional ecosystems.

In 2008 the House of Commons Environmental Audit Committee concluded that the UK had failed to halt the loss of biodiversity and that we were not going to meet our 2010 Biodiversity Objectives. The EU has now set a new target "to halt the loss of biodiversity and the degradation of ecosystem services by 2020." Another firm commitment but what are the chances of success if we just try to do more of the same? Indeed time and again we hear firm political commitments to nature conservation, whether it is the Wildlife and Countryside Act, the Convention on Biological Diversity, commitments to deliver Biodiversity Action Plans, or warm words in local authorities' Local Development Frameworks. We may think we are getting somewhere but in practice the gains are at best small. Loss of biodiversity continues, at global and local scales, unfortunately confirming that we are indeed in the middle of the sixth global mass extinction event.

Economics – friend or foe?

Evidence from studies such as The Millennium Ecosystem Assessment (2005), The Economics of Ecosystems and Biodiversity (TEEB) and now the UK National Ecosystem Assessment (NEA) are confirming what ecologists have known for decades – nature provides the services on which we depend for all aspects of human well-being (The TEEB material will be reviewed in the next ECOS by John Bowers). Ecosystem services are provided by a healthy, functioning environment but at present many of these are unknown and unvalued. This is already having direct economic consequences. TEEB, for instance, has estimated that the economic loss through damage to ecosystem services from the degradation of forests alone is far greater than the economic losses experienced during the worst of the recent recession. As ecosystems degrade further, these losses will increase.

In brief, nature is continuing to be degraded but we rely entirely on a healthy, functioning nature for our economy, sense of well-being and ultimately for our very existence. Whilst past approaches to nature conservation have had some success, the failure of the current system to reverse the long-term trend of biodiversity loss indicates that we need a paradigm shift in the policies and approach we adopt for our natural world.

Pressure for change

Before the general election the Wildlife Trusts lobbied the main political parties to create a major new driver for the natural world to achieve a Living Landscape. One result of this, in September 2009, was the formation of a review group to look at England's ecological network by Hilary Benn, the then Secretary of State for the Department for Environment, Food and Rural Affairs. 'Making Space for Nature: a review of England's Wildlife Sites and Ecological Network', was therefore set up and chaired by Professor Sir John Lawton, a highly respected ecologist from York University. Even as the Lawton review was underway we turned our efforts towards gaining cross party commitment for a White Paper, with the support of other Non Government Organisations. The General Election and subsequent change of government in May 2010 could otherwise have put paid to this, but the new Secretary of State, Caroline Spelman, was totally committed to the White Paper.

The completed Lawton Report[1] was submitted to the Secretary of State on 16 September 2010. The Lawton review asked the basic question "do England's wildlife sites comprise a coherent and resilient ecological network?" In essence it asks whether our current approach can deliver an ecological network where "biodiversity is enhanced and the diversity, functioning and resilience of ecosystems re-established in a network of spaces for nature that can sustain these levels into the future, even given continuing environmental change and human pressure." An ecological network should restore species and habitats to levels better than in 2000, restore the ecological and physical processes that underpin ecosystems, enhancing the capacity to provide ecosystem services, and provide accessible, wildlife rich, natural environments for people to enjoy and experience.

Our environment faces huge challenges, from demographic change, economic growth, new technologies, societal preferences, and changes in policy and regulation, for example. All these will have huge consequences on the environment. Establishing a coherent and resilient ecological network will help wildlife to cope with these changes. It will also improve the ability of our environment to provide the range and quality of ecosystem services upon which we all depend.

The Lawton agenda

The review essentially concluded that **our current scatter of wildlife sites does not comprise a coherent and resilient ecological network**. Perhaps this is not a surprise, but it is significant that a government commissioned report, drawing on a wide range of evidence and expert opinion came to this conclusion.

The Lawton review then sets out 24 recommendations for what needs to be done in order to make the coherent, resilient ecological network that we need. Together these recommendations provide a key check-list for what we should be expecting from the new Natural Environment White Paper.
First, the review recommends that ecological networks should be identified and protected. Looking after what we have is the basic starting point. Importantly, however, this includes areas for ecological restoration, and thus not solely focusing on the areas that are currently of high quality.

A key theme is the delivery of landscape-scale ecological restoration. This, it proposes, should be done through the establishment of Ecological Restoration Zones (ERZs) - "large, discrete areas within which significant enhancements of ecological networks are achieved, by enhancing existing wildlife sites, improving ecological connections and restoring ecological processes". It also promotes making space for nature along river catchments through the expansion of wetlands and the restoration of natural processes. Coastal management should also take full account of the natural dynamics of the coast, thereby allowing habitats to move and evolve.

The proposals were summarised in four words – "more, bigger, better and joined."

The review suggests that the process should start with the development of 12 Ecological Restoration Zones around the country. The Wildlife Trusts view is that this would be far too minimal; indeed to limit ambitions to just 12 ERZs would be to ignore a large amount of work that has already taken place. As a comparison the biodiversity partnerships in the South East of England have got together to develop a map of large scale Biodiversity Opportunity Areas (BOAs). This process has involved a large number of partners, extensive consultation and is now accepted as the basis of the South East Biodiversity Strategy. It did feed into the South East Plan (before it was abolished by the new government) and should now feed into the more local strategies that replace it. So a lot of work has been done. In Sussex alone we have identified some 75 BOAs.

Ideas into action – large or small?

Sometimes it is helpful to think of a real area in order to put some 'meat on the bones' of some of these general strategies so I'll talk briefly about one such location in Sussex. The Sussex Wildlife Trust has a West Weald Living Landscape project in a large area on the Surrey-Sussex border, to the south east of Haslemere. This is an agglomeration of Biodiversity Opportunity Areas that can broadly be described as a forest matrix, containing within it some of the most important ancient woods for nature conservation in Europe. We know the nature of the ecosystems there, and partnerships of key organisations have been established and landowners are involved. This has all led to a good understanding of the ecological processes at work and the various ecosystem services delivered. Work is underway here already, although better support would see far more achieved. The point, however, is that this could provide a model for future ERZs.

In practice, Ecological Restoration Zones should surely be on a scale similar to that of the West Weald Landscape project. If so then ERZs must ultimately be identified in every part of the UK and therefore there should be a large number of them, all interlinked to form what truly is a coherent ecological network. Just 12 such projects scattered around the country will be far too few to have much positive effect on a failing country-wide ecological network.

The Lawton Report does not claim to offer accurate estimates of the cost of its recommendations but it does touch on how they might be implemented. Current financial mechanisms (such as Environmental Stewardship and tax incentives) need to be improved, and new ones brought in. Economic approaches are needed that favour conservation management by stimulating new markets and payment for ecosystem services, to ensure that the values of a wide range of ecosystem services are taken into account in decisions that affect the management and use of the natural world.

Nature paying its way?

Payment for ecosystem services is a growing theme. It was addressed in the Lawton review and options and examples are currently being researched by Defra. The UK National Ecosystem Assessment aims to describe the state and value of the UK's ecosystem services. If this value is properly understood, then the need for healthy, functioning ecosystems should also be recognised. The natural environment should then start to have due primacy in policy, legal and economic decision making.

There are, however, dangers in ascribing an economic value to the natural world; there are more fundamental, over-riding ethical considerations that justify nature conservation at a higher level than its utilitarian value. Some scientists described an economic valuation of ecosystem services as a "poor approximation of infinity" – how can you put a price on something that you can't do without. Furthermore I would argue that our economy is not the over-riding system we imagine it to be. It is essentially a sub-system that relies totally on the whole system which is the environment itself. It is odd to value the over-riding system (the environment) according to the values of a sub-system (the economy). Thus whilst economists may ask us to justify the environment in terms of its economic worth we should rather be asking the economists to justify the economy in terms of its environmental worth. Furthermore, such ecosystem services are essential, non-tradable and required by everyone, so should largely fall above economic value.

Nevertheless, it is difficult to express the essential worth of the environment in a world so heavily biased towards economic value. As Pavan Sukhdev, leader of the TEEB initiative, has said, putting a monetary value on something does not mean you are creating a market for it. Furthermore, when economic evaluations of nature are carried out TEEB shows that economic benefits of environmental protection are often between 10 and 100 times greater than the costs.

The value of nature therefore needs to be embedded into decision-making at all levels. The current link of damage to ecosystem services and biodiversity loss on the one hand with economic growth on the other is in practice a market failure of greater severity even than that which has led to climate change. Indeed the need to disconnect economic growth from negative environmental impact is perhaps the greatest challenge of our time. Re-internalising the costs to nature and the benefits from nature into policy and practice will help set the basis for an economic structure that is symbiotic with nature rather than parasitic upon it.

The work of the UK NEA could provide a framework in this respect, categorising ecosystem services into a hierarchical structure:

- First are the **Primary Ecological Functions** fundamentally supporting all subsequent ecosystem services. These include all supporting services and the major regulating services.
- Second are the **Final Ecosystem Services** including the remaining regulating services and all cultural and provisioning services. These underpin the goods we receive.
- Third are the **Goods** themselves which have a financial or non-financial value to humans.

In order to avoid double counting, 'value' is attributed at one stage – usually from the 'goods' received at the end of the hierarchy (and even then some goods are valued while others are not). In practice goods are often seen as competitive, with any area of land providing one or another good. Even worse a 'good' may be seen as competitive with its underpinning ecosystem services and even with the primary ecological functions that support all services. Intensive food production is an example of the bias in the way we currently evaluate services. In this case food is the only good that is evaluated. All other goods provided by that area of land are either degraded, unvalued, assumed to be free or assumed to be infinite. Food is an essential provisioning service but if produced at the cost of all other goods then it is a very inefficient use of land, and if it is provided at the cost of the ecosystem services and ecological functions on which it depends then it is ultimately self-destructive.

Furthermore, with our valuing system so biased towards a small number of goods, biodiversity can be relegated to a small, special interest in a sub-group behind one of the goods (a sub-set of recreation perhaps). In practice, however, biodiversity
- forms the basic building blocks of the ecosystems that underpin ecological functions;
- is an indicator of ecological health;
- is valued by people; and
- provides genes and species for crops and other products.

Building up credit

A key principle from an ecosystem approach should be the delivery of multiple ecosystem services from an area of land; any forces acting on that area should be supportive of rather than counter-productive to ecosystem service delivery. A consequence for the forthcoming White paper could be that all activities should be ecosystem and biodiversity 'proofed'. If an activity negatively impacts on biodiversity or ecosystem services then it should pay a realistic cost to reflect that impact, but if it has a positive effect then it should receive some form of ecosystem or biodiversity credit.

When ecosystems are seen as not only essential but also providing an economic benefit, then this might put a rather different complexion on the apparent 'costs' of implementing Lawton's 24 recommendations. Instead of being seen as costs perhaps it should be seen as paying for the benefits we are (or should be) receiving from healthy ecosystems. If we don't pay for them, we may not get them. That will have much larger economic consequences.

I suggest there are two main themes that come out of the Lawton review and the UK National Ecosystem Assessment:

• First: **Major landscape-scale ecological restoration** – Ecological Restoration Zones, river catchment restoration, re-instatement of natural processes and a large 'ecological network' philosophy. England has failed to meet its 2010 biodiversity objectives so we need to scale-up the future action.
• Second: **Recognising the value of functional ecosystems** because of the ecosystem services they deliver and so developing financial mechanisms to pay for them. We can no longer ignore the value of what nature provides for us. Both these elements must be fully addressed in the forthcoming Natural Environment White Paper. If successful this should create a paradigm shift in our attitude towards the natural world, returning primacy to environmental quality rather than economic growth. We must aim high.

Reference
1. Lawton J, Brotherton P, Brown V, Elphick C, Fitter A, Forshaw J, et al. (2010) Making space for nature: a review of England's wildlife sites and ecological networks. London: Defra.

Lakeland valleys and Somerset hills - a tale of two managements

ECOS 31 (3/4) 40-44 (2010)

Just as there can be a world of difference between two Lakeland valleys depending on their management, so apparently can there be between regions of the same organisation.

PETER TAYLOR

At the end of September 2010 I had the pleasure of walking Ennerdale in Cumbria with its custodian managers of the Forestry Commission, the National Trust and United Utilities (who own the lake), surveying the evolution of habitats since the whole valley was subject to landscape-scale 'rewilding' at the turn of the Millennium. At the head of the valley the changes were hardly discernible – reduced sheep numbers had been augmented by cattle, and the longer term aim under discussion was a cattle-only option. The sward was still cropped low and streamside tall-herb vegetation showed no sign of recovery. But the problem with reducing sheep numbers is that neighbouring flocks then invade the valley and defeat the manoeuvre! Then there were the areas of clear-felled Sitka – some showed no regeneration of this exotic and were sprouting a new native wildwood of birch and rowan, whilst others were rampantly regenerating another Sitka stand. Such outcomes depended on the age of the stand when cut and the latent seed-bank. Should the battle be waged further, or simply surrendered? And further down by the lake, old meadows were now grazed only by cattle, which also had access to the old conifer woods along the valley sides – they were rougher and wilder and much fencing had been removed. Most exciting of all, the river Liza had been allowed to breach her old containment and wander across the valley bottom, creating new meanders and pools. The pace of change is slow – rather painfully slow for the rewilding faithful on the management advisory group, but there is something in the slowness that is very educational.

*The River Liza in Ennerdale - in the process of carving out a new channel.
(Peter Taylor)*

Floods and ecosystem services

As Alison Parfitt pointed out at our meeting, this part of Cumbria is a tale of two rivers. The one at Cockermouth last year, just over the valley watershed, that flooded the town, took out a bridge and claimed the life of a local policeman. That valley was grazed flat and the river totally contained along almost all its courses. When so highly charged, like an angered deity, the river had retaliated with enormous power. In this valley, Liza had reclaimed her wildness and was a subject of awe to us all, as if her wild spirit got under the skin and we all realised just how much we gained from sitting with her and simply watching and listening.

Is there a lesson for other valleys? How so when the economy of hill farming requires every inch of valley in-bye land for bringing the sheep down off the hill? Generations of farmers have cleared the boulders and built the levees, and the sheep have razored the banks as well as the fields. Long gone are the breeding lapwing and curlew and the flower-rich meadows, even within the borders of a National Park. It doesn't have to be like that, of course, but an alternative would require a major cultural shift – a surrender of hard-won grazing land, uneconomic cattle instead of uneconomic sheep, restoration of streamside vegetation and meandering pools, and all to be paid for under a system of ecological service provision (water quality, flood alleviation, carbon sequestration and increased biodiversity). That is not so difficult, considering the whole upland sheep economy is paid for by the EU taxpayer anyway. All that is required is a shift in what the recipient is expected to provide. And of course, as the Lawton report may presage, such a shift is underway – conservation has finally found a way to package the whole lot into the service economy.

At the pace of cultural change

But of course, a cultural shift is required, and this is slow. That's why the National Trust keeps sheep on the hill in Ennerdale and it is Galloway cattle that come when you whistle in the woods, and not the scary-horned and potential health-and-safety nightmare of an aurochsian Heck, or a wild moose or wood bison. Cultural change is slow, and here the National Trust is committed not just to consultation with local communities, but actually implementing their wishes. The locals like the elderly and majestic Spruce and Larch and so they remain. Paths and bridleways are maintained.

The radical in me wants to lobby for a fully wild valley, ethnically cleansed of its aliens, with beaver, elk, aurochs, and boar. And if the neighbours can be convinced to keep cattle on the fell instead of sheep, then lynx would be feasible. But as we sit around the table, I know that everyone else knows that this is for future generations to decide and we will proceed slowly. I like it when I am invited and listened to, and it is nice to give something back and experience some open-minded and progressive conservation.
Walton Hill, SSSI

I returned then to my own patch of the wild. Across the little B-road outside the house, lies Walton Hill, owned by the National Trust and managed in conjunction with local grazers – who kept the rights, and as part of a small landscape-scale project to maintain the Polden Hills – a string of sites of limestone grassland knolls and a mosaic of woodland that bisects the Somerset Levels. I have been walking the same few hundred metres of path around the hill for over ten years. Here I found my first bee orchid. One early spring, I watched as a goshawk pair completed their almost suicidal diving courtship, and though the wood is narrow along the side of the hill by the old windmill, there is a corner where it is dense with under-storey and I never did locate their nest from which I know they reared two or three youngsters. One year I was annoyed that sheep were staying later on the hill and would eat all the orchids. I contacted the Trust's ecologist – he told me there was not much he could do, that the grazer was tricky to control. I discovered that the original agreement was with Clark's estate (the shoe people) and a simply letter was dispatched about responsibilities to nature (the site is also an SSSI, but I did not know that at the time). The sheep left the very next day.

81

Earlier this year, I noticed that the brush-cutter's van was parked much longer than usual – long after he had cut back the brambles, nettles and old thistle stands. A little walk confirmed my fears – the chainsaws had been at work on the other side of the hill. Gone were the thickets under and around the goshawk's hide-out of oak, maple and ash in that little quiet corner. Thirty or forty-year old hawthorns had been neatly sawed into piles. All the blackthorn and similarly aged elder had been cleared and burned. Some had been just a metre from the boundary fence which was now neat and open for all to see. Even where some thorn trees had been left at the top where they had been in open ground, they had been cleansed of bramble and their aged clematis and honeysuckle lianas hung limply a few feet from the ground. I guessed the site was being returned to "favourable condition" – the key goal for any SSSI.

Walton Hill: Clearing of scrub to add a few percentage points for limestone grassland (Peter Taylor)

This had been my favourite spot. It had long ceased to be a quiet place – the farm below the wood had been converted to a skeet-shooting business, day in day out the hill now sounded like a battlefield. It complemented the now ever-present helicopter gun-ships built down the road at Yeovil Westlands. The B-road now suffered from the curse of Sat-Nav and there is a daily rush hour that starts at 7am. Lorries trundle past throughout the night and there is a patch of road that causes them to bump and rattle their contents, as well as the foundations of the house. I often think of its former life, when the windmill provided flour and the house was a bakery for the nearby villages – it must have been so quiet!

And now, after so many years, the National Trust was another enemy of that which I love. At first sight of the clearances, I found the chain-saw ecologist on the hill and asked him about the cleansing. I didn't talk much because my heart was beating part of anger part of grief. I made a plea for the rest of the hill and especially the stand of older sloe bushes which always put on such an amazing display. And I pointed out the forty-year elder and hawthorn and how much we in the house loved their spring show. He responded that they needed to protect the grassland which was very special but he would take into account what I had said.

Informing not consulting

So – early in this October, I was concerned to see a note in the local paper that the Trust would meet with local residents one Saturday morning to outline their plan for the hill. It did not speak of consultation. My sister and I were the only people to show. The ecologist and a naturalist from Millfield, who also manage woodland nearby, were there to explain the plan. I asked if it was a consultation. They looked perplexed. No - they were outlining their plan. And he then went on to explain about limestone grassland and the rare and threatened species it contained. I said I understood a little about the issues - and was there not a debate about the common and the local, public values and pleasure and how to balance that with professional scientific, target-led conservation?

Apparently not here on Walton Hill. It had already been decreed and here was a map. It showed how in nineteen sixty-something the hill had been grassland all the way to the fence and so a lot of rare habitat had been lost. All they were doing was restoring it to its previous condition.

No amount of persuasion was going to alter anything. The key man was going to brazen it out and the other just kept smiling. I pointed out that they might get an extra 5% more grassland, that the grass would be shaded still by the bigger trees left standing and by the boundary wood, and that the soil where the thickets had been was already enriched. I pointed out that in ten years, the brambles had not encroached and that the grazing regime was the key to maintaining a balance. I emphasised the word balance. I talked of nest sites for blackcap and thrush, long-tailed tit and bullfinch; of feeding for bees and countless insect species; of the thrill of the spring show of elder, may-blossom and blackthorn, summer clematis and honeysuckle....how though these were all common species, you would have to walk miles to find anything like the show we had here. No avail, not against the chalk-hill blue (one of a dozen small blue butterflies that all look the same to the uneducated eye) and the Lady's bedstraw (we already had a fine meadow of these this summer and that is dependent on the right grazing regime). And they knew what they were talking about with regard to what they expected to achieve – with lots of experience at restoring grassland...and I said, 'Okay, I am a generalist'. What do I know but from a practised ecological eye? And then at the end, the smiling man said, 'well, if after 40 years we don't get it, we can change the plan'.

Of course! The longer term. And here was I concerned about my own selfish patch and the next 10 or 20 years of my enjoyment. My sister remarked, 'So, like he said, it is all an experiment'. No, I told her, 'It is a target from headquarters. There will be a grant system somewhere. A box to tick.' And I thought, that box will be called 'returned to favourable condition'.

I had said to the Trust's man, as a parting plea, 'instead of hyper-managing this last little patch of wild hill, why not buy the next one along – right next door, a meadow and hillside that would add 50% to the reserve?' But, apparently the Trust has no spare money.

And then, as I resigned to the loss, with a little prayer as we passed the blue-berried beauty of the old sloe that he might spare that one if I made a very special plea (he didn't – the other day it lay on its side still loaded with berries), I realised this was not the National Trust I knew. That other Trust would have remembered where I lived, that I was a local resident who cared and showed an active interest and would have visited and shared their plan and asked for feedback and listened and compromised, even if it were just for that one fine old blackthorn.

Fresh woods and pastures new

ECOS 25 (1) 26-33 (2004)

Is the way that nature conservation is carried out going to alter in response to CAP reforms and new agencies, or will organisations continue to focus on small-scale site protection measures?

KEITH KIRBY, HEATHER ROBERTSON & REBECCA ISTED

There is a growing feeling among conservation practitioners that nature conservation needs to be large-scale, rather than just site-based, if we are to conserve successfully wild plants and animals. Non-mobile species in small isolated sites may face an uncertain future if their climate space changes around them.

In addition many practitioners consider that there should be more emphasis on allowing natural processes to operate, rather than relying on prescriptive management regimes[1,2,3] that have been the traditional means of treating small sites (see also articles in *ECOS* 16(2), 18 (2)). This article considers some of the ways that English Nature has been taking forward these ideas, particularly with respect to woodland conservation.

Keeping habitats as they are – the recent history

In parts of the world it may be possible to set aside large areas of perceived wilderness, where human impacts are minimal, and then just leave the wildlife to get on by itself. However, when the government conservation service was established in 1949, the starting point, especially in England, was a managed landscape in which farming and forestry were the primary land uses. Key habitats and species tended to have survived in relatively small patches that were dependent on direct intervention by farmers or foresters for their continued survival.

Different types of protective mechanism evolved, from legally-protected sites to changes in general land-use policy.[4] The Nature Conservancy and its successors, initially concentrated on the protected-sites series, although the damaging changes elsewhere in the countryside were all too obvious.[5] Increased protection for special sites, through legislative changes (most recently the *Countryside and Rights of Way Act*[6]), tended to shift the balance of effort away from broader landscape conservation, in part because of the accompanying checks and balances on how the legislation operated.

85

Nevertheless the wider landscape was not ignored. From the late 1980s onwards, agri-environment schemes have spread conservation effort considerably beyond statutory sites. English Nature's Natural Areas programme[7], the Habitat Restoration Project[8], policy inputs to CAP reform (Agenda 2000 and the recent Mid-term Review)[9] were all aimed at trying to improve the prospects for wildlife in the countryside as a whole - not just special sites. Much work is being done on habitat restoration and creation as part of the Biodiversity Action Plan process. However, for the most part, these programmes still assume an interventionist approach. For instance, a large block of new heathland will subsequently be managed to keep it as heathland.

In the past one reason for intervention was because conservation had to be tied in with farming and forestry practice, but these are changing. The impact of the recent CAP reforms is as yet unclear but combined with tough world market conditions could lead to major changes in British agriculture. Forestry has struggled to be profitable and much of the publicly owned forests now have public access and enjoyment and nature conservation as key objectives rather than just timber production. Therefore, as well as larger scale conservation projects, perhaps we can now be less prescriptive in our conservation management.

Levels of intervention in nature conservation management

What scope is there for giving natural processes more opportunity to operate? There are problems of defining what is 'natural', such as considering if humans have a role, and whether we are considering past or future natural conditions.[10] Consequently it might be better to pose the question: How widely are we prepared to set the acceptable limits of change for a site (or landscape) in terms of habitats, species and processes, before we deliberately intervene to shift the balance back towards our preferred outcome?

In most Sites of Special Scientific Interest there are key features that we wish to maintain and often there are set prescriptions to keep these features within quite tight limits (Figure 1a); in a totally natural system there might be no limits at all (Figure 1c). This latter is not likely to be an option in England, except perhaps with respect to some coastal and marine features. In between, however, are sites and landscapes where the limits could be broadened to various degrees (Figure 1b), so that most, but not quite anything, goes.

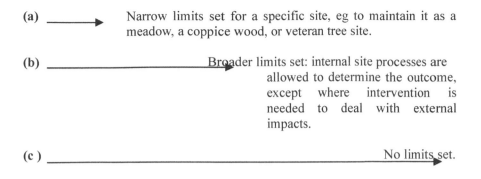

(a) ⟶ Narrow limits set for a specific site, eg to maintain it as a meadow, a coppice wood, or veteran tree site.

(b) _____Broader limits set: internal site processes are allowed to determine the outcome, except where intervention is needed to deal with external impacts.

(c) _____No limits set.

Figure 1. *Possible extents of acceptable change in (a) a cultural (b) a naturalistic and (c) a natural system.*

The degree to which the limits can be widened may depend on the size of the site: small areas usually require very tight limits of acceptable change if they are to maintain their interest. This may be the case in large sites as well - some large heaths are managed with quite precise prescriptions for heather cover - but there is at least the option of having broader limits. An explicit assumption with having more dynamic systems, with broader limits, is that within these limits, species or habitats or processes may fluctuate quite wildly, or even disappear. If we are not prepared to let this happen then we are not accepting the natural process.

Widening the limits of acceptable change in woodland

There are many woods where the emphasis is on maintaining or restoring 'traditional' management regimes (coppicing, pollarding, controlled-grazing) or some modern variant of these regimes. This may be because there is evidence that these regimes will produce the combination of habitats and species that are desired or simply because traditional management is felt to be a worthwhile option in itself, and part of the character of the place. In other woods new treatments such as continuous cover forestry are applied, because they are expected to produce the desired outcomes and may be better adapted to modern economic systems. Implicitly or explicitly quite tight limits are set (Table 1a).

This prescriptive approach is often essential, but may be based on little direct evidence that it is actually necessary in the longer term. What would happen if we were less prescriptive and interventionist? For some sites an alternative 'minimum intervention' approach has therefore been adopted, perhaps most famously at Lady Park Wood in the Wye Valley.[11,12]

Lady Park Wood and other long-term study sites have provided us with considerable insight into the dynamic processes that may influence the structure and composition of woods, from one-off events (1976 drought, 1987 storm) to longer-term changes such as increasing deer pressure. A more coherent and organised system of minimum intervention areas should be part of the process of improving our understanding of the impacts of management (whether traditional or modern) and of longer-term changes (eutrophication, climate change) that may be masked in other sites by the more immediate management effects.[12,13]

Some intervention may be agreed to be necessary from time to time; most commonly this has related to the impacts of invasive non-native species, or of increasing browsing by deer. Often, because most minimum intervention woods are relatively small (<50 ha), the impact is a consequence of changes in the surrounding, managed landscape. The logical move therefore is to enlarge the 'minimum intervention' area so that more of the processes can be internalised, and hence the intervention may become unnecessary.

The New Wildwoods project

There is uncertainty about the future of the upland areas of England and Wales, particularly in the light of changes in agricultural subsidies and the collapse of the commercial timber market. The conservation agencies therefore decided to explore the scope for a substantial increase in woodland cover with a higher proportion of native species, more reliance on natural processes for regeneration and more dynamic boundaries between open and closed habitats.[14,15,16] These studies considered not just the nature conservation aspects of such a change, but possible implications for agriculture, tourism and broader environmental questions such as soil and water conservation (Table 1).

Table 1. *Examples of possible benefits/disadvantages from developing 'new wildwoods' in the uplands.*[14]

Sector	Possible benefits	Possible disadvantages
Conservation	Increase in woodland and mosaic species	Possible loss of some open ground species
Recreation /tourism	Diversified landscape Improved recreation opportunities Increased visitor numbers	Some loss of long distance views Some areas become less accessible
Farming	Possibilities for diversification Improved shelter for farmland Locally available wood-products	Increase in pests (foxes, deer) Reduced agricultural output
Forestry	Small quantities of quality timber or other wood products	Loss of bulk wood production
Shooting	Improved options from wood-open mosaic	Some loss of grouse shooting
Water resources	Improved quality of water Possible reductions in some flood risks	Possible changes in water yield Possible increase in damage to bridges from trees

During the discussions about this work the potential for taking a similar approach in the lowlands was also raised. It might be on a somewhat smaller scale (hundreds rather than thousands of hectares) but there are a number of recent initiatives that are shifting lowland farmland out of agricultural production, for example the Great Fen project in East Anglia. A key part of the discussions was the idea that the new landscapes would be a mixture of open and closed habitats with some grazing continuing within the woodland. Indeed grazing could be the key to management of such landscapes.

A new interest in naturalistic grazing

Frans Vera's book, *Grazing ecology and forest history* [17] was published in English while this other work was in progress. Vera proposes that the former natural woodland cover was more like a modern wood-pasture than closed high forest, as a consequence of the activities of large herbivores such as bison, wild horse and aurochs. That the role of large herbivores in past landscapes has been underestimated is now widely accepted, but there is still debate as to whether the pre-Neolithic landscape was really that open or functioned in the way that Vera proposes.[18,19,20] English Nature has recently commissioned a study, looking particularly at the fossil invertebrate record, to explore further the evidence for the structure of the past natural forests.

However even if Vera is wrong about the role of large herbivores in the past, his ideas may still be relevant to their use to create and maintain a mosaic of different habitats and conditions outside of conventional agricultural or forest management. Initiatives such as the Grazing Animals Project have already brought together considerable information on the practicalities of using grazing under relatively controlled conditions.[21] Re-introduction of grazing to enclosures in the New Forest, at Sherwood Forest and Epping Forest has been carried out as part of initiatives to help deliver the Wood-pasture and Parkland Habitat Action plan, while large-scale heathland grazing regimes are being explored for example at Ashdown Forest.[22,23] These grazing regimes are still largely tied to creating or maintaining specific habitat conditions – for example if grazing animals don't lead to more heathland vegetation at Ashdown, then other management measures, such as burning, may have to be introduced.

Controlled grazers in Hatfield Forest (Keith Kirby, Natural England)

Table 2. *Some issues associated with developing a large-scale reserve managed by naturalistic grazing regime (not exhaustive!)*

What size of area is needed?	The larger the area the less the intervention that may be needed.
What species and numbers of animals are introduced?	Is the aim to mimic the Atlantic period fauna, for example with Heck cattle, or to use purely domestic breeds?
How are animal numbers to be controlled?	What methods, what time of year, how many animals, and what is the basis for deciding which to take?
Are there any current habitats or species that must always be present, and at what levels?	If the area starts with a high degree of semi-natural habitats, is it acceptable if some of these are lost; is there any limit on, for example the extent of openness, or the extent of forest?
Are there start-up works needed?	Are there habitat management works to be done before initiating the regime, eg removing non-native invasive species?
Are there public safety issues?	Are there public rights of way, or rights to roam across the site, adjacent roads, water courses that might be contaminated by dead animals etc.?
What is the animal welfare situation?	If the animals come under domestic stock regulations then there are a series of legal requirements (water, regular checking) that may not apply if they are wild. Even if wild animals are involved would sick/starving animals be just allowed to die on site?
What is the 'escaped animal' contingency plan?	What happens when (not if, remember Jurassic Park!) an animal escapes - even domestic cattle if they are not regularly handled may present safety problems particularly if they get on to roads.
What are the 'contagious diseases' emergency plans?	What will happen if there is a Foot and Mouth (or some other contagious stock disease) outbreak?
What monitoring is needed to tell if the system is producing the expected benefits?	Monitoring systems need to be put into place to show that this approach is providing more cost-effective biodiversity and other benefits than alternative systems.

Is there scope for going a step further and creating something closer to the situation at the Oostvaardersplassen Reserve in the Netherlands,[24] where feral and wild herbivores are not controlled, and where the vegetation and species mosaic that develops is completely unpredictable? Could state forests be rejuvenated to provide areas that recreated a wilderness experience?[25]

Understanding the science and practice of naturalistic grazing

A different type of conservation philosophy and approach would be required for such a landscape than that which we currently apply (and would need to continue to apply) to most other reserves and managed landscapes. Even if the land is available, and there is public and institutional support, it is not simply a case of putting a fence round the area, chucking in a few beasts and stepping back (Table 2). English Nature is exploring what the potential is for taking further steps down the naturalistic grazing road by addressing these issues. We would welcome views via a web-based discussion site set up by CEH at http://forums.ceh.ac.uk:8080/~naturalised-grazing.

Conclusions

For the foreseeable future most conservation is likely to take place in small sites constrained by their surroundings; therefore closely specified habitat or species targets and management regimes will remain common. However there is a need to have sites where these limits are relaxed to varying degrees to ensure that our management is achieving what was expected and to pick up unpredictable events and longer-term trends.

English Nature also believes there is scope for developing lower-intervention landscapes, with naturalistic grazing regimes. We expect these will have a high biodiversity value, albeit some of the habitat and species mosaics may not be ones that we are familiar with today. For such landscapes to develop they will need sound scientific backing, as well as public and institutional support. The research and demonstration work that English Nature is undertaking should provide the information needed to generate this support.

References

1. Gay, H and Phillips, A (2002) Dynamic nature - managing the assets. *ECOS* 22(1), 1-2.
2. Harvey, J (2002) The role of large areas in nature conservation. *ECOS* 22(1) 13-18.
3. Woodland Trust (2002). *Space for nature.* Woodland Trust, Grantham.
4. Kirby, K J (2003) Woodland conservation in privately-owned, cultural landscapes - the English experience. *Environmental Science and Policy.*.
5. Nature Conservancy Council (1984) *Nature conservation in Great Britain.* Nature Conservancy Council, Peterborough.
6. *Countryside and Rights of Way Act*, 2000, The Stationery Office, London.
7. Batten, L, Kirby, K J, Marsden, J, Wilkinson, M and Whitmore, M (1996) England: natural areas and prime biodiversity areas. In *Perspectives on ecological networks*, edited Nowicki, P, Bennett, G, Middleton, D, Rientjes, S, and Wolters, R, pp 71-92. European Centre for Nature Conservation, Man and Nature series, volume 1.
8. Thomas, R C (2000) *Habitat restoration project, final report.* English Nature (Research Report 377), Peterborough.
9. English Nature (2003) *Options for reform of the Common Agricultural Policy*, English Nature's response to consultation.

10 Peterken, G F (1996) *Natural woodland.* Cambridge University Press, Cambridge.

11. Peterken, G F and Jones, E W (1987) Forty years of change in Lady Park Wood: the old growth stands. *Journal of Ecology,* 75, 477-512.

12. Peterken, G F (2000) *Natural reserves in English woodland.* English Nature Research Report 384, Peterborough.

13. Mountford, E (2000) *A provisional minimum intervention woodland reserve series for England with proposals for baseline recording and long-term monitoring proposals.* English Nature Research Report 385, Peterborough.

14. Worrell, R, Pryor, S N, Scott, A, Peterken, G F, Taylor, K, Knightbridge, R and Brown, K (2002) *New wildwoods in Britain.* LUPG Research Report, Joint Nature Conservation Committee, Peterborough.

15. Rogers, S and Taylor, K (2003) *New wildwoods: removing barriers to development and implementation.* LUPG Research Report, Joint Nature Conservation Committee, Peterborough.

16.   Penny Anderson Associates (2003) *Vegetation change in the English uplands following removal of management.* Draft (unpublished) report, English Nature, Peterborough.

17. Vera, F W M (2000) *Grazing ecology and forest history.* Wallingford, CABI.

18. Svenning, J C (2002) A review of natural vegetation openness in north-western Europe. *Biological Conservation* 104, 133-148.

19. Kirby, K J (2003) *What might a British forest-landscape driven by large herbivores look like?* English Nature Research Report 530, Peterborough.

20. Rackham, O (2003) *Ancient woodland* (new edition). Castlepoint Press, Dalbeattie.

21. Oates, M and Tolhurst, S (2001) *The Breeds' Handbook.* English Nature (Grazing Animals Project), Peterborough.

22. Goldberg, E A (2003) *Wood-pasture and Parkland Habitat Action Plan 3rd annual advisory group meeting.* English Nature (Research Report 539), Peterborough.

23. Marrable, C J, (2003) *Ashdown forest – a review of grazing.* English Nature (Research Report 535), Peterborough.

24.   Kampf, H. (2002) Large herbivores and government policy. *Vakblad Natuurbeheer (special issue) Grazing and grazing animals,* May 2000, 56-59.

25. Garforth, M and Dudley, N (2003) Forest renaissance. Published by WWF, Godalming and Forestry Commission, Edinburgh.

This article is derived from a series of studies carried out for English Nature, many in conjunction with other bodies (Countryside Council for Wales, Scottish Natural Heritage, Forestry Commission, Environment Agency, Countryside Agency). Various colleagues inside and outside of these bodies have contributed ideas and comments on this subject. We are grateful for all their positive thoughts, but any errors or misinterpretations are ours alone.

Rewilding and the role of large herbivores

ECOS 25.3/4 59-62 (2004)

This article looks at the role of large herbivores in rewilding processes: what animals can be used, how do we balance gains and losses of habitats, and how do different interest groups react?

KEITH KIRBY

Nature conservation in England is largely about maintaining habitats and species that are survivors of former farming and forestry systems. Often the best way to protect them is to try to continue with something like the past management practices. However we can and should explore the scope for allowing alternative systems to develop that depend less on direct and regular human intervention.[1]

There are no situations in England where human influence can be withdrawn completely, although on the coast, sea-walls have been breached to allow the development of salt-marsh as part of managed retreat programmes. Inland, more limits are likely to be set on the degree to which natural processes are allowed to determine the outcome.

'Rewilded' areas may end up bearing some resemblances to 'original-natural' landscapes but will be moving towards a 'future-natural' state. This will create new patterns and assemblages of species, which raises some interesting questions in terms of current target-driven approaches to nature conservation.

Rewilding and domestic stock

Domestic stock, particularly cattle, have been suggested as part of rewilding projects as substitutes for lost herbivores such as the aurochs.[2] If they are to be included in rewilding projects their role needs to be clear. It is quite distinct from that in conventional farmland (where they are essentially a product or producer) but also from that in most nature reserves where they are used as management tools, for example to prevent tree regeneration on heaths or maintain short turf conditions on chalk grassland (Table 1). If domestic stock are themselves to be part of the 'wild' system then we need more information about their ecology and their impact under such low-intervention conditions.

Table 1. How grazing animals fit into different types of system

System	Role of animals	State of most vegetation	State of animals
Intensive Farmland	Primarily agricultural output – potential for nature management too	Highly productive, low conservation value	High yield important, healthy, productive
Semi-natural habitat management	As management tools to produce desired habitat	Desired semi-natural habitat present	Yield less important, basic health and welfare rules apply
Re-wilding areas	Integral part of the ecosystem. Large herbivores are essential drivers of ecosystem processes.	Whatever the grazing and other processes produce	Health and welfare guidance adapted for self-reliant animals

What numbers and sorts of animals do we use?

Cattle and ponies grazing a landscape will generate a different vegetation dynamic than cattle alone: if small numbers of animals are used then a different pattern of vegetation is likely to develop than if a larger herd is established at the outset.

To some extent these decisions will be influenced by whatever 'vision' there is for the expected outcome of the rewilding project. If the expectation is that a relatively open landscape should be produced (for example a 50% open park-like landscape) the tendency may be to encourage a high density of animals initially; if the expectation is that woodland should predominate then the starting numbers may be lower. There is unlikely to be one inevitable outcome on any one area – the starting conditions will influence the result - so the reasoning behind the initial stocking decisions should be stated.

Is the rewilding area meant to have some similarity to the Atlantic period landscape – a 'Holocene Park'? If so we might exclude ponies because Yalden considers they had died out in Britain by that time.[3] We would also need to consider eliminating more recent additions such as rabbit and fallow deer: is this feasible? The cattle (aurochsen mimics) would be chosen for their wildness. If we are not interested in the analogue with the past and also want to attract people to the area, then we might deliberately include ponies, and the cattle might be chosen from breeds that look 'wild' (eg Highland) but are not too aggressive. Again the reasons for choosing one set of animals over another need to be clear because it will influence the outcome.

Losses and gains

Rewilding is likely to lead to changes in habitat and species assemblages, so the balance of gains versus losses needs to be assessed. An area with a diverse mix of habitats and species to start with has more potential to develop new interesting assemblages and patterns than one that is poor to start with. However, the potential losses are also higher from a rich starting point.

For example the Sussex Wildlife Trust has an area of farmland that is being shaped via grazing into a more mixed mosaic of habitats: the current interest of the actual fields is low. A relatively low level of grazing is proposed initially, but there is little to be lost if the scrub develops more rapidly than expected (see Tony Whitbread's article in this issue). On a site with a high current interest, for example extensive heathland communities, there would be potentially more serious nature conservation losses from rapid scrub. Therefore a high initial density of animals might be used to ensure the maintenance of at least a minimum area of heathland. In the spread of scrub in the North Pennine, the losses of some open ground waders might be more acceptable under a rewilding project if black grouse colonise and spread than if they do not.

So should we be looking for areas of intensive farmland to rewild on the grounds these can hardly fail to improve in wildlife terms, even though the potential of the area may be limited by high soil fertility levels and poor current species content?
Wherever is chosen, an adequate system of monitoring the gains and losses needs to be put in place to justify what has been done.

Perceptions of rewilding

The third area that needs to be explored is the social acceptability of rewilding. It is taken as read in this article that any area can only be taken forward for rewilding with the full support of the land owners and managers.

However even in raising the concept of rewilding in discussion, there has been criticism that it is sanctioning 'land abandonment', 'land nationalisation', 'dereliction', 'rural depopulation', 'spread of unsightly scrub', 'production of only boring secondary woodland'. Each of these perceptions and complaints can be countered, but they reflect the passions that are raised and the care with which this idea needs to be pursued.

People have concerns for the countryside because of its appearance and historic elements such as field patterns and ancient monuments, and for many other values. Rewilding could lead to changes that may not be welcomed. Cattle and ponies are not wild animals in legal terms and the appropriate welfare and disease control legislation must be adhered to. It may be that special allowances can be agreed for the animals in a particular site, but this cannot be taken for granted. Even if legal agreement were reached, public opinion is strongly against allowing what might be perceived as allowing animals to suffer.

People are injured and sometimes killed by domestic stock at present. There is a risk that animals allowed to graze under more naturalistic conditions could present more of a potential threat because they are less used to people. Areas considered for rewilding will probably either have public rights of way across them or be 'open access land' under the *Countryside and Rights of Way Act*. So we will need to build support for the concept with for example walkers.

Stimulating public interest

English Nature is interested in the rewilding concept. We have been researching the use of naturalistic grazing regimes in landscape conservation and will be reporting on the results in 2005. Developed carefully, it has the potential to catch the public imagination and to generate new landscapes and patterns of wildlife.

References

1.   Kirby, K J, Robertson, H J, & Isted, R (2004). Fresh woods and pastures new: from site-gardening to hands-off landscapes. *ECOS* 25 (1), 26-33.
2.   Vera, F W M (2000) *Grazing ecology and forest history.* Wallingford, CABI.
3.   Yalden, D. (1999) *The History of British Mammals.* Poyser.

Uncontrolled grazing in Oostwaadersplassen (Keith Kirby)

Ecosystem effects of wild herbivores – lessons from Holland

ECOS 27 (3/4) 58-60 (2006)

This article discusses the effects of wild herbivores in the Dutch National Ecological Network and the Oostvaardersplassen.

NEIL HARRIS

Wild and large herbivores have been used in the development of the Dutch National Ecological Network in a variety of ways. The choice of species has been guided by factors including public opinion, public use of the land, neighbouring agricultural considerations, and the style of land management.

In the wetlands and grasslands of the Oostvaardersplassen, animals have been introduced which are more suited to the passive, hands-off management techniques and natural processes which sustain the ecology of the site. Heck cattle, Konik ponies and red deer were introduced whilst roe deer were already present on the reserve. Wild boar have not been introduced in Oostvaardersplassen because of the neighbouring pig rearing industry and the possible risk of introducing swine fever.

Surprises and indirect habitat effects

The area grazed by the cattle does not have open access to the public allowing the choice of a de-domesticated, potentially dangerous (in terms of conflict with members of the public) breed of cattle. Population dynamics are still evolving as the herbivores find their own place within the ecosystem and create their own surroundings by influencing the development of vegetation. The populations of the introduced herbivores have grown steadily since their introduction and each species exerts a different influence on its surroundings. There are many examples of the cattle, deer and horses both directly and indirectly influencing the habitats available to other species. For example, elders are palatable to red deer which is preventing regeneration of this species. Should the red deer population decline, an increase in stands of elder is the likely result. Similarly, willows are eaten by deer and horses which keep them in check. The large herbivores have created extensive areas of low grassland vegetation which is particularly attractive to geese, swans and waders. The tens of thousands of geese which have returned to the reserve to graze the grasslands also feed on young reeds during the moulting season, keeping the marshlands open. Carrion from dead carcasses provides food for white-tailed eagles and ravens.

The Veluwezoom heaths

In the heathlands of the Veluwezoom, a more active style of management is carried out in the semi-natural landscapes, for example tree removal on some areas of heathland, but large areas are managed as a nearly-natural landscape using natural processes. Twenty years ago cattle and horses were introduced to the woodlands and heathland of the area to prevent grass invasion and create a mosaic of open spaces and woodland. The area is open to the public through a network of walking and cycling trails and this has influenced the choice of cattle introduced. Highland cattle were chosen for both their hardiness and also their passive nature. Where natural processes are being allowed to develop on previously managed areas, changes in the vegetation result from the grazing and browsing preferences of the herbivores present. Some areas of heathland within the Veluzoom are no longer being actively managed and these areas are being colonised by conifer saplings which are unpalatable to the cattle, horses, deer and wild boar present. In time, conifer forest will replace the existing heathland. This has led to debate on the introduction of European bison which could be capable of tackling conifers. Carcasses of fallen animals (apart from cattle and horses which are removed if their location is known) are tackled first by the wild boar and subsequently by birds and insects.

Beavers, birds and eco-bridges

In the Biesbosch National Park, a freshwater tidal area, cattle are used to graze the polders and other areas to retain their openness and prevent natural succession back to forest. Because the Biesbosch experiences large seasonal fluctuations in water levels, cattle are required to be housed in the winter months. This type of management is more comparable to traditional agricultural practices. Beavers have been successfully introduced to this wetland site and have had an impact on the landscape and ecology. Beavers are capable of cutting down large trees to get at the tree-bark and leaves of the branches which are their preferred food item. They act like coppicers, creating glades in woodland where successional scrub develops, increasing habitat diversity. Bird species like nightingale and marsh warbler move into these temporary areas, as do many species of invertebrates.

Large herbivores and other mammals in these wild areas would live in ecological isolation without the creation of wildlife corridors to connect them up. The ability to migrate and disperse from one area to another via, for example, ecoducts and eco-bridges under and over main roads, and via ecological corridors, and to encourage genetic variation, is the path being used in the Netherlands to construct complete ecosystems. Visitors to, and residents of these nature areas have been involved in planning processes. This has led to a wider public support of the message that grazing management plays a positive role in healthy ecosystems.

Heck bull and deer in Oostwaadersplassen (Hans Kampf)

UK wildlife and climate change
Nature's disaster or dynamics?

ECOS 28 (3/4) 33-39 (2007)
Are our professional instincts on how wildlife responds to climate change better than any available modelling, and how should we protect wildlife from the impacts of climate change mitigation measures?

PETER TAYLOR

How to assess the impact of climate change on UK wildlife? There are perhaps two approaches: one would be to ask experienced naturalists to assess what they have seen over past decades and project this into future decades assuming the same progression of climate changes. That would be fraught with difficulty – they would have to make selections to reflect the changes, and how would they isolate other factors, such as the intensification of agriculture? The other approach would be to build a computer model using more 'objective' indices.

As far as I know, significant government resources have only been put behind the computer model approach – and the MONARCH project[1] is the most extensive review of the potential impact of climate change on Britain's fauna and flora – taking seven years, involving four major research bodies and consultancies (ADAS, CABI, BTO and ERM) and funded by a partnership of just about all the relevant government departments and agencies from the Forestry Commission, the JNCC, SNH, CCW, NE, Defra, and voluntary bodies such as the National Trust, the Woodland Trust, WWF and RSPB, plus the UK Climate Impacts Programme at Oxford.

Having read the conclusions of phase 1 of MONARCH and as a practising ecologist with some responsibilities in advising on land management and climate change strategies, I have to say that it is next to useless. But, as an independent consultant, how to say this to just about every hand that might ever feed me? And why do so when the recommendations for action support the goals of the more creative approaches to biodiversity that many of us have been advocating over the last decade? My only answer is my belief that we need an awareness of the limitations of our methodologies. Otherwise these studies could backfire and endanger the goals of landscape-scale conservation that everyone acknowledges is required to make our wildlife more robust to change.

To be fair, the MONARCH study states some of the important limitations of the methodology it has chosen – selecting a relatively small number of species not for their particular susceptibility to climate change, but because good data existed across Europe that could be used with the model chosen to calculate an index called 'climate space'. This index determines how much room a particular species has in Britain to 'move'. But only in so far as climate factors are concerned – it does not address actual habitat or a species' ability to physically move across or through any biological barriers it might encounter. The only biology used is a measure of climate adaptability drawn from knowledge of the species' range in Europe.

But there are greater problems than the ones acknowledged and which would challenge any methodology. The first relates to the degree of confidence in largely computerised and hence un-validated predictions of future climate regimes; the second involves the way in which UK biodiversity is measured and valued; and the third to the timescales for the effects of any policy initiatives such as adaptation might direct. The fourth is the horseman of mitigation strategies and their impact on the very biodiversity they are meant to protect. Unfortunately, MONARCH assumes an unjustified progression in future climate regimes, accepts UK BAP targets and definitions with little reflection on their wider bioregional significance, and fails completely to model the interaction of mitigation responses with adaptation strategies.

Uncertain climate futures

Despite the prevalence of 'best guess' projections – as advanced by the UK Climate Impacts Programme with its use of regional computer models (either based at University of East Anglia's Tyndall Centre or the Met Office's Hadley Centre in Exeter), there is considerable scientific uncertainty as to the future unfolding of UK climate in a 'warming' world.

This is the case even without any major critique of the 'global warming' model driven by carbon dioxide. The translation of the so-called consensus model to regional levels is still very uncertain. Accelerating warming in the Arctic could potentially lead to a cooling of the NE Atlantic region as the Gulf Stream is slowed by freshwater inputs to the northern end of the 'conveyor' system. Other models of the main climate driver, not favoured by the IPCC, are based on giving greater weight to solar cycle changes and their link to cloud cover. Some solar scientists expect a rapid downturn in northern hemisphere temperatures in coming years. Despite the opinion of the UN and the majority of science institutions, including, it would seem, all the funders of this study, it is a *political* decision to exclude this model, not a scientific one. It is based upon the needs of the policy makers for a single answer.

Thus, any reviewer is faced with choices:

1) provide projections for change in either direction,
2) provide projections for the 'best guess'
3) provide timescales based upon various global emission scenarios
4) provide timescales based on solar cycle projections.

In practice, there are forces militating against exploring the first and last of these scientifically valid choices. Funding bodies do not like uncertainty and policy makers likewise – so exclusions are made. Thus, the only major study of climate impacts on UK biodiversity provides only UKCIP's 'consensus' model with three timescales (2020, 2050 and 2080) and two global emission scenarios and all the other non-specialist bodies on climate in the MONARCH consortium collude with this.

UK Biodiversity indices and values

There has been a long running debate within *ECOS* on the values inherent in the UK Biodiversity index and its Action Programme, but despite such intelligent critique the BAP remains as the central plank of UK policy. Its limitations are doubly highlighted when used as a basis for climate impact studies.

Firstly, the UK BAP, despite the provision for habitat plans, is species focussed and most importantly, relates to species that are already *threatened* – that is to say, in decline or in vulnerable small populations. The list of BAP priorities is also strongly representative of professional scientific conservation interest – wherein there has been little self-reflection on the *value* of species, not only in relation to ecosystem function, but to the wider public psyche. As I have argued in *Beyond Conservation,* a scientistic approach to nature conservation has probably contributed to its ghetto status, especially with respect to governmental priorities.[2] There has been a failure to translate the public affection for nature and wildlife into effective indices and actions.

When climate change is considered, the species focus compounds these problems. Many 'rare' species are limited in their UK distribution because they are already on the edge of their range. They are not necessarily threatened with respect to their wider distribution. That wider distribution is also likely to have a climatic component to its limits. The British Isles is a maritime climate province bordering the wider continent, thus, in the north and west of the island, there are habitats and species that are restricted to this maritime border, with some smattering of endemic species or subspecies and some very important major populations – some of which are abundant and not particularly threatened (e.g. seabirds, coastal heath flora). However, the south and eastern parts of the island touch the range of continental species adapted to drier environments; whereas the northern provinces may capture the southernmost populations of essentially northern and often circumpolar species.

Within this context, each species also faces threats in the modern era from other dynamics – especially agricultural intensification and loss of habitat, plantation forestry, water extraction, disturbance, persecution and invasive introductions. This compounds attempts at identifying climate change as causative in any past changes in distribution, and hence predicting future responses.

On a biological level, it is hardly ever recognised by conservation programmes that species are always 'threatened' with extinction or under pressure, some more than others at any particular time. Species are the sacrificial front-line troops of the evolutionary process and like the generals in the rear, it is the *Genus* that usually persists and hence evolves. Species come and go as the environment, including the climate, changes, or new competitors come along. For example, there are several *Fritillary* species in the genus, all hardly distinguishable by lay observers – the same for leaf warblers of the *Philloscopus* genus, but whatever happens to the climate and niches they occupy, some of them will likely make it and the genus will survive and potentially radiate another supply of species. What is nature conservation doing when it interferes with this process? I am not saying here that conservationists should do nothing, only that they make their interventions transparent, especially to the public that pay the salaries and put up the research funds.

The nature of the 'threat'

Thus, any map of rare and threatened species of Britain and Ireland will not necessarily reflect that species' global status nor its vulnerability to climate change. When it comes to evaluating species' response to change, there seems little awareness of the way in which 'rarity', 'charisma' and 'nationalistic' values come into play. In some sense *all* species are going to be affected by climate change, and obviously not all species from nematodes to fritillaries are equal, whether to the conservation scientist or the public mind. In this respect, the bluebell is of observedly higher value than the cudweed. But it is the cudweed that features in the shortlist for MONARCH.

Timescales for adaptation and mitigation

In the orthodox scenario, the UK climate warms to 2080 by as much as 2 C. But what will this mean for habitats and species? The projection is for drier and hotter summers and warmer and wetter winters – but as the summer of 2007 demonstrated, the average can be punctuated by extremes – in this case of flooding. There is also a potential for late frosts and gale damage. These are not easily factored into the model. Sea temperature changes and resultant food chain effects may also be marked. It is not clear that these kinds of uncertainties are reflected in the simple index drawn from a species' wider distribution.

Some changes are already evident. Spring has advanced by two weeks and the growing season is longer. Winters are warmer and wetter (though some have been very dry) and summers drier with a marked drying out of upland habitats and eastern agricultural land. Larger insects have noticeably declined in abundance. But isolating effects upon fauna and flora is not easy: the past two decades of warming (previously the globe cooled from 1945-1980) have also coincided with major agricultural change – in particular the winter sowing of wheat, early cutting for silage, grass monoculture and loss of species-rich meadows; new and powerful veterinary biocides have been introduced that affect dung-fauna and have wide-reaching knock-on effects. There may also have been major habitat changes in the winter range of summer visitors such as warblers.

These changes make it difficult to ascribe current declines to climate change. Conversely, some 'gains' are clearly climate related – such as the colonisation by little egrets of the southern and western estuaries and marshes.

It is not an easy matter therefore to identify potential changes in a warmer or cooler Britain as individual species' responses are not well understood – but certain generalisations on habitat (using the orthodox warming model) could be made:

- there is likely to be further loss of wet pastures, particular in river valleys in the south and east; and upland (and coastal) heath and grassland will be drier and more susceptible to fire damage;

- there will be a gradual retreat of the sub-alpine zone on northern hills, with some habitat being replaced by scrub.

One does not need a computer model to draw these conclusions – any competent naturalist could do so. And equally, most naturalists would be able to estimate 'climate space' and then add on the crucial element of how much real habitat exists within that space. But computer modelling is a modern necessity if studies are to bear weight.

And actually, naturalists with a feel for their particular birds, bats or butterfly ecotype distributions usually know enough genetics to be cautious in the assumption that just because a species occurs in Caledonian and Balkan pine forests the former will have genetic access to the latter's climatic adaptation – this seems to be a fundamental flaw in the concept of 'climate space' upon which the MONARCH study depends.

However, there is one further factor mentioned at the outset – the widespread impact upon habitats that mitigation policies may bring. The recently announced EU biofuel targets will likely lead to widespread intensification of agriculture and forestry in the UK; wind turbines already threaten raptor populations, such as the sea eagles in the Hebrides and kites in Wales; and estuarine barrages will impact upon waterfowl habitats. Which mitigation strategies are going to save *our* redshanks and lapwings that have been so recently decimated by agricultural intensification is far from obvious, but the growing global demand for woodchip to burn is certain to suck in habitat as far away as Latvia; likewise biodiesel and ethanol targets will affect Brazil and Indonesia.

In its final analysis of 32 species the MONARCH report identifies, as one might expect, a proportion of losses (8), gains (15), and no change (9), though it warns the proportion is not representative so no conclusion can be drawn. Despite this, the report then concludes that *"loss or shift in climate space for British and Irish wildlife will be more severe unless greenhouse gases are cut"*. It recommends more conservation effort, better habitat management, and the creation of a more resilient and permeable landscape. The study purports to have identified the potential consequences of *"failing to reduce emissions and strengthens the case for action"* such as the *"need for the conservation sector to advocate the development and implementation of a robust mitigation policy"*.

The latter conclusion is dangerous political and ideological polemic dressed up in the guise of a scientific and objective study. It goes way beyond the science and in particular the very limited science of MONARCH's methodology. At the outset the study talks neutrally of impacts – but by the end it drops into the ideology of 'threats'. How have they evaluated the gain of a little egret in the Somerset Levels – which I watched with great pleasure today, against the loss of an obscure bat that I and 99.9% of the public are never likely to be able to distinguish from any other bat? The same argument will apply to all the families and orders affected.

And what business is it of the likes of WWF, RSPB, Woodland Trust, Natural England, SNH, CCW and the National Trust to call for mitigation strategies when they provide no study of the likely impacts of these (which are huge!), and no analysis of the timescales for mitigating actual climate change (at least 50 and probably 100 years before emissions can be stabilised at *current* levels which are apparently already driving the changes).

More rigour, less collusion...

Of course we need action to address human welfare needs and environmental stability in case climate change becomes more severe. But in my view there has been an unacknowledged collusion of government agencies, NGOs and other parties in assuming climate change is strictly bad news for the UK's fauna and flora in all situations. This is a grossly simplistic outlook. They make an *a priori* assumption that the balance of impacts can only be a net *loss*, despite there being little solid evidence in their analysis to support this. They seek to justify the targets of emission reduction in order to mitigate such losses but with not even a reflection upon the impact of those mitigation strategies on the biodiversity it sets out to protect.

Even though there is an equally forceful call for adaptation strategies such as larger scale habitat creation, this collusion doe not serve the wider public campaign for nature. The report is transparently weak and as such unlikely to influence policy makers engaged in what is perceived as a battle to save the planet. At a time when Friends of the Earth and other environmental NGOs argue for major sacrifices of Britain's few remaining wild areas to wind turbines, I doubt we are going to convince anyone that *biodiversity* matters with these kind of studies. There is a complete absence of treatment of recent and high profile gains, especially to the nation's much loved avian fauna – such as little egret, purple heron, and great egret, and spoonbill may follow (the great bustard and sea eagle have come from re-introductions and enhanced management).

I would argue that the main drivers for enhanced biodiversity are habitat creation, agricultural extensification and raised public awareness and willingness to pay for these programmes – climate change is in my opinion virtually irrelevant. By joining on the climate bandwagon and ignoring the scientific uncertainties and inherent problems of indices and value, more support may be gained for habitat creation, but there is a real danger of backlash once all of this becomes transparent, and more particularly if the carbon dioxide model has been overplayed. A little more circumspection and critical appraisal of modelling would not go amiss.

References

1. MONARCH – Modelling Natural Resource Responses to Climate Change - *A synthesis for biodiversity conservation.* **www.ukcip.org.uk**

2. Taylor, P. (2005) *Beyond Conservation* Earthscan, London

Abbreviations
ADAS: Agricultural Development and Advisory Service consultants
BTO: British Trust for Ornithology
CABI: Commonwealth Agricultural Bureaux International
CCW: Countryside Council for Wales
Defra: Department for the Environment, Food and Rural Affairs
ERM: Environmental Resource Management
JNCC: Joint Nature Conservation Council
NE: Natural England
RSPB: Royal Society for the Protection of Birds
SNH: Scottish Natural Heritage
WWF: World Wide Fund for Nature

A response to key points in this article has been made by representatives of the MONARCH consortium. This can be viewed on the Blog section of BANC's web site at *www.banc.org.uk*

Scary or what?

ECOS editorial 27 (1) 1 (2006)
GEOFFREY WAIN

A female beaver emerged from her release pen in the Cotswolds last October. She ambled around for 10 minutes, nibbled some willow, and returned to her pen to sleep, oblivious to the hordes of watching cameras. Minutes later she and five others were released at a lake at Lower Mill Estate. Around her was a scrum of TV crews and tabloid reporters. No matter that an electric fence encloses the lake, which is what allowed the Defra licence - something charismatic was coming home to the British landscape and the country's media were desperate to see.

The rest of Europe would be amazed at such a fuss. The beaver can be found even along dykes on German golf courses, yet beaver reintroduction in Scotland was blocked last year after rigorous trials in Knapdale, and much public support. Ambushed by establishment figures, the Scottish Executive used the fine print of law on Special Areas of Conservation to halt progress on beavers.

Much of this edition looks at prospects for reintroduced species and their potential for reinvigorating our ecosystems. Reintroduced species will be exciting for both the ecology and the economy of remote places. Tracts of Scotland could be branded as Lynx Country, and beaver could help parts of Wales become rewilded and rejuvenated. Associated new wildlands could involve regenerating woodland, better water retention, and carbon-absorbing soils.

Years of debate and feasibility work have kept government bodies busy dallying over reintroductions, but meantime private landowners in England and Scotland are already on the blocks with projects involving wild herbivores and carnivores. Elsewhere, nature and humans have also conspired to make reintroductions real, because the boar, and, wait for it, possibly the lynx, have bolted. Clusters of wild boar are now free-living as we know, and big cat researchers have told ECOS that lynx are breeding in Scotland, and possibly in SW England, following escapes and clandestine releases. Yes, this top predator may already be back and influencing deer numbers.

Views on reintroductions vary – conservation, farming and game organisations all have different enthusiams and anxieties amongst their members, sometimes over the same candidate species. From the rednecks to the strictest BAP-minded ecologists, all the parties must be engaged if we're to make headway on reintroductions - the incentives, the compensation, the visitor management, the public information, and the role of game organisations must all be addressed.

It's easy to get paranoid over the effects of creatures we have parted company with for a few centuries, such as wild boar. But our European neighbours cope with these creatures and their disease potential and agricultural disturbance. These are management issues that come with the deal. They are not reasons to be scared of rediscovering our wilder roots, and shaking up Britain's bland ecosystems

Britain's predators in tooth and claw

ECOS 27 (3/4) 17-22 (2006)

The tale of Bruno the brown bear who wandered the German-Austrian border in spring 2006 gripped audiences across Europe, until the decision to shoot him in June. In Germany the media prioritized the story over the country's World Cup campaign. Predators capture our imagination and release deep emotions...

PETER CAIRNS

Faced with the vastness of North America's rolling plains, early Puritan ministers were quick to remind European colonists of their Christian obligation to "destroy that which is wild and make something of the land". In 1756 John Adams wrote: "This continent is one dismal wilderness, the haunt of wolves and bears and more savage men". The ecological destruction that unfolded across America over less than two centuries, redefined a deep-seated prejudice embedded in the western mind. Where towns were built and forests felled for pasture, there was no room for mountain lions, coyotes, bears and wolves. No one knows how many predators were killed across America during the nineteenth and early twentieth centuries, but estimates run into millions. Between 1883 and 1918, 80,730 wolves were bountied in Montana alone.

Conservation-minded Britain?

It is too easy to blame previous generations for their apparent disregard of nature's wealth. The concept of ecological niches and recognition that all life is inter-dependent, is a relatively modern science and the preserve of educated, affluent societies. American settlers based their attitudes towards nature on what they read in the bible: man was placed on this earth to have dominion over the rest of creation.

In these more enlightened times, it is hard for us to imagine such mean-spiritedness towards creatures like wolves. We no longer have to compete with these animals for food and our increased ecological awareness has nurtured a greater tolerance towards natural predator-prey mechanisms. Or has it?

In conservation-minded Britain, we are quick to jump to the defence of India's tigers, Africa's lions or closer to home, Europe's increasing wolf populations. We expect the working rural people of these countries to accept the difficulties that large predators bring and condemn the apparent obsession with which some species are hunted down and killed. But where are our wolves? Where are the bears and lynx who once stalked our forests? Our perception of and benevolence towards predatory species is still, at best, fickle.

For many, the sight of a hen harrier quartering a remote moorland or a peregrine stooping into a swirling wader flock are spectacles of nature, key components in the ecological integrity of our countryside. For others, predators are nothing more than an inconvenience, a financial drain on rural businesses. Predators undoubtedly mean different things to different people but very few with an interest in the British countryside remain indifferent.

The fact that predators need to kill to survive sets them apart. What they kill and how they do it influences how we feel about them, how our emotions respond. Our increasingly suburban and regulated existence has changed our relationship with nature. For the most part, our needs are easily met and we perceive no need to engage with the natural world; we consider ourselves spectators on, rather than part of, natural processes. Predators strike at the very heart of our notion of civilization – they threaten our sense of control. This, rather than religious conviction or an instinctive need to eliminate competition simply to survive, is now what shapes our attitudes and perceptions.

Additionally, species like foxes and seals have become political symbols, pawns in battles between different socio-economic or special interest groups, each filtering selective information to the public which best serves their particular agenda, often at the expense of biological fact. The complex issues surrounding predator management embrace a web of social politics: rich versus poor, town versus country, national policy versus local tradition.

Managing predators in Britain today is rarely about the animal itself – it is about managing people's perceptions – what we believe, what we value and how we look upon our dependency on nature.

Predators and their consequences – the debate

So how does modern Britain really feel about predators and how do those feelings continue to be influenced by culture, myth and economics? Can the shooting of birds of prey to protect human leisure interests ever be justified? Should the impact of pet cats on small birds and mammals be controlled? Should we really consider returning wolves to our wild areas having worked so hard to eliminate them?

Tooth & Claw (www.toothandclaw.org.uk) is a photo-journalistic project which sets out to find the answers to these and other questions. The project's authors are photographers and writers, not biologists. They wanted to get under the skin of contemporary predator issues and explore different facets of our lives alongside those animals that kill other animals. "We want to know how the British public feels about predators - to reach beyond corporate policy and speak to those who encounter the actions of predators on a regular basis – farmers, keepers, researchers, tourism operators and recreationists" says Mark Hamblin, one of Tooth & Claw's photographers.

Eurasian lynx (Peter Cairns/Northshots)

Tooth & Claw is independent and non-judgmental. "We want to encourage a wide range of people to relay their experiences and feelings. We also want to nurture greater empathy between different viewpoints and move away from the culture of conflict which continues to divide rural policy. Ultimately, our role is to inform and inspire rather than persuade" continues Hamblin.

Through a series of case-studies, Tooth & Claw is bringing predator issues to life. Using imagery and anecdotal contributions, the project is exploring various aspects of our relationship with predators. "Although we are looking at different species from varied viewpoints, there are common themes which crop up" says Ian Rowlands, the project's journalist. "It is the inconsistency in people's attitudes that belies a deep misunderstanding of predator biology. We have had many contributors who are outraged at raptor persecution yet detest sparrowhawks for their 'audacity' of raiding garden bird tables. Another contributor had watched an otter drowning a mallard and considered himself privileged at witnessing such an event. The same man – an educated gamekeeper – was then livid when a pine marten raided *his* goldeneye box and killed *his* incubating female. Feelings change when it becomes personal."

It is hardly surprising that value judgments are made instinctively when there is such apparent inconsistency in predator management. An obvious illustration is the persecution of hen harriers for their impact on red grouse. This is not only almost universally condemned but now attracts a custodial prison sentence. The shooting of foxes to protect ground-nesting birds however, is a commendable act of conservation, carried out routinely by the RSPB and others. Legalities aside, these are not dissimilar routes down the path of selective management. Tooth & Claw is ultimately a project which explores our changing relationship with nature. It asks questions of all of us; it exposes our fears, our inconsistencies and our prejudices. We are reminded of our own place in nature as the most powerful predator of all.

Priority species

It is less than 20 years since pine martens were protected by law and they have since enjoyed a rapid increase in numbers. For many people this improves the chances of an encounter with an elusive nocturnal predator, and entrepreneurial wildlife tourism operators have been quick to recognise this opportunity. The marten's 'success' however, comes at a price and not everyone welcomes their return. Pine martens prey on other rare (nationally at least) species such as red squirrels. This raises the thorny issue of priorities. Is one species more important than another? Should martens be 'controlled' to protect red squirrels? Some people think so.

Pine marten
(Carl McKie/ Derek Gow
Consultancy)

Scottish wildcats (Chris Robbins/ Derek Gow Consultancy)

Living room lions

The British public love cats – an estimated 8 million of them. They provide companionship, contact with 'nature' and for some enthusiasts, are an extension to their own personalities with visits to the hairdressers and 'cat boutiques' quite routine. This is an animal that polarizes opinion however. Their impact on garden birds and small mammals is estimated at 250million annually, making it by far our most significant 'wild' predator. For all the millions of cat supporters, there are just as many who resent this toll on our native wildlife. Behind the politics that rage over domestic cats, their wild ancestor is in serious trouble. Statistics are patchy and research inadequate but some biologists suggest there are now only 400 pure-bred Scottish wildcats in existence. Despite huge budgets spent on other flagship species, it seems the wildcat has been forgotten – an irony indeed.

Sea eagle in Scotland (Mark Hamblin/ Northshots)

The return of iolaire suil na greine

The sea eagle's return to Scotland's west coast is one of modern conservation's landmark successes although the restoration has not been without its setbacks: egg theft and illegal poisoning remain a threat even today. But amidst the furore surrounding the tourism potential of this icon in places like Mull, there is a danger of forgetting that not everyone welcomes the prospect of living next door to a powerful predator. Crofters have lost lambs and game interests perceive a threat to their quarry. There was also opposition, verging on "militancy" according to the National Farmers Union for Scotland, to the reintroduction having been *forced* on rural communities by a national government headquartered 600 miles away. Although it took some time to engineer, Scottish Natural Heritage's Natural Care scheme now provides financial incentives to Mull's farmers to look out for eagles. Does this provide a possible template for greater tolerance of predators elsewhere? According to wolf biologists working in Germany, there is no doubt. They told Tooth & Claw: "If society wants predators, society must be willing to pay."

A wolf at the door?

A century on from the systematic persecution of wolves by American settlers, this animal has become one of the most studied on the planet and its recent return to America's northwest has been globally scrutinized and widely celebrated. Yet bizarrely, the wolf remains widely misunderstood and continues to embody fundamental divisions in our feelings towards predators. Here in Britain, despite theoretical public support for wolf restoration, we have not yet been asked to once again live alongside this or any other large terrestrial predator. Things may change but scratching under the surface of our relationship with foxes, hen harriers, seals, peregrines… in fact any predator with any impact on our lives, it is apparent that we are far from equipped to deal with an animal that would place such demands on our political and social infrastructure.

For predator supporters this consideration should be taken seriously. Science should rightly inform predator policy but a more imaginative engagement with a wider, mainstream audience is essential in order to influence decision makers. The public is entitled to consistent evidence and information but they must also be excited by nature, and inspired to celebrate the processes that come with it. It is not the law that will ultimately protect Britain's predators, it is the people.

A problem bear or a problem for society?

Finally, back to Bruno the Bear, Europe's most famous predator of 2006, who didn't follow the script when he was part of a project to reintroduce brown bears to northern Italy. He ventured into Austria and Germany, where he killed sheep and even roamed into villages. He was the first wild bear seen in Germany since 1835, and Europe's media closely followed his adventures from May to June.

After efforts to stun and capture Bruno, Bavaria's environment ministry announced in June that he could be shot because he was getting too close to humans as he searched for food. He was shot in late June near the town of Zell in southern Germany by an unnamed marksman. Italy's Environment Minister Alfonso Pecoraro Scanio was angered by the killing saying the bear, a protected species, should have been shot with tranquillisers and transported back to Italy. He also demanded the return of Bruno's body to Italy. Two Bavarian villages close to where Bruno was shot also vied to have his stuffed remains on show, no doubt aware of the potential visitor revenue. But Bruno's corpse is destined for the Museum of Humans and Nature in Munich.

Bruno's killing provoked intense reaction. Members of the public filed legal complaints against the Bavarian ministry, memorial websites were created, and many newspaper web sites across Europe developed long discussion threads from readers' e-mails. Bruno's innocent offences in the wild and the struggle of the authorities to cope with him pricked many people's conscience. Maybe he will prompt Germany to once again co-exist with bears, and as we address predator issues in Britain, perhaps we should take heed of the passion over Bruno played out in Bavaria.

The return of large carnivores to Britain – the hunters and the hunted

ECOS 29 (3/4) 25-32 (2009)

The return of iconic species like lynx and wolf to Britain will affect hunters and the success of any such projects may depend on them. This article explores the pivotal role of game interests in the debate on reintroductions.

DAVID BLAKE

The September 2008 conference at Findhorn on species reintroductions, 'Wild free and Coming back?' included a specific workshop on game interests. I have a strong interest in wildlife management through natural processes and my first professional training was as a gamekeeper and deer stalker, so I was pleased to convene that particular session of the event. In what follows, I reflect on some of the main discussion in the workshop and on reactions I have had from fellow hunters since the event. I have included them because I would not want anyone to be in any doubt as to how many, perhaps even the majority, of game managers and hunters will react to the proposals to reintroduce large carnivores to the UK.

We started the conference game session off by describing the parameters for the discussion and setting some definitions: The introduced predators could be lynx, wolf, or wild boar, but also a predatory bird such as Sea Eagle or a fish species. It was also useful to differentiate between those people with a professional or commercial interest in hunting and those for whom it is a sport or part of their way of life. During the discussion we used the term "Game manager" to mean a professional, in full or part-time employment as a gamekeeper, or a land agent, landowner or contractor providing a hunting or culling service. We used the term "Hunter to mean a private individual who hunts for sport and food and for whom hunting has a deep cultural significance. This could be a recreational deer stalker, a fisher or shooter.

I had prepared a SWOT (Strengths, Weaknesses, Opportunities, Threats) analysis to form the basis for the discussion, as set out below. The fact that the Weaknesses and Threats out-weighed the Strengths and Opportunities, served to emphasise how difficult and contentious any reintroductions would be for the hunting and land-owning community.

Reintroductions and game interests – a SWOT analysis

Weaknesses

- In the UK, it is the land owner that receives financial support via agri-environment schemes and the Single Farm Payment and makes any game management decision. Hunters and game managers are not often consulted on long-term land-use policies and estate management decisions that affect the land over which they work and hunt. They are therefore peculiarly powerless to effect long-term change and this encourages short-term thinking and planning in all aspects of game management and hunter attitudes to resource protection.
- It would be very easy for a land owner who cooperated in a reintroduction to pass the cost of the predator's impact (such as loss of game birds) and any control of that impact (such as additional fencing) on to the hunter. Hunters and game managers could then experience rising costs as well as a deterioration in the availability of game.
- Any reintroduction programme would have to meet the requirement and cost of training hunters and game managers to understand the threats, opportunities and technical adaptations to their operations regarding the introduced species.
- Behavioural predictions for introduced species must be treated with caution, predators have been introduced to many ecosystems, often accompanied by an expectation that they will have some positive effect, sometimes with disastrous results.

Threats

- The reintroduction would be another predator of game when game managers have their hands full coping with the ones we have got already, such as carrion crow and red fox, not to mention the protected species such as badger, buzzard, hen harrier and raven.
- The reintroduction would be another predator of game that did not have a predator before, such as roe deer.
- There would probably be conflict with wild game conservation, such as red grouse and grey partridge, and species conservation programmes on land managed for game, such as capercaillie and stone curlew.
- The reintroduction could be a vector of current or novel disease, such as internal parasites. This is already an issue with wild boar in the South West of England.
- If game managers are not fully supportive of a reintroduction programme, then they would be able to halt the programme by killing the reintroduced individuals.

119

Opportunities

- The reintroduction would be another game species to generate additional revenue and greater sporting opportunity, this has happened with the arrival of wild boar in South West England.
- Land that has a low sporting value, such as upland forestry plantations, may become enhanced by a new sporting opportunity, such as wild boar hunting.
- Game managers would be of great assistance in any reintroduction programme, providing information, technical expertise, human and financial resources and local political support.

Strengths

- The reintroduced species might occupy a higher trophic level than the current predators of game species, such as lynx predating red fox, thereby assisting in the conservation of wild game such as grey partridge and red grouse.
- The reintroduced species may provide new or enhanced ecosystem services, such as hunting opportunities, wildlife tourism, enhanced germination of tree seeds or beneficial grazing.
- While there are many records of failed or misguided reintroductions (introduced predators have been responsible for the total extinction of 61 avian taxa, 33 of which were caused by the introduction of the domestic cat to novel ecosystems, most of the others were caused by the deliberate introduction of Small Indian Mongoose to unsuspecting island fauna[1], there are also some very successful ones, such as the otter being welcomed back onto chalk streams fisheries in southern England.

The workshop group was then asked to consider three questions, as highlighted below, and I have recorded the answers, as bullet points below, that we came up with.

1. What factors will encourage game interests to embrace a reintroduction programme?

- Will land and sporting values increase or decrease with re-introductions? There must be a clear economic benefit for any reintroduction programme to gain the full support of the land owning and game management community.
- Reintroduced large predators would have to be added to current Firearms Certificates to allow humane and safe culling of individuals.

- Any reintroduction programme should consider the inclusion of hunting activities such as wild boar drives and the sport hunting of large mammalian predators, such as lynx.

2. What can game interests and other stakeholders learn from each other, when considering potential re-introduction projects?

- We could learn from the successes and challenges of the otter's return to intensively managed fisheries.
- We could learn from the informal development of hunting activity in South West England that has occurred after the return of wild boar. This could inform a planned development programme to run alongside future reintroductions.

3. What can game interests contribute to reintroduction projects, and how can these benefits be harnessed?

- A vital contribution would be the innovative and pragmatic approach that game and land managers are used to adopting as they have to constantly adapt techniques and plans to changing circumstances.
- Land owners and game managers would be able to contribute vital local knowledge and be of great influence in the formation of opinion amongst their neighbours, and their peers and contacts, both locally and nationally.
- Game managers would want to see a long term commitment from the reintroduction programme that would safeguard their earnings, livelihoods and culture.

The voice of hunters

Since the conference at Findhorn, I have tested the idea of reintroducing large predators to the UK by starting a discussion thread on a web site devoted to all kinds of hunting with contributors from all over the world. I wanted to get an impression of the gut reactions of hunters not just in the UK but from people who live with, cope with and hunt large predators within the species' current range. This exercise was not at all scientific, but below I have relayed some of the responses, heavily edited by myself, which I think are pertinent, or typical, or offer food for thought.

In response to my suggestion to reintroduce lynx, the following came from a Swedish hunter:

"You must be either joking or, and this I am saying with the utmost respect, be a few cards short of a full deck. ... In Sweden the return of the four large predators, wolverine, bear, wolf and lynx, causes a great stress on the relationship between rural and city, between hunters and conservationists ... I would sooner turn loose rats, rattlesnakes and roaches in my house than to do anything that would increase the local wolf and lynx population. I am dead

serious and not saying that to be cute. The roaches and snakes are far easier to kill. Your forefathers eradicated lynx and wolves for a reason. Well, as I typed that I realized mine did too. But now the government gives them protection. I have noticed that the president and governor do not have wolves, lynx, bears, and bobcats in their backyard as I do. If they lived here for a year they would change the law to put a bounty on the beasts ... I don't think any one should be punished by having the lynx back in the wild."

Also from Sweden:

"I don't think the animal fanatics would really care [about the damage to game and rural interests]... *but when you have had enough and want to shoot them, the whole world will 'care' ... a couple a years a go when they shot 3-7 wolves here ... freaks from all over Europe came to protest"*

There was a great deal of anecdotal evidence given for lynx and wolf having a disastrous impact on populations of wild and reared game, how hunting becomes difficult due to the timidity of quarry species increasing when a predator is in the locality, and the dangers of using dogs such as retrievers that could run into a lynx or wolf. There were also some links to government web sites that gave up to date figures for losses of domestic livestock to large predators.

Conversely, this message was left by a hunter from Estonia:

"Here in Estonia we have all of the animals you pointed out, lynx, wolves, bear and wild boar. All those species have their part in our environment. I'm hunter and I'm really lucky to be a part of such rich nature. So it would be better to ask from someone who has experience before making such untrue statement [that lynx and wolves ruin hunting]. Regarding lynx and roe. Our lynx population hasn't been so numerous for a long time and the same goes for the roe at the same time. So where is the truth?"

But the response from hunters in the UK was mostly negative. This was more positive than most:

"It is often the case that animals now lost to our lands were eradicated for a reason. Something that may not be immediately apparent to someone without an understanding of all the facets of sharing your ground with a new species. I love the concept of a 'wild Britain' but contact with German and Scandinavian hunters has given me a better understanding of what it actually means to have wild boar, lynx, wolf and bear on your hunting grounds. Sometimes I long for the chance to regularly see pigs on my ground - but seeing the damage a sounder will do to pasture in just one night convinces me that perhaps our countryside is already ideal for the hunter, farmer and sporting shooter."

These were more typical:

"I have to say that the proposal to reintroduce the wolf to the UK is a lunatic scheme as a) domestic stock would be easy prey, b) they need a huge territory which would cover many estates and c) they would have to be European Wolves which are scarce and almost impossible to harvest for reintroduction. The proposal for the lynx is slightly less lunatic but I think we have to be very very careful before reintroducing a top predator back into these islands."

"There are too many people in this country that claim to want to re-establish predator populations both mammal and avian without thinking about the consequences. The RSPB, the leading bird charity here, is spending (and raising) huge amounts of money in order to re-establish various raptors. We have releases of Buzzards near us and they are releasing harriers and all manner of other raptors on the northern moors. No one pays attention to the overall damage any single species conservation attempt does to biodiversity."

A hunter from Switzerland left this interesting post:

"I'm not going to try to argue one way or the other on the issue of lynx re-introduction. But I would like to point to the experience with that exact endeavour here in Switzerland. For whatever reasons or with whatever background, the western part of Switzerland (most notably part of the Jura mountains and the Canton of Bern) had lynx reintroduced some decades back. Apparently, reintroductions were both planned (legal) and unplanned (illegal), the latter presumably done by "well meaning" greenies...

For the hunters in the areas concerned, this has turned out a VERY controversial issue. No, it is not like the lynx have eaten every living roe or chamois (on top of more than a few domestic sheep etc). Rather, the game animals have become extremely shy and almost impossible to hunt. Needless to say, the introduction of the large predator has not been to the liking of the hunting community. This in turn has resulted in more than a few (illegal) shootings of the lynx - some of which have been radio collared. That in turn has generated more bad blood, and needless to say, the press has had a field day being able to portray the hunters as blood thirsty outlaws, and themselves (and associated greenies) as shining examples of nature conservation.

Much to the consternation of the hunters, some lynx were even resettled from the now too large population in the original release area. Mind you, the intended area of settlement has been rejected by the lynx, who have sought out their own territory. Proving yet again, how successful man often is when planning 'controlled' releases of non-indigenous game."

The reality check

I am grateful to my fellow hunters for taking the time to respond to my thread. Their comments come from a self-selecting sample of people who have definite opinions based on varying amounts of experience and knowledge. Most of them are expressed in a second or third language. Of course the above quotes convey some strong views, and we do not know how representative they are of game interests across Britain. However, they give sufficient indication of the strength of feeling that prevails in some quarters of the hunting fraternity. This feedback has taught me was that the discussions we had at the Findhorn event were not too far off the mark and that if any reintroduction of a large predatory mammal was seriously proposed it would have to have the enthusiastic support of the hunting community, and gaining that support will take an enormous effort. I would particularly draw the attention of *ECOS* readers to the comments about how the reintroduction and protection of predators has exacerbated the friction between those who are wary of coexisting with large carnivores and those who advocate the reintroduction of these predators, many of whom would not have to experience the consequences. In addition, the topic of carnivore reintroductions needs handling sensitively, otherwise it could drive a wedge between 'conservationists' and 'hunters'. I would hope that any move to reintroduce large predators would not leave any group of people feeling disenfranchised, forgotten or under-valued.

There was a strong consensus at the conference that any plans for reintroducing iconic species like lynx or wolf should not be foisted upon people. The views from the hunters above have proved this thinking is wise, and that efforts to bring them on board are vital. I would urge proponents of returning predators to consider the following steps, in collaborating with game interests to consider programmes for returning predators:

- Invite game managers to become involved in the programme.
- Design the programme so that game interests are at the very least preserved and enhanced if possible.
- Treat the input of game managers and hunters with respect and value it as highly as that of conservation organisations.

References

1. Jackson, JA, 1977 Alleviating problems of competition, predation , parasitism and disease in endangered birds *Endangered Birds pp75-84, Madison, Univ of Wisconsin Press*

Aliens among the British mammal fauna

ECOS 26 (3/4) 63-71 (2005)

As we debate the consequences of alien mammals we need to factor in the effects of the human species and the land-use consequences of its domestic farm stock.

DEREK YALDEN

When the Channel was flooded about 8,500 b.p. to turn Great Britain into the British Isles, we had a mammal fauna of about 48 terrestrial mammals plus two seals. We have since lost eight of these, including the largest rodent, artiodactyls, and carnivore species. These losses have been numerically more than compensated for by the introductions of at least 21 alien species that have established breeding mainland wild populations, plus at least two others on smaller islands. Some of these were accidental (house mouse, black and brown rat, plus Orkney vole and Scilly shrew); some were food animals (brown hare, rabbit, fallow deer); some were fur-bearing (mink, muskrat, coypu); or specifically for amenity value (edible dormouse, grey squirrel, sika, muntjac, water deer, wallaby). Two of these were subsequently exterminated, and two are now very scarce or nearly extinct.

About 50 percent of the biomass of British wild species of mammal is now contributed by the alien species. It is not surprising that we notice the impact of the aliens when they get too numerous, but in such debates the impact of the domestic stock (and ourselves) tends to be forgotten. The largest impact has come from the introduced domestic mammals, whose collective biomass now outweighs the combined wild species by about 18 times. Our own biomass too s about 11 times that of the wild species.

The ebb and flow of climate and species

18,000 years ago Northern England was actually periglacial, if not under ice. None of the terrestrial fauna or, indeed flora that we have now could have existed here. Therefore, what we have now has happened since then and we know from the pollen record that this started about 15,000 years ago. A warming led to birch scrub invading Britain. There was a cooling, the younger Dryas period at about 11,000 years ago, which caused the birch to retreat and the tundra-type vegetation to expand and then at about 10,000 years ago it really got warm, with 8 degrees centigrade warming of summer temperatures in 50 years or less. Because of the warming, first the birch re-invaded, then the hazel, then the pine and a bit later, oak and elm and alder. Therefore, for a period the country was essentially deciduous woodland. On top of this, because the whole climate was warming up so fast, ice caps were melting, sea level was rising, and the world sea level curve rose to about 34 metres, 8,000 – 9,000 years ago, so cutting Britain off from Europe.

Thus, what had been a continuous land mass across the North Sea, with Britain a sort of peninsula of modern Europe, got flooded, and the British Isles formed. The mammals that had got into Britain, and most of the terrestrial plants that had got into Britain by then, were the natives.

The concept, of course, does not apply so well to perhaps insects, birds and bats that can fly and a few plants that can also 'fly'. Some, such as the tongue orchid that has recently arrived, are still doing so and for some plants the Channel is no barrier. Nevertheless, for terrestrial mammals what we had then are the native mammals and what we have since are aliens.

My guess is based in part on a couple of early archaeological sites that we know well and a little bit of interpolation for the small mammals. These are not terribly well recorded in archaeological sites. I suspect that we only had 33 or so native terrestrial mammals: 5 insectivores, 10 rodents; a hare, interestingly more species (11) of carnivore than there were rodents, and then half a dozen large ungulates.

Of course, the list is not what we are used to historically - we have lost some of them, including Reindeer, and, though we are not sure its history here, wolverine. We think we lost elk about 4,000 years ago. The root vole survived at least on the Scilly Isles until Bronze Age times, and aurochs disappeared in about Bronze Age times. Brown bear certainly survived through to Roman times. Lynx actually got through into Anglo-Saxon times. Then in historical times, we have lost beaver, wild boar, and wolf. We can lose aliens as well. We have managed both to introduce and then to eliminate two alien mammals: coypu and muskrat. It is possible. It has been done, and might give us some hope

Native terrestrial mammal species at 9,000 b.p. (Extinct species in italics) Based on Star Carr, Thatcham, etc. (from Yalden 1999[1])	
HEDGEHOG	WEASEL
PYGMY SHREW	STOAT
COMMON SHREW	POLECAT
WATER SHREW	PINE MARTEN
MOLE	OTTER
	BADGER
MOUNTAIN HARE	*GLUTTON?*
	RED FOX
BEAVER	*WOLF*
RED SQUIRREL	WILD CAT
DORMOUSE	*LYNX*
BANK VOLE	
FIELD VOLE	*WILD BOAR*
ROOT VOLE	ROE DEER
WATER VOLE	*ELK*
HARVEST MOUSE	*REINDEER*
WOOD MOUSE	RED DEER
YELLOW-NECKED MOUSE	*AUROCHS*

Losses and gains

We have done rather too well at making up for all those losses, for those extinctions, by introducing species that clearly are not native. At the top of a list of 22 aliens there are 4 early-Neolithic, farming-introduced, livestock and a little bit later the horse as well. A point to which I will return, that sheep and goats are not native to Europe at all; they were most certainly introduced. Almost certainly, the cattle and the domestic pigs that were introduced came with them from the Middle East. They are not descendants of their native wild relatives - the aurochs and the wild boar respectively.

We do not know exactly when Orkney voles came to Orkney or when lesser white-toothed shrews were introduced to the Scilly Isles, but they have been around for about 4,000 years. Those two came in from the south, probably by accident. The house mouse probably also came in by accident but originally from the Middle East, again with farming but taking a bit of a long time to get here, arriving in Iron Age times. 10 years ago brown hare would not have been on this list but we now know that it was introduced, again in Iron Age times. Genetic evidence confirms what we have come to believe, but we are not sure why it was introduced, but possibly as a cult animal. Romans introduced black rats, again by accident, from India but through the Middle East. They might have died out after that and were re-introduced about 1100 AD. We do know that the Normans introduced the fallow deer and the rabbit. The botanists, I think, would identify these as "archeophytes" or, I suppose, archaeozoons; that is as ancient, well-established animals. But they are not native. The rabbit is native probably only to Iberia and the fallow deer is not even native to Europe. It comes from the Middle East, probably from Anatolia, from Turkey. In New Zealand, the brown rat was introduced before the black rat and the black rat replaced it. In Britain, the black rat was introduced before the brown rat and the brown rat replaced it. Something odd is going on there - it is something to do with relationships between climates and ecophysiology. The black rat is a more southern species than the brown rat and it sounds like the New Zealand climate suits it fine. The British one does not. Then, more recently of course, many species were introduced for amenity, or in some cases for fur.

Some of these introductions have had a massive effect on the fauna, and on the ecology in general. Maps show the native range of the wild sheep in the Middle East, as well as archaeological sites where early wild sheep were discovered, and from there they were taken first across into Greece about 8,000 years ago and spread up through Western Europe. In that part of the world as well, fallow deer were introduced about 8,000 years ago.

Species introduced since 5,500 b.p.		
SHEEP	5400 b.p.	FOOD
CATTLE	5400 b.p.	FOOD
GOAT	5400 b.p.	FOOD
SWINE	5400 b.p.	FOOD
HORSE	4000 b.p.	TRANSPORT
COMMON VOLE	4500 b.p.	ACCIDENT
LESSER WHITE-TOOTHED SHREW	4000 b.p.	ACCIDENT
HOUSE MOUSE	2500 b.p.	ACCIDENT
BROWN HARE	200 b.p.	CULT?
BLACK RAT	200 A.D.	ACCIDENT
FALLOW DEER	1100 A.D.	FOOD
RABBIT	1150 A.D.	FOOD
BROWN RAT	1728 A.D.	ACCIDENT
SIKA	1860 A.D.	AMENITY
GREY SQUIRREL	1876 A.D.	AMENITY
EDIBLE DORMOUSE	1902 A.D.	AMENITY
REEVES' MUNTJAC	1922 A.D.	AMENITY
MUSKRAT	1927 A.D.	FUR
RED-NECKED WALLABY	1940 A.D.	AMENITY
COYPU	1944 A.D.	FUR
CHINESE WATER-DEER	1945 A.D.	AMENITY
AMERICAN MINK	1958 A.D.	FUR

I have explained that fallow deer and rabbit were Norman introductions for food. Coneys, adult rabbits, were kept in warrens initially, carefully protected, and did not become a pest for 500 years or so. Fallow deer were introduced to parks, for venison on the hoof. The Fallow is a more suitable animal for parks than either red deer, which are a bit too big and suffer if they're overcrowded, or roe deer because they are woodland browsers and territorial. Fallow are grazers, and live in herds, so they were an ideal park animal. They were also protected but some were introduced to hunting forests like the New Forest and Epping Forest, and others have since escaped. They established themselves over the last 200 or 300 years, and of course in England they are now the most common deer.

The landscape amenity introductions

Leading on to the amenities, we may mention grey squirrels and sika as two of the later aliens, and again these are animals which are increasingly common. They were introduced because they looked nice, and have done very well thank you.

The black rat had massive historical impacts, since it was the one that carried the fleas that carried the Black Death, the Bubonic Plague, in 1348, then again in 1665. The brown rat did not displace it until some time after, but that too can carry some nasty diseases and they are two aliens we certainly would prefer not to keep. Having said that, the black rat is now so rare it only occurs on a few offshore seabird islands – see Helen Meech's article in this issue.

Deliberate introductions

Deliberate introductions are much more numerous than the accidental ones. In particular, many deliberate introductions have made massive pests of themselves. The edible dormouse was released at Tring Park in 1902. It is a species very much of beechwoods, so the Chilterns make an ideal habitat for it, and it has not spread very much. In a wonderful paradox, it is illegal to release edible dormice back into the wild, as a Schedule 9 Alien Species under the *Wildlife and Countryside Act* 1981. As a dormouse, it is a member of the Gliridae, and it is therefore protected under the *Berne Convention*. It is a bit of a pest of houses and nests in the attic or raids food stores. It also hibernates, usually underground in drains and the like. Of course, they are strictly nocturnal and they are a bit bigger than ordinary mice, so half a dozen of them thrashing around in the attic tend to be noticed. You are not allowed to kill them, and you are not allowed to return them to the wild either. Consequently, people take them to places where they should not occur at all and surreptitiously let them go, like the New Forest. I expect this is a species which is going to do considerably better, and which we might be worrying more about it in the future. It has on occasion damaged commercial forestry.

An interesting contrast is between Reeve's muntjac and Chinese water deer, which are similar-sized deer. There is a concern that the world population of Chinese water deer is not very big and that we have about half of the mainland race and about 15% of the world population, even though this is very limited. Reeve's muntjac, which is a Chinese muntjac, is not at all well known there in the wild. It has done very well here, particularly turning itself into a deer of suburban countryside, frequenting gardens and eating roses. It can live inside bramble patches, on railway embankments, and it is a frequent road casualty. Its introduction possibly started about 1920 with escapes from Woburn Park. Muntjac do not turn up in far away places, such as up into Scotland, as a result of natural spread from Southern England. However, they are quite often hurt in road accidents, taken in and rehabilitated and the RSPCA, who ought to know better, take them elsewhere to let them go. This is illegal, but nobody ever stops the process. It is illegal to release grey squirrels in the wild, but they do that too. The Duke of Bedford, who had muntjac originally in his park, was also deliberately spreading them into the wild. He would take groups of five or so and let them free at places some distance from Woburn Park to make sure they survived in the wild. One introduction in Kent did not work, but I think that muntjac will get there shortly anyway.

Does it matter?

Should we get uptight about aliens? It matters, I think, very much in several senses. First, part of the interest of British mammal fauna is that it is 50 separate species. It does not improve the biodiversity of the world in general to bring in alien species from all over the place and produce a mish-mash. If we are not careful, we will have a world mammal fauna that includes house mouse, brown rat, black rat, fallow deer, grey squirrel, rabbit, brown hare, and little else. That is not improving the world's biodiversity and I do not think it's improving Britain's biodiversity, or the importance of this fauna and flora, to bring in every 'rubbish' species from anywhere around the world and add it on top.

Second, we do not always succeed in adding it on top. We think we have improved our biodiversity by having two species of squirrel. But we are actually getting one, which is an alien species we should not have, and we are losing the other. It took us a long time to realise this. Monica Shorten did point out in 1945 that there seemed to be a strong correlation between the places where grey squirrels had been established in and around London by 1930, and places where red squirrels had gone by 1945. Nevertheless, the link was not taken seriously. It might have been possible, for instance, if people had taken it seriously, to have got rid of, say, the Scottish grey squirrel.

The grey squirrel was a pest but no-one took much action, and through the 1970s we saw the grey squirrel spreading even further, particularly into Wales. It had not spread into East Anglia at that point, but by the end of the 1970s it had and, sure enough, the red squirrel continued to decline. The maps show the picture in 1990. That is now considerably optimistic. We lost the Peak District ones; the last one was seen in 1994, but unfortunately in the talons of a goshawk. The grey squirrels were taking over and the red squirrel was already on its way out. The Cannock Chase population went at the same time, as did the Suffolk heathlands population. Craig Shuttleworth in his paper to the *Loving the Aliens 2005 Conference* gave details of red and grey squirrels, in Wales. The ranges shown for Wales are certainly optimistic, and the red squirrel has certainly retreated from the southern Lake District as the grey squirrel has continued to expand. I do not see that as a good replacement. It will take a while longer yet, but unless we do something serious about it, we're going to lose red squirrels completely.

Mink and Voles

Another case is the American mink, first reported breeding in the wild in 1956. The Ministry of Agriculture, Fisheries and Food said there was no problem. We are now all aware of the major impact of mink on water voles, so there is the relationship between water vole latrine counts and mink occupation across the country. Water vole has done very badly, where mink are numerous. However, it is actually the last phase of a much longer decline. As you go back to Neolithic and Bronze Age faunas, water voles are at least as common as field voles. Two of those other aliens have also had a massive impact on water voles. Water voles in continental Europe are not confined to water. They are known much more widely to be an agricultural pest. They occur in pastures, in meadows, and in apple orchards. Here in Britain they seem to be confined to waterways. We think this is because sheep and especially rabbits also eat the grass, the cover that water voles need. So three aliens have had a massive impact on water vole numbers in Britain, and part of the interest of Britain should be that water voles are very common, but they are not and mink are just the last straw as far as water voles are concerned.

More on deer and cats

Sika is a Japanese relative of the red deer and does very well in plantations of another alien, sitka spruce. Sika have done moderately well, for instance, in the Dorset/Hampshire/Poole Basin area, and they are particularly abundant in the Scottish sitka plantations. They are very difficult to shoot to cull in dense forestry plantations, so they have done really well.

Unfortunately, sika is also quite closely related to the red deer, though the two species do not normally hybridise. Rather obviously, red deer is a lot bigger, with sika about the size of a fallow deer. Sika stags do not stand a chance of rivalling red deer stags when both species are around. However, when they are not, then sika stags will try and mate with the first year red deer hinds because they are fairly small and they sometimes force themselves. What does happen is that hybrids are then fully fertile both ways. So hybrid red/sika deer could be anywhere between sika and red deer in phenotype, and quite indistinguishable. The consequence is that the remaining population of red deer is almost certainly doomed. There will not be red deer in Scotland in 50 years' time and the advice of the geneticists is that changes have already gone too far to be reversed. Though I do wonder whether that is true as no one has tried reversing it. I suspect, of course, the hunting lobby prefer to shoot large red deer stags. That is actually the worse thing they can do. What they should be shooting is small sika stags, but that will not happen and I suspect that, yes, we have already lost the red deer as a mainland species. It will take 200 years, but it seems we will lose our largest mammal.

A similar problem exists between wild cats and feral moggies. They are more closely related than red and sika deer are. The domestic moggy is almost certainly descended from the African race of wild cats. Nevertheless, released into the wild it can certainly interbreed with Scottish wild cats. Since the wild cat is now in such small numbers, a migrant moggy and migrant wild cat are more likely to meet each other than wild cats are to meet other wild cats. We have an estimate of 3,500 wild cats in Scotland, but they may comprise about 1,000 wild cats and 2,500 hybrid cats.

A wider perspective

Therefore, there are a number of cases where these aliens really are problems. Because we have so few mammal species to worry about, the mammal ecology and conservation people certainly have been recording these changes and are concerned about them. They hope to turn that concern into positive action.

A plot of individual body masses against abundance for all the British terrestrial mammals shows a negative relationship (see diag). The regression line is not quite 2/3 (0.67), it's more precisely 0.72, but this is the relationship between abundance and individual mass for terrestrial mammals. It leaves out the bats, because bats clearly ecologically belong to a very different category. We do not know what a native bat is because some of them certainly have crossed the Channel. They actually fall on the bird line which is parallel to but lower than the mammal one.

I have also left out domestics, for which I'll return later. The point is, of course, that you'd expect a small mammal to be more numerous than a big one - so indeed pygmy shrew, common shrew, field vole, for example, are at the upper end and at the other end is our largest, terrestrial, native mammal, red deer. Scarce mammals include black rat, wallaby, and small feral populations of reindeer and wild cattle. Therefore, there is a relationship, which tries to quantify how abundant small mammals should be or how abundant large mammals should be on a common scale. What we want to know is where the aliens fall on this. The message is that mostly these aliens fall in with the native mammals. Some of them are restricted because they were introduced into small areas, like lesser white-toed shrews on Scilly, red-necked wallaby, or only survive in small areas, like black rats. But notice particularly how abundant rabbit is compared with mammals in general. Some other aliens have done quite well, for instance fallow deer and sika. Look how much more successful grey squirrels are now than red squirrels on the estimates that we have.

So how does this compare with how things were in the Mesolithic, when all we had were native mammals and farming had not interfered with things? It's estimated there were 535 million Mesolithic mammals, and the biomass of 300 thousand tonnes of mammals was very much dominated by the big ungulates, the aurochs, elk, red deer, roe deer, and the wild boar, many of which have gone extinct. There were rather more large rodents around then because there were beavers as well as a lot more red squirrels. The native species are now reduced around half numerically, to 222 million and by mass to a fifth, 61 thousand tonnes. But the introduced species, collectively, number about 57 million, while the deer, rabbits, and brown hares mostly, provide about the same amount of biomass, 68 thousand tonnes, as what's left of the native mammal fauna. That is bad enough, but remember that I left off the four domestics of farmed sheep, cattle, horses and pigs and we could add, perhaps, a spot there for ourselves.

Collectively we and the domestic ungulates number 68 million, but contribute a biomass of 6,614 million tonnes, over 50 times the biomass of the wild (native and alien) mammals. Of course, we notice when either native species or, indeed, the introduced species, get rather more abundant than we think they ought to be because, basically, the resources have been taken up by ourselves and domestic stock. One of the main messages here is that there's not much habitat left for wild mammals.

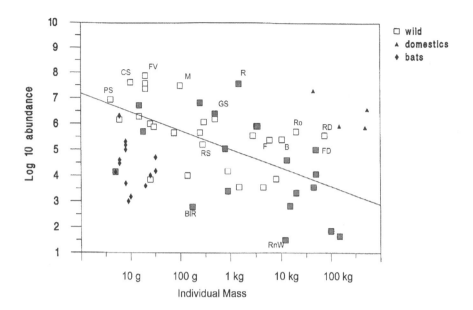

Labelled species:
B Badger; BR Black Rat; CS Common Shrew; F Fox; FD Fallow Deer; FV Field Vole; GS Grey Squirrel; M Mole; PS Pygmy Shrew; R Rabbit; RnW Red-necked Wallaby; Ro Roe Deer; RD Red Deer; RS Red Squirrel.

References

1. Yalden, D. (1999) *The History of British Mammals*. Poyser Natural History, London
2. Harris, S., Morris, P., Wray, S & Yalden, D. 1995. A review of British Mammals: population estimates and conservation status of mammals other than cetaceans. JNCC, Peterborough.

Future Natural – the unpredictable course of wild nature

ECOS editorial 27 (3/4) 1 -3 (2006)
Without any target or action plan to drive it, Britain is witnessing a re-wilding of its landscapes. These transformations are enriching ecosystems and bringing lyrical power to the land.

MARK FISHER

In the conclusion to his book *Fenced Paradise*, Richard Mabey identifies a missing zone from amongst the many specialised habitat domes at Cornwall's Eden Project. His recommendation would be for a new, uncovered area of the quarry to be left to re-vegetate from the surrounding native species. His experience of that location and the re-vegetation of similar disused industrial sites, suggests that furze (gorse) would be an early returnee, which would produce a characteristic landscape that he delightfully labels the garrigue of Cornwall.[1]

I think Mabey's prescription for the Eden Project should be one for all areas of Britain, missing as they are - for the most part - landscapes that are given the opportunity to decide how they will clothe themselves with vegetation, and to whom they will give sustenance. The exciting aspect of that prescription is the prospect of watching nature do its own thing: the quick returns that are ephemeral; the later returns that stick around; and the opportunistic but inappropriate directions whose moments of glory may succumb to an ultimate course.

Wild action – documenting the projects

Examples do exist in Britain of landscapes regaining greater self-determination, and which can give us inspiration. The Wildland Network has recently compiled a database of re-wilding projects, available on its website (see Ward, Fisher and Carver article). It is worth exploring some of these projects as they indicate a range of circumstance in which this greater self-determination can take place.

In woodland regeneration, time-limited exclosure to eliminate grazing pressure is the simple act that often initiates transformation. Trees for Life in Scotland will beguile you with tales of the springing into dramatic growth of native conifers, infantilised from decades of over-grazing, as well as the flush of new seedlings as constraints are removed to the re-formation of the Caledonian Forest.

In Suffolk, an aim is to defragment two ancient woodlands, Spouses Vale and Arger Fen, through natural re-vegetation of the field that lies between them. In the upland areas of the limestone Yorkshire Dales (South House Moor) in the eastern Lake District (Royalty Allotment) and Snowdonia (Cwm Idwal) natural re-wooding is taking place after a few years of a break in livestock grazing.

Water is a potent driving force for native wetland habitat regeneration. The new coastal wetlands at Abbott's Hall Farm and at Wallasea Island, Essex, are a stunning compensation for wetland losses elsewhere (see May, Hall and Pretty article). In smaller scale, Cors Dyfi a new reserve of the Montgomeryshire Wildlife Trust someway inland on the Dyfi estuary, saw a Sitka spruce plantation cleared and the water drainage reversed. A mere eight years on and there is infiltration of wetland again with reeds, bulrush, bog myrtle, flag iris and willow, recolonising from sufficient remnant species around the reserve.

Perhaps outside of a framework of simple transformation, the re-vegetation of a Pembrokeshire coastal farm shows the lengths that have to be taken in realising the return of a particular habitat on farm land – in this instance coastal heath. Fields at Trehill Farm, with their centuries of agricultural improvement, have undergone a stripping-off of topsoil followed by dressing with a sulphur waste product from the local oil refinery to re-acidify the soil. Coastal forbs quickly returned but heath species needed seeding from the brash cut from heathland elsewhere.

The return of natural vegetation cover can accompany the re-introduction of lost mammalian species. Perhaps the example with the highest profile is the Alladale Estate of Paul Lister in the Scottish Highlands (see Roger Sidaway's article). The plan for restoring the original Highland ecology of this former hunting estate began on a small scale to explore the success of habitat recovery, with a replanting of native trees (saplings of juniper, willow, rowan, birch, aspen, Caledonian pine) and a reduction in grazing pressure through a culling of the local deer population. Red squirrel, wildcat, and wild boar will be reintroduced on a 1000 acre site, the aim eventually being to re-introduce these to the whole of the estate, along later with the wild grey wolf, lynx and brown bear.

The estate will be enclosed with high fencing to prevent release of carnivores into the wild, but will the open access provisions that exist in Scotland mean that everyone can benefit from this restoration? This is the main challenge for the project – enclosing the predators while keeping access groups content. Alladale will be an opportunity to study how the re-introduction of wolves and other native predators in the longer term can restore a natural balance in the deer population without the need for further culling. Lister is seeking the co-operation of surrounding landowners to double the potential area of wild reserve to 50,000 acres. He believes that this area of land could support two wolf packs (12-15 animals in each pack), three pairs of lynx, and up to 30 brown bears.

Predicting nature's accidents

In all these transformations, unpredictability could never be a factor that is obviated, and it is ever so with nature. We trust to the future that giving a freer rein to the forces of nature will pay dividends in improved integrity for ecologically functional landscapes. This future natural state was articulated by George Peterken, when he set out a vision for the natural evolution of new temperate wildwoods in Britain.[2]

Peterken accepted the unpredictability by pointing to the contemporary factors such as extinctions, and climate and soil changes that meant that this woodland would never be a re-creation of the past – the original natural woodland. The concept of future natural is thus wider than just woodland, certainly embracing wetland restoration, and maybe even habitats such as heathland where other factors are sometimes able to prolong its often short existence in the absence of our interference.

It is that latter point – the active involvement and management by people and their instruments - which marks out a divergence in views about how a future natural state can be achieved. Already there is a presumption for natural reseeding and re-wooding over tree planting for new wild woodland, with recourse to the latter only when the location lacks a sufficient seed bank or source. But a different course was given a big push when Frans Vera published his theories about the relationship between woodland regeneration and wild herbivores, and the establishment of a major demonstration project in Holland's Oostvadersplassen (a place which receives much attention in this issue).

Becoming parasitized?

It is easy to see the seductive nature of Vera's theories, as they sit effortlessly within the landscape management orthodoxy of conservation professionals in Britain. Not unsurprisingly, significant progress has been made in a few short years on the animal welfare issues in preparing the ground for adoption of the approach here, as reported in this issue by Matthew Oates. Where perhaps less effort has been applied is in understanding and realising the state of landscape vegetation to which this herbivore pressure can be re-introduced, and which has any hope of survival if we contribute to get the balance wrong. Can the balance ever be 'right' or 'natural' if what we have to do is fence in these surrogate wild herbivores rather than allow for their natural passage? I am often reminded of the wisdom of Leopold, writing some 60 years ago, when he said "By grazing all the woods we eventually exterminate the woods".[3]

I should make less of this divergence and instead recruit it to the diversity of transformative approaches that a future natural state can arise from. An important factor for this future natural state will be its relationship with the land around it. As is becoming clear across the world, isolated enclaves of wild nature are less effective than if they are networked together by wildlife corridors[4], and bounded by buffering with semi-natural land.[5] The key for all of these aspects of future natural will be our exploring of it with an open mind and heart, managing our expectations of it, as much as we should resist over-managing the processes themselves.

Returning to Richard Mabey's concluding remarks in *Fenced Paradise*, he throws in a natural horror to his vision of the natural re-vegetation of an area of the Eden Project quarry: the gorse becomes parasitized by common dodder, a climbing and twining plant common to the SW that he likens to a serpent. Dodder barely roots in its life cycle and gives nothing back. Mabey gives us a brutal caution when he says that people have much in common with dodder when we do not consider equably our relationship with the natural world.

References

1. Mabey, R., 2005. *Fencing Paradise: Reflections on the Myths of Eden*. Eden Books

2. Peterken, G.F., 1996. *Natural Woodland – ecology and conservation in Northern temperate regions*. Cambridge University Press

3. Leopold, A. Do we want a woodless countryside? *In*: Calicott J.B. & Freyfogle E.T., 1999. *For the Health of the Land*. Island Press

4. Humphrey, J., Watts, K., McCracken, D., Shepherd, N., Sing, L., Poulsom, L., Ray, D., 2005. *A review of approaches to developing Lowland Habitat Networks in Scotland*. Scottish Natural Heritage Commissioned Report No. 104 www.snh.org.uk/pdfs/publications/commissioned_reports/f02aa102_2.pdf

5. Forestry Commission, 2005. *Keepers of Time - a statement of policy for England's ancient & native woodland*. www.forestry.gov.uk/keepersoftime

Grazing systems and animal welfare – matters of life and death

ECOS 27 (3/4) 52-57 (2006)

Animal welfare interests and nature conservation groups are working together to address key requirements for extensive and naturalistic grazing systems. This article discusses some of the main issues that confront them.

MATTHEW OATES

Since the late 1970s the UK's nature conservation practitioners have been experimenting in grazing with domesticated stock. Experimentation has been precipitated largely by agriculture's increasing reluctance and inability to deploy stock in the marginal land which expands and contracts according to economic forces. These efforts have been based on some recognition of the role domesticated large herbivores have in driving the ecology of grassland, heathland and pasture-woodland habitats. This role of herbivores has often accompanied activities such as burning, cutting and even drainage.

Conservation effort has at times functioned with natural processes, and in other situations raged against them. Conservation grazing activity has sought local solutions both from within and beyond agriculture. The abilities of a diversity of breeds of cattle, sheep, ponies and goats to help with the maintenance and/or enhancement of sites managed for nature has been explored in a glorious but uncoordinated experiment.[1] The wheel has therefore been invented and reinvented locally, often in sublime ignorance of comparable experience elsewhere. The Grazing Animals Project (GAP, see www.grazinganimalsproject.org.uk) was established in 1997 largely to improve communication on issues relating to grazing in UK nature conservation.

In Agri-land where the shadows lie...

Agriculture has made significant steps towards embracing nature conservation, notably by providing significant funding. Yet, in consequence, and because of our dependency on stock grazing, nature conservation has been invaded by the burgeoning bureaucracy that agriculture has become. We now have to comply (with agri-environment specifications) and cross-comply, and our ability to opt out of, or outmanoeuvre, the agricultural system has effectively disappeared. A great deal of land managed for wildlife is now tied into well-meaning but narrow agri-environment schemes. Moreover, whereas Biodiversity Action Plans help the process of prioritisation, they add another massive tier of bureaucracy.

Agriculture is now firmly the default-setting baseline for nature conservation, and for our engagement with nature and landscape. Of course, it does not have to be that way, as Frans Vera argues[2], but the inadequate philosophical and psychological basis for nature conservation does not enable us to outmanoeuvre agriculture at all easily (Oates, in press).[3] So, our landscapes and their habitats largely reflect agricultural values and endeavour, present and past in that order, and are set now to reflect agricultural bureaucracy.

Past, present and which future?

The real issue for nature conservation is the extent to which our perceptions of the past can and should prime future actions. We cannot answer this 'which past – which future?' debate until that basic philosophical question has been addressed, and we lack a mechanism for doing so. I believe that the thinking around 're-wilding' or, more appropriately, 'wilding' must engage in that debate.

Of course, we cannot go back. Time is forward-bound, and is essentially the dimension within which change occurs. The philosophy of time is, therefore, like nature conservation, strongly concerned with the relationship between past, present and future. However, nature conservation is also primarily concerned with seeking a future for features of significance, for things that people value. It should also be concerned strongly with the relationship between people and nature.

Proxies and analogues

The aurochs has gone forever. A massive amount of perception and mythology has developed surrounding its ecological role in the minds of modern ecologists, but despite admirable recent work (notably Hodder, Bullock & Kirby, 2005) we will never know the true extent to which it functioned as an ecological driver. Frans Vera has developed the concept of modern large herbivores acting as proxies or analogues for extinct ecological drivers such as the aurochs.

But how do we determine the most appropriate analogues for extinct keystone species? At what estimate percentage of approximation should we buy-in to a proxy? Our decisions will be guided by legislation, social perspectives, and the landscape situation within which nature conservation effort functions.

The Grazing Animals Project advocates that for the more challenging grassland, heathland and pasture-woodland habitats, stock of an appropriate 'type' need to be deployed.[5] The key components of 'type' go beyond species and breed, and encompass age, sex (and no sex at all, with castrates) and, most importantly, 'background'. The latter includes husbandry and social group history, and in many conservation grazing systems seems to be the most crucial attribute of 'type'.

Embracing animal welfare

Animal welfare is one of the main contexts within which nature conservation functions. This is not a constraint but something that nature conservation should actively embrace, for positive engagement with animal welfare can only strengthen the nature conservation case with the public and politicians. Furthermore, attending to animal wellbeing enables domesticated stock to function to the best of their ability in challenging situations, and in so doing are most able to make genuine impacts on the vegetation that conservation seeks to control. (In ruminants, this wellbeing is largely a matter of rumen function). Animals whose wellbeing is compromised are less able to perform their grazing function adequately. However, grazing animals should not be perceived or labelled as 'grazing tools'; such terminology sends out the wrong messages to the public and, moreover, is incorrect as grazing animals manipulate vegetation in their own way.

The legal framework for animal welfare is based on avoiding unnecessary suffering, though this obviously involves significant grey areas. The general way round any difficulties here is to endeavour to function within the spirit of the concept. The new Animal Welfare Act now imposes a duty of care, which is likely to encompass animals introduced to naturalistic grazing systems.

The welfare of domesticated herbivores has been further developed through the Five Freedoms, produced by the Farm Animal Welfare Council (*www.fawc.org.uk*) and upon which are based the various Defra codes of recommended husbandry practice. The Five Freedoms are not an impossible council of perfection but are to be used as a practical guide, particularly to identify the strengths and weaknesses of any husbandry system. Stated blandly, they are:

> Freedom from Hunger and Thirst.
> Freedom from Discomfort.
> Freedom from Pain, Injury or Disease.
> Freedom from Fear and Distress.
> Freedom to Express Normal Behaviour.

At face value the first four Freedoms seem irrelevant to naturalistic grazing, if not to nature itself. In the wild animals regularly experience the first four, often to significant extents. But the fifth Freedom, so readily denied in domesticated systems, often allows them to be able to do something to alleviate suffering. The Five Freedoms are aimed at avoiding situations where an animal's stresses exceed its ability to cope. Most fears are imagined, and stresses can be natural circumstances, and the welfare issue is really over the degree rather than the quality of stresses. It is, of course, difficult to measure stress, though this has been achieved in the case of hunted Red Deer.[6]

The Five Freedoms address both physical and mental welfare and aim to reduce or avoid stress in order to prevent the high degree of suffering that may occur when an animal becomes unable to cope with stresses that have become too severe, complex or prolonged. In particular, an animal will suffer if it cannot take action to relieve or avert the stress it is suffering. A good example here is the fact that animals in the Oostvardersplassen in Holland are contained and cannot escape or migrate when food becomes scarce in winter - which is does. Indeed, the heavy poaching along the eastern perimeter fence there on my last visit, in March 2005, was on a scale reminiscent of images of the Western Front.

The naturalistic grazing movement needs to engage with animal welfare organisations to develop the concept of the Five Freedoms within the context of extensive grazing systems involving free-ranging large herbivores, plus and minus large carnivores.

The process of feralisation
One difficult welfare area which is pertinent to naturalistic grazing systems is the issue of de-domestication, the process of feralisation. At Oostvardersplassen, one of the three introduced large herbivores was already 'wild' – Red Deer – and the other two – Konic ponies and Heck cattle - were chosen in part because they were felt to be breeds most able to bridge the gap between domesticated and feral animals. This was a deeply thought out attempt to introduce animals of appropriate 'type'. However, the ponies and deer are better able to graze the sward closer than the cattle, and to strip bark. They therefore may out-compete the cattle. To an extent, then, the cattle's welfare may have been compromised by human decision, for it was known from the onset that this competition might occur.

It is not easy to devise criteria for determining when animals have become truly wild. The problem here is assessing when and how does our dominion over introduced animals end, if at all? Moreover, animal behaviour patterns in naturalistic grazing situations always will be influenced by human decision, even if the decision to do nothing has been taken. A further complication would be the decision to add large carnivores, in order to replicate natural systems. The impact of large carnivores on large herbivore dispersion is likely to be of more significance than their role in population control (see David Bullock's article in this issue).

Death shall have no dominion...

The greatest area of difficulty in animal welfare is death and dying. However, most of the animals in the Oostvardersplassen have a better quality of life than many farm animals, though those that effectively die of 'starvation' must experience 'unnecessary suffering' near the end.

In naturalistic grazing systems, there are two possible ways around these problems: through developing criteria for culling, and through the concept of carrying capacity. Neither are easy. Culling criteria are based on our ability to determine that an animal is beyond hope – assuming a marksman can find it, for many animals seek to die in the bushes (which may well say something about their attitude to death). Attempts are being made to fine-tune this thinking at Oostvardersplassen, though the best we can go on is Condition Scoring (which was developed for agricultural systems wherein animals are handled), and different people will set the intervention threshold variously. The difficulties with carrying capacity are, first, that it denies natural population fluctuations and cycles, which clearly influence vegetation dynamics; second, that it inevitably leads to the culling of healthy and young animals; and third, that it is difficult to calculate what a carrying capacity should be.

I would argue that the real issue here is the lack of any coherent philosophy covering death...

Overcoming our fears

Animal welfare and nature conservation need to come closer, because the two movements have much in common, and because both are capable of becoming radicalised and alienated. Animal welfare is primarily about human perception and value judgements, as is nature conservation. The good news is that there is a Conservation Grazing Animal Welfare Working Group, convened by GAP, which brings the thinking of the two movements together to agree, hopefully, through Defra, some form of code to guide naturalistic grazing systems within the spirit of the new Animal Welfare Act. This group can help with the development of the Five Freedoms thinking within the context of naturalistic grazing. Above all, the group is encouraging depth and breadth of thinking, and forward-planning, on issues relating to nature conservation grazing.

The main issue holding back progress towards the eco-system approach to nature is not animal welfare concerns, but the fears most nature conservationists have over loss of valued features (primarily species and habitats), and the bureaucratic processes put in place to prevent such losses. These concerns emanate largely from the lack of any philosophy for nature conservation (and Nature) in the UK: there are no criteria for accepting decline and loss, basic pragmatics apart, and no conceptual thinking for handling the processes of change. We need to engage in such discussions...

References

1. Oates, MR & Tolhurst, S. 2000. Grazing for Nature Conservation: Rising to the Challenge. British Wildlife 11:5: 348-353.

2. Vera, FWM. 2000. Grazing Ecology & Forest History. CABI Publishing.

3. Oates, MR. In press. The Dying of the Light. British Wildlife.

4. Hodder, KH, Bullock, J & Kirby, K. 2005. Large Herbivores in the Wildwood and Modern Naturalistic Grazing Systems. English Nature Research Report, No. 648.

5. Tolhurst, S & Oates, MR (eds chosen in part because they were felt to be breeds most able to bridge the gap between domesticated and feral animals. This was a deeply thought out attempt to introduce animals of appropriate 'type'. However, the ponies and deer are better able to graze the sward closer than the cattle, and to strip bark. They therefore may out-compete the cattle. To an extent, then, the cattle's welfare may have been compromised by human decision, for it was known from the onset that this competition might occur.

6. Bateson, P & Bradshaw, EL. 1997. Behavioural and Psychological Effects of Culling Red Deer. Proc. Royal Soc. B. 264: 1-8.

Rewilding the Human

Living on the edge
the risks of going wild

ECOS 24 (3/4) (2003)

Peter Taylor reflects on the experience of nature, parenting, control, safety and rebellion, and the rise and rise of managerial safety.

When I was a teenager, I courted death though I would never have called it that. Out of sight of parental view I explored sea-caves, having to wade chest deep when caught by the incoming tide; slid to the edge of an untimely end down crumbling chalk at the edge of a two hundred foot drop; and there was a near-miss of dislodged rock on an (un-roped) climbing escapade. In my 20s, I was more philosophically aware, and the Eiger in winter, or crossing the oven-heat of the southern Sahara, was clearly a counterpoint to the slow death of office life. I thought then, I pushed the envelope, because to live on that edge was to affirm life – one false move and you were dead! As a parent, life looked decidedly different. It took great effort to allow my children the same freedom, and now I know why I never told my parents of my escapades.

Troublesome teenagers

A Mayan shaman, a teacher for these, my later years, reckons that the Gods of Death stalk teenagers especially.[1] His culture's darker deities hunt down the creative spark of men and can only be appeased by poetry. If they like it, they let you live. But then, you are truly alive, because good poetry can only come from those who really live. For those who fail, those who seek comfort and security, those who would hold on to their life so dearly and try to cheat death, they die. Not materially, of course. Not immediately. The dark Gods have no need of that as ultimately, it happens to everyone and is therefore immaterial. They become the walking dead, and they belong to the Gods of Death.

Other indigenous cultures, perhaps also, our own now distant, have similar understandings, and similar Gods that might gobble up the unwary poet or lop off the head of an arrogant warrior, all to ensure life moves forward with a meaning beyond mere survival. In all of these tribal cultures, young people are initiated into poetic realities, usually at 14 years of age. Here began art, song, music and dance to add to the hunt, to warrior combat, and courtship. Life took on a greater meaning and the risk of life also.

My Mayan friend looks upon our modern troublesome teenagers with delight. They risk all for ecstatic dance or a wild car chase, and rock-and-roll still lives on the city streets. They may get locked up, or worse, but they will have lived on the edge. He sees in that the potential for poetry in all its forms, for the creative spark of human life, at least with the aid of a little mentoring and focus. Oddly, these kids, when faced with an initiation as simple as a night walk in the forest, get truly fearful. The adrenalin still flows, but the mind makes a far bigger deal of the risk!

Initiation - built by teenagers at Cae Mabon for storytelling, poetry, music and nightwalks in the forest (Peter Taylor)

Until recent times, the most trouble from the uninitiated arose from boys. Now girl gangs are becoming more of a problem. Both sexes benefit from encounters with the wild, with the girls just as eager to experience that edge. But indigenous cultures always have very separate initiatory rites, and I wonder not so much as to whether our unisexual approach does any harm, rather, what it is the girls may be missing. There is now little trace of an ancient wisdom on that

146

score, the churches having systematically eradicated the uncooperative 'wise women' healers, diviners, and herbalists of Europe over a 500 year time span.

Nature co-opted

Most children, the ones that do not rebel, are over-parented and un-adventurous. If they get to visit the great outdoors, they are usually accompanied by adults with one eye on the twin Gods of insurance and litigation. They may go white-water rafting, kayaking, mountain biking, abseiling and orienteering, but all hell will break loose if a supervisor is negligent in an unwatchful moment, or their protective gear is not appropriately checked. The mountains and rivers of our National Parks abound with well-zippered goretex. Nature is co-opted in the enterprise. Our young people must be given a wild experience, exposed to some risk, just as long as it is well-managed.

This, to my mind, is little better than the criminal car chase or the pilled-up buzz of the rave. Indeed, it is the same uninitiated craving, but lesser, because it is well managed, and both types of adrenalin junkies, if you left them alone in the forest, by twilight would be crying for mum.[2]

This is a bizarre circumstance. Young people crave risk in an over-civilised society. And their greatest physical risks, from car accidents, drug abuse, or violence, arise within the very bounds of that supposed civility, yet they fear most that which is in the unknown land beyond the city gate. Then they grow up and become managers! Countryside risks get fenced off. Up go the notice-boards. Beware: Deep Water, Falling Rocks. And further – not even a humble beaver allowed to disturb the comforts of fishermen and cattle-grazers, let alone a lynx, a bear or a wolf.

In the pioneering Dutch experiment of turning a 5000 ha polder into a paradise for wild cattle and horses, along with deer and boar, visitors are shepherded around in safe safari vehicles. Perhaps that has to be, but the local authorities soon put a stop to the carcasses lying around, dying variously from disease, starvation, or combat, and left to rot. Too much risk of disease.

The risk averse and the hypocrisy

There occurs within this risk-averse mindset, a curious hypocrisy with regard to natural processes of death, whether by predation or decay. The supposed 'safe' world of civil order, including its agricultural counterpart, is actually very dangerous. City streets, and even country roads are dangerous places, especially for children. Farms and their produce are full of disease and death. Foresters and hunters cull deer, and occasionally, inadvertently, themselves. Yet, I have heard Vosges shepherds and hunters decry with great emotion, the introduced lynx for the deer and sheep they kill, and Norwegian sheepherders likewise the wolf, not

147

only for its livestock depredations, but also for its apparent potential to attack children. This same Norwegian community continually ignored pleas to cull a pack of domestic dogs gone wild, and then lost a child to a grisly death, something regularly documented in civil Europe; whereas no European wolf has ever been recorded killing a human. In the Vosges, cars killed more deer than the hunters, and in Norway, pneumonia kills a good many more sheep than the wolves.

Avoiding the darker Gods

At one time I used to believe this madness was the fault of the Christian God. The Saviour spoke in glorious wisdom of lilies and sparrows, but not a jot about eagles and wolves, and the Divine Mother always hovered around in the background wondering where He was. The Christian feminine deity, ever nurturing of the boy-child God-to-be, is a far cry from Ceridwen the crone, able to shape-shift and pursue Taliesin to the final transformational devouring. Other cultures seemed to understand the psyches need for an accord with death, decay, and mortality, whereas our own sought to cheat all three. Has this now carried over into massive investments in anti-biotic warfare, on the fields and inside the body, where all bacteria, invasive fungi, and pesky insects are subject to military campaigns. Cancer has become a 'big enemy', yet cancer-wards, for all the fear, can be places of immense healing and insight into life.

Rationalist modernity, despite its disavowal of the spiritual, hardly differs in approach, indeed, it takes the whole operation further. After several decades of wielding ever more powerful technological weapons against pests and diseases, the war seems to have made the enemies stronger! When one is knocked down, as with cancer and diseases, another appears. And the pests evolve genetic resilience and come back with supercharged aggression.

We also now have a whole science of risk analysis, to which can be added costs and benefits. Probabilities are ascribed and comparative assessments made. Yet, within that process, the same prejudices operate. The emotional content and meaning of risk is removed and reduced to statistics. One apologist even said that the childhood leukaemia deaths hypothetically ascribed to the discharge of radioactivity to the food chains of the Irish Sea should not be called deaths, rather, 'life-shortening', for everyone dies someday! Such statistical life-shortenings could then be added up and compared to those from burning coal, or getting hit by a truck carrying coppiced willow. Surprisingly, on this level, there is not much difference between one fuel cycle and the other.

Lessons from Romania

The sanctification of 'man apart' by the Christians, and the sanitisation of a desacralised nature by their descendents, I thought at least must be contributory

148

factors to this collective myopia, until I visited Romania. The Carpathian forests are quite salutary. They are replete with bear, wolf and lynx. The former regularly kill people and cattle, the wolves never people, but sheep rather often, and the lynx....well enigmatic as ever, for there is no data, taking a few sheep but certainly, no threat to people. Yet, these tolerant Romanians are as Christian in their history, as any other, despite their hard road under Communism. Some clue exists along the roads and pavements, where extreme caution is necessary. Any hole is simply left as it is for the unwary drunk or over-exuberant child. Some of these gaps in the path are yawning people-traps that would, in any Western country merit a manhole cover, or at least some bright warning tape. Here physical risk seems to be courted, though sadly that also extends to burning the rubbish, plastic and all, in huge open fires on the edge of the town or village.

Romanians milking sheep - traditional pens and guard-dogs protect from wolf, lynx and bear in what is otherwise an Alpine landscape.(Peter Taylor)

Here I had my only encounter with wild bears. Distance 30 feet. Place, Racadau housing estate on the edge of Brasov. Time, 10.30 pm. Circumstances – three bears rummaging in the skips serving the blocks of flats adjacent to the forest, as they do every night, just a service road's width from open windows and TV soaps. The taxi drivers do good business with tourists who get to hear, and want an encounter. These bears are big, sometimes with cubs, and though nervous, potentially very dangerous, yet there is no oversight and no regulation.

Whether conscious or not, the holes and the bears mean that every Romanian learns to live with risk, to take care and watch where they are going.

As I left the Carpathians, the New American Century announced that Romania was their new frontier and they would be building a big new factory for helicopter gunships. In exchange, Romania will get new roads, dams, power stations, PVC windows, satellite TV, and a drug culture, to add to its rampart sex trade. No doubt the streets will be paved, traffic regulated, holes covered, forests fragmented, livestock subvented, and the countryside more managed. Wildlife will have to become economic if its risks are to be tolerated. I had an unsubstantiated suspicion, though, that Carpathian shepherds, hunters and foresters, though well Christianised, had retained some pagan sense of joy and poetic ease with wild nature, and I hoped they would fight to retain it when the new Gods arrive.

The wild bites back

In all this, there is, however, a slow turning. The wild with all its risks, is coming back. There are wolves in the Brandenburg forests close to Berlin, and new tracks in the Cevenne and Pyrenees. Bears have been trans-located from Slovenia to Austria and France. Scotland brought back the Sea Eagle and Osprey. Norway has agreed to tolerate one wolf pack as long as it stays in one place. If we are to re-establish natural processes in our wilder land, with herds of large herbivores such as reconstituted aurochsen and tarpan, boar, bear and wolf, then risks to life and limb will have to be accepted. And along with risks, and with time, perhaps will come benefits to local economies. Even our wayward panthers and pumas, once confirmed as more than mere spectres, might get a fair crack of the symbiotic whip from a public increasingly willing to accept the presence of something wild, unpredictable and potentially dangerous. If so, conservationists might take a few risks themselves, and stick their necks above the office parapet with a bit more of the wild dream.

1. Martin Prechtel, see *Secrets of the Talking Jaguar.*Element, 1998.
2. It is a common experience of those who take delinquent boys into the wild that the hardest often show the greatest fear of the simplest things, like darkness.

(Editor's note: Eric Maddern and co-workers continue to do much good work on initiation and wilderness training at www.caemabon.org.uk)

Wild by Nature: activating the wild psyche

ECOS 26.1 (2005)

In ECOS *24 (3 / 4) Peter Taylor wrote of living on the edge – the risks of going wild. This article explores the edge within our essential wildness and freedom of spirit, which when absent, is an extinction of experience.*

DAVID RUSSELL

The invitation to write this piece was prompted by a chance remark I made at a Wildlands Network meeting. I said it's not just nature that needs to become wilder, but also the psyche. I hadn't given much thought to what now looks like a rather glib remark. Now I have been asked to say what it was I meant.

Wild Nature

I want more often than not to leave nature to itself. One reason that nature matters to me is because it is simply *there*. Wilding, to me, is walking away and accepting and enjoying whatever happens. Why is that so difficult? I guess somewhere behind the idea of such an abandonment lies a different sense of nature. Partly it's this: for me, nature has never been in need of protection because nothing can harm it. Nature encompasses everything, mass extinctions, even annihilation if it is in the nature of the universe to collapse back into a singularity at the end of time. How can such a thing ever be harmed? In fact, it seems to me, we always most hurt *ourselves* in the way that we relate to the world around us. Maybe we need to know more about that hurt. John Fowles, the novelist, wrote about nature in his short book *The Tree*:

> "The subtlest of our alienations from it [nature], the most difficult to comprehend, is our need to use it in some way, to derive some personal yield"

It feels important to me to be able more often to let go of the need to get something from nature or to do something to it. This might seem impossible, after all we need to sustain global biodiversity and management is surely essential. There are also issues around public accountability. I've tried to suggest elsewhere that maybe we don't have to assume that intervening less and giving more space to wild nature will mean less biodiversity. Yes, I do recognise the immense pleasure and inspiration that people get from working in nature. But giving in to our desire to shape it to our own sense of what wildness should be is an aspect of the alienation that John Fowles describes.

Wild Man

> "There is something in the nature of nature, in its present-ness, its seeming transience, its creative ferment and hidden potential, that corresponds very closely with the wild, or green man, in our psyches."

This is John Fowles, again. I am conscious of the wild man in myself. The Wild man or Green man has been part of the collective psyche from the dawn of consciousness: the close, masculine, correlate of the Great Goddess. He is represented in cave paintings. He seems always to have had a role in the initiation of male children into the world of men. The account of the Iron John legend by Robert Bly, explores the psychological content of a tale in which a young boy releases the wild man, Iron John, from imprisonment in his father's castle using a key stolen from his mother and is then carried away to the wilderness before coming into his inheritance. In the ancient Sumerian tale of Gilgamesh, the help of Enkidu, the wild man, is needed to bring the young king Gilgamesh into his maturity. I also think about the bible story of Jesus going into the wilderness and then encountering John, the hairy wild man who baptises (or initiates) him into his new role.

The experience of the correlation John Fowles describes between inner and outer wild nature is always ecstatic. Something happening outside is experienced inside or vice versa. Wonder and terror are forms of ecstasy. We can be moved to tears or jolted out of shape by our experience of nature. If we need our own creative ferment, our own presence, our own transience, our own hidden potential, we need wilderness and perhaps most of all an encounter with its seeming purposeless-ness. (If there is a purpose it is locked in the mind of God). I have done this now for the past two years on retreat on Bardsey island. Although not really a wilderness, time is the rhythm of the sea and the seasons of the farm, where money is not needed, where there are no vehicles and where it is possible for a while to be purposeless too.

The thrust of modern environmental management and policy making largely misses all of this. It seems to me that managers and policy makers (like everyone else in the world) are increasingly preoccupied with standards and performance targets. Those who are caught up in this will tend to see nature not so much as a presence but a resource; managers manage resources so what else should we expect; even people become human resources in this lexicon. The language engenders a particular and even dehumanising way of understanding and experiencing nature (and people!). I have to allow that I am particularly averse to standardised practices and regulations, so I need to be careful before I generalise, but I am convinced that we are in danger of seriously eroding the real importance of nature of itself. Can we understand and relate to nature as being of itself? Can we allow wonder to guide our actions at least as often as the standards and good practice guidelines? And I would like to think that it is more often possible to leave nature completely alone. Be that as it may, there's still the human spirit to celebrate so let's remind ourselves that it's through inspiration not regulation that we get the big results.

Finding the Edge

I remember some years ago reading a paper given by a senior executive of Shell. I think it was in the context of a discussion about the inner city that he suggested that it's not more policemen we need so much as more poets. I liked that then and I still do. Poets (and not just those who are wordsmiths), the modern day wildmen, are the people that can give us the *impudence* to ignore all the trivial bits of silly authoritarianism, the *insight* to see into the soul and what moves it, and the *inspiration* to celebrate our individual unique human-ness.

Just by chance, after I had written that paragraph, I pulled a book off the shelf. Alasdair Maclean (no not that one!) a poet from Ardnamurchan in Scotland, seems to have captured this notion in the opening verse of his collection called *From the Wilderness*.

I am not bondsman to your least shout,
Nor friend; perhaps, if I choose, more foe.
Only it is my trade to lead you carefully
Astray in lands where no mapmakers go.

It will not serve to whistle then nor pray
Nor quote authority nor put on speed.
What keeps you upright in your shoes, your needle
To the poem's north, is a sort of greed.

I leave the foothills of the images
And climb. What I pursue's not means but ends.
You may come if you've a mind to travelling.
Meet me at the point where the language bends.

Poets can often find an edge, the point where something bends. What happens if we accept the poet's invitation to flirt at the edge of safety, where authority doesn't serve; the point where something gives; to keep alive our ability to challenge our own fears? If we choose to stay within a comfort zone we can find the edge closing in. Somehow life gets smaller; this is the extinction of experience.

Wild City

It is our wild nature that contains the energy we need if we can dare to maintain our individual unique human-ness. Often images of our wild nature like the green man can seem relatively harmless; a new age symbol of environmental harmony. But, in a quiet garden retreat from seventeenth century Wiltshire we find another manifestation of our wild nature. In the seventeenth and eighteenth centuries it was fashionable to include a wilderness in the formal garden. Here is the wilderness created at Wilton in Wiltshire in the 1630s. Compared to what we think of as wilderness no doubt it seems pretty tame, but perhaps not so far from our ideas of wilderness as we might at first think. Our own wild nature projects, while they contain a core of wildness, are just as hedged around by the neat order of our theories, strategies, expectations, aesthetic preferences and the paraphernalia of funding and public accountability as the core of wild nature at the heart of the wilderness at Wilton. The Wilton Wilderness is still a valid metaphor.

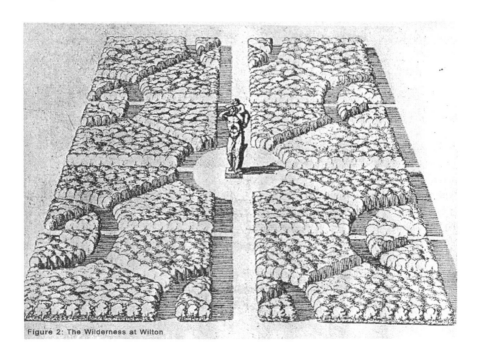

Figure 2: The Wilderness at Wilton

The Wilderness at Wilton with a statue of Bacchus. Engraving from Isaac de Caus, Le Jardin de Wilton, c 1645

The core of wild nature, the figure at the centre of the wilderness, is Zeus bearing the infant Dionysus or Bacchus the god of ecstatic or wild nature; both inner and outer wild nature. He was a principal deity of late classical Greece, a relative late comer. He was one of a wave of new Gods who arrived when the cities were already well established. While many cities allowed the cult and gave space to occasional wild festivals, several cities resisted the cult. One was Thebes. The stories tell of Pentheus, ruler of Thebes refusing to give entry to Dionysus. Pentheus insisted on the rule of reason and the need for security. In Ted Hughes' translation Pentheus is the ruler whose "two eyes ... so sharply supervise everything and see nothing." Dionysus rewarded well the rulers who allowed him entry but sought vengeance when he was denied. When Dionysus entered Thebes to punish the ruler Pentheus, he drove the population to frenzy, binge drinking, gluttony and drugs. His followers, mostly women, ran out into the countryside in violent frenzy, eventually tearing Pentheus apart with their bare hands because they mistook him for a lion.

Myths can be understood at different levels but they often have something to say which is of deep significance for our collective and personal psyches. Oedipus and Narcissus are more familiar examples. In this case we hear that if we allow wild nature in to our collective psyche (and personal psyches) we will be rewarded; the hidden potential, the creative ferment will be ours; if we deny it, something which is in the way will be torn apart. But we can also see that however it happens a new equilibrium is restored; since before the time of Christ, Dionysus was known as Saviour.

It would be reasonable to argue that there is a great deal in life which can challenge the sense of individual unique human-ness. I don't want to give the impression that we're all going under, far from it, but not everyone can keep their head above the rising tide of regulatory systems and the turbulence of ever changing strategies overseen by new watchdogs and other official regulators in Europe and at home. Add to this the tumultuous nature of often spuriously urgent social change, the demands of technology, or the pressures for conformity. As the sociologist Richard Sennett puts it:

> "How can we decide what is of lasting value in ourselves in a society which is impatient, which focuses on the immediate moment? How can long term goals be pursued in an economy devoted to the short term? How can mutual loyalties and commitments be sustained in institutions which are constantly breaking apart or continually being redesigned?"

In the story it is the controlling influence of Pentheus' that has to be torn apart. This allowed the creative and positive space needed for an expression of people's unique human-ness. If we continue to build a highly regulated social order that makes it hard to sustain our individuality we may need either to take dire measures to express it for ourselves in extreme risk or violence or abandon it altogether in the oblivion produced by addictive substances, the denial of experience. Addiction begins with a yearning to belong; to be a real person in a real situation. The moral of Dionysus is that it really is not more controls that society needs but more freedom for the individuality of its members to be realised.

But there are those who insist on the glory of their individual-ness. Free-running is an extraordinary example: athletic, gymnastic and wild. If like me, as a child, you explored the ways to circumnavigate your house without touching the ground, you have been an embryonic free-runner - add a touch of Spiderman and you've got it. It has been elevated to the roof tops. The free-runners move across the city on the wild surfaces; they claim the wilderness of the rooftops, walls and railings. They flirt at the edge of fear. The only rule seems to be never to show off; the only discipline always to know where the edge really is and to respect it. Each free-runner moves and dances in his or her own way. It is an assertion, an act of liberation, a celebration of the individual in him or herself; the Dionysian dance at the edge, a lust to be really alive. It would still be exhilarating but something would change if for example, the roof tops were designed for free-running, or if courses were laid out with marshals or if formal risk assessments were required.

Wild by Nature

The inspiration I feel in free-running comes from the way that the freedom is *claimed,* and individuality is exuberantly celebrated. The wild psyche needs to get us to the places which are not regulated, where we have to be ourselves, where everything depends on knowing the edge and respecting our own capacity as an individual. Not wild by design, but wild by nature.

Wild roots to wild wings

ECOS 26.1 (2005)
The unstructured and unspoken contact we make with nature when small has a profound impact on our values.Raising inter-connected children who can relate well to their own wild-ness is crucial for the wilderness.

HANNAH PEARCE

One of my strongest childhood memories is that of sitting 'encapsulated' beneath the fronds of a large weeping willow tree in the front garden of the house where I lived until I was five or six. In the years before I went to school I spent many hours playing in the sanctuary of backlit colour and subtle texture created by the leaf curtain of that tree.

As an older child I would often prefer to sit through an hour of Quaker silent meeting rather than join the clamor and company of Sunday school. Like the snapshot I hold in my mind of the willow, those recollections have an uncluttered quality where deep silence is suffused by light passing through lace-like tree canopies that fill the expanse of sky visible through the high casement windows set around the room.

Thirty years later I fell in love with and bought a flat that sits at the top of a four storey Edwardian town house and now live - in effect - at the same level as the tree canopy in a set of large sunlit rooms that command a bird's eye view of the entire London skyline.

A childhood outdoors

Until I was seven I grew up to the west of London in the semi-suburban sprawl between Beaconsfield and Slough. Like nearly every other child of my era I walked to school with other children, and spent many long lazy afternoons dawdling home again. We picked daisies, blew dandelion clocks, made posies of wild (and probably not so wild) flowers and were substantially free to move in and out of each other's homes and around the local area with few restrictions. We made dens, cycled everywhere and generally kept our mothers in ample washing.

When I was nine we moved to a more rural village in northwest Essex. We had less garden here but there were many more places in and around the village where I could wander along paths, down lanes, and around the field margins, often for hours at a time on foot or by bike. So like most of my peers I grew up substantially outdoors, literate in weather and seasons, confident, responsible, resourceful, independent, persistent and blessed with great stamina.

Today young people are widely pilloried for lacking these qualities, but is it any wonder given how little freedom and experience they get and how much they are required to remain indoors?

Moving into wildness

My first encounter with truly vast landscape was probably in Kenya where I went on a three week secondary school expedition that took in Naivasha, the foothills of Mount Elgon, a climb up Mount Kenya and a week in the Serengeti. Returning later as a student I was drawn to the east side of Turkana and out into the desert of black volcanic sand around Marsabit.

My fascination with deserts had crystallised in Nevada at the age of 19. After surfacing out of an extended coma sustained in a car accident my native American nurse placed my bed in front of a picture window that provided an unrestricted view across the surrounding desert for a period of several weeks. Through every angle of the sun this offered an array of extraordinary backdrop, but as each day died the horizon would catch fire and transform into a furnace of vivid indigos, reds and purples. Mute, amnesic, riddled with pain and immobile in a shattered body, I duly rejected the valium drip and let my heart-mind find its refuge wandering out into that unrestricted soul of colour.

Journey into vastness

Having a memorable near death experience in a desert while crossing the boundary between youth and adulthood left me with an archetypal taste for vast and unhindered landscapes. I have been riveted ever since by the relationship between internal and the external wilderness, and by what scholar John O Grady once called "the loosening selvage of the ego". It was nearly a decade however before I went somewhere that would ultimately resolve that obsession. In 1992 I was taken by a Tibetan lama to stay with the Kharnakpa, a small community of nomads who herd yak, goat and sheep over a series of valleys to the north of the Zanskar mountain range on the edge of the Ladakhi Changthang.

In his book *Practice of the Wild*, Gary Snyder suggests that the experiential quality of wilderness is that of 'presence'. Walk into Kharnak you would know instantly and instinctively what the man means as you become 'completely encapsulated and insignificant' in the face of nature and the elements.

Wild child

Since 1997 I have lived predominantly in London, raising a daughter, now seven, who is half Ladakhi, though not as it happens half Kharnakpa. Given her mountain background and my job as an environmental journalist I try to ensure that, despite a predominantly urban upbringing, she grows up with a firm

158

understanding of both nature and of the wild. I also believe it is not only possible to do this while living in the city, but essential that more parents make this effort in order to counter and prevent the 'extinction of experience' described so well elsewhere in this issue of *ECOS*.

My daughter loves our allotment. It sits in the middle of a large site completely enclosed by a high fence with locked gates. This is possibly the only place in our locality where since she was four she has been able to wander around at will and without significant hindrance. She can climb trees, build dens and play freely without close supervision. She is now frequently the person to initiate a visit and upon our return she always explains why she appreciated being there.

I also take my daughter at least once a year to Spirit Horse, a valley in Wales where in her own words "I have almost unlimited space to play in the steams, the woods or the meadow and lots of other children to create anything we want with!"

Spirit Horse Camp in central Wales (www.spirithorse.co.uk)

Spirit Horse is now in its fourteenth year and experience has shown that letting the children run free in ways that few if any can do elsewhere is starting to deliver a very out of the ordinary young adult further down the line. Several in recent years have begun to ask the community to create ceremony and rites of passage by which they may pass ritually into adulthood. As part of this they formally leave their parents and move for a year into the home, care and tutelage of other adults within the community. There they undertake a combination of voluntary service, wilderness quest, travel and if possible a period of initiation with spiritual elders from another culture. Those accepting responsibility to serve as guardians for the year are also supported collectively to carry the costs of their obligation.

It's a new and evolving process that has so far supported only a handful of young people but the passion for it from all sides - elder, participant and wider community - is huge and gaining considerable momentum. Moreover, so far the new adults returning from the process have shown an exceptional degree of personal insight, compassion, strength of identity and clarity of purpose. They also possess tightly framed values, strong environmental and social concerns, and clear intent for their futures. Overall, the work provides a small but interesting example of what can be achieved when as adults we rise to the challenge. The Campaign for Leadership expresses this as: "personal and social change through self-determination in the context of a living community and contact with nature".

Teaching ourselves and believing that we can raise capable and respected young adults skilled at living in a more interconnected manner is the real challenge for modern parents.

The wolf at the door?
Imagine urban nature running wild

ECOS 28 (1) 67-72 (2007)

The current debate on new wilderness in Britain largely focuses on sparsely-populated areas. Are there opportunities for bringing an element of wilderness closer to home, in and around our towns and cities?

MATHEW FRITH & PETER MASSINI

In his book *Beyond Conservation – A Wildland Strategy*, Peter Taylor provides a compelling and powerful argument for the re-wilding of key landscapes in the remoter parts of our islands.[1] His discourse on the return of wild herbivores and (more controversially) wild carnivores and the restoration of ecological processes is matched by a plea to rediscover the 'wildness' within that part of our psyche which is part of, not separate from, nature. Taylor, aptly, in poetry, points out that: "*…we are afraid/afraid of the wild heart/that we will not look into the fire directly/We live in our job-protected lives/behind the ramparts of a life insured/and keep the wildwood at bay.*" It is a paean to the unprocessed, to remoteness, to isolation, and a vision that eschews the man-made, the built, the teeming, frenzied, maddening city.

Wild nature on the rebound

We, of course, have been creating the circumstances where the (false) boundary between natural and unnatural is blurred. Whilst the imposition of our settlements onto existing wildlife habitats has, either by design or happenstance, enabled some wildlife to survive and flourish in their new urbanised circumstances, others – having been banished from our immediate environs in the past – are returning. The wild boar populations which are less than 100 kilometres from London and the south coast towns are unlikely to stay put, and the burgeoning peregrine falcon population, together with the apparent attack by a 'panther' in Sydenham, south London, in 2005, suggest that it doesn't take much for nature (or our imaginings of nature) to exploit the opportunities that we create. Elsewhere moose forage in Wisconsin drive-by fast-food outlets, black bears saunter into the fringes of New Jersey, brush-tailed opossums colonise the lofts of Melbourne suburbs, troops of chacma baboons mosey through the gardens of Cape Town's southern quarters, and wolves pad around the outskirts of Leipzig. Nature has a remarkable way of ignoring the strictures of human endeavour and ecological romanticism; that "*there is no true wildlife anymore, only urban and suburban wildlife, adapting to yet another human-warped landscape with terrible patience*" is a notion that is gaining some resonance.[2] Whilst these 'rebounds' in no way compensate for the damage we have dealt to natural environment, they demonstrate the resilience of some parts of nature.

And the creation of special places for nature, re-introduction programmes and escapees will all play their part in re-wilding the urban environment. It maybe only a few years before red kites are seen again in the skies over Kidbrooke (OE; *the brook over which the kites fly* - the location of the Ferrers Estate, where Jamie Oliver went to eradicate turkey-twizzlers), but the country's burgeoning deer population is already making ingress into many conurbations, to the irritation of many gardeners. Indeed, in some countries over the past few decades this process has been accelerated by the establishment of urban biosphere reserves; the creation of relatively large areas of open space at close proximity to cities in which natural processes are allowed to function with varying degrees of freedom, but with benefits for people and biodiversity, for example Kampinoski on Warsaw's outskirts, and Kogelberg outside Cape Town.[3]

Britain's urban areas – getting greener and wilder?

Even in Britain, notwithstanding the continuing developmental pressure upon green spaces and the inevitable impacts of traffic, pets, diffuse pollution, and the like, there have, arguably, been advances for the natural environment within our towns and cities over the past 30 years. The creation of hundreds of urban nature reserves and Community Forests, enhancement in the management of public green space and waterways for biodiversity, growth in gardening for wildlife, and the improved understanding (if not performance) of developers and planners in recognising and providing for biodiversity through the planning process, have all contributed towards this. These actions to improve urban areas for biodiversity are continuing to evolve to meet the demands of early 21st century Britain, through the promotion and adoption of sustainable drainage systems, green infrastructure, green roofs, sympathetic development practices, and questions over the future role of the Green Belt.[4] Policy is undoubtedly largely moving in a positive direction, and we can but hope that practice on the ground follows suit.

The current drivers for adopting these greening practices are twofold; adaptation to and mitigation for climate change, and, albeit more tenuously, health. Multi-functional greenspace, first articulated in the 1990s,[5] is becoming embedded in the jargon and slowly worming its way into policy and guidance. Whilst there are undoubted merits of designing and managing urban areas with a green infrastructure approach, this falls short in one particular respect when viewed from Peter Taylor's perspective.[6] It appears functional, almost robotic, to be applied to reduce costs for, say, the future management of flood waters, or the supply of valium. Although "*urban [regeneration] experts love the future, they*

162

rarely think ahead", and there is already a danger that an opportunity is being missed, as has been shown in the timidity of some of the future visions of the Green Belt.[7] Where is the 'wild heart'? It seems to have little of the essence that he and others might perceive as 'wild'; no room for nature to be unleashed from our utilitarian straitjacket.

Wild at heart?

Is it a fear of the uncontrollable, or ignorance of the art of the possible, that prevents urban planners, and perhaps conservationists, taking a leap of faith? Surely we must rediscover the 'wild heart' through promoting and encouraging a sense of wild(er)ness in the places where most of us live and work - in our towns and cities? Green infrastructure does not currently include this spiritual component nor the philosophical one of putting nature first, presumably because we think that the wild heart cannot - or more tellingly – can not be allowed to beat here.

But it can. Despite the increasing dominance of glass, steel and concrete in the centres of our towns and cities, and an approach to public space which appears to favour clean-lined squares and fountain-filled piazzas (but not necessarily demanded by the public), the wilding of our towns and cities, as we have seen, is taking place. This is not a wilding which will replace bricks and mortar with flora and fauna. It is one that enables the return of the untamed by restoring some of the ecological processes (naturalising rivers, for example) that will help make our cities more sustainable. It is a wilding that gives time and space to nature, and that celebrates 'the return of the native', as species once banished from the urban environment return to make the wild heart beat faster. For who can gainsay that the peregrine that stoops for pigeons over the Millennium Dome is any less wild than its cousin putting rock doves to flight over Celtic cliff-tops?

Inevitably the wilding of our towns and cities will be less extensive, less dramatic and perhaps less inherently 'natural'. However, it may be, in a botanical sense, more colourful, as plants from both within and without Britain take hold in ever more unusual mosaics - are the remaining sparse prairies of evening-primrose on the wastelands of south Liverpool any more manipulated than the machair of the Scottish isles? The colonisation of post-industrial land in the 1960s and 70s by a wide range of native and non-native plants was, arguably, a wilding (there was little guiding hand from us apart from preparing the canvas). Astutely championed by Richard Mabey for seeing what nature what was doing when we took our hand off the tiller, these places and processes took time for most conservationists to recognise, let alone accept, most probably because they involved species and places that didn't – and possibly still don't – fit in with what is believed to be truly natural. As Mabey remarked, "*no amount of human planning could have produced... the remarkable orchid colonies that*

163

[grew] up on the lime-rich chemical tips near the old soda factories of Manchester".[8] Alas, these and many others post-industrial wildernesses – our 'unofficial countryside' - have subsequently disappeared or been landscaped into 'new' green spaces.[9]

Unless some non-natives cause economic or social problems, matters of a wild plant or animal's provenance will surely be largely academic; they are unlikely to be of concern to the wider public. In short, wilderness is largely about philosophies and processes, and in and around our conurbations any application of wilderness principles should be considering the palettes of wildlife that are already there – and likely to join in – whether they are 'old-school Brits' or 'foreign interlopers'. Purist applications of a wilderness founded on Celtic, pre-Roman or other ancient temporal contexts will undoubtedly fail if xenophobic – or, worse, anti-people – agendas are entwined in what at times can appear to be a distinctly anti-modern philosophy. Wilderness must be about now and the future rather than returning to a 'better' rural past.

And for our conurbations it should be no less wild. Overall the wilderness may be less fierce (but less scary?) than that planned for the remoter wildlands. And this wilderness may be more subtle; understood and appreciated by an experience of natural processes (flood, storms, seasonality, migration, etc.) rather than encounters with wild nature on the grand scale. Ironically, the challenges of climate change perhaps provide significant opportunities; "*it reward[s] imaginative lateral thinking [and an] awareness of the importance of giving nature room for manoeuvre*".[10] With the need to green our cities in order to make them more comfortable and to alleviate the impacts of extreme weather events, wilderness has a role to play if we are willing to take a gamble. Why not large herbivores and the odd, fleeting, parry from a big predator amongst a backdrop of windblown trees, and scrubby out-of-town wilds to bring back a bit of excitement on our fringes? In the Wigan Flashes, Don Valley north of Rotherham, the Wakefield coalfields, the Potteries, Tees Estuary, the Mersey Basin, and even the Thames Gateway, putting a bit of the wild into the mix might make a difference. Although if urban society is as unprepared for a light flurry of snow as it is a tornado or two (as in Birmingham and London in 2006), then the might and unpredictability of nature could kick back at attempts to bring a little wild(er)ness on a more permanent basis.

The debates and initiatives around implementing wilderness within Britain are exciting means to address the future of biodiversity and its relationship to modern society. In particular, the fears of an increasingly individualistic society disconnected from the natural world perhaps indicate that the nature conservation sector's emphasis on protecting what we've got (in short, emasculated, fragmented, e(xc)lusive and not that exciting) may not be that well-supported. Indeed, BBC's *Springwatch*, focusing largely on the familiar wildlife on the doorstep, and the media's attention on scare stories (e.g. leopards in Peckham), suggests that an element of the wild close to the home could be just the trick.

There is, of course, room for both the remote wilderness and the metaphorical wolf at the door. Indeed they are bound together; Taylor's vision for wildlands and his *crie de couer* for the 'wild heart' can only be achieved by encouraging wild imaginings in the urban mindset. For whilst we may never get to have an urban lupine experience within our lifetime, we long for nature's pawmarks in the city to become wild enough to put us in our place.

References

1.Taylor, P. (2005), *Beyond Conservation: A wildland strategy*, Earthscan, London.
2. Matthews, A. (2001), *Wild nights; the nature of New York City*, North Point Press, New York.
3. Hadley, M. (Ed.) (2002), *Biosphere reserves; Special places for people and nature*, UNESCO, Paris.
4. Massini, P., Cook, R. and Robertshaw, E. (2004), *London's Natural Values*, English Nature and London Wildlife Trust, London.
5. Barker, G. (1995), *Nature is good for you*, English Nature, Peterborough.
6. For example the draft East London Green Grid Framework, in public consultation during the winter 2006-07, see www.london.gov.uk/auu/elgg
7. Groundwork and the Countryside Agency (2004), *Unlocking the potential of the rural urban fringe*, Groundwork, Birmingham.
8. Mabey, R. (1980), *The Common Ground; A place for nature in Britain's future*, Hutchinson and Nature Conservancy Council, London.
9. It is no irony that the developers of the Greenwich Peninsula in preparing the site for the Millennium Dome exclaimed their pride in "*transforming over 300ha of wilderness less than 3 miles from the City*" in a report of 2000.
10. Adams, W. M. (2003), *Future Nature; a vision for conservation*, Revised Edition, Earthscan, London.

Facing the predator – the inner drama

ECOS 28 (1) 51-55 (2007)

A playwright researching a play about the reintroduction of wolves to the Highlands writes about her growing engagement with conservation and its challenges.

SAMANTHA ELLIS

I'm surprised to find myself writing this. A year ago, the world of conservation was a mystery to me—let alone challenging conservation.

I was researching Leviathan for a play I was writing about Noah's Ark when I came across a website on which Aboriginal women were campaigning against conservationists who wanted to reintroduce the crocodile to a nearby river. The women didn't want the crocs back. They'd been glad when the last one was killed. Now they feared for their children.

Encountering the concept of faunal rewilding

It was the first time I'd encountered the concept of faunal rewilding. My Leviathan research had also turned up David Quammen's book Monster of God. He argues that we need the crocodile, and other predators. In caging, fencing and hunting our alpha predators to extinction, we have lost a sense of ourselves as prey, and we have become disconnected not just from the food chain but from the circle of life. He quotes a Transylvanian shepherd who calls the bears, for all they eat his sheep, the treasure of the forest, saying "A forest without bears—it's empty".

There seemed to be a play in all of this—particularly when I found out that faunal rewilding was a possibility closer to home. I'd been vaguely aware of the beaver debate, but only as a half-serious story on the end of the news. I live in London and it's easy to be completely ignorant about conservation. I had no idea that the sea eagle had been reintroduced to Scotland, nor that the beaver debate was still raging, nor that anyone would want to bring back anything else. As I started finding out about this, a director asked me to come up with ideas for the Edinburgh Fringe. I saved a document on my computer as "faunal rewilding" and I was off.

What attracted me to the subject was that I couldn't understand it. I've always been scared of predators. I'm not even very good with dogs. I've never had a pet apart from goldfish. I've almost always lived in London, far from anything that could be considered to be wilderness or even wild land. So it was really hard for me to understand why anyone would want to reintroduce predators.

Of the creatures on the list of potential reintroductions, it was the wolf that scared me most. I could see that the charismatic megafauna were just that—charismatic—but not why anyone would want to bring back creatures that might kill people. It seemed perverse—a forced return to a harsher, more terrifying past—and I couldn't think about wolves without thinking about Red Riding Hood. They were—they are—our iconic monster. Here are some of the things my friends said when I told them there were people campaigning to bring the wolf back to Scotland:

> *"Why would we want to bring back wolves? We turned them into dogs..."*

> *"They eat children, don't they?"*

> *"Have these people seen Grizzly Man?"*

> *"Isn't Scotland full of sheep?"*

A friend who grew up in the Highlands, when I told him, said that if wolves came back, it would mean that when he went hillwalking, he'd take a gun. Certainly there was no shortage of opinion on why we *shouldn't* reintroduce the wolf.

When I watched *Grizzly Man* I felt much less in sympathy with Timothy Treadwell calling the bears "my animal friends" than with Werner Herzog telling us in voiceover, "I believe the common denominator of the universe is not harmony, but chaos, hostility, and murder." Despite the shock of the film, I couldn't shake the feeling that bears were less terrifying than wolves. But the moment where Treadwell's mother is filmed hugging her dead son's teddy bear got me wondering whether I'd feel differently if I'd been given a teddy wolf as a child.

Learning to like the wolf

I read Barry Lopez's *Of Wolves and Men* on the promise that it would make me see the point of the wolf. I didn't think it likely I would change my mind. Every time I saw the cover with the wolf staring out, its yellow-green eyes wild and strange, I felt chilled. Lopez begins in a cabin in Alaska where *"the cold sits down like iron, and the long hours of winter darkness cause us to leave a light on most of the day"* and takes the reader out into the "gray daylight." He urges us to *"Go out there. Traveling for hours cross-country you see only a few animal tracks. Perhaps a single ptarmigan or a hare. Once in a while the tracks of a moose. In the dead of winter hardly anything moves. It's very hard to make a living. Yet the wolf eats. He hunts in the darkness. And stays warm. He gets on out there."*

I so wanted to resist Lopez's invitation to go into the cold and darkness where the wolves are. I didn't want to like the wolf. But by the end of the book, I began to see why people might be fascinated enough by wolves to want to bring them back to live among us. It was being able to get a glimpse of this perspective that made me think I might have a play.

Next, I re-read Clarissa Pinkola Estés' *Women Who Run With The Wolves*. She's writing counter-myth, recasting the wolf as a symbol of the wildness we (women particularly) have lost. As a teenager, I read it as a sort of self-help book in being tougher. This time round I argued with word of it. She seemed to want me not just to like the wolf but to empathise with wolves. To want to be one. She argues that as wolves were hunted, and paradise was paved, so women's wildness, instincts and passion were preened and crushed and tidied away. *"We are all filled with a longing for the wild,"* she writes. *"We were taught to feel shame for such a desire ... But the shadow of the Wild Woman still lurks behind us ... No matter where we are, the shadow that trots behind us is definitely four-footed."* A few chapters in, I start to see her point too.

I still couldn't imagine why someone would actually want them out there. Not in my backyard. Not even in Scotland. Wolves can run at up to 40 miles per hour. Only when they're on the hunt, only for short sprints, but nonetheless, the Caledonian Sleeper's average speed is only twice that. It wouldn't take long for them to get down south.

I went on to the internet to find the people who really did want to reintroduce the wolf. I wanted to find out why, but I also wanted to know how. Was it, I wondered, possible to do such a thing? Could it happen? If I was going to write a play, I wanted it to be a what-if play, not a total fantasy. I wanted it to be about something that might actually happen, just as it had in 1995 when wolves were reintroduced to Yellowstone Park.

168

Endangered Mexican wolf (Peter Taylor)

My thinking on predators was still pretty limited. The word conjured images of slavering beasts with enormous teeth. The Tooth and Claw questionnaire at www.toothandclaw.org.uk points out that Britain's 6 million pet cats kill 270 million birds and small mammals every year. On the Wolf Trust's website, I read that when the last wolf in Scotland was killed in 1743, people still believed in witches—I started wondering whether our fears of wolves are equally ill-founded. And after all, how scared was I of wolves? I was advised to go to the Anglian Wolf Society where people who'd had nightmares about wolves all their lives had found themselves in tears, hugging a wolf. I still haven't been mainly because hours after scoffing at the notion that I'd have a nightmare about wolves I watched Angela Carter's The Company of Wolves. Despite the schlocky sound effects, the animatronic wolves and plastic bats, that night I dreamed a wolf burst through my window.

I'd been talking to people who wanted to reintroduce wolves, calling up and trying to find out why, but it was still a shock to go to the BANC and Wildland Network event 'Scary or What?' and find myself in a room with 80 people who mostly wanted to bring back wild predators. For me, the most startling moment was looking at David Hetherington's feasibility studies on the lynx and seeing that the lynx was, in fact, feasible. When I'd booked my place, I'd feebly booked the field trip to look at the Lower Mill Estate beavers. But when I got there, I realised I had to try and face my fears. A few hours later, I found myself looking for wild boar. I didn't know whether to be relieved or disappointed that the closest we got were some hairs stuck in a tree.

A couple of weeks later, I saw wild boar for myself. I was in the Highlands and I visited the Alladale estate, where the plan is to create a fenced-off wilderness reserve for everything from the red squirrel to the bear. A posse of wild boar were already in residence and I forced myself to walk into their enclosure. I'll admit I was still scared of them but I had done it, gone in among them, and I felt exhilarated.

Why write a play about it?

I was mainly in the Highlands to research the other point of view. I heard sea eagles called "shitehawks", I visited wolf stones marking the spots where notorious wolves were killed, and most of all, the people I talked to wanted to know *why*. Why would anyone want to reintroduce the wolf? They were asking the same questions I've been asking, and am still asking. I'd never want to write a play where I came down firmly on one side of an argument. It's the trying to understand both sides that appeals to me, and I hope this means that the plays I write end up giving audiences a chance, through the characters, to feel things they don't usually feel and to think things they don't usually think, to rehearse choices they might make in real life. Theatre might not be much good in a campaign or in conflict resolution but perhaps it can contribute to what I've heard called conflict transformation.

If this all sounds a bit grand, I also think theatre's an exciting place to explore faunal rewilding because I realised when talking to conservationists in favour of reintroduction that our disciplines are not so very far apart. There is a clear parallel between opportunity-mapping a landscape and asking an audience to imagine they are in another place. The consultation conservationists do before making changes to a place is not a million miles from a playwright inviting an audience to enter into an imaginative complicity.

I wonder how much of the campaign for faunal rewilding is about engaging with imagination rather than intellect. I was fascinated, at BANC's workshop on big cats and Britain's ecology, by the tension between the desire to prove that big cats are out there, versus a desire to preserve the mystery. When it comes to reintroductions, members of the Wild Beasts' Trust have claimed that they have already reintroduced lynxes to the Borders and have wolves ready to go. They say that a guerrilla reintroduction would mean that the wolves would be truly wild—not radio-collared, not GPS-monitored, not counted out by biologists. It would also mean that they were wild in the way that big cats might be. We wouldn't be certain that they were out there at all, but the possibility might reconnect us to the wild. Maybe we don't have to reintroduce the wolf at all— maybe we just need to believe that they are out there.

Of course, this is a writer's view - the view of someone who spends too much time imagining things and too little time experiencing them. I've just finished a draft of my play and while I hope I know how my characters feel about reintroducing wolves to the Highlands, I am less clear on my own feelings than when I started. One thing is different, though. All this thinking about the prey and predator relationship and the place of man in the ecosystem and the food chain has changed me. Recently I ended eighteen years of being a vegetarian: I took a bite of beef and became if not a predator then at least a carnivore, and a tiny step closer to the wolf.

A version of this article was first published on www.ashdendirectory.org.uk, an environment and performance website. Please see the website for updates on the making of the play and performance dates.

Native behaviour – the human and land-use implications of returning key species to Scotland

ECOS 29 (3/4) 2-8 (2009)

Feedback from participants at the recent 'Wild, free and coming back?' conference raises a range of issues to do with human-wildlife relationships and points to possible ways forward in returning key species to Scotland.

STEVE CARVER

Chairing a conference as opposed to participating as a delegate can give one the opportunity to step back from the nitty-gritty of the debate and take a wider view from the podium. This article is my own attempt to summarise and make sense of key debates at the 'Wild, free and coming back?' conference, jointly run by the Wildland Network and Trees for Life in September 2008 to consider the return of key species in Scotland. After some thought provoking talks by speakers, delegates considered key issues pertaining to reintroductions in six groups, each focusing on one of the following issues:

- Perceptions of predators
- Livelihoods from reintroductions
- Farming and forestry issues
- Game issues
- Community-based reintroduction projects
- Ecosystem restoration – how reintroduced species can drive it

While it is not possible to summarise here the full breadth of debate on each of these points, below I have pulled together a few of the main themes that give a flavour of the richness of this debate.

Perceptions of predators

The British public has very mixed opinions about its predators. On the one hand we are fascinated by them, being avid watchers of TV wildlife programmes, and are keen that countries with remaining populations of big cats, bears and other top predators do everything in their power to protect and promote their welfare. On the other hand we, by and large, do comparatively little to protect our own indigenous predator species; witness the fate of the Scottish wildcat of which there are only about 400 left. Indeed, we have, as a nation, systematically persecuted our predators over the centuries to worryingly low numbers and in many cases to extinction. Some continue to do so today. There is a clear need for more research on reintroductions, particularly on predator-prey relations, habitat requirements and human-wildlife interactions that will address our lack of knowledge, not only of the species themselves, but also our relationships with them. It can be argued that the stumbling blocks to reintroductions are largely human ones and that the ecological conditions are already fit for lynx[1, 2] and for wolf.[3] Fear, prejudice, and a lack of clear, unbiased information from non-partisan sources are all at fault in creating these barriers. If we are to move forward in predator reintroductions we need to work hard to remove these and create a level playing field for meaningful and productive debate. Finding the common ground (if such a thing is possible) is an essential pre-requisite for reintroductions at any scale. One way to achieve this is through better education as to just what predators are, what they do and how they can help improve the functional landscape of Britain. This should start in schools at a young age, but extend to all demographic levels as needed. This can be achieved in numerous ways such as positive reporting in the media and creative programming on TV and radio, but there is no substitute for direct experience through close contact with the animals themselves, for example through wildlife parks such as *Wildwood* in Kent, and the *Highland Wildlife Park* on the edge of the Cairngorms, or travelling 'wildlife displays' such as the school visits run by the UK Wolf Conservation Trust.

Livelihoods from reintroductions

Whatever education initiatives and targets are pursued it is likely that there will be strong resistance to reintroductions from some, if not many, amongst the farming, forestry and game lobby. This is not without due cause because livelihoods are potentially at risk through economic losses due to livestock predation, crop damage, and the like. The example of the long-running saga of beaver reintroductions in Scotland is a good case in point.[4] The answer here is to legislate for a system of financial incentives that will make the presence of predators in the landscape economically advantageous, for example, through increased tourism and visitor revenues or government grants and payment schemes. This has been shown to be successful in other European countries (e.g. Sweden) and could be successful here.

It is crucial that the necessary infrastructure is built to make the most of revenue potential from wildlife watching. Such facilities will include visitor centres, car parks, catering services, interpretative trails, hides and captive viewing areas. This should involve land managers from a very early stage to ensure the right facilities are installed in the right places such that they are well placed to capitalise on both direct and indirect spin-offs from increased tourism.

Valuable lessons can be learnt from the history of sea eagle reintroductions on the Isle of Mull in this respect where wildlife tours and bird watching safaris have become part of the local business culture. There is a clear need for an advisory service to support the development of local and regional wildlife economies where reintroductions take place. The FWAG (Farming and Wildlife Advisory Group) model of trusted advice may be relevant here. Such a service could provide advice and outreach to farmers, land managers, land owners, businesses and local government on how best to adapt to the inevitable changes that reintroduced species will bring and how to capitalise on the associated opportunities.

Farming and forestry issues

Reintroductions can bring concerns about physical and economic damage to farming and forestry operations, although predator populations are actually more likely to bring associated benefits from reduced herbivore populations due to predation and changed behavioural dynamics. Nonetheless, farming and forestry operations may see new and unexpected costs associated with reintroductions, for example in livestock protection, ensuring public safety and the employment of wildlife rangers or wardens. Farmers are often regarded as stewards of the land and therefore managing reintroductions could be a logical extension of that role, in overseeing changes to the landscape that reintroductions might bring. Connectivity of wildlife habitats is a key issue in creating a landscape that is more 'permeable' to wildlife, that allows free movement of both predator and prey species across the country, along corridors between core natural areas and around or over obstacles such as transport routes, urban, industrial and intensively farmed land. The cooperation of all land owners is essential here together with appropriately designed and located infrastructure (e.g. eco-bridges), though legislation will be needed to modify planning policies and provide the funds for capital projects. This approach has been successfully demonstrated in the Netherlands and adjoining partner countries in the Pan European Ecological Network (PEEN).[7] Nonetheless, experience has shown in regard to existing reintroduction success stories such as the sea eagle, osprey and red kite, that local involvement and commitment is required to ensure a successful and uncontested outcome.

Game issues

In many respects the game lobby promises to be the most difficult nut to crack. For hundreds of years game interests in the British Isles have focused their combined might on eradicating the countryside of its predators and other 'pests' so that man would have no competition in his quest for good game or high crop yields. This started on a large scale with the Tudor vermin laws and has continued largely unabated into Victorian times and up to the First World War. It still persists even today in the hardened attitudes of some old-school land managers who believe the countryside will be better off without its eagles, badgers, otters, pine marten and wild cats. This arises out of the entrenched and erroneous view that less predators equals more game. I am reminded of the words of Aldo Leopold (again) at this point when he realised that fewer wolves did not necessarily mean more deer and hunters' paradise because removing natural predator control merely passes the job onto humans who are unable to keep pace with prey species' birth rates leading ultimately to over grazing and poor quality hunting stock. Of course this is, ecologically speaking, rather a simplistic view but in general, the practical experience usually shows that things never go right for an ecosystem after the removal of the upper tiers of its biotic pyramid.

Despite legislation providing legal protection to the rarer predators, views on predators do remain somewhat polarised and wildlife crime persists in some areas (e.g. illegal poisoning of golden eagles and shooting of hen harriers). It is of course, not all doom and gloom as we have seen some great steps being made toward increasing predator populations. For example, otters are increasing in number and spreading back into their old haunts and are even showing up in urban catchments. Any change must be shown to have clear economic benefits, however, as landowners will not tolerate additional cost, especially under the current fiscal climate. Greater emphasis needs to be placed on new revenue streams such as might be found from improved quality of existing stock, improved quality of the hunting experience and the availability of new target species (e.g. boar hunts). In addition, headway must be made in stressing the beneficial controls larger predators have on the numbers of lower order predator species. For example, it has been shown from research on the continent that lynx can control fox populations[5], while otters have a similar effect on mink. In this manner, the game lobby can and must be brought on board and so become a powerful ally and an informed advisor in species reintroductions. See Dave Blake's article in this issue for a longer discussion on the game issues.

Community issues

History tells us that the reintroduction projects most likely to succeed are not necessarily those backed by good science and strong legislation alone, but those that are organised and led by local communities (e.g. osprey reintroductions). Community owned reintroduction projects are the way forward, as without community backing (including the farming, forestry and game interests mentioned already) the outcome is uncertain at best. For this to work, economic benefits need to be seen to be distributed widely throughout the community be it through government incentives, new infrastructure, tourism income, trickled-down effects and direct and indirect employment. Again, history has shown that if communities really go for it then they are unstoppable, even in the face of government uncertainty and antipathy, and distributed wealth creation will ensure widespread support.

Ecosystem restoration

Ecologically speaking, whole ecosystem restoration that combines landscape-scale habitat restoration with species reintroductions makes perfect sense, with benefits accruing to all sectors and at all levels. For example, interest in the trial reintroduction of beavers in Scotland has opened up the debate on riparian issues, salmon fisheries, forestry and hydrological processes. Environmental resilience and ecosystem services are two important themes here. Diverse and spatially connected ecosystems that are well aligned and integrated with our productive and urban landscapes are likely to be more robust to external forces such as climate change. Building this kind of resilience into the landscape mosaic will be important in helping both humans and nature adapt to changes as they occur. At the same time, natural areas provide additional benefits in the form of ecosystem services such as carbon sequestration and storage, flood water retention and groundwater recharge, nutrient and sediment stripping and protected clean water supplies, habitat and wildlife protection, environments for tourism and recreation, etc. All these facets of ecological restoration, including reintroductions, need to be packaged and carefully marketed in a way that leaves no doubt that the overall benefits outweigh the costs. In many respects, we already have a good idea about habitat networks and big ecosystem opportunities, especially from lessons learnt abroad, and can therefore be opportunistic in regard to influencing policy development and implementation in the UK. It may be that we can effectively piggy-back whole ecosystem restoration onto higher profile initiatives to reintroduce charismatic species. These are more likely to grab the public imagination than tree planting or river restoration schemes, and yet these will necessarily form part of the reintroduction programmes.

Sooner or later...?

A great deal of expertise and experience was brought to bear on the topic of species reintroductions at the 'Wild, free and coming back?' conference, and these notes are merely a summary of that discussion. Standing in at the edges of some of these conversations it seems clear to me that there is a great deal of enthusiasm among the (albeit self-selecting) people who promote the worth of reintroductions. Looking further afield it is possible to identify a much wider constituency of stakeholders who might not be so enthusiastic or, in some cases, will be down-right hostile. These are the people who we need to engage with in a much wider ranging debate to see if we can identify common ground and establish a consensus based on a clear exchange of facts and exploration of the benefits and opportunities afforded by ecosystem restoration and associated reintroductions. Amongst the general public I feel confident that there is sufficient existing interest and support for wildlife and countryside issues that we might term 'the SpringWatch' factor. Further careful media programming, government backing and education will bring a great many of these people firmly on board in due course, if they are not on-message already.

Two speakers at the conference gave very different challenges on the timing of reintroductions. Alan Watson Featherstone of Trees for Life laid down some carefully considered and detailed timelines for the reintroduction of beaver, lynx and wolf into selected areas of the Scottish countryside. These were based on the idea of 'back-casting' or identifying the milestones needing to be achieved and steps taken in order to reach the overall aim of a successful reintroduction at some specified point in the future (e.g. first wolves reintroduced into the Highlands in 2043). Roy Dennis was more blunt, saying that we just need to get on with it... now. I suspect they are both correct, as the lead times will be quite lengthy as we have seen with the beaver. In the meantime, while we prepare the ground for practical actions on reintroductions there remains much work to be done in conserving current populations of rare and endangered species such as pine marten, wild cat and capercaillie. With limited resources, the question inevitably arises as to how we might prioritise complementary conservation and reintroduction activities. Community-led programmes may well be the most efficient and successful approach so long as they are backed up by clear and strong government policy and well-funded systems of financial support that are underpinned by the EU Habitats Directive and linked legislation. It is then up to the rest of us to provide support 'in kind' be it through giving of our time, muscle, expertise or custom.

References and notes

1. Hetherington, D. (2006) The lynx in Britain's past, present and future. *ECOS* 27(1), 66-74.
2. Hetherington, D.A. and Gorman, M.L. (2007) Using prey densities to estimate the potential size of reintroduced populations of Eurasian lynx. *Biological Conservation* 137(1), 37-44.
3. Nilsen, E.B., Milner-Gulland, E.J., Schofield, L., Mysterud, A., Stenseth, N.C. and Coulson, T. (2007) Wolf reintroduction to Scotland: public attitudes and consequences for red deer management. *Proc. Royal Soc.* 274(1612), 995-1002.
4. Gow, D. (2006) Bringing back the beaver. *ECOS* 27(1), 57-65.
5. Carver, S. (2006) Connectivity of nature in the Dutch landscape. *ECOS* 27(3/4), 61-64.

Rewilding the political landscape

ECOS 30.3/4 (2009)

Rewilding has been branded a political gimmick by some. In fact it represents a grass-roots shift in thinking towards creative landscape-scale conservation with multiple benefits.

PETER TAYLOR

Whilst rewilding has seemed too daring for some NGOs and agencies to embrace, politicians have not been so cautious. David Milliband flagged it first in a speech when he was environment secretary, and Hilary Benn, his successor, endorsed the concept as a new way forward in conservation at Labour's 2009 party conference (Jonathan Leake, *Sunday Times*, 27 September 2009). Some journalists dismiss the notion as a political gimmick demonstrating a lack of appreciation of the real issues in the countryside (Terence Blacker, *The Independent*, 30 September).

Over the past five years, the Wildland Network has initiated a series of regional seminars and exchanges to promote the initiatives of the National Trust (e.g. at Ennerdale[1] and Wicken Fen[2]), the Forestry Commission (Ennerdale and Glen Affric), the Woodland Trust, RSPB, the Wildlife Trusts and the public subscription projects of Trees for Life[3] and Carrifran[4,5] as well as individual landowning developments in Alladale[6,7] and at Knepp Castle Estate.[8] Additionally the Network has focussed attention upon the restoration of key species, such as wild grazers and their predators.[9,10,11,12,13] Thus the 'rewilding' wave is not a new political gimmick but a response by government to this new wave. A Wildland Research Institute has been launched at Leeds University and there are ongoing studies at Aberdeen University on the potential for wolf re-introduction in Scotland. (wolvesandhumans.org and see also Paul Eccleston, *Daily Telegraph*, 29 November).

In the agricultural wilderness

In eastern Britain, fenland and coastal marsh restoration projects co-exist with high production wildlife-free zones, creating a potential mosaic. The recent recolonisation of the region by the common crane, a large bird that requires disturbance-free nesting zones more readily associated with Scandinavia and Eastern Europe, is an indication of major progress toward wilder land.

The trends toward intensive agricultural production and the concomitant loss of wildlife on both arable and pasture land can be partly addressed by smaller scale mosaic approaches that make use of wild headland, margins, coastal strips, streamside and corridors, using extensive grazing by special breeds and targeted subsidy. In this strategy, even the wildlife-deserts of the grain-belt can be improved without significant loss of production, employment and changes in rural life. No one is advocating wolves in East Anglia, Dartmoor or Exmoor, but with the Forestry Commission now officially admitting they have feral panthers in the Forest of Dean,[14, 15] and lynx being regularly sighted across Britain, including in the Mendips[16], there must be a case for official return of Eurasian lynx, especially in regions afflicted by an over-abundance of roe and muntjac.[17]

Progress in this area would be made much easier if land-owners could get payments for any acreage taken out of production and given over to this kind of 'neural network' of connectivity.[18, 19] Where such networks acted as corridors between core reserves, the latter might contain wild grazers such as free-ranging cattle, deer, ponies and boar.[20] We would encounter issues of road-safety, disease control, pedestrian safety and public rights of way[21], as well as crop damage and given the over-developed Health & Safety culture, prospects are perhaps not so good, but then rewilding also has to be extended to the human psyche.[22] In Romania in the mixed landscape of the Carpathians, I was struck by the absence of fences and warning signs – even in the towns where road-works presented dangerous holes to the unwary – the whole culture was wilder in the sense of not so incredibly uptight about risks. If you have bears in the woods, the best protection comes from a cultural knowledge (and acceptance) of the risks, not fences with warning signs to the uninitiated.

But again, in the English *farmed* landscape, wolves and bears are not a prospect, and though lynx might be, the main concern is with bird species, flowers, insects, rodents, amphibians and reptiles. The sea eagle in East Anglia might pose more of a challenge given its (undeserved) reputation for taking lambs – but this is (again) more of an issue of education and responsible media-coverage.

These issues are topical. A recent seminar by the British Ecological Society and Flora Locale tackled the theme: would it be better to have separate land for wildlife, or have more wildlife-friendly farming methods? The event took a closer look at the prospects for rewilding agriculture but positing the false dichotomy of reform versus separation. An eclectic mix of speakers attempted to come to some conclusion. It was clear to me that farmers, an example being Robert Sutcliffe near Winchester, who leave large field margins, cut hedges at the right time, eschew silage for hay and who farm for quality – whilst also supplying TESCO, can achieve a great balance. His operations are clearly economic yet he maintains the biodiversity of farmland typical of three decades ago. He works with satellite-based precision drilling and fertiliser techniques and has reduced nitrogen dressing fourfold.

Tim Benton, presented the million Euro results of his models at Leeds University showing that organic production would not necessarily benefit wildlife – contrary to every expectation drawn from previous studies, and this encapsulates the problem. Defra and the EU fritter ever more funds away on computerised assessments (with dubious methodology) at academic institutions, rather than the footwork of networking best-practice followed by communication at a grass-roots level. What is clearly required is a cultural shift – and neither they nor the academics are capable of leading such or nurturing it.

Equally, a cultural shift in diet and purchasing habits would cause huge differences to the analysis of conflicting land-use for food and biofuels. With world population set to add another billion mouths to the nearly seven billion of today within the next 10 or 15 years, and the EU pressing biofuel targets upon the same cultivation area, the prospects for wildlife on farms and even marginal land, do not look good. However, the degree of intensification required also depends upon the market for meat products – which consumes seven times the land directly needed for vegetable protein. Simon Fairlie presented some intriguing, if rough, calculations on organic/chemical and meat/vegetarian/vegan alternatives. As livestock pastures are lost to arable there are gains for woodland and hence the potential for wildland. Patrick Whitefield showed how highly productive permaculture units as small-holdings could repopulate the land and also create small-scale havens for wildlife.

Climate-change reared its all-pervasive head, with Defra concerned for food security as well as low-carbon farming and ecosystem services such as carbon sequestration and flood alleviation, but there was no detailed assessment of how biofuel or woodchip targets would be met and what impacts are expected – largely because the targets have been set without any such assessment. Agriculture in general aims to reduce its carbon footprint by 30% by 2020, but apart from the advantages of restoring soil carbon and organic/permaculture systems that have less reliance of fossil fuels, mainstream farming is fossil-fuel intensive though mechanisation, fertilisers and pesticides and it is hard to see how production can be maintained as systems revert to less intensive energy use.

The question uppermost in my mind remained unresolved: is it better to separate wildland (and biodiversity issues) from agricultural land – including within the same farm? This boils down to answering how effective have agri-environment schemes been at halting the loss of biodiversity, and from the limited analyses on offer, I could not discern an answer. The higher-level schemes of subsidy are voluntary and still a small proportion of farming operations, whereas the more pervasive entry-level schemes offer little that is convincing. Nothing at this meeting convinced me that separation was not the best way forward – and that this would work either as part of the farm's own zoning, or as a targeted purchase strategy on the part of wildlife groups.

Rewilding and conservation: are they at loggerheads?

In my own neck of the woods in the South West there is a good example of the opportunities for wildlife groups to purchase strategic agricultural land. On the Somerset Levels just west of Glastonbury lies the Avalon Marshes project. In this area of flooded peat workings, the RSPB, Natural England and the Somerset Wildlife Trust own several contiguous patches of land covering several thousand acres. The project has created a nationally significant amount of reed-bed interspersed with open pools, alder woodland and adjacent wet pasture with ditch boundaries. Recently the Hawk and Owl Trust purchased over 100 acres of former arable land adjacent to the National Nature Reserve at Shapwick toward the western end of the marshes.

Is conservation wild enough?

This purchase well illustrates the forces at work that counter wildland initiatives. First, several kilometres of new barbed wire fences were erected and the culverts repaired. A small car-park was created, with new gates and information boards. The arable land was to be grazed by sheep and cattle – domestic, of course. On my last walk down the long and now wired-in drove I was led right up to an ancient oak with a large gabled box conspicuously hammered to the trunk. It sported a neat little perch. All that was missing was a sign saying 'Owl's House'.

The Levels are nationally important for their Barn Owl populations, hence the interest of the Hawk and Owl trust in buying land, with the aid of numerous charitable foundations. A good proportion of the population is maintained by such nest-boxes. I was interested, therefore, to attend a talk given by the naturalist Chris Sperring, conservation officer for the Trust, entitled 'Is conservation wild enough?' In his soul, Sperring clearly didn't think so, but he outlined the advantages of HLS payments per acre of land as long as it was grazed in an environmentally friendly way. The Trust gets an income stream. He felt that this also made scientific sense in that nutrient rich arable land would gradually be depleted and returned to herb-rich pasture. Currently, there are no specific schemes whereby land such as this could be turned over to non-agricultural use or wild-grazers. It would require NE to bend the rules – which we know it sometimes can, but more, for landowners like the Trust to know what is feasible. For example, Charlie Burrell managed to do a great deal on 3000 acres of the Knepp Estate in Sussex with English Longhorns, Exmoor ponies and Tamworth pigs.

How far could we go in an environment such as the Levels? Or elsewhere in England such as in the Great Fen project. How far is the Knepp estate a useful pilot? What projects might succeed on Dartmoor, Exmoor or the North Pennines, with greater potential for landscape-scale projects? And in Wales, in the Cambrians or Snowdonia? Or in Scotland – with much larger contiguous land-holdings in Glen Affric, Alladale and the Cairngorms, where there are some very significant private sector initiatives.[23]

Wildland values extend beyond biodiversity

The pitfalls of biodiversity indices and targets have been well rehearsed in *ECOS*. Yet, in many discussions I witness there is little appreciation of the limited meaning of the numbers and the operation of species and specialist bias. Thus, the same old arguments resurface about rewilding compromising biodiversity targets. The theme lay unacknowledged in Tim Benton's study which compared organic farms with the same land category, region and farming mix as non-organic – which was probably scientifically accurate, but if the starting base is in the middle of an East Anglian prairie then a farm with lower inputs into such an artificial and wildlife-poor environment could well register less biodiversity. The study aimed at correcting a bias created by most organic farms being in the west and most conventional equivalents being in the east of the country – all very academic, but of little help in deciding whether an organic policy would have overall benefits for biodiversity.

he key issue so often not addressed by groups focussing upon biodiversity and established 'conservation' concerns, is that defining wildlife is a cultural issue as much as a scientific one, and even the science contains often unacknowledged cultural bias. The value of wilder cultural landscapes (as in Ennerdale), rural crafts, traditional farming and forestry, eco-tourism and the health and educational benefits that accrue to people's welfare are as important as the conservation of individual species or habitats. At the other end of the spectrum, there are large holdings of 'wildland' with very little of the original flora and fauna remaining, yet they have strong appeal in the absence of obvious human artefacts - as the John Muir Trust demonstrates. These large wilderness areas are candidates for interventionist rewilding with the return of seed-trees and eradicated species – as in the Trees for Life vision for Glen Affric.

Other large area initiatives demonstrate techniques of wildlife-friendly land use more appropriate to buffer zones and corridors: for example the extensive farming and forestry in Ennerdale, where stands of exotic conifers have been removed and fell-sheep replaced with cattle breeds capable of roaming both forest and moor. This joint National Trust and Forestry Commission plan does not have a fixed end-point. It starts from where the land and the people are now and moves at the community's pace in a generally wilder direction, but it is adjacent to other FC and NT holdings and the prospects are there for a very wild core area to be developed if funds could be made available for a transition from traditional practices to wild grazers and perhaps even the lynx as predator.

There is a recurrent theme in discussions on these potential core areas – a tendency to think *either/or* as if any new idea or pilot implies a complete rethink (and funding scheme) across all sites. It doesn't of course. There is a great deal of sense in targeted grant schemes available for selected areas, such that they do not compromise or interfere with other areas where practices might have other objectives – for example, in the maintenance of heathland by domestic grazing.

Rewilding conservation

So, what are the prospects for a rewilded conservation sector being given a better political environment? People are more questioning of scientific authority when they see it led so often by corporate goals and managerial convenience coupled to specialist interests they cannot comprehend. There is greater popular defence of the grey squirrel than would have been anticipated, as also with Sika deer and other aliens that are well suited to cultural landscapes. As conservation groups have reached out and won broader public subscription they are, perhaps, having to take on public rather than specialist values. This can be a double-edged sword, however, and as with the eradication schemes for hedgehogs in the Hebrides, the balance can be awkwardly tipped by lack of ecological understanding.

The problem with conservation is not just a matter of getting the right subsidy regime – it lies with the mentality of management, goals, corporate structures, econometric minds and the whole language of ecosystem services and the 'customer' paradigm that goes with these times. Bill Adams[23] picked up on this in last edition of *ECOS* and it is heartening to see academia taking a stand, but the conservation sector is now big business, accounting for £500m of expenditure in the countryside (about five times the whole upland subsidy for Wales), and whilst that presents a tremendous opportunity, it also constitutes a major constraint. If we are going to move beyond the pilot projects we have monitored for the past 10 years, conservationists are going to have to go wild themselves! Someone has to start taking risks, and pursue the prompts from Labour Environment Ministers.

References

1. G. Browning & R. Yanik (2004) Wild Ennerdale – letting nature loose
ECOS 25 (3/4) 34-38
2. A. Colston (2004) Wicken Fen – realising the vision *ECOS* 25 (3/4) 42-45
3. A. Watson Featherstone (2004) Rewilding in the north-central Highlands – an update
ECOS 25 (3/4) 4-10
4. P. Ashmole & H. Chalmers (2004) The Carrifran Wildwood Project
ECOS 25 (3/4) 11-19
5. H. Chalmers (2007) Ecological restoration without all the pieces – early news from
Carrifran *ECOS* 28 (3/4) 89-95

6. R. Sidaway (2006) Alladale's fenced wilderness – making a breakthrough? *ECOS* 27 (3/4) 30-35

7. P. Taylor (2008) Alladale's wilderness – seeing through the fence. *ECOS* 29 (3/4) 18-24

8. P. Taylor (2006) Home counties wildland: the new nature at Knepp. *ECOS* 27 (3/4) 44-51

9. N. Harris (2006) Ecosystem effects of wild herbivores – lessons from Holland *ECOS* 27 (3/4) 58-60

10. M.Oates (2006) Grazing systems and animal welfare – matters of life and death *ECOS* 27 (3/4) 52-57

11. D. Blake (2007) Deer in Britain: the challenges for nature conservation *ECOS* 28 (2) 41-49

12. P. Hadfield (2009) Too hard to bear? People and large carnivores in Slovakia *ECOS* 30 (2) 76-84

13. D. Hetherington (2006) The Lynx in Britain's past, present and future *ECOS* 27 (1) 66-74.

14 J. McGowan (2007) Big cats in Dorset: the evidence and the implications *ECOS* 28 (1) 73-78

15. P.Taylor (2002) Big cats in Britain: restoration ecology or imaginations run wild? *ECOS* 23 (3/4) 30-64

16. Moiser C. (2002) On the prowl, Lynx in the British Countryside, *ECOS* 23 (2) 9-13

17. D. Hetherington (2009) The history of the Eurasian lynx in Britain and the potential for its re-introduction. *British Wildlife* 20: 77-86

18. A.Parfitt (2006) New nature in Holland – attitudes and achievements *ECOS* 27 (3/4) 65-69

19. S. Carver (2006) Connectivity of nature in the Dutch landscape *ECOS* 27 (3/4) 61-64

20. N. Harris (2006) Ecosystem effects of wild herbivores – lessons from Holland *ECOS* 27 (3/4) 58-60

21. M Oates (2006) Grazing systems and animal welfare – matters of life and death *ECOS* 27 (3/4) 52-57

22. P.Taylor (2005) *Beyond Conservation*. Earthscan.

23. Adams, B (2009) Conservation and consumption. *ECOS* 30(2) 2-10

PART II

Projects

The data base: re-wilding projects in the UK

ECOS 27 (3/4) 5-7 (2006)

VICTORIA WARD, MARK FISHER & STEVE CARVER

While a number re-wilding projects have been underway in Britain 30 years or more, it is only in the past few years that rewilding (and indeed just 'wilding') initiatives have really got underway. The need for a one-stop-shop for such information has never been greater, thus the Wildland Network is collating information on all such projects in the UK. This information is now available in an online resource and will be updated as and when new developments occur. The database was devised with a some key aims in mind:

- To provide a comprehensive description of the number and range of different re-wilding projects currently underway in the UK;
- To show the current potential for the development of connections between areas of wild land, and ultimately, the creation of a network of core wild areas and nature corridors across the UK.

The needs of all species

The growing interest in the potential for re-wilding parts of Britain's landscape has led many to rethink the practicalities of the UK's fragmented pattern of nature and wildlife designations. Echoing the sentiments of many, Salwasser sums up the reasoning behind this, arguing that wild land, unless it possesses millions of acres "cannot sustain a broad enough distribution of seasonal habitats to supply the needs of all species" which depends upon "favourable conditions in many places and freedom for individuals to move throughout a population of large size" (Salwasser, 1988, 87).[1] It is this thinking, which has led to the promotion of more joined-up thinking about nature conservation in the UK. Such an approach foresees the development of an effective network of wild lands and nature corridors which will stretch throughout the UK, encompassing not only large core areas of wild land, but also smaller isolated nature reserves and re-wilding projects and providing safe pathways for wildlife to move through areas of intensive agriculture and across our towns and cities. In order to plan this network it is necessary to have some idea of the current state of wild land or potential wild land in the UK.[2]

The gazetteer of re-wilding projects will provide details of where projects are currently operating and the steps they are taking to return land to a more wild and natural state. Moreover, further information on the size of projects and methods being undertaken is paramount in assessing the viability of linking projects together. The benefits of the projects database are summarised below

---

- Seeing the whole picture may encourage others to become involved or start up their own projects.
- The database will act as a resource for those considering setting up their own project in demonstrating the range of potential for management options, partnerships, funding opportunities and methodologies.
- The database will identify areas of possible land linkage, and show the different routes other projects are taking.

What's included...

The database contains certain basic details about every known project, including name, location, an overview of the re-wilding methods being used, and a list of contact details. Information on land designations covering in the area, ownership, management and administration details, funding sources, year the project commenced, size of the area covered, habitats present, a list of target species and planned reintroductions. To date, the details of 41 projects have been entered into the database.
.

Use of the database

Making the database open to everyone has the advantage of publicising re-wilding efforts as widely as possible, and allowing gaps in the database to be spotted. Already in the English Midlands there is interest in adding to the data base, so the region can represent its efforts to pursue natural processes and wild nature. New entries will be submitted online, thus keeping the database up to date. In the meantime, while permissions are finalised, a simple list of project names is available on the Wildland Network web site (www.wildland-network.org.uk). The authors would be grateful if any omissions are notified via email.

References

1. Salwasser, H, (1988), Managing Ecosystems for Viable Populations of Vertebrates: A Focus for Biodiversity, in Agee, J, K, Darryll, R, J,(Eds), (1988), Ecosystem management for parks and wilderness, University of Washington Press, Seattle

2. Bates, S, (2004), Nature Maps: visions for wild landscapes, *ECOS* 25 (3/4): 55-58

The South East

Home Counties wildland – the new nature at Knepp

ECOS 27 (3/4) 44-51 (2006)

The 3500 acre Knepp Estate in West Sussex is a mix of ancient parkland, woodland, arable and pasture. Five years ago its owner, Charlie Burrell, decided on a wildland project for the estate 'where natural processes predominate and long term financial stability is achieved outside of a conventional agricultural framework'. The project is providing a baseline ecological and economic study for potential rewilding in the English lowlands.

PETER TAYLOR

I knew it was possible, even sensible, but I had never actually seen it happening – fields upon fields of once arable land becoming wild again. Each field was different – some had been intensive rye grass for dairy production, others for winter wheat, and the pasture was wilding up slowly, with bird-sown sloe and dogrose, and sprouting jay-stashed acorns. The hedges were rank and brimming with berries. Where arable fields had simply been left, there was a mass of thistle heads, willowherb and fleabane, but some fields had been tilled and resown with wildflower mixes, then cut and the hay removed to drain the over-nutrients. It was October so I had to imagine what the spring would be like.

Nature in abundance

For Charlie Burrell the most significant thing about spring at Knepp is the *sound*. In all his years as a farmer he had not known what was missing. In spring the once silent fields are now buzzing and humming with a myriad insects and the cascade of bird songs. For me, in this balmy autumn, it was the *feel* of the place that was extra-ordinary.

We approached a part of the estate known as the lags – an old channelled stream system where the rewilding had blocked up drains and instigated little tree-dams to bring back the meanders. What were formerly neatly grazed bare meadows were now a mass of sallow and wet pools, home for snipe and very soon, it is hoped, some beaver. The sallows had already invaded half the adjacent field.

Suddenly, Charlie's acute hearing picked up a grunt and out of the scrub trundled seven massive red-brown pigs – right up to our legs, nuzzling recognition and prodding for nothing more than affection. These were a free-living group of Tamworths – adapted to forage and requiring zero maintenance. They can turn over half-an-acre of pasture in one night snuffling for roots and grubs. They will even eat carrion. The disturbed ground gets colonised very quickly – one patch was now a mass of dock.

Charlie's one sadness is that local farmers look in horror at what they perceive as a 'mess' of invaded fields and rank hedges. But it is early days. This is a rewilding, for sure, but it also contains compromises that may be of more relevance to some farmers than they might at first realise. The Tamworths will provide high-quality organic pork for market. There are now some 60 head of old English Longhorn cattle, also requiring minimal maintenance and no supplementary feed, and the organic free-range beef will be sold at a premium to local markets. Thus far, about 1400 acres of former farmland are rewilding around a core of ancient parkland, currently being restored under a Countryside Stewardship scheme. The restoration is focussed upon its former role as a deer park, and fallow deer have been re-introduced with the intention to extend wild grazing to the whole estate, which will be ring-fenced, and diversify the mix of herbivores. A small group of Exmoor ponies has been introduced and we visited Knepp's first foal – its mother keeping a good distance from our intrusion, and the herd with one stallion will soon build up. Roe deer are plentiful on the estate.

The gameplan for going wild

Most internal fences in the park have now been removed – but the currently impassable A272 cuts across the northern half which is grazed by a second group of Longhorns. Having moved on from the deer-park ideal, the objective is now to allow this land to scrub up before the grazing is increased. Ultimately, if the A272 can be crossed by an eco-bridge or tunnel, and minor roads crossed with cattle grids, the whole 3500 acres, including a few hundred from a collaborating neighbour, could become southern England's first functional 'wildland' site. There is the potential to link to the Sussex Wildwoods project to the west and to create wild river corridors with other collaborating land owners.

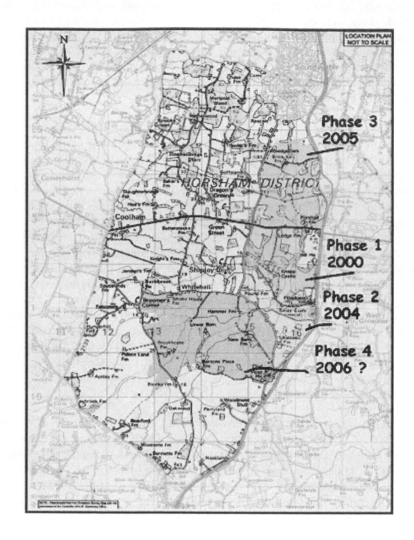

The Knepp Estate planning phases

At present the project is open-ended. Charlie would like to see a full-spectrum of wildland emerge – the Longhorns would be replaced with truly wild Aurochsen (Heck cattle), beaver would be introduced, perhaps the European wood bison, and red deer. Wild boar are likely to colonise – they are now only a few miles distant. Lynx would be the only effective predator – but this animal would require a much larger range – in the richest habitat about 20 km^2. Even if

190

Knepp were extended to twice its size it would provide only one such territory and thus would have to be part of an ecological network. However, there are rumours of lynx being released by activists – of what kind of activist, or lynx, no one seems to know, and there are regular sightings further west in the Mendips and the Dorset heaths.

Charlie is well-advised on the techniques and dynamics of rewilding – his oversight group includes Hans Kampf and Joep van der Vlassaker with advice from Franz Vera, the pioneers of the Oostvaaderspkassen in Holland and the Large Herbivore Foundation that now supplies a steady stream of projects throughout Europe with wild cattle, horses and bison. Knepp's advisers also includes experts from English Nature and the National Trust who are studying the project with great interest, and consultants are examining the economic implications of the venture and the various markets it is creating.

The crucial question is… how relevant is this to other wildland projects? Is it a model that interested farmers could follow? To my mind, there are two key issues: what are the economic implications, and is there potential for a network of such sites? There are other issues regarding long-term sustainability and ecological objectives, but these are perhaps less pressing and can be answered only by observation as the project unfolds.

The viability of a wild estate

The economic aspects are the subject of detailed study by Natural England. At present the CSS deer-park restoration is central and there is an annual grant for the land it covers, with some relaxation of the original criteria to cover the new objectives of rewilding. The rest of the project is covered by the Single Farm Payment scheme which can be applied because the project is still 'farming' in the sense of production of pork and beef. These two sources of finance will be supplemented by expansion of the Longhorn herd and the Tamworth pigs, with some small income from wild venison. Overheads are very low – but all the animals with the exception of the deer, are subject to daily inspections and normal veterinary regulations. Animal welfare and regulatory issues concern whether or not to intervene at difficult calvings, supplementary feed in hard winters, castration of bull calves (to mitigate fighting), weaning and removing calves before the next year's calving (lowering the risk of the calves being abandoned) and the introduction of Heck cattle's wilder and more feisty genes with consequent risks to stockmen, visitors and the quality of meat for market.

I could have pored over the economics – there is a mass of data and a thoroughly worked business plan available for scrutiny, but this kind of study is of limited relevance. The crucial questions relate not to current incomes or projected incomes under current schemes, but what will happen to agri-environmental grants in the not-so-long term of 10 or 20 years. Most landowners have long-term security in mind for their families and heirs, and rewilding is reversible but at a cost. There is, of course, no clear indication that the EU schemes will continue at current levels of support – and a clear indication that they will not, given the twin pressures of GATT (global agreements on trade) to liberalise markets and the expense of new EU membership in eastern Europe. What is required to secure wildland projects and ecological networks is a new long-term assured grant structure specifically designed for two levels of wilding – the non-productive core which would operate as a sanctuary, and productive buffer zones that could use semi-domestic stock, shooting and other appropriate enterprises to support its economy. My own preference is for core areas not to be shot over for sport, but culling would almost certainly be necessary.

The changing farm infrastructure

Charlie Burrell and his family are cushioned to some degree from these uncertainties – the estate's core business is now property management and the 20 staff are secured by employment in this business. However, there are some useful lessons for other estates: the dairy and arable farms were closed down meaning reduced employment overheads and a net loss of jobs, and farm buildings were suddenly redundant. It came as a shock to be shown one of these buildings now let as three separate light industrial storage spaces with an income of £18,000 per annum equivalent to the average net profit of the 300 acre farm unit! This story is apparently repeatable all over southern Britain – and indeed, my own *Somerset Gazette* carries a farming piece this week on that theme – farms can earn *more* by letting their outbuildings than they can from farming the land. The Knepp estate has a flourishing business in light storage, craft workshops and other small operations running from its old farm buildings. There are important planning implications here of course, although national guidance is for local planning authorities to show as much flexibility as possible in the new use of farm buildings.

Most farmers would be reluctant to give up 'farming' and become property managers – there is a social and psychological component here that is not to be under-estimated. They have been schooled by a production ethic. They are 'progress' minded and do not like to 'step back in time'. As many ecologists advising farmers will testify, money does not necessarily buy cooperation in biodiversity objectives.

True wildland will entail no domestic stock, so grants schemes need to be evolved that do not require conventional 'production'. The dilemma is that farmers may not come on board unless they can still 'farm'. In this respect, Knepp offers a useful test-bed in this early part of the rewilding jouney. There is a market for organic beef and pork, as well as wild-shot boar and deer. In the Forest of Dean, as we learned on a recent Wildland Network outing with the

Forestry Commission, surrounding farmers have been making a surreptitious £300 per night letting to shoot the frequent wanderers of a small forest herd of wild boar that has been there since 1989.

Strategic thinking on wildland

Whether such a mixed enterprise would be viable without some kind of public-funded support scheme will emerge from the more detailed study commissioned by Natural England. This mix of woodland and pastoral production does not, however, have to be an effective economic model for larger-scale agricultural change in order to be of great relevance. The future for nature lies with corridors and buffer zones linking core areas – the ecological networks pioneered by the Dutch. On a longer timescale of a few thousand years everything we do for biodiversity in England will be trammelled by a wall of ice. In terms of European temperate zone species survival what happens between Latvia and Romania is crucial – without an effective corridor for migration, north-west Europe's mammal fauna (at least) is doomed. If Western Europe can influence what happens in south-eastern Europe, we will have done far more than anything our own national species targets can achieve. Scarce public funds could be targeted to special areas – rather than dispersed, perhaps ultimately ineffectively, over a generalised agricultural support scheme.

The future for agriculture is now bound up not only with EU subsidy schemes, but also a developing markets for biofuels. Reduction of subsidy at one time was thought to mean more marginal land for rewilding, as happened in New Zealand – but the opposite can happen – where production is intensified for biofuels, as well as generally to compete with global low-cost production of basic foodstuff. The future for the natural world would be grim – isolated natures reserves amidst ever-intensified farming, unless there was a programme of enlarged core-areas and corridors.

In such a programme there would be a spectrum of wildland – buffer zones and wildlife-friendly corridors can be a mix of organic farming, productive forestry, and appropriate small business enterprises. Knepp also runs a Polo Club, clay pigeon and pheasant shoot. Pony trekking and wildlife-watching, mini-conference centres and school visits can all play a role in such conversions.

English Longhorn cattle and grassland at Knepp (Charlie Burrell)

Animal welfare and public perceptions

Charlie Burrell is not motivated toward the 'safari-park' end of the business model. If it were economic, he would be happier to see the full spectrum of wildland with no domestic or semi-domestic stock and a low level of visitor disturbance – in other words, to act as a core-area where natural processes held sway. He is not averse to wild-shot game meat – whether pheasant, boar, cattle or deer (horses, even wild ones, are never included, of course!). And in any case, populations would require culling not just for the sake of the woodland flora and regeneration, but also for animal health reasons.

The latter is a major issue for wildland practitioners. If domestic stock are used as analogues for natural grazers – as with the Longhorn and Tamworths (and also with regard to Exmoor ponies, which though truly wild animals, are not perceived by the public as such) then farming and animal welfare regulations apply. This means daily veterinary oversight and intervention during poor winters. Carcasses have to be removed, disease controlled, and injuries ameliorated. Starving animals would engage public interest as well as regulatory concern. Animals would have to be removed to an abattoir for killing.

These rules do not apply to 'wild' animals such as deer – even though these species are just as sensitive to pain and starvation. Deer and wild boar can be shot on the land and the meat marketed locally. Such regulations would not likely be extendable to wild horses, and maybe with some difficulty to wild cattle or bison – at least not in relatively small areas in southern England. The Dutch projects have had trouble with public reaction to carcasses lying around as the populations adjust via natural death to winters or competitions for mates.

At a few sites we visited points where the wildland of the estate abutted private dwellings. Charlie had the rough edges removed in a buffer strip of mown grass sufficient not to disturb sensitivities – mostly with regard to blown thistle down! Clearly, public education on wildness may be a long process – but one that could bring dividends. The estate welcomes school parties and is currently engaged in efforts to assuage local parish council concerns – which are mostly about tidiness of the countryside.

An ecological network in lowland Britain?

What then is the potential, whether by core areas at Knepp or corridors and buffer zones, for an ecological network in southern England – and elsewhere in the lowlands? The land at Knepp is part of the Sussex Low Weald natural area – heavy bolder clay, with much woodland and ancient iron workings. There is some interest from neighbouring estates and a 10,000 acre connected block is not out of the question in the long term. Linkage to the nearby Sussex Wildwood Project would entail a 'good many fields' in the four miles distance – but Tony Whitbread, chief executive of Sussex Wildlife Trust, and a long-term advocate of wild grazing regimes for woodland, is on the advisory group. There are potential river restoration schemes within the Knepp estate and also extending outward. Pulborough Brooks, the RSPB reserve is a few miles to the west on the river Rother. Links could perhaps be made to the extensive woodland of the Weald and the South Downs.

The lessons of Knepp could be applied to other potential large land-holdings as core areas, and also to buffer zones along rewilding river corridors. Truly wild woodland zones with natural grazers would likely be a mosaic of canopy trees, glades, scrub and riparian pasture – home perhaps for a lynx or two (and doubtless of benefit to our naturalised puma and melanistic leopard). Buffer zones on marginal former agricultural land that were partly productive with organic beef and pork would be resilient to predators such as lynx, as well as providing undoubted additional biodiversity benefits.

A mosaic of surprises

As I was leaving Knepp, I spied a pair of stonechat. They were not on the baseline-survey list of 2005, and not a species I would expect of pasture and parkland – they like it a bit rougher! This land would doubtless bring back many bird species and prosper others on the Estate that are struggling such as turtle dove, skylark, marsh tit, yellowhammer and reed bunting (it is thought the decline in woodland and farmland birds is a combination of intensive practices such as winter sowing and a general decline in insect numbers). Four pairs of buzzard have colonised – and we saw one fly up from a rabbit kill. Red kite are recorded and there are lapwing, stock dove, barn owl, green woodpecker and nightingale all likely to increase as the meadows and woods develop. Currently water shrew is the most notable wild mammal – but otter may come, and European wildcat could be introduced. Knepp offers current refuge for several nationally scarce Lepidoptera – including silver-washed fritillary, some scarce beetles and bees, great crested newt, and the great yellow cress as the only unusual plant.

But biodiversity targets are not the only benefit, or even the main relevant criteria for success. Knepp offers a glimpse not only of the potential for cores and corridors, and to act as a test-bed for wildland and buffer-zone economics – it offers an *experience* of what nature can be like and of what it may feel like to lessen control and slow down enough to listen – not just to the sound of birds and insects, but also to the human heart that somehow got lost along the ways of a crowded and busy world. In all these respects, Charlie Burrell is a pioneer and I came away vastly encouraged not just by the sights and sounds of a rewilding land, but also by the professionalism of the project, the focus of expertise and open minds, and, to their great credit, government agencies willing to support an open-ended project such as this, and learn alongside it.

Further reading:

Greenaway T.E. (2006) Knepp Castle Estate baseline ecological survey. *English Nature Research Reports* No 693.

Hootsmans M. & Kampf H. (2004) Ecological Networks: experiences in the Netherlands (from h.kampf@minlav.nl)

Hodder K.H. et al (2005) Large herbivores in the wildwood and modern naturalistic grazing systems. *English Nature Research Reports* No 648

Kirby K.J. (2003) What might a British forest-landscape driven by large herbivores look like? *English Nature Research Reports* No 530.

Vera F.W.M. (2000) Grazing ecology and forest history. CABI Publishing.

Wicken Fen – realising the vision

28.3/4 (2008)
To secure the future of Cambridgeshire's fenland wildlife and to re-establish lost species, the National Trust is taking action beyond the existing fragments of wetland.

ADRIAN COLSTON

Wetland expansion – thinking big

The National Trust is proposing to acquire up to 3,700ha of farmland to the south of Wicken Fen in Cambridgeshire over the next 100 years. This extension of the wetland will provide exciting benefits for people and wildlife. Recent considerations on the plight of Cambridgeshire's wildlife have concluded that radical approaches are required to achieve real improvements.[1]

The landscape of Wicken Fen (National Trust)

The whole of the proposed new reserve at Wicken lies within the boundaries of the Swaffham Internal Drainage Board. The wetlands of the area would be restored by a combination of natural regeneration and the raising of water levels via a reduction in drainage pumping and the use of sluices.

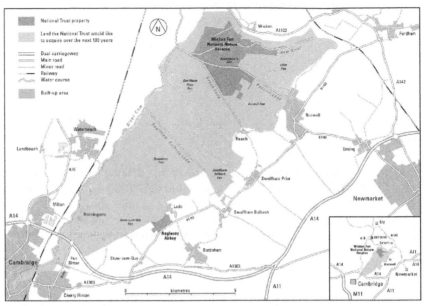

The National Trust's fenland vision

Recreation opportunities

Access to the countryside around Cambridge is currently limited. There is an extensive public footpath network but the area could not be described as 'good walking country' on account of the arable nature of the landscape. The Wicken project can enhance recreation opportunities by the creation of cycle paths, footpaths, horse trails and circular routes from the city centre to the countryside. It can provide a positive link between city and countryside.

It is essential that access to the new reserve does not rely on car transport. The desired creation of the corridor at the southern end of the area into the centre of Cambridge offers great potential for cycle, horse and foot access. In addition, the railway station at Waterbeach and the possible new station at Chesterton also increase the access potential. There is also a good bus service linking the Fen Edge villages with Cambridge, again encouraging access to the area by public transport.

The Cambridge phenomenon

Cambridgeshire's economy is experiencing some of the fastest growth in the UK. There is a huge desire within the University, the City and the local councils to promote Cambridge as the high technological capital of Europe. Consequently there is much inward investment occurring with many prestigious multinational firms locating to the area to utilise the highly skilled workforce and the research potential.

By 2025, it is predicted that 105,000 new houses will need to be built in the county. There is currently a vigorous debate surrounding the publication of the Regional Planning Guidance and the review of the County Structure Plan as to where and with what environmental conditions these new houses should be built. The Wicken Fen Vision offers a counter-balance to the inevitable housing development. It would provide a green lung of open countryside accessible to the public, and with a wide range of environmental and amenity benefits.

Tourism and the local economy

Whilst the urban areas of Cambridgeshire are flourishing, economic development in the farming sector is depressed, including in the Fens. The new reserve has the possibility of providing additional jobs in the locality as a result of employment on the reserve. There is also the possibility of additional economic activity from visitors to the reserve, and there may be new demand for accommodation, and increased visitor spend in pubs and cafes.

Konik ponies in Wicken Fen (Adrian Colston)

Sharing the vision with the community

For the new reserve to be successful and popular it will need backing from the local community and the business sector in Cambridge, along with a large number of voluntary and statutory bodies. The idea of creating a new large wetland in Cambridgeshire was debated at a Citizen's jury in Ely in 1997 and was favourably received.[2,3]

If this ambitious project is to proceed the National Trust will have to work in partnership with many diverse organisations and individuals. Development of partnerships will be the main thrust of implementing the ideas for expanding Wicken, so much effort is being devoted to establish these vital links.

Following a series of meetings during 2000 the National Trust has approved the principle of implementing the Wicken Vision and the project now forms part of the recently published National Strategic Plan.[4] The project has been widely discussed and much useful advice has been received internally ensuring that the Trust has adopted a holistic approach to the initiative, rather than viewing it simply as a nature conservation initiative.

In addition the Trust has sought views widely outside the organisation to determine the feasibility and desirability of the project. Over 350 presentations have been given by the Wicken Vision Team and to date the reception has been overwhelmingly positive. The Trust has also contacted all the landowners in the project area informing them of our ideas and we have met over 70 in person.

The vision takes shape...

In October 2000 the National Trust acquired the first area of land at Guinea Hall Farm (115 acres) which is immediately adjacent to the east of the existing reserve. This was funded entirely from resources within the National Trust. All future purchases will have to include partnership funding.

A second purchase of 415 acres of Burwell Fen Farm was acquired in October 2001 for £1.7m including a grant of £933,500 from the Heritage Lottery Fund.

In 2003 the Trust was offered £800,000 from the Office of the Deputy Prime Minister to acquire land to assist with the creation of the green lung north of Cambridge. Negotiations are currently underway for an additional 500 acres of land.

Wildlife, landscape and livelihoods

This Wicken Fen project being pursued by the National Trust is putting wildlife back into the countryside on a landscape scale. It is integrating the requirements of wildlife with the needs of local people, the economy, and tourism. It is this holistic approach which has encouraged such widespread support. The project will help demonstrate how a new era of nature conservation in the lowlands can develop where habitats for wildlife can be restored without being divorced from the needs of people.

References

1.Colston A. (1997) 'Conserving wildlife in a black hole', *ECOS* 18 (1) 61-67.
2.Aldred J. (1998) 'Land use in the Fens: lessons from the Ely Citizen's Jury', *ECOS* 19 (2) 31-37.
3. Friday L.F. & Moorhouse T. (1999) *The Wider Vision,* University of Cambridge.
4. National Trust (2001) *National Strategic Plan: Summary. March 2001 February 2004* The National Trust. London.

A more detailed account of the Wicken Fen project can be found in 'Beyond preservation: the challenge of ecological restoration' in Decolonising Nature, *Edited by WM.Adams. Earthscan (2002).*

The Wicken Fen Vision: the first 10 years

ECOS 28 (2) 58-65 (2009)
In 1999 The National Trust launched the Wicken Fen Vision. Here we review progress and evaluate the public support in the first 10 years of this century-long project.

STUART WARRINGTON, CHRIS SOANS & HOWARD COOPER

The Vision – what's it all about?

In 1999, the National Trust embarked on a 100 year project, the Wicken Fen Vision, to encourage the development of a landscape-scale nature reserve for the benefit of people and wildlife across 5,300 hectares (53 km^2) of land between the National Trust's Wicken Fen nature reserve and Cambridge. One of the early drivers for this project was the concept of thinking big and trying to deliver nature conservation on a large scale, rather than just working even harder on our existing high quality 255 ha designated site. The ecological reasons for working on a larger scale are well understood, with support from topics such as species-area relationships, island biogeography, minimum viable populations, metapopulations and habitat fragmentation. Large areas may also address some of the issues relating to the effect of scale on conservation efforts, potentially also improving ecosystem functions and climate change resilience.[1]

There was also the recognition, passionately expressed in ECOS by Adrian Colston[2], that we need to do much more for wildlife in the 'black hole' of inland, central England, in counties such as Cambridgeshire where less than 3% of the land has the status of Site of Special Scientific Interest.

The National Trust developed the guiding principles below and the Vision strategy with the help of many advisors, both internal and external. The four guiding principles for the Wicken Fen Vision are:

    1. We will manage the land to enhance its nature conservation value, protect the depleting peat soils, secure sufficient water resources and seek to preserve and interpret the cultural heritage.

    2. We will ensure that the Vision has a sustainable financial future and supports the local economy.

    3. We will work in partnership with local people, landowners, businesses, government agencies and voluntary and conservation organisations.

    4. We will encourage, public access and recreation, scientific research, volunteering, community engagement and learning

For nature, the aim is to allow the development of a mosaic of habitats, such as wet and dry grasslands, reed beds and shallow pools, woodland and scrub, largely where soil, topography and hydrology dictate. The actions of large grazing animals will help to develop the habitat mosaic along with control of hydrology. Right from the start the Vision was also about providing significant public benefit such as improved access for local people and visitors to the countryside of the area, a 'green lung' for walking, cycling and horse riding, and also a boost to the local economy through tourism opportunities.

Why the National Trust and why at Wicken Fen?

The National Trust has been in existence for well over 100 years and it has the experience, expertise and resources to make this long-term project a reality. The Trust has made a commitment to "plan and manage on a landscape scale to create a network of high quality habitats" in its nature conservation policy.[3] The Trust also has the unique ability to declare its land 'inalienable' which means it cannot be sold or mortgaged. We do not, however, have the powers of compulsory purchase and will have to approach all of the 120 landowners in the area to see if they might sell us their land now or in the future and then raise the necessary funds.

Wicken Fen is an ideal place from which to launch a landscape-scale project. It is an internationally important wetland, but even at 255 ha in area, the designated site is too small to guarantee the long-term survival of all of its numerous rare and special species. Wicken Fen is vulnerable to damaging influences from the surrounding more intensive land uses and is isolated and quite some distance from other wetland reserves. It has often been described as an 'island nature reserve in a sea of arable agriculture'. The Fen is at the north edge of a very shallow basin, with gently rising ground to the north, east and south and the embanked River Cam to the west.

Land drainage for farming over the last 300 years, and especially in the last 80 years with efficient pump-drainage, has resulted in significant shrinkage and oxidation of the peat in this basin and the land levels have dropped by up to four metres, leaving the undrained peat of Wicken Fen well above the farmland. The land in this basin forms a single hydrological unit and this is the 5,300 ha area of the Wicken Fen Vision. About 2,000 ha of peat soils remain in this basin. This peat is of variable depth and quality but it may form the basis of fen habitat creation in the long-term. The area can also be divided into different management units, if necessary, by roads and Lodes (the local name for an embanked small river). Thus habitat and especially wetland creation could take place in stages during the deliberately long timescale of the project.

The worth and relevance of the project

We would argue that the project is even more important now than when it started. The Government has admitted that it is not on course to meet its 2010 biodiversity target and biodiversity is still declining especially in the wider environment outside of designated sites.[4] Furthermore, halting biodiversity loss must not be the end-point for nature conservation and our ambitions should go beyond this to enable growth in biodiversity into the future.[5] Large landscape-scale habitat creation and restoration projects will make a major contribution to this growth in biodiversity. In addition, issues such as ecosystem services, carbon storage and sequestration have grown in importance since 1999 and landscape-scale projects may well have the scope to offer these wider environmental benefits.

Also, the development pressures have increased significantly in East Anglia in recent years. The city of Cambridge is forecast to grow to over 250,000 people by 2025. Access for people to green space is a key target on the Government's health and well-being agenda. As it develops, the Wicken Fen Vision will be providing improved access to a greener landscape close to the city, and it could provide a key focus within the emerging Cambridgeshire green infrastructure strategy.
Vision to reality?

One of the greatest strengths of the Wicken Fen Vision and the related Great Fen Project[6] near Peterborough is that they are much more than ambitious plans. These projects are tangible, with action on the ground. In 2004, Adrian Colston[7] provided a 5-year review and reported that 215 ha of land had been purchased in two parcels. Since then, a further 203 ha has been purchased in 5 parcels. Overall, the Trust now owns 857 hectares in the Vision area (16.2%). There is no set target, but we wish to acquire about 500 ha each decade, thus there is good progress in the first 10 years. The project has already secured over £4m in grants to assist with the land purchases from farmers and subsequent site management, including improved public access.

Big creatures - big attractions

Conventional approaches to habitat creation and restoration are often highly prescriptive and intensive in their approach. The results can be wonderful and can make a significant contribution to Biodiversity Action Plan targets, but these projects can be financially costly both in their creation and subsequent management. The Wicken Fen Vision approach is deliberately less intensive. As land is acquired, we allow natural regeneration of vegetation, in places supplemented with seeding at low rates with appropriate grasses. We aim to isolate land from the farm drainage systems and to control water levels as far as possible without affecting drainage of neighbouring farmland.

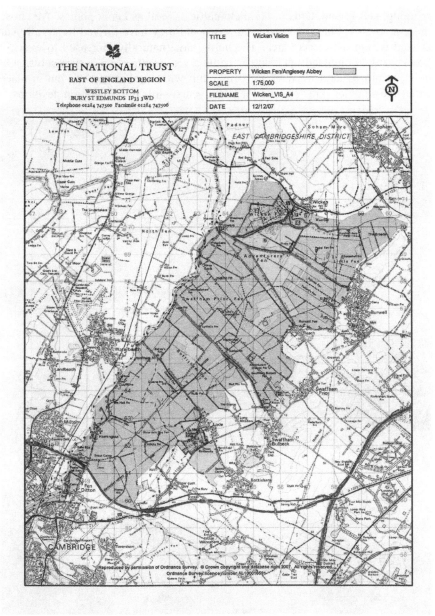

TITLE	Wicken Vision

PROPERTY	Wicken Fen/Anglesey Abbey
SCALE	1:75,000
FILENAME	Wicken_VIS_A4
DATE	12/12/07

THE NATIONAL TRUST

EAST OF ENGLAND REGION

WESTLEY BOTTOM
BURY ST EDMUNDS IP33 3WD
Telephone 01284 747500 Facsimile 01284 747506

The vision unfolds -purchases by 2007

Once vegetation is developing we introduce large grazing animals. Grazing animals are critical for adding a vital element of dynamism to that created by the variations in water levels. On the first purchased areas, we have introduced free-roaming, self-reliant herds of highland cattle as well as konik ponies. We chose these animals as they are 'fit-for-purpose' and they have thrived living all-year around within the project area. The herds have naturally increased to over 30 koniks and 40 highlands and have become a visitor attraction in themselves. On newly acquired land we work in partnership with local farmers to put in place extensive summer cattle grazing for a few years while the vegetation develops.

Konik ponies (National Trust)

The exact composition of the habitat mosaic that develops is less predictable but we believe it will be more responsive and adaptable to long-term environmental change. The Trust is deliberately aiming for a 'lighter touch' for the management of the Vision land, and we believe this will also be more financially sustainable. We continue with our intensive conservation management on the classic old fen, with sedge harvest, litter cutting, ditch slubbing and the like.

Extensive grazing with highland cattle and Konik ponies (National Trust)

How are the habitats progressing?
A great deal of research has been carried out at Wicken Fen over the years[8], including fundamental ecological research by Godwin, Tansley, Walters and many others. Research and monitoring also underpin the Vision project. We have investigated the water, soils, topography, archaeology and land use of the Vision area and recently have commissioned further research into the hydrology and carbon budget, taking into account climate change predictions.

Surveys into the wildlife of the area are carried out by professionals, University students and by volunteers (some of whom are national experts). Of special note is the Fen Restoration Monitoring Project[8], hosted and supervised by Anglia Ruskin University and funded by the Esmee Fairburn Foundation, which is investigating both the Wicken Fen Vision and Great Fen projects with vegetation and soil surveys, hydrological monitoring, aerial photo analysis and further studies. There are new projects underway to investigate carbon flux, dung beetles and grazing animal behaviour. The fundamental point is that you need to know how your project is developing and fill in the gaps in your knowledge. Wicken Fen has a Research and Recording Group to help organise, monitor and steer this vital work. Communicating the research results both within the project team and your own organisation and to a wider audience is also very important.

Gaps to bridge?

Helping people enjoy the Wicken Fen Vision area is a key target and we have made major progress in creating a spine route that crosses the area from north to south. In early 2008 a new bridge was installed over Swaffham Bulbeck Lode opening up new routes for walkers, cyclists and horse-riders and linking with paths we had made on land recently purchased. We are planning another bridge over Reach Lode to be completed by summer 2010, which will link into a new Sustrans cycle route as well as greatly extend the footpath network. We have also commissioned a Transport Plan to look into current and future ways for people to access the Vision area.

Do people support the Vision?

As with almost all large 'greenspace' projects, there is a close alignment and strategic fit between existing Regional and County strategies and our Vision strategy. The Environment Agency and Natural England are strong supporters of the project.

Well over 500 talks and guided walks have been given over the last 12 years about the Wicken Fen Vision. There have been newsletters distributed from the Visitor Centre, via the web and delivered to all local households.[9] The project gets regular local and regional media coverage, especially when a new parcel of land is bought. With all of this activity, it came as a surprise that feedback revealed that a significant number of Cambridgeshire people said that they had not heard of the Vision project and would like to know more.

Thus in Spring 2008, the Trust embarked on a major consultation exercise, with eleven meetings in local villages and drop-in sessions in the towns of Cambridge, Ely and Newmarket. Thousands of Wicken Fen Vision booklets, including a questionnaire, were distributed by hand to every local house and from the Fen. The Wicken Fen website also allowed online feedback. The objectives of the exercise were: a) Raise the public profile of the Wicken Fen Vision; b) Build public support and manage expectations for the Vision; c) Engage the public in the strategy consultation process; d) Create methods for dialogue; e) Position the Trust as a consultative, open organisation.

We got a range of valuable feedback on people's views and desires for the countryside and the Vision. In summary, 83% of the 500 respondents to the questionnaire thought the Vision was an excellent or good idea, 11% had some reservations and 6% were against. We believe this shows that there is considerable support for the Vision. To maintain and develop our work locally, we have also set up a Parish Council Chairs' meeting and a Recreational Users Group, both of which meet at least twice a year.

Junglyfication – good or bad?

Oppositional views do exist. There are opinions expressed that the farm landscape should not be changed and it should remain agriculturally productive and must not be 'junglyfied'. Letters have been regularly written to local newspapers and there is currently an e-petition.[10] As has been found with many projects, small opposition groups can make a lot of noise and they have learned to use the power of the press and now the internet very effectively. They do not have to get their facts right, they can hijack meetings and they write to the local press and politicians with astonishing frequency. Countering these claims and correcting mis-information can use up much energy, time and resources. For example, in November 2008, the Trust paid for a one-page 'advertorial' in the local Ely Standard paper, to deal with some of the misconceptions, such as that the Trust wants to flood the fens and that malaria will result. The lesson to be learnt is that you have to be prepared to invest a lot of time communicating, listening and working with local communities and that you have to keep up this effort throughout your project. Further drop-in meetings in each local village will take place in 2009. However, strong support has been forthcoming from many influential commentators, such as Tony Juniper.[11]

Lessons for now and the future

Here is some advice we can relay from our experiences so far:

Integrate multiple objectives: Large, landscape-scale projects must recognise that to actually deliver this new approach to wildlife conservation in our crowded island requires integrating the requirements of wildlife with the needs of local people, the local economy and tourism.

Build widespread support: You need to get support at all levels, from politicians and statutory organisations as well as local people and organisations.

Help people experience the place and the wildlife: Creating new opportunities to gain access to and experience this developing and inspirational countryside on foot, bike and horse are an essential part of these projects and this can be the most significant and positive way to generate financial and public support.

Finally, **hold you nerve**: you know what you are doing is right and really important and you are in this for the long-term benefit for wildlife, people and the environment. In time, these large landscape projects will make a hugely positive contribution to our wildlife and to people's wellbeing in this busy and congested country.

References

1. Harvey, J. (2001) The role of large areas in nature conservation. ECOS 22 (1) 13-18.
2. Colston, A. (1997) Conserving wildlife in a black hole. ECOS 18 (1) 61-67.
3. Nature and The National Trust (2005). Our nature conservation policy and strategy.
http://www.nationaltrust.org.uk/main/w-nature_conservation_strategy3.pdf
4. Natural England (2008) State of the Natural Environment. www.naturalengland.org.uk/sone/default.htm
5. Environment Audit Committee (2008) Halting Biodiversity Loss. Thirteenth Report of Session 2007–08. The House of Commons. The Stationary Office, London.
6. The Great Fen Project (2008) www.greatfen.org.uk
7. Colston, A. (2004) Wicken Fen – realising the Vision. ECOS **25 (1)** 42-45.
8. Wicken Fen (2008): Research www.wicken.org.uk/research.htm
9. The National Trust (2009) The Wicken Fen Vision: Our Strategy. www.wicken.org.uk/vision.htm
10 We the undersigned petition the Prime Minister to Stop the National Trust flooding or junglefying our Cambridgeshire Fens.
http://petitions.number10.gov.uk/SaveOurFens/
11. Tony Juniper (2009) Wicken Fen - A magic week in April. The Guardian 16 April 2009.

{Editor's note: We have not had an ECOS article yet on the Great Fen project referred to in the article above - and this is a major omission which we hope will be rectified soon. It is an ambitious and recently very successful project that has mapped out a potential 9000 acres of future wetland habitat in the vicinity of Woodwalton Fen and Holme National Nature Reserves near Peterborough. The partners - Huntingdon District Council, the Environment Agency, the drainage board - Middle Level Commissioners, and the local Wildlife Trusts, have recently won a Landscape Partnership Project grant of £8.9m from the Heritage Lottery Fund, with a remit to create new greenspace for people, new opportunities for recreation, education and business - as well as for wildife. The project's 'masterplan' as well as consultation history can be downloaded at www,greatfen.org.uk There is much emphasis on recreation and celebrity involvement, with a major visitor facility planned, new access routes and interpreted walks. Whilst this would compromise the wild element of the fens, the current land surrounding the NNRs is intensively farmed and there is much to be gained by connecting the reserves: 'nature conservation objectives are therefore major influences on the masterplan – to link habitat between Holme Fen and Woodwalton Fen and to create linkage of woodland through natural regeneration of the isolated woodlands to the south of the site. Although there are isolated pockets of nature conservation interest elsewhere within the Great Fen area, the land is generally intensively farmed and of limited wildlife value. A primary objective of the masterplan is to transform this situation – to greatly increase wildlife and habitat diversity across the whole project area, and to buffer and link the currently isolated designated sites of national and international nature conservation importance'.}

From Weald to Wild

ECOS 25 (3/4) 46-49
The Sussex Wildlife Trust's work at Butcherland is using less prescriptive management to create processes that will lead to prime pasture woodland.

TONY WHITBREAD

Connections across the Weald

The Weald of Sussex and Surrey is a strong candidate for rewilding in lowland England. It is well-wooded, has a high degree of habitat connectivity, retains many forest species and has a network of non-wooded habitats. It is against this background that the West Weald Woods Project was established.

Ebernoe Common - north, and Butcherlands, west, looking to North East. (Rich Howorth, Sussex Wildlife Trust)

The clay vale of the Low Weald in West Sussex and Surrey is bordered to the west and north by a greensand ridge, while river valleys mark the eastern and southern edges. The area is highly important for nature conservation, having two candidate Special Areas of Conservation (cSACs), one National Nature Reserve

(NNR), three Sites of Special Scientific Interest (SSSI) and many Sites of Nature Conservation Importance.

Woodland type varies from managed broadleaves at Chiddingfold Forest to pasture woodland at Ebernoe Common and old growth forest at The Mens. Species found in these woodlands reflect past and present management. For example, rare butterflies, typical of forest glades and rides occur in Chiddingfold Forest while Ebernoe Common NNR is exceptional for its rich lichen flora, typical of large trees in open areas and for bats. The Mens is particularly important for fungi, being the only known site for three species of *Russula*. A key challenge is to improve connectivity across the landscape unit. This will benefit a range of species at a variety of scales.

The Mens at Crimbourne Stud, looking North East.(Rich Howorth, Sussex Wildlife Trust)

Why a landscape-scale approach?

The above question can be addressed by looking at two example species groups – bats and butterflies. Bats require a wooded matrix between woodland blocks, while butterflies require a connected patchwork of openings within woodland, as the following two paragraphs explain.

Ebernoe Common is an important roost site for the barbastelle bat, but this species relies on the surrounding landscape for feeding. In early evening these bats disperse using hedges, belts of trees and woodland edges as flight lines. Individual bats will hesitate where there are gaps in this network, waiting for darkness before venturing further. Breaks in woodland connectivity reduce the bats foraging efficiency and reduce the value of the area to this species. Conserving individual sites in favourable condition is not enough, this species needs a functionally connected forest habitat network throughout the landscape.

Butterflies tell a similar story. The distributions of wood white, pearl-bordered and small pearl-bordered have all reduced considerably. These species require a connected matrix of woodland clearings within the forest. They have poor powers of dispersal so need 'permeable' habitats through which they can move in order to spread and interact with other populations. Favourable sites alone are not enough if they are going to make up lost ground, what is needed is a functionally connected landscape through which species can move, interact and colonise.

Superficially these examples may seem just interesting ecological cases rather than an argument for rewilding. Nevertheless the common theme is the need for a functionally connected forest habitat network. In the past, traditional agriculture and forestry provided this connectivity, but this is not the case today. Current land management practices tend to fragment the landscape. Rewildling may provide an alternative vision that could re-build a connected landscape.

Rewilding a landscape - the practical implications

A rewilded tract of Sussex and Surrey is a long way off, and may not even be desirable in a landscape with so much current and historically recent human influence. Nevertheless there may be steps that can be taken to getting more naturalness, an incremental rewilding, that might deliver this connected, permeable landscape required by a range of threatened wildlife. Such a landscape might function better ecologically, and so would be more adaptable to changes such as from climate change. It is also likely to be an attractive landscape with many social, economic and amenity values. Tourism and local woodland produce are obvious examples, but how about the controversial idea of 'wilderness meat' from wild, de-domesticated grazing animals?

What are needed are practical projects that shape the landscape in this general direction. One such project is being developed by the Sussex Wildlife Trust in this West Weald area – the Butcherland / Ebernoe project, explained below.

Butcherland and Ebernoe Common - no end in sight

Ebernoe Common is a fine example of pasture woodland. There are, however, ecological conflicts here. Lichens require large old trees in open-canopy pasture woodland while Bechstein's and Barbastelle bats require dense old growth forest. This conflict indicates the need for more structural diversity at a larger scale. The current site is too small to accommodate the range of habitat requirements.

In 2002, the Sussex Wildlife Trust purchased Butcherland, 80 ha of farmland adjoining Ebernoe Common. This consists of old arable fields, set-aside land, hedges and strips of woodland. Our objective is to create pasture woodland, expanding the features found on Ebernoe and enhancing habitat connectivity. This will be achieved through a near-natural approach rather than the traditional form of management planning. Normally, a clearly defined end-point is set and the land is managed to achieve this. However, setting such an end-point would be against the principle of a near-natural approach. Instead we have just a broad a vision of pasture woodland and will encourage the natural processes that will lead to its establishment.

The lack of a clear end-point, however, means that measuring progress is difficult. A system is required which allows the area to develop towards pasture woodland, but is not prescriptive about what habitats develop where. This may be achieved by setting broad limits of acceptable change. If the site moves outside these limits, action will be taken, by influencing the processes that deliver the required habitat. In the case of woodland cover, for example, the normal approach might be to plant or regenerate trees where we wanted the woods to be. The near-natural approach, however, sets broad limits for acceptable change such that woodland cover across the whole site is between 30% and 70%. The natural processes involved, natural regeneration and grazing could then be influenced to maintain these limits.

Butcherland scrub-edge (Rich Howorth, Sussex Wildlife Trust)

This is the approach that is being trialed at Butcherland. Our short-term management is setting up the conditions for longer-term natural functioning. In this case it means altering the site from a pattern of fields and hedges to one of open and closed woodland, and wooded glades.

The site is poorly wooded at present, so woodland and scrub expansion, and future forest glades, are being encouraged. The project has four broad phases, as summarised below.

Phase I	Agricultural land prior to set aside being established. Hard boundaries between fields and woods.
Phase II	Set-aside land fenced, mown areas developed in old fields to establish future preferential grazing areas.
Phase III	Commercial stock introduced at very low stocking densities. Scrub and tree regeneration developed and future woodland glades become established.
Phase IV	Fencing removed, leaving just perimeter fencing. Change to traditional cattle breeds acting as wild herds within a wider area including all of Ebernoe and Butcherland..

Butcherland 50 years on...

A defined habitat pattern will not be set as an end point, but a recognisable pasture woodland ecosystem should be forming after about 50 years. Ecotones between wooded and open areas should be wide, tree regeneration in patches of thorny scrub should be scattered throughout the area and preferential grazing areas should have turned into permanent forest glades. There will be a dynamic between wooded and open habitat, driven by regeneration on one hand and grazing pressure on the other.

The approach at Butcherland should illustrate what could be done in the wider West Weald Woods area. The objective is to develop a naturalistic grazing regime that allows the development of pasture woodland and through this, a complex network of open and wooded habitat. Applied over a large scale, this should deliver the habitat connectivity that is required by species of conservation concern in the area.

Managed retreat in Essex: rewilding the coast at Abbots Hall

ECOS 27 (3/4) 36-43 (2006)

The coastal re-alignment at Abbots Hall Farm involves the creation of 87 hectares of saltmarsh, saline lagoons and grazing marsh resulting in a more sustainable coastal defence. This article describes how the project was achieved and the benefits it has delivered.

ANDREW MAY, JOHN HALL AND JULES PRETTY

> "Ours was the marsh country, down by the river, within, as the river wound, twenty miles of the sea... I found out that the dark flat wilderness beyond the churchyard, intersected with dykes and mounds and gates, with scattered cattle feeding on it, was the marshes; and that the low leaden line beyond, was the river; and that the distant savage lair from which the wind was rushing, was the sea.."

Charles Dickens, Great Expectations (1860-61)

Salt-marshes provide a valuable environmental service – a sea wall with no salting in front of it can costs £5m per kilometre to construct, but only a tenth of that if there is a salting. But salt marshes are disappearing.[1, 2, 3] They are squeezed against sea-walls, damaged by pollutants, and drained for farmland and housing. Should we continue to invest in repelling the sea, with costs likely to spiral, or should we bring back biodiversity to the coast?

The Blackwater estuary is a land and seascape of massive skies that stretch forever. This coastline is home to hundreds of thousands of wetland birds, including Brent geese, dunlin, knot, shelduck and redshank. The fisheries amongst the marshes contain important stocks of oysters, cockles, herring, bass, mullet and eels. Fronting the north bank of the Blackwater estuary is Abbotts Hall farm, until recently a 280 hectare conventional arable farm. This farmland is protected by a two-metre seawall, on the river side of which are remnants of saltmarsh. The farm itself dates back at least to the Domesday Survey of 1085. In 2000, with the support of several organisations, the Essex Wildlife Trust purchased the farm with a grand landscape redesign in mind. This is productive farmland, yet the Trust researched, planned and managed five breaches in the sea-wall in 2002, and allowed salt-water irrigation to create new saltmarshes, coastal grazing, reedbeds and saline lagoons.[4, 5] The remainder of the farm is now devoted to sustainable agriculture methods and habitat improvement, including the reinstatement of hedgerows, ditches, copses and field margins.[6,7]

Abbotts Hall Farm – the dynamic context

The Essex coastline stretches some 480 km and supports an abundance of wildlife. However Essex is losing 2% of its saltings area each year. Sea level rise is already placing pressures on hard coastal defences, such as sea walls. These are in turn preventing the saltmarsh and inter-tidal areas from migrating inland, which they would do as a response to sea level rise. As a result, the outer edge of the saltmarsh and the fronting mud-flats are undergoing erosion at a rate of up to two metres annually. Coastal re-alignment is therefore a potentially useful approach for both habitat creation and coastal defence. The rationale is based on a combination of flood defence requirements and habitat creation to replace lost inter-tidal habitats.[8]

Further sea level rise will reduce the intertidal area of mudflat within an estuary, especially in an estuary constrained by sea walls. However mudflat area on its own may be unimportant for birds. What is important is the biomass and availability of invertebrate food which depends ultimately on primary productivity and the time the mudflat is available to birds by being exposed by the tide. Thus sea level rise could carry a double problem for wading birds – reduction of saltmarsh productivity and a decline in the time their potential food is available. Estuaries and saltmarsh creeks are also important for commercial shellfisheries and nurseries for marine fish, and their functions too would be threatened.

The Blackwater estuary is one of the largest estuarine complexes in East Anglia covering 4395 ha.[9] It has extensive areas covered by three types of statutory designations: Ramsar, Special Protected Areas and Sites of Special Scientific Interest (SSSIs). In 1996, the mid-Essex coast had 70% (3,237 ha) of the saltmarsh habitat in Essex and 7% of the total area of saltmarsh in Britain. Up to 50% of these inter-tidal flats have been lost over the last 30 years.[2,8]

The Crown estate delegated its consent to English Nature. Above the saltmarshes and often behind sea walls there used to be extensive areas of grazing marshes. Traditionally these old enhanced saltmarshes have been grazed by sheep all year round, or by cattle in the summer months, such as today at Tollesbury Wick, an Essex Wildlife Trust reserve. In 1946, the War Commission changed 90% of grazing marsh into agricultural land. Essex has an extensive area of arable land - a proportion of which falls within the coastal zone. Furthermore, sea level rise is particularly relevant to Essex where the coast is predominately low lying. The 1953 floods illustrated this when a tidal surge from the North Sea caused 1,200 breaches in the sea defences of East Anglia, pushing sea water up to 3 km inland and resulting in 307 deaths. As a result many Essex sea walls were reinforced and raised, thus increasing the impact of coastal squeeze on the inter-tidal habitat.

Delivering the project and working with its stakeholders

In October 2002, some 80 hectares of new intertidal habitats were created by breaching 3.5 kilometres of sea wall fronting Abbotts Hall Farm along the Blackwater estuary in Essex. The scheme was undertaken by Essex Wildlife Trust, supported by the Environmental Agency, World Wide Fund for Nature, English Nature and the Heritage Lottery Fund. Two planning application were made. The first covered the construction of the spur walls, hides and jetty, raising the track and the excavation of a lake. The second application covered the excavation of the creek systems, the breaches of the sea wall and tidal flooding. The Environmental Statement supported the application. For works that affect flood defences and coastal protection additional regulations apply. Consent for land drainage was required from the Environment Agency under the 1991 Water Resources Act and from English Nature (now Natural England) for the coast protection work. The Trust also had to obtain a Water Abstraction licence under the Water Resources Act (1991) to fill it with freshwater from a local watercourse. For Abbots Hall Farm the Crown Estate owns land below the mean high water mark. Consent was also needed for the construction of the jetty as this extended below the mean high water mark.

Removal of the sea-wall and flooding of pasture land. (Archive)

The older consultation for the scheme was with 30 organisations, and the latter consultation was with over 100 individuals. The BBC included interviews and opinions from many local people, water users and those that live in the floodplains protected by the sea walls. At the same time the BBC Wildlife Unit at Bristol made a documentary about the project before it had been constructed or planning permission granted. The resulting film was seen by an estimated 1.5 million viewers (with four repeats) and won best environmental programme for 2003.

The second consultation was created in two ways as a result of the initial communication strategy. The design features were to be inclusive, e.g. the jetty, new footpaths, restraining sill to breach B, feeding of the sewage treatment works at Wigborough through the new lake, and by a communication strategy that was both formal (meetings with the oystermen, newsletters, and leaflets), and informal, comprising of chats and meetings with those that had concerns or wished to develop products and outcomes. This included expansion of oyster grounds, sheep grazing, samphire harvesting, asparagus, guided walks, plus the opening of a visitor centre. To address the early concerns of the Blackwater Oystermen, additional monitoring was agreed to and a specialist advisor on oyster culture was appointed to act as` professional arbiter if required.

On 4 November, a large spring tide flooded through the five breaches in the sea wall. Elliot Morley MP, the then Parliamentary Secretary for Fisheries, Water and Nature Protection welcomed over 1,000 people to mark the sea water coming back onto the land and the beginning of new coastal marshes. Local people were invited to sail their small craft through the breach and to be the first to navigate on the marsh since it was enclosed 400 years ago.

The breach at high-tide (Essex Wildlife Trust)

221

Habitat and species gains

Since the coastal re-alignment in October 2002, 10 species of fish have been found to be using the area for feeding and breeding, including sand smelt, three spined stickleback and common goby. Most notable are sea bass and Blackwater herring. Other marine species include shore crabs, common jellyfish, lugworms and common shrimp. Water voles have been recorded on site as well as great crested newts and all four species of the commonly encountered British reptiles. The sea slug (*Tenellia adspersa*) has been rediscovered on site adjacent to the sluice where it was found during the original borrow dyke survey.

In the autumn of 2003, hundreds of over-wintering waders and wildfowl arrived to feed on the new wetlands. These included teal, mallard, spotted redshank, black tailed godwit and golden plover. Above this the new ESA grassland attracted brent geese, with wintering counts peaking at 1,700. Little egret numbers peaked in autumn 2003 with some 30 roosting in the willow by the new lake and feeding in the inter-tidal areas.

Considerable numbers of birds using the Blackwater SPA are also making use of the new realignment. The peak overwintering count during 2003-04 was 2275 for all species. This included wigeon (186 and also roost on site), teal (270 and also roost on site), little egret (13), lapwing (1050 and roost at low tide), golden plover (820 and roost at low tide), dunlin (75), ruff (15), spotted redshank (23), greenshank (6), redshank (81), snipe (50) and linnet (250). In addition, water rail has been observed on two occasions within the new re-alignment. The number of breeding birds of note on the re-alignment include shelduck (7 pairs), oystercatcher (7 pairs), avocet (3 pairs), redshank (5 pairs), skylark (27 pairs), and yellow wagtails (6 pairs), whilst on the new lake, pochard (10 pairs), tufted duck (7 pairs) and occasional teal, shelduck and avocet.

Since October 2002, saltmarsh plants have rapidly colonised the inter-tidal habitat.[10] Plants relatively tolerant of the conditions associated with immersion by seawater first colonised the bare sediment. The plant community at Abbotts Hall is now dominated by glassworts (*Salicornia* spp.), grass leaved orache (*Atriplex litoralis*), sea spurrey (*Sperguloria* spp.) and annual sea blite (*Suaeda maritima*). Shrubby sea blite, shrubby glasswort and sea purslane are now beginning to establish. Particular efforts are now being made to re-establish Sea Hog's Fennel (*Peucedanum officinale*). This is one of the rarest coastal plants in Britain, and occurs in only three isolated populations, the largest being in the Walton Backwaters, with most growing on the Essex Wildlife Trust reserve, Skippers Island. It is the exclusive foodplant of Fisher's Estuarine Moth (*Gortyna borelii*). In the UK, this moth occurs only in the Walton Backwaters area (and one other secret location in Kent), with the majority of the population confined to Skippers Island.

Both of these species have been adopted as a Biodiversity Action Plan (BAP) species for Essex and consequently are the focus of research and conservation effort. The plant also supports another rare moth *Agonopteryx putridella* that is a national BAP species and occurs both in the Backwaters and Kent. The long-term viability of the Sea Hog's Fennel population and its dependant moth species is threatened in the Walton Backwaters. Skippers Island is low lying with deteriorating sea walls. As a consequence of sea level rise, inundation at some point in the future is inevitable. The resulting prolonged immersion would have a severely detrimental effect on the plants and moths. The ideal solution to safeguard the plant and its dependant moth species would be the creation of a string of coastal sites which are not threatened by the sea and could be sympathetically managed and protected. Sea Hog's Fennel has thus been planted at Abbotts Hall Farm which is now in an ideal location to introduce the Fisher's estuarine moth too.

Visitors and interpretation

Since April 2004, Abbotts Hall Farm has been open to the public. Although not fully open all week, eight thousand people were shown around the farm to view the coastal re-alignment in its first year. In addition, many group visits have been arranged, including for partner organisations, farmers, community groups, clubs and coastal management professionals. A major attraction for the public is the birds and the first of several hides have been installed including a recycled plastic hide. Regular leaflets, newsletters, publications and media correspondence have been produced.

Combating the problems of coastal erosion and loss of associated habitats will be linked to the concept of sustainable fisheries. This is an important message for visitors and the local community, whilst at the same time retaining these habitats to support wildfowl such as brent geese and waders such as curlew and to retain the character of the estuary landscape. There will be a major interpretation and education focus on this important subject in view of climate change and coastal realignment.

Economic and ecosystem benefits

The new wetland was designed to function over at least a 200 year timescale. By having no landward counter wall, the entire habitat can migrate landward to accommodate future sea level rise without the need for any further interference or construction. The main economic benefits have been as follows:

Flood alleviation: the project has saved an estimated £500,000 over the next 20 years on sea wall maintenance. It has also provided improved flood defence at the terminal counter walls to east and west.
Wastewater treatment: the project has improved the water quality of the estuary

by further treatment of the Wigborough sewage treatment works by feeding the outfall water through the new lake and the developing reed bed. This also assists in control of stormwater flows from the works with direct improvements to the water quality of the estuary.

Recreation: the scheme has provided a new barge jetty for people to land and have a bridge between the sea and the land. There are also 50 hectares of restored high tide navigable water for small craft, and about 5km of new permissive footpaths on the farm itself.

Ecotourism: the project has ecotourism benefits not only at this site, but through the potential of joining up with the adjacent landowners at a future date on an enlarged wetland that stretches from West Mersea to Tollesbury and covers over 3,000 hectares.

Fisheries: independent monitoring has shown that the site is an important provider as a habitat for fish fry, in particular commercial fish such as herring and sea bass. An EU wide estuary fish monitoring methodology is now being developed, based on Abbotts Hall.

Water quality: research has shown that new saltings, created by realignment, improve water quality by soaking up both heavy metals and agro-chemicals. 80 hectares of new habitats at Abbotts Hall will assist in this function for the estuary.

New food sources: sheep are being raised, and alternative crops of samphire, asparagus and sea spinach are now being sold to local restaurants.

Taking the experience to Wallasea and beyond

Experience from Abbots Hall has been used to establish a second major coastal realignment at Wallasea, Essex, in 2006. This comprises 115 hectares of new wetland built to replace similar areas that had been destroyed by development at Lappel Bank on the Medway and Fagbury Flats on the Orwell at Felixstowe. The final phase of breaching took place in July 2006, creating 115 hectares of wetland, comprising 90 ha of mud flats (including lagoons and 7 artificial islands) and 25 ha of saltmarsh. 1,600 roosting birds and 76 species are using the managed realignment. A comparison was made between the high tide data from the winter and passage tidal counts and the national populations, taken from WeBS Core Counts. This showed that the managed re-alignmenmt is nationally important for ruff in the winter, with 1.2% of the UK population and for avocet (2.2%), greenshank (1.3%). This shows that the Abbott's Hall managed realignment site is already making a significant contribution to the winter bird usage of the Blackwater Estuary SPA.[11]

New habitat after re-alignment (Essex Wildlife Trust)

Essex had 30,000 hectares of saltmarsh 400 years ago. As a result of enwalling and erosion this was reduced to 2,800 hectares by the early 20th century. Only 50 hectares had been re-created in the decade before Abbotts Hall Farm and Wallasea added 200 hectares. The experience and evidence from these schemes now give prospects of further rewilding along the Essex coast.

References

1. Long S P and Mason C F. (1983) *Saltmarsh Ecology.* Blackie. pp.133.

2. English Nature. (2000) *The Essex Coast beyond 2000.* English Nature, Peterborough.

3. Pretty J. (2002) *Agri-Culture: Reconnecting People, Land and Nature.* Earthscan, London.

4. May A. 2003. The largest coastal re-alignment in Europe – occurred in Essex. *Essex Naturalist* (New Series) 20, 108-110.

5. May A and Smart D. (2003) Managed retreat of the Essex coast. *Geography Review* 17 (1), 38-41.

6. May A and Smart D. (2004) Enriching our landscape – an Essex success story. *Essex Naturalist* (New Series) 21, 117-120.

7. May A and Smart D. (2006) Arable farming and biodiversity: can the two exist? *Geography Review* 19 (4), 24-28.

8. Gilbert O L and Anderson P. (2000) *Habitat Creation and Repair.* Oxford University Press, Oxford.

9. English Nature (1995) *RAMSAR citation for Blackwater Estuary.* Peterborough.

10. Rodwell J S. (ed). 2000. British plant communities, volume 5, Maritime communities and vegetation of open habitats. JNCC.

11. Natural England (2006) *Monitoring of Bird usage at Abbotts Hall managed realignment site, work carried out during the period 2003 to March 2006.*

Acknowledgments

Essex Wildlife Trust is grateful to the project's main partners WWF (UK), English Nature, Environment Agency, HLF, and Defra. We would like to thank Blackwater Oystermen, Colchester Borough Council, Maldon District Council, Winstred Hundred Parish Council, Essex County Council and the University of Essex for their encouragement and support.

MIDDLE ENGLAND

Rewilding Middle England

ECOS 27 (3/4) 8-16 (2006)
Must the central lowlands of England forever be tame? The opportunities for wild land in the region, and the threats to it, are explored in this article.

MICHAEL JEEVES

Ordered, planned and predictable

Browse through the magazine or website of Trees for Life1, the inspiring nature conservation organisation working in the Scottish Highlands, and the idea of what rewilding is about is easily understood, even though it is a difficult concept to define. Restoring woodland to where it once was, together with lost predators and grazing animals, allowing natural processes to function, people interfering as little as possible, with few or no pre-determined outcomes, are just a few factors involved. Forrest Gump's mother said, "Life is like a box of chocolates, you never know what you are going to get". Well, nature conservation should be a bit like that, except that targets and planning are taking over to such an extent that the surprise factor is now missing. Whether it be 'x' hectares of reedbed, 'y' percent of scrub or 'z' pairs of lapwings, we know the plot from the outset.

Nowadays the Highlands are a spectacular and wild-looking landscape even if they are often said to be degraded, holding much less wildlife than they once did. Down in Middle England, however, it is all very different. The landscape from the East Riding of Yorkshire right through the Midlands, towards the South Coast, but extending eastwards into East Anglia, is 'champion' country, or what Oliver Rackham calls the 'planned countryside'.[2] Most of the woodland long having been removed, the open field system was developed here, from Anglo Saxon times into the Middle Ages, and the region was later subjected to the Enclosure movement. The result is little biodiversity and an extremely tame, neat and ordered landscape – the Black Hole of Middle England.[3,4] Common land is generally scarce and there are few places that are not used intensively for something by people, who are present in huge numbers, together with their buildings and roads. The cities, towns and villages too are increasingly tidy, with little room for wild nature.

Take a look at the Wildland Network Rewilding Projects Database[5] and it appears that little is happening in Middle England. The situation is not quite as bad as this, but the challenge of rewilding this region is surely greater than anywhere else in Britain. So, what then are the main issues, threats and opportunities?

Attitudes of people to wild land

At a nature reserve open day a while back a woman and her children looked at display boards showing two large colourful images, one of a meadow full of green-winged orchids and another of an oilseed rape field. To the amazement of the staff in attendance the woman pointed to the oilseed rape photograph and said "isn't that wonderful children!" It was a good lesson in not assuming that everyone likes the same things. So, do people want wild land? Perhaps there is a need to find out.

It is probable that many people are happier when wild land and fierce animals are in remote places. There is certainly also a strong contingent that wants nature reserves to be like parks, with surfaced paths, dog bins and other formalised features and facilities. Others do value wilder land and more might if they had the chance to experience it. What is certain is an imperative to engage more fully with people over the rewilding issue and perhaps to acknowledge that different levels of wildness are appropriate for different situations.

Predators, large herbivores and other keystone species

Wolves, brown bears, lynx and wild cat disappeared long ago from Middle England, and most of the smaller, less fierce animals have been exterminated or severely reduced in number. Recently some have returned, for example otter, red kite, buzzard, sparrowhawk, raven and polecat. Exotics such as big cats (especially melanistic leopard, puma, and the former native Eurasian lynx) are considered by some to be established here and ospreys have been released at Rutland Water.

Osprey at Rutland Water (John Wright/LRWT)

It is said that large predators and herbivores are essential to enable ecosystems to function properly[6], but they make nature more exciting for people too. Only a few years ago Buzzards were rare visitors to most of Middle England, now they are a common and spectacular sight. It should not be too long before red kites are widespread too, but it will be interesting to see whether ravens and polecats are welcomed back in the same way that the birds of prey were. Persecution is still a problem, especially of corvids, although stoats, weasels and foxes suffer too. Attitudes to predators are mixed, as is discussed elsewhere in this issue.

Although it is unlikely that the region will ever have wolves or bears again, there could be stronger populations of some of the species already present and perhaps the re-introduction of pine marten and goshawk in places such as the National Forest. Here and elsewhere there might be possibilities for re-introducing beaver and maybe other keystone species like wood ants. Large herbivores are already being utilised on some conservation sites and their involvement in nature conservation should be explored further. These animals are much admired by human visitors too, and can stimulate people's interest in a nature reserve or wild place.

Existing sites and reserves – their wild credentials

Middle England has, of course, some good places for wildlife. There are National Nature Reserves such as Sherwood Forest, with its fantastic veteran trees, and many other nature reserves and SSSIs. Together these only cover a small percentage of the area, and moreover not all of them are really very 'wild'.

Take nature reserves, for example. They are a real success story in nature conservation, but how wild are they? Table 1 has been adapted from the National Trust for Scotland's Wild Land Policy 2002 and includes suggested indicators of wild land in Middle England.

Table 1. **Indicators of wild land in Middle England**

Positive indicators	Negative indicators
Natural processes allowed to function – 'nature in charge' e.g. natural regeneration, extensive grazing, flooding, predators not controlled, non-prescribed management outcomes	Natural processes constrained – 'people in charge' e.g. tree planting, hedge laying, mowing, flood defence, dams (reservoirs), predators controlled, prescribed management outcomes
Sense of remoteness	Closeness of built-up areas
Large size	Small size
Scenic grandeur (rough terrain, cliffs, rocks, flowing water, sea)	Uninspiring scenery
Solitude	Presence of crowds or group activity
Quietness	Man-made noise
Absence of re-assurance in a hazardous and challenging environment (risk)	Security, tameness
Extreme weather such as gales, heavy rain, frosts and blizzards frequent	Extreme weather rare
Absence of man-made structures e.g. nest boxes, tern rafts, hides, seats, surfaced paths, fences, roads, pylons, overhead wires, buildings, signs	Presence of man-made structures

By scoring each indicator between one and five (negative to positive), but multiplying the natural processes score by a factor of three to reflect its importance, admittedly crude wild land values of individual sites can be compared. The total possible score is 55 and for illustration some of the nature reserves of the Leicestershire and Rutland Wildlife Trust when assessed using this system give some interesting results (Table 2).

Table 2. Wild land values of some Leicestershire and Rutland Wildlife Trust nature reserves

Reserve	Score
	(out of max 55)
Launde Big Wood (SSSI)	37
Charnwood Lodge (NNR)	34
Prior's Coppice (SSSI)	32
Cossington Meadows	28
Rutland Water (SPA)	18
Cribb's Meadow (NNR)	17

The Trust's wildest reserve at present is Launde Big Wood, a good-sized, fairly remote ancient woodland, most of which is purposefully 'managed' with minimum intervention. Next comes Charnwood Lodge, a very large varied reserve with rough terrain, rock outcrops and low-key management. Other LRWT ancient woodlands score highly too, such as Prior's Coppice. Here there are repeated calls for the muddy rides to be surfaced, but these have been resisted so far in order to preserve the wild feel of this marvellous woodland, not to mention the wildlife that lives on the rides. Next on the list is a wildish floodplain wetland, Cossington Meadows, and then a gap to lower scoring reserves.

Grasslands such as Cribb's Meadow are carefully managed through grazing, mowing and 'weed' control to achieve a desired sward height and elimination of unwanted species. While it is a lovely and relatively remote place, Cribb's Meadow is not especially wild. Rutland Water Nature Reserve is remarkable in that it holds a tremendous amount of wildlife, but the reserve scores poorly in terms of wildness. This would probably be true for most of the large wetland reserves in Middle England, where attracting large numbers of visitors is a high priority and there are therefore hides, surfaced paths, interpretation centres and so forth, as well as controlled water levels and intensive management. Colin Tubbs wrote passionately nearly 30 years ago about the paradox of increased wildlife but reduced wildness where nature reserves are created. He thought that "too many reserves have lost their appeal through the safari park approach of their managers...".[7] Clearly some places do require a high degree of human control in order to maintain traditional practices such as hay making and others like Rutland Water provide an important role in introducing people to wildlife, but a better balance needs to be struck between honey-pot, ordered reserves, and wilder ones.

For comparison, Chee Dale, a superb nature reserve in the Peak District, just outside of the region being considered, appears to score highly with 43 using the indicators in Table 1, while Beinn Eighe National Nature Reserve in the north of Scotland amasses a hugely impressive 51.

There must be potential for some reserves to be wilder and they could be used as demonstration sites to promote wildness as a concept. It is another matter on SSSIs and other legally protected sites, at least at present. The objective of getting SSSIs into 'favourable condition' through prescribed means severely restricts the scope for wildness. For example, a lowland reservoir in Leicestershire notified as a SSSI for its draw-down zone plant communities developed a wonderful tangle of wet woodland along its margins in the absence of grazing. This woodland, itself an important habitat, is being cleared in order to try and restore the specialised draw-down zone plant communities, even if that is near impossible to achieve because of eutrophication of the water. Also, on heathlands, one of our wildest landscapes, despite the fact that they are the product of centuries of management, suggestions have been made that one Leicestershire SSSI should be compartmentalised with fencing to facilitate control of grazing. On another stock must be removed in the winter, so the whole concept of extensive naturalistic grazing is undermined. This is all to achieve defined levels of scrub, bracken, bare ground and ericaceous shrub cover. There seems to be little room for the dynamism of nature.

Farmland

The notion of letting nature have a little more say is a difficult pill for many farmers to swallow. Even the conservation-friendly farmers want to be in charge, so realism is necessary when contemplating the rewilding of farmland. The new Single Payment Scheme has already produced narrow field margins of rough grass and the Environmental Stewardship Scheme is surely going to benefit wildlife. These schemes will not, however, result in a wilder looking land, where the emphasis is still on prescribed outcomes and control. Abandonment of much land in the rich area of Middle England seems unlikely, but if farmers were paid through these schemes to set-aside areas for several years, on a rotational basis with much less interference than hitherto, then that could create some wild places in the countryside. If these places were located next to rivers or existing good sites, that would be even better. There are a few examples of this happening and they are producing encouraging results. Negative perception of so-called 'weeds' is something that will have to be overcome.

The creation of more woodland on farmland should be encouraged and it will surely be necessary to link existing woodlands to make them more viable ecological units, especially with the threat of a changing climate. More land is being bought by people who do not necessarily want to farm, so there must be potential to find a few who are interested in doing something exciting and different. A large private estate in south Warwickshire, known as the Forest of Dennis, is already being established by one (Felix Dennis, a wealthy publisher) who is aiming to create an area of woodland extending over an astonishing 25,000 acres (approx. 10,000 hectares).[8]

Rivers and floodplains

If the opportunities for rewilding are limited on farmland, the situation on floodplains is much more promising. There are currently many conservation initiatives along river valleys, often taking advantage of old gravel workings. New reedbeds are springing up everywhere, as well as marshes grazed by wild-looking longhorn cattle, wet woodland, lakes and more reedbeds. River valleys are recognised for their existing and potential value to wildlife. There has even been some restoration of rivers that have been engineered in the past, such as the River Tame at Middleton Hall.

Numerous gravel pits, grants to enhance them, the scarcity of arable farming and relatively small land holdings, wet land, enthusiastic non-governmental organisations, a dedicated government body (the Environment Agency) and support from water companies and local authorities have all combined to facilitate successes in river valleys. With more gravel extraction inevitable and a probable decline in the profitability of floodplain farming, perhaps even more can be achieved in these places. There are still threats, such as high land prices in pony paddock areas, development and climate change. The latter may lead to drastic measures to reduce increased danger of flooding of towns and cities through the construction of dams, thereby taming rivers again.

Existing woodland

Although the cover of woodland in Middle England is generally low, there are some denser wooded areas, like Rockingham Forest in Northamptonshire. In most of the region, though, there are only quite small, scattered ancient woodlands and fox covers. A few places have concentrations of relatively new and sometimes large conifer plantations, often on former heathland. Many of the older woods were once intensively managed by regular coppicing, but during most of the twentieth century were either neglected or planted with conifers, and then neglected. This has resulted in the loss of some wildlife, but neglected woods are wilder than those with carefully mown rides and coppice coupes surrounded by tall fences to keep deer out. Ironically perhaps, deer are considered by many conservationists to be a major threat to woodland biodiversity, yet others see the absence of large herbivores in ecosystems as a critical issue. It all depends on the circumstances of course, but there are mixed messages being sent here.

Woodlands are the best places in Middle England to find wildness. They can offer a refuge from twenty-first century civilisation, at least as long as internal roads, tree tubes, external noise and the like are kept to a minimum. Natural processes are being used to rewild a number of damaged ancient woods, for example in Forest Enterprise woods such as Owston Woods in Leicestershire.
Area-based projects

Conservation, landscape and recreation work has increasingly become focused on defined areas. One of the best examples is surely the National Forest. This initiative started in the early 1990s and through its innovative Tender Scheme the area of woodland in the Forest has been increased substantially. The Tender Scheme rewards landowners handsomely for carrying out not just tree planting, but conservation, access and recreation work. It is certainly a model that could be used elsewhere. Community Forests (the smaller tracts of mixed woodland helping to revive the edge of many cities) would benefit from having similar grant schemes, because encouraging farmers to plant trees is difficult. A farming representative memorably said recently that there are only two things that will make farmers plant trees - money and mental illness!

The Great Fen Project, Sherwood Forest and OnTrent are other exciting area-based initiatives. There are more in the early stages of development throughout Middle England. The challenge is to get rewilding higher on the agenda of some. There must be the potential in the National Forest for wild land, if only because much of the new woodland may well end up unmanaged. Hopefully increased wildness can be achieved in a more positive way though.
Biodiversity Action Plans

BAPs are now a well-established part of nature conservation, enshrined in many a strategy. The principles on which they are based are good – strong partnerships, agreed priorities, objectives and targets. Of course there are problems, not just a shortage of resources to actually do much, but also an implied message that biodiversity can only be increased through targets, planning and control.

Notwithstanding concerns from both sides of the argument, BAPs can be used to further rewilding initiatives. It really depends on how the plans are written. The fact that so many grant schemes now demand that projects contribute to BAP targets means that BAPs must be taken notice of. The important thing is to ensure that the plans include rewilding concepts. Local

BAPs perhaps have more flexibility for this than national ones and for example the Leicester Leicestershire and Rutland floodplain wetland Habitat Action Plan was used to help secure funds towards the purchase of 100 hectares of land adjacent to the River Soar.

Quarries

In addition to the numerous sand and gravel pits on floodplains and elsewhere, Middle England also has, because of its geological diversity and location, many other quarries. These have considerable potential for restoration to benefit wildlife and wild land too. The key is the creation of a varied topography with a nutrient-poor substrate and the use of natural processes as drivers in the evolution of the site.

Lafarge Aggregates started one innovative project in the mid 1990s, in the largest granite quarry in Europe, at Mountsorrel in Leicestershire.[9] Following the construction of a new landform, the original restoration plan was to topsoil the landform and then plant trees. The Leicestershire and Rutland Wildlife Trust suggested that instead no topsoil be used and that the trees be left to regenerate naturally (the land has on one side an ancient woodland). To its credit Lafarge was keen on this idea, no doubt partly because of the scarcity of topsoil, and it was supported strongly by its forestry consultant, Leicestershire County Council and English Nature. The results were remarkable, with up to 58,700 trees per hectare growing within five years (R. Pakenham pers. comm.).

Public perception is important and certainly Lafarge had to think hard about what local residents would say about a quarry company appearing not to do anything on land it had turned into a 'wasteland'. In the event little adverse comment was received.

With many quarries still being worked and more undoubtedly to come, opportunities for wild land are there to be taken. Often mineral companies do not actually own the land they are working, which is a problem, and that the planning system does not seem to be able to adequately ensure the long-term future of restored sites.

The wild side of towns

Wild land is now very scarce in many towns and cities. Open space is at a premium and even where it occurs twenty-first century wealth enables ordered landscaping to rule the day. Acres of grass are regularly mown, trees and shrubs are planted and maintained, and householders increasingly concrete, slab or brick over gardens. One conservationist was galvanised into a scathing attack on the destruction of wild land in London and its replacement with landscaped wildlife areas, making the point that planted or sown trees and other plants are not actually wild.[10]

Contemplation of wild land in urban and suburban situations begs the question do wild places have to be big? There is much discussion of large areas in conservation circles these days, but small wild places have value to wildlife and can bring much pleasure to people too. If more gardeners could be encouraged to let just a small part of their land go wild and local authorities did the same with parks, a great deal could be achieved. The culture of the neat and tidy approach is a major obstacle and wild land is frowned upon as the product of the idle.

A new era of conservation?

While sound science and policy are familiar themes in nature conservation, philosophy is rarely mentioned. The truth is that nature conservation is as much an idea as anything else and ideas have changed over time. We look after what we like, especially charismatic and attractive species. Of course policies and science are both important, but opinions are many and varied on what we are trying to achieve. Long may it be so. Wild land, or wilderness, is certainly an idea and everyone will have an opinion on it.[11]

But if there are exciting wild land projects being developed in the Scottish Highlands and other upland parts of Britain, why bother with Middle England? Aldo Leopold, the great American wilderness advocate, when considering the apparent acceptance that Grizzly Bears were going to become confined to Alaska in that country, wrote that "relegating Grizzlies to Alaska is like relegating happiness to heaven; one might never get there".[12] We need some wild land everywhere.

References

1. See: www.treesforlife.org.uk
2. Rackham, O. (1986) *The History of the Countryside* Dent. London
3. Colston, A. (1997) Conserving Wildlife in a Black Hole *ECOS* 18 (1) 61-67
4. Jeeves, M. (2005) News from the Black hole *ECOS* 26 (3/4) 95-103
5. See: www.wildland-network.org.uk/projects/wn-rewild.database.htm
6. Dennis, R. (1995) Scotland's Native Forest – Return of the Wild *ECOS* 16 (2) 17-21
7. Tubbs, C. (1979) Poor Substitute for Wildnerness *Birds: Summer Issue* pp 26-27
8 .Dennis, F. (2005) The Forest of Dennis *Tree News Autumn/Winter Issue pp 50-52*
9. Pakenham, R.A. (2000) Landscape Restoration – An Alternative Approach *Quart. J. of Forestry* 94 313-318
10. Bertrand, N. (1999) Putting the Savage Back into Wild Flowers *BSBI News* 80 39-41
11. Oelschlaeger, M. (1991) *The Idea of Wilderness: From Prehistory to the Age of Ecology* Yale University Press. New Haven and London
12. Leopold, A. (1949) *A Sand County Almanac* Oxford University Press. New York

THE SOUTH WEST

Towards the wild - A Dartmoor trail

ECOS 25 (3/4) 50-54 (2004)
A local charity is helping people contribute to improving heath and moor on Dartmoor, and shaping a wilder future landscape.

ADAM GRIFFIN

Moor Trees – reviving Dartmoor

Moor Trees is a charity based in the Dartmoor National Park. We began our work in 1997 with a vision to restore a natural forest dynamic back to Dartmoor. From the inspiration of Alan Featherstone and Trees For Life we grew into a community organisation linked by a strong sense of the tree as a symbol of life.

Moor Trees wanted to bring balance back to the overgrazed moorlands and undervalued woodlands, to create an initiative for new, near-natural or wilding zones. We decided to implement this by:

- planting trees and encouraging natural woodland regeneration
- promoting the value of a natural forest ecosystem, and
- encouraging people to get involved in ecological restoration.

Our national conference in 1999 explored new approaches to grazing systems and conservation in National Parks. Equally it served as a reminder of the wound of the lost UK forest wilderness and it challenged the mindsets that are species-centric and headage payment orientated in National Parks.

Moor Trees has created the Wild Dartmoor Forum, to continue the dialogue between key landowners local authorities, agencies and environmental groups. Interest grew in a feasibility study for an experimental wilding area, but the weight of opinion at the last meeting was to first start learning from similar studies and experimental areas, as there were no immediate resources for our own study.

Native trees and the wild heart

The Dartmoor National Park Authority 2001 management plan states that "it is impossible to predict with any accuracy what the scale and speed of the effects of global warming will be on Dartmoor's landscape and wildlife." The plan goes on to say "National park experts are only now beginning to think about how to measure such concepts as the "wildness" of Dartmoor, even though many would agree that this is Dartmoor's most special quality."

Spurred on by this recognition of wildness in the management plan, we began practical projects, growing and planting trees and implementing several educational projects including traditional storytelling and informative walks and talks on the ecology of Dartmoor.

Our tree planting work linked ancient and secondary native woodland and creating new woods for wildlife benefit. George Peterken's guidelines on minimum managed size of 25 ha (or if unmanaged 50ha)[1], have helped us towards developing our *Wildwoods Service* for landowners. This is a free service, which provides help with making grant applications, free trees from our local community tree nurseries and volunteer help to plant and maintain the trees for up to five years. In return we ask the landowner to enter into a 20-year agreement to safeguard the trees against exploitation. We offer management agreements further beyond this time frame, but asking for more that 20 years could take us into another generation and this may put people off.

In its first year, our *Wildwoods Service*, helped plant over 4.6ha of new woods which linked or extended nearly 50 ha of ancient and secondary woodland. Our seven community tree nurseries around the moor are currently growing over 10,000 local native trees. The species we grow are mainly those that make up the fragments of upland or Atlantic oakwoods that remain on Dartmoor. We only collect from ancient woodland, as it is this genetic heritage which is most adapted to the local conditions, but it may also be the best to survive climate changes.

Wildwoods Community Tee Nursery (Adam Griffin)

The challenge of climate change

As a response to climate change, there is much speculation as to what we should be planting and how we should manage it. The integrity of natural processes and the ability of an intact natural forest dynamic to heal itself, has much to teach us. This is why we try to mimic natural woodland regeneration and encourage our volunteers when planting to learn about this vital natural process. It's fun and quite a challenge to engage with something that is, by its nature, chaotic, particularly as we are often trying to avoid it in activities at home or work.

We get hundreds of people coming out in all weathers to help sow, weed, plant and nurture the trees. For many it symbolises a giving back to the earth from which we take so much and the benefits of the chain reaction that occurs once a tree is established.

Not just trees

The last tracts of a biologically intact wilderness in the British Isles, have long gone, but often the interest in stories of the wild and what it was like to have bears fishing on the Dart and wolves tracking herds of Aurochs, stirs great interest. Our traditional storytelling and our 'time machine' slide shows have been a success and a step towards reclaiming what might be 'forest wilderness' in British terms.

Many people come to these events with the perception of a plantation 'forest'. To quell any fears of our vision being just about trees, we remind them of the medieval hunting forest that still annotates our older maps. We also explain the habitat diversity of past UK forest and of many present temperate forests abroad. This is, however, one end of the spectrum and often hill farmers are at the other end. Hill-farming subsidies have dramatically altered the character of remote regions like Dartmoor. As a result of livestock headage payments, the UK sheep population rose 37% between 1981 and 1993 to reach nearly 44 million.[2] In 1999 alone, £2m was spent on subsidies for hill farming on Dartmoor.[3]

Restoration of heath and moor

Large areas of heather moorland on Dartmoor have been turned into grass moor (now 5,300ha) due to the "'heavy grazing of the heathland, a habitat of far greater wildlife value".[4] As a result, the primary purpose for designating Dartmoor as an Environmentally Sensitive Area (ESA) in 1994, was to promote the restoration of upland heathland, by reducing grazing numbers. It is good news, then, that by February 2004, 70% or 60,000 ha of eligible land in Dartmoor ESA was under agreement, with all of the 36,000 ha of Dartmoor Common Land either in ESA or under discussion.[5]

Planting at Harbourneford, South Dartmoor (Adam Griffin)

With over 1,000 registered Dartmoor commoners with grazing rights, it has been a remarkable feat for DEFRA to gather most of them into the Environmentally Sensitive Area scheme. It will be interesting to see the effect this has over the next five years. Now the ESA scheme is changing to Environmental Stewardship (ES),[6] the challenge is to continue to take farmers and landowners forward into a new era of conservation land management on Dartmoor.

Bracken has been regenerating rapidly, particularly in the southern half of the moor. It has shaded out important heathland and provided cover for gorse and rowan to start the next step in succession. Now there are over 5,000ha of it, and this could be for several reasons. Overgrazing forces sheep to move to areas often much further away, giving time for the bracken to colonize quickly. The reduction of grazing could also mean cattle are no longer present to push through it and trample it down, and of course rising temperatures due to climate change may also be a factor.

Rediscovering the wild

Along with poor quality grass moor and the change to the agri-environment schemes, these bracken areas present an opportunity for change. There is a chance to create new experimental wilding areas; natural networks of habitats linked in a patchwork to allow species to move in response to climate change and for the possible reintroduction of species extinct from the area. Places where natural regeneration could be allowed to develop with no loss of biodiversity from the other internationally important habitats alongside them.

Whatever the different stresses and priorities on wilding, or rewilding, amongst practitioners, at least we are starting the process of discovery. Moor Trees continues to grow and develop as a practitioner of ecological restoration. We are helping to trigger debate and stimulate action to achieve new, near-natural areas. My hope is that tomorrow we will be linking up Dartmoor with other areas across the country, from Bodmin Moor to the Lakes, from the

Norfolk Broads to the Yorkshire Moors, from wildlife corridors to habitat highways!

Extending the woods on Dartmoor (Adam Griffin)

References and notes

1.   Peterken G. (2002) *Reversing the habitat fragmentation of British woodlands*, WWF, Godalming.
2.   Harvey G. (1997) *The Killing of the Countryside*, Vintage
3.   Moor Trees (1999) *Towards the Wild*, Conference Report, Dartington Hall, 20.11.99, Moor Trees, Dartmoor.
4.   Dartmoor National Park Authority & English Nature (2001), *The Nature of Dartmoor*, A Biodiversity Profile, DNPA & EN, 2001
5.   DEFRA Rural Development Service Feb 04
6.   See DEFRA website page:-
         http://www.defra.gov.uk/erdp/schemes/es/default.htm

The Neroche Scheme: transforming landscapes, working practices, communities and lives

ECOS 32 (in press, 2011)
A leading example of landscape scale transformation that includes woodland grazing, habitat recreation, improved access and educational projects is nearing the end of its first phase and engaged in securing a future for multi-purpose forest management with an ethos of public service as well as timber production.

GAVIN SAUNDERS

The scarp slope of the Blackdown Hills south of Taunton has an almost continuously wooded horizon, much valued by local people for its wild secrecy compared to the relatively open moors of Exmoor, the Quantocks and the Mendips. Hugely varied, these woods span the full spectrum from deeply ancient combes of oak, ash and hazel, through planted pine, larch and spruce, to scrubby willow and birch which has only recently reclaimed former wet pastures on the springline.

The larger part of the woods here, close to the border between Somerset and Devon, is leased by the Forestry Commission and collectively this holding is called the Neroche Forest. Neroche derives from the ancient Royal Forest of that name which covers part of its area, and the Norman hillfort of Castle Neroche which overlooks it. The word Neroche has an obscure derivation, thought to originate from the Old English words *nierra* and *raecc-wic* meaning *'the place (kennels) where rache (hunting dogs) were kept'*.

The Forestry Commission leased the estate in the late 1940s, shortly after its acquisition by the Crown Estate Commissioners in lieu of death duties, following the death of the last Lord Portman. The Portmans had held the lands for more than 500 years before that, during which their successive lordships had created lavish deer parks and built a family seat (now vanished) which for a century or so was the finest early Renaissance manor in southern England. They also captured the Duke of Monmouth in a Somerset ditch in 1685, enclosed the ancient commons from the waste and pioneered modern agricultural and forestry techniques, amassing a fortune and a name manifested in the title of Lord Chief Justice and a London residence in Portman Square. But all that had gone by the end of the Second World War, and the Crown, while retaining the fertile pasture lands of the estate for lucrative tenancies, gave over the rest to the new state forestry service.

Neroche forest from the air (Gavin Saunders)

Neroche Forest was never a very good bet for a decent return from plantation forestry. The steep, wet slopes grew excellent Douglas fir and some other species, but the cost of getting them out was always likely to neutralise their value. But nevertheless the imperative to increase the size of the national forest estate drove the planting of these hillsides, and by the 1960s much of the former rough heathland commons had been populated by conifers, while some of the broadleaved woods had given way to mixed plantations.

Fast forward forty years and the Forestry Commission had matured into a much more multi-purpose organisation, seeking to provide a public forest which met the public's desire for places for recreation, the conservation lobby's demands for a secured biodiversity, and the continuing exigency of a viable timber supply. Neroche, viewed during the 1980s and early 90s as a low-priority commercial forest and even considered for disposal, rose to the top of the pile when the cards were re-shuffled in favour of the new multiple environmental objectives.

However, though it presented a great landscape spectacle, and though it contained a concentration of SSSIs, the environmental attributes of Neroche were under severe threat, and its recreational value was poorly realised. Creating a modern forest required a re-balancing, with a shift away from dense conifer towards a more diverse forest structure, re-visiting the truer definition of a forest as a mixture of trees and open space. The fact was that much of the rarest and most iconic wildlife in the Neroche forest needed more open space, albeit sheltered within a matrix of woodland, and even the wildlife of deep woodland could not thrive under the dense shade of spruce, fir and hemlock.

Thus the scene was set for a new investment of funding, expertise and popular interest into Neroche. In 2003 the Forestry Commission began to develop a bid to the Heritage Lottery Fund under its emerging Landscape Partnership Scheme, and with the support of the Blackdown Hills AONB, Somerset and Devon county councils, English Nature and a partnership totalling 17 different organisations, it secured £2 million from the HLF in 2006, as part of a programme totalling £3 million.

The Neroche Scheme proposals were initially driven by the biodiversity-centred goal of restoring a landscape-scale network of open space within the forest. But the HLF's Landscape Partnership Scheme required a wider, more comprehensive approach to heritage in all its forms, and the new partnership was encouraged to address a much broader palette. That impetus was crucial, and ensured Neroche become much more than just a landscape-scale habitat project.

The Scheme set out to address all aspects of landscape heritage through a suite of 23 separate projects[1]. These invested in the fabric of the heritage (habitat restoration and built heritage conservation), sought to make it accessible to all (physically and intellectually), and improved people's ability to look after it into the future (through true community participation, volunteering, and skills training). The Scheme set out to do more than simply address each of these themes in isolation: it sought to weave together the delivery of overlapping solutions and innovations which require different groups to work closely together. In this way it set out to work with the landscape as a many-faceted whole, and connect that whole to the everyday experience of its people.

The Scheme has been governed by a Partnership Board comprising representatives of the funding partners and members of a Local Stakeholders Group (LSG). The LSG comprises eleven members of the local community who were closely involved in the design of the original bid (and acted as arbiters over which projects found their way into the final delivery plan), and have acted as ambassadors for the Scheme amongst their communities. As a consequence of that experience, latterly the LSG decided to establish itself as an independent charitable company, the Blackdown Hills Trust, to take forward the spirit and objectives of Neroche into the future.

Delivery of the Scheme was led by a core team, employed by the Forestry Commission and based with the Blackdown Hills AONB Partnership in Hemyock. The team comprised a Project Manager, an Access & Interpretation Officer, a Community History Officer, a Forest Works Supervisor, a Forest Schools Officer and two Admin assistants.

Landscape-scale habitat restoration

The dilemma for the Forestry Commission was that, in order to maintain larger areas of open space in the forest, the only practical and sustainable type of management would need to involve grazing. But to create areas of forest large enough to sustain grazing livestock, conifer harvesting would need to be rapid and on a large scale – despite the Commission's preference for continuous cover forestry. The ecological and psychological shock of this was unavoidably severe: however informed local people were of the proposals, once the forwarders and timber trucks moved in, the change was traumatic.

Seven separate blocks of forest were selected for major harvesting to create open ground. All of them were areas which historically had been open before the Commission plantings in the early 1950s. 220 hectares were opened up between 2006 and early 2009, for restoration as open space and wood pasture. A further 40 hectares of conifer was removed from plantations on ancient woodland sites. On each site, stumps were lowered and brash raked and burned on site. For six months after felling, the newly opened areas looked raw and quite bleak. Within a year the land had begun to re-cloth itself, but the shock of that initial change – regardless of the fact that it was only the conifer cover which had been removed – was too much for some local residents who had been used to the old character of the Forest. Some of those remain, to this day, deeply unhappy about what was done.

As a result of this period of upheaval, nearly sixty years after the Commission had first started its afforestation programme in the area, a new landscape began to take shape within the Neroche estate. The network of re-establishing marshy grassland, wet heath, scrub and wood pasture began to be managed using a herd of English Longhorn cattle, acquired by the Neroche Scheme using Lottery funding, and managed for the project by a local farmer.

People-friendly Longhorn in forest meadow (Gavin Saunders)

248

Longhorns – a new ingredient with an old pedigree

Livestock grazing in woodland, on a large scale and with a positive environment purpose, is not a common feature in South West England, though it has a long pedigree elsewhere. For Neroche, a breed of cattle was needed which would suit a public forest, would thrive in the unconventional conditions of former conifer plantation, and would bring individuality to the Forest, in keeping with its character. Experience from Sherwood Forest and elsewhere led the Neroche Partnership to the English Longhorn.

Maintaining the sward -Longhorns in Neroche forest meadow (Gavin Saunders)

The English Longhorn is an ancient and beautiful breed. Once an official Rare Breed, Longhorns came close to extinction in the middle years of the twentieth century but have proved themselves to have a valuable role to play in conservation management. They produce high quality beef, they are hardy, thriving on poor, variable forage, and importantly they are docile and deal well with the public.

The longhorns have acquired a strong following, with many people already regarding them as an iconic part of the Neroche forest. There were to be problems for the new project in its first few years however, with some ill feeling towards the cattle, based partly on remaining unhappiness about the change in the forest, partly on discomfort felt by some at the idea of large livestock in a public woodland setting, and partly welfare concerns about the cattle themselves. This came to a head in 2010, when a very small group of local individuals mounted a surreptitious campaign against the project, with secret filming of overwintering facilities and allegations of welfare breaches by the projects' grazier. Fear over the potential effects of this on the farmer's wider business forced FC to end the relationship with him in late 2010 and take the herd away from the Blackdowns for the winter to escape unwelcome attention. At the time of writing, a new arrangement is being finalised with two new graziers splitting the herd between them, financed from Higher Level Stewardship.

Rebuilding biodiversity

The small open glades within the previous conifer plantations owed their survival to the efforts of the local Branch of Butterfly Conservation, who had managed them by hand over many years, keeping back the woody scrub and cutting and raking the grass. Thanks to their efforts, small, vulnerable populations of rare butterflies were hanging on. These small reservoirs of open habitats were expanded and connected by the Neroche felling programme into a wider network.

Nature abhors a vacuum, and very quickly a new tide of vegetation began to sweep across the new clearings. Within three years, ground which in 2006 had been under deep conifer shade and devoid of almost all flora, had amassed up to 15 species of flowering plant per square metre [2]. Volunteers who worked with the Neroche Scheme in these early years were able to track this change, recording the reappearance of important butterfly foodplants like cowslips, vetches and trefoils. Alongside this monitoring, Butterfly Conservation's volunteers continued to record the presence of the most threatened butterflies. Wood white responded to the new conditions almost straight away, but poor summer weather made for two successive bad years for butterflies in 2008 and 2009. 2010 was better, but the tenuous prospects for these iconic insects remain difficult to predict. The recovery of the newly cleared areas into the fullness of their new character will take some years: a fully stable vegetation will probably not be reached until a decade after the initial clearance of the trees. Retaining the butterflies and the rest of the wildlife they represent through that period will require good fortune as well as careful management.

A modern forest for people

Despite the prominence of the felling and grazing work, the wider set of projects in the Neroche Scheme gave it many more dimensions, and a far greater immediate relevance to local people. Creating safe, easy access for all into the forest was a key objective, together with exploring the cultural and historical heritage of the area, investing in the conservation of built heritage features, and widening the scope for education, training, volunteering and the arts.

The Scheme conserved the important Iron Age and Norman fortress at Castle Neroche, and supported the National Trust in work to conserve the iconic Wellington Monument, a 19th-century obelisk built to commemorate the Duke of Wellington. A popular Community History Project helped establish three new local history groups, and built capacity in a range of groups and individuals to research, explore and document their local heritage. Amongst the key achievements of this work was a popular community excavation of a lost medieval village site on the edge of the forest, and the publication of a major heritage book, 'Along the Wild Edge', containing over 30 chapters by local people exploring the area from an archaeological, artistic and ecological perspective [3].

Storytelling in the forest (Gavin Saunders)

Neroche adopted the Blackdown Hills AONB's long-cherished plans to create a long distance off-road trail in the area, and developed a popular 13 mile circular walking and horse riding trail, called the Herepath Trail, to enhance the public's experience of the Blackdown Hills landscape. Named after the Saxon word for 'People's Paths', the Herepath attracted 20,000 visits in its first three years. In addition an all-ability 1km loop trail was established through part of the FC forest to a major new viewpoint over Taunton, creating a highly popular destination for a range of audiences including the elderly and disabled users. In total the Scheme has created, enhanced or interpreted over 60km of off-road trails.

Neroche chose to develop a close relationship with the local arts community throughout, using natural sculpture, storytelling and music to convey the qualities of the heritage in new, arresting ways. The approach was to create art works which were ephemeral, or made from local materials, and add to people's enjoyment of the landscape without marking the landscape permanently. A music and storytelling programme in 2008 reinvigorated local folklore and culminated in an event called Punkie Night, bringing 300 children and parents into the forest after dark for a hugely memorable lantern procession. The interpretation programme for the Scheme also developed innovative hand-held Digital Trail Guides to enable people to carry words, pictures and sounds describing the landscape with them on their explorations.

Learning in the landscape

Neroche chose to use the Forest School approach to outdoor environmental education to enable children from all primary schools in and around the area to experience the forest landscape as a normal, regular part of their learning. The Forest School ethos focuses on the child rather than primarily the environment, using learning styles that maximise the emotional, social and developmental benefits of education, in an outdoor setting. Practitioners use learning and teaching strategies that raise self-esteem and develop confidence, independence and communication skills, and use woodland settings for the tools they offer – space to explore, materials to use, and boundless stimuli for all the senses. The project has invested in training nearly 40 local school teachers to become qualified Forest School Leaders and Assistants to OCN Level 3 or Level 2, thereby embedding outdoor learning into the ethos of more than 20 schools. The impact on children and teachers themselves has already been profound.

Forest school (Gavin Saunders)

Meanwhile a diverse events programme has used a variety of themes and approaches for attracting people into the forest, including bushcraft, outdoor art courses, green woodworking, archaeological survey, wildlife tracking and practical habitat conservation. Family Bushcraft days have catered for some 300 people, and have been an especially popular way for families to spend time together in a natural setting. The approach here has been to use the forest as a setting, not for didactic teaching about the environment, but simply as a space in which people can be – interacting as families, and finding out more about themselves. The Scheme also included a Health Walks project which has brought hard-to-reach audiences from nearby urban areas into the forest for guided walks and other activities, while a partnership has evolved with the mental health team at Somerset NHS Trust to use bushcraft on a long term basis with patients with psychotic illnesses.

The Scheme worked hard to establish an active volunteering programme, providing opportunities for practical site conservation, wildlife recording, local history research, oral history recording and other activities. Initially the numbers of volunteers were limited, but after about three years the effort suddenly began to pay off, and latterly the number of tasks organised for and by the Neroche Conservation Volunteers has doubled to meet demand. Since 2007 over 1100 volunteer days have been accrued.

Finally, the Scheme ran a successful apprenticeships project, training a team of three local young people to NVQ Level 2 and 3 in Forestry and Conservation Management, to enable them to develop local careers in the countryside. This laid the foundation for a further pilot across the Blackdowns and East Devon which began in 2010, testing a new model for a national forestry apprenticeship.

Evaluating a complex landscape programme

Neroche has provided valuable lessons – good and bad – on the value of a collective approach to heritage conservation, which seeks to transcend barriers between professions and approaches to the management and celebration of landscape. Many of the most exciting moments of the Scheme have come where very different practitioners interact, and previously distinct perspectives coalesce.

The Scheme has learned much about the practicalities and ultimate value of true community involvement, and the investment of time needed to keep people on board effectively. Through the support of the Heritage Lottery Fund the Forestry Commission has been able to put its principles about multi-purpose forestry into practice at Neroche, and reinforce its commitment to maximising the value of the heritage it manages and influences.

An evaluation of the Neroche Scheme carried out by Forest Research in 2010[4] chose the word 'transformation' to describe both the physical and psychological effects of the programme. It summed these up as follows:

- "Transformations in the landscape – the physical opening up of the Neroche forest benefited wildlife but also affected how some people now relate to and experience the landscape.
- Transforming work practices - participating in a holistic project encouraged a broader perspective and inspired some partners to be innovative and visionary, as well as building up knowledge and confidence.
- Transforming lives - some individuals, groups and families found a new sense of enjoyment and wellbeing through activities offered or initiated by Neroche. This gave people opportunities to connect with family and nature and experience their natural environment, local history and cultural context, which they would not otherwise have had.
- Transforming small communities to become 'Big Society' - members of the rural communities of the Neroche area were encouraged and empowered to use their abilities to influence the planning and management of projects and activities in their area, discover new interests and roles in supporting conservation and community activities, and take responsibility for their upkeep through professional training or volunteering."

Future plans

Generating an on-going momentum for legacy projects to succeed the 5 years of Lottery funding for Neroche has proved difficult, frustrated by the recession and causing anxiety about the longevity of the Scheme's achievements. Some legacy funding is secure, but the future of the public forest estate and the Forestry Commission makes the future uncertain. The HLF-funded Neroche LPS comes to an end in September 2011, but the Neroche Partnership remains committed to continuing and building on the progress of the last five years.

The Forestry Commission remains fully committed to the forest grazing programme in the recovering habitat network created by the Neroche Scheme, and is now working with the new Blackdown Hills Trust which will take on a lease over the grazing units, and receive HLS payments to finance the involvement of the new graziers. Putting this project on a long term, economically sustainable footing, by creating an added-value product and/or a valuable pedigree breeding herd, remains the aim, but the partnership has found this a longer, harder road than perhaps it anticipated, with a clear need for HLS support for the next few years to buffer the project while the new graziers establish themselves.

Meanwhile, building on the challenges and successes of the forest grazing project within Neroche, FC has worked with Butterfly Conservation, the Blackdown Hills AONB and Natural England to initiate a new conservation grazing project across the wider AONB, called Beef & Butterflies. The overriding intention here will be to bring the Neroche approach to community participation to bear on the thorny issue of collaborative working within the livestock sector, seeking to persuade owners and managers of marginal wetland habitats on the Blackdowns to work more closely together, sharing experience and finding common solutions. Beef & Butterflies has secured funding through the Blackdown Hills' Local Action for Rural Communities (LARC) programme for an initial three year project.

Neroche has also secured funding through the Woodland Carbon Task Force, which has also been placed with the new Blackdown Hills Trust, for a programme of new work exploring the scope for more effective community engagement in managing underwood in FC woodlands, and for encouraging an increase in new woodland planting across the wider Blackdown Hills.

Alongside these programmes, the enthusiasm and vigour of the volunteer network created by Neroche is beginning to be focused onto the evolution of a new, permanent community woodland centre at Young Wood, in the heart of the Neroche Forest, where the spirit of Neroche – people and nature in a forest for all – can take deeper root.

References

1. See www.nerochescheme.org

2. *Neroche Project 2010 Monitoring Survey*, Somerset Environmental Records Centre, February 2011

3. *Along the Wild Edge – A journey through the northern Blackdown Hills*, compiled by Tanya James, Neroche Partnership, March 2011

4. *Enabling Positive Change: Evaluation of the Neroche Landscape Partnership Scheme*, Claudia Carter, Liz O'Brien and Jake Morris, Forest Research, January 2011

THE NORTH EAST

Eee, it's wild oop north!

ECOS 25 (3/4) 29-33 (2006)

This article describes some of the issues and progress on wild land and rewilding in Northern England, including Geltsdale and the North Pennines AONB.

STEVE CARVER & PETER SAMSON

The wilds of the North

Thousands of years of human history have created a mosaic of different land uses, in which even those that appear to be wholly natural are in fact the product of human action in recent or more distant times. Nevertheless, there are parts of northern England that do retain a feeling of wildness; of wide open vistas uncluttered by obvious signs of human action, a sense of remoteness, solitude, tranquillity and of nature in the raw.[1] These areas tend to be in the uplands, though selected forests and coasts also engender some of the same feelings. Recent changes in the economy of upland agriculture in England and Wales, brought on partly by economic forces and partly by crises such as BSE and FMD, have created an opportunity for re-wilding in marginal or less profitable areas.

Defining wild

Definitions of wildness, wilderness, wild land and natural areas are frequently contested. James Fenton goes some way towards providing us with working definitions of wilderness and wild land.[2] These are:

> **Wild land:** An area where natural ecological processes are paramount (can be of any size).

> **Wilderness:** An area little affected by current civilisation where nature and natural processes are in charge, and where people can isolate themselves from other people." (After Fenton, 1996, p.17)[2]

257

Although northern England possesses some of the largest tracts of land outside of Scotland that fit this definition of wild land, the emphasis in England and Wales might best be placed not only on conserving existing areas, but on developing new wild lands where the opportunities arise.

The National Parks in England and Wales, and now in Scotland, are together with other conservation areas such as Areas of Outstanding Natural Beauty (AONBs) and National Nature Reserves (NNRs) are key candidates for rewilding schemes because of favourable management and planning structures and the wilder character of these landscapes. Indeed, the notion of rewilding got a major prompt in 1991, when the Edwards review of National Parks of England and Wales proposed "a number of experimental schemes on a limited scale should be set up in National Parks where farming is withdrawn entirely and the natural succession of vegetation is allowed to take its course".[3]

The Council for National Parks (CNP) then outlined plans for enhancement of the wild qualities of National Parks in its 1998 publication *Wild by Design*.[4] The document describes two broad categories of wilder areas:

> **"Semi-natural areas,** which appear natural but are in fact influenced by management for agriculture or forestry.
>
> **Near-natural areas,** where the land is totally divorced from agricultural or forestry use – in which natural processes are encouraged to maintain the diversity of habitats, and vegetation is free to vary naturally with variations in the physical environment."

Mapping what's wild

The authors have mapped landscape variables pertaining to wildness and rewilding potential using Geographical Information Systems (GIS) and national datasets to map the wilderness continuum according to remoteness, both from settlements and mechanised access, and naturalness of the landscape in terms of absence of obvious human artefacts and ecological integrity of the land cover.[1] This approach has been published in an interactive form to survey public perceptions of wild land in Britain. http://www.ccg.leeds.ac.uk/teaching/wilderness/.

A typical map of the wilderness continuum for England and Wales is shown in Figure 1, with inset of the northeast in detail. Boundaries drawn on the inset map show how wild land areas intersect with designated conservation area boundaries including the Northumberland National Park and North Pennines AONB.

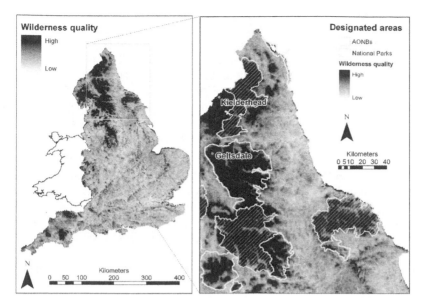

Fig. 1 Mapping wilderness quality in the North East

Rewilding the North-east

Several rewilding projects are local to the Northumberland National Park and North Pennines AONB and their respective management plans refer to enhancing naturalness and biodiversity through appropriate land management and agri-environment schemes. With the renewed interest on natural processes as drivers for nature conservation, a number of areas in northern England illustrate different approaches. There are examples on privately owned land (e.g. shooting estates and utility companies), areas in public ownership (e.g. Forest Enterprise and Ministry of Defence) and reserves owned by conservation bodies (e.g. Wildlife Trusts and RSPB). Some examples are set out below.

Kielderhead (Forest Enterprise)

One of the longest standing examples of rewilding (although this term is not used) without the influence of agricultural grazing has taken place at Kielderhead, deep in the Kielder Forest on the border between Northumberland and Scotland. The area had originally been intended to be planted with conifers, but by the time the foresters reached the area it was realised that the altitude and climate were too severe. As a result, this 3,500 ha area has remained unplanted. The eastern half remained split between three agricultural units, with the western half having no management input over 30 years. The site forms part of the Kielderhead and Emblehope Moors SSSI.

259

In the case of Kielderhead 'no management input' means no sheep grazing, other than from occasional escapees from the neighbouring farm units, grazing by a flock of feral goats, varying in size but currently at about 70 individuals, natural grazing by deer, no pest control and no burning. The impacts of this has been development of a lush vegetation with heather regenerating naturally, very little development of shrubs because of the grazing by goats, and little in the way of seed source, some regeneration of Sitka spruce and an interesting bird community with moderate numbers of red grouse, hen harriers, peregrine falcon, merlin, golden plover, dunlin and other upland waders.

This area was the subject of a report commissioned by the Countryside Agency on the social and economic effects of developing new wild land. The report concluded that taking extensive areas out of agricultural production for rewilding projects would lead to negative social and economic impacts for the region, but did concede that opportunities exist for extending and enhancing areas of semi-natural habitat and developing nature-based tourism across the region.[5] However, the report was published ahead of recent CAP reforms, and so may paint a less than true picture of rewilding opportunities under the new regime of the Single Farm Payment.

Geltsdale

The RSPB Reserve at Geltsdale in the northwest corner of the North Pennines AONB is one of the RSPB's largest reserves in England. The reserve consists largely of high moorland and blanket bog, with a substantial coverage of woodland on the lower slopes. An ambitious project is now under way to redevelop the open woodland coverage of the historic wood pasture known as the 'Kings Forest of Geltsdale'. The project will create a 200 ha area of woodland pasture, combined with the retention of farmed areas, which will enhance the local landscape in accordance with AONB Management Objectives. The area has been temporarily isolated by fencing, and trees have been planted to kick-start the regeneration process. Planting is at a variety of densities with up to 40% open space. Extensive cattle grazing will be introduced once the canopy cover is beyond browsing height.

Wild Ennerdale

Since 2000 the National Trust and the Forestry Commission have been devising proposals for a combined management plan for Ennerdale in the Lake District. The wild character of Ennerdale was identified as being of primary significance. In 2002 United Utilities joined the partnership and a vision for the project was agreed: "To allow the evolution of Ennerdale as a wild valley for the benefit of people relying more on natural processes to shape its landscape and ecology".

The project is enabling natural forces to become more dominant in the Ennerdale Valley. It hopes the resulting area will provide special conservation habitats and an inspirational visitor experience. The project is explained in full elsewhere in this edition.

Naturalness and wild land

Both the management plan for the North Pennines AONB and that of Northumberland National Park Authority identify large sites where a minimum intervention approach can be established, monitored and reviewed. The North Pennines AONB Management Plan states: "Though active management has resulted in the countryside we see today, in some places the intensity has been such that wildlife has survived in spite of it, rather than because of it." It suggests that an approach that promotes naturalness in conservation can have the following advantages:

- scrub, woodland and rocky ecosystems will be restored more cheaply and less contentiously;

- natural dynamism will be restored which, in time, will promote habitats of increasing complexity;

- such landscapes would be richer in wildlife which is visually appealing, with more texture and seasonal colour;

- more natural landscapes can provide refuge for species needing a range of habitats, such as black grouse; and

- promotion of the conservation of common resources to help us understand the capacity of nature to recover form unsustainable exploitation.

The locations of these rewilding projects are shown in Figure 1a. These projects already lie within some of the wildest parts of the countryside, but are amongst large tracts of wild and remote country that offer up further potential for re-wilding projects.

Seeing the benefits for real

In *Wild by Design* the CNP highlights the challenge of rewilding as having "the commitment to leave minimal intervention areas on a much larger scale (landscapes of thousands of hectares) and over much longer periods (hundreds of years)".[4] The real challenge is the successful integration of rewilding objectives with primary industry such as farming and forestry, or in Fraser-Darling's words "Wilderness <u>and</u> Plenty".[6] The key to the challenge will be

261

selling the benefits of rewilding to the farmers, landowners, planners, politicians, conservationists, pressure groups and local and visiting public, as an alternative to existing land uses. Already, a number of dedicated organisations, individuals and embryonic groups are attempting to do this.

More projects like Geltsdale and Wild Ennerdale, that illustrate the issues for real, will help us all learn from the experience.

References

1. Carver, S., Evans, A. & Fritz, S. (2002) Wilderness attribute mapping in the United Kingdom. in *International Journal of Wilderness*. 8(1), 24-29.

2. Fenton, J. (1996) Wild land or wilderness – is there a difference? *ECOS* 17(2), 12-18.

3. Edwards, R. (1991) *Fit for the Future.* 4. (Recommendation 6.3) Report of the National Parks Review Panel. Countryside Commission, Cheltenham, CCP 334.

4. Council for National Parks (1998) *Wild by Design in the National Parks of England and Wales: a guide to the issues*. CNP, London.

5. Countryside Agency (2002) The Social and Economic Effects of Developing New Wild Land in Northumberland. Final Report by Natural Capital Management. pp.167.

6. Fraser-Darling, F. (1970) *Wilderness and Plenty.* Houghton Mifflin Co., London.

Rewilding the Tweed

ECOS 25 (3/4) 24-28 (2006)
This article looks at habitat improvement work focused on the River Tweed and its tributaries. Concentrated in the sparsely populated headwaters, in a landscape dominated by the effects of overgrazing, the work shows how organisations working in partnership can have an effect at the catchment scale.

LUKE COMINS

The river, its catchment and its landscape

The Tweed Rivers Heritage Project has begun to have a real impact on the expansion of native habitats of parts of the Scottish Borders and North Northumberland. The Tweed catchment is over 2000 square miles and straddles the English-Scottish Border. It is a rural area with farming, fishing and forestry being some of the mainstays of the economy, against a background of decline of the once famous textile industry. The river and its associated heritage is one of the region's biggest assets. Tweed Forum is an umbrella organisation which promotes the wise and sustainable use of the Tweed and its tributaries through integrated catchment management and planning. There are 30 members including many organisations with an interest in the management of the Tweed on either side of the English-Scottish border.

The Tweed Rivers Heritage Project (TRHP) was borne from a desire of the membership to take river management beyond the confines of the channel and look at the wider picture. The Project was developed by the membership "to conserve, enhance and promote the natural, built and cultural heritage of the Tweed and increase the recreational opportunities and quality of life in the region." After a thorough consultation process; rigorous project rationalisation and integration, the resulting project consists of 50 schemes with a total spend of £9m. Half of this comes from the Heritage Lottery Fund whilst the rest is made up of a complex funding package with over 60 different funding partners.

The project recognises that the landscape is a function of natural, social and economic history and in managing this 'tapestry' it is necessary to look at all the threads that make it up. The 50 projects fall into four main categories: the natural heritage including wildlife and landscape conservation; built and cultural heritage associated with the river; access and recreation improvements in and around this heritage; and education and interpretation of the river and its heritage.[1]

The rewilding work revolves around key species, habitats and landscape. The majority of this work has been carried out in the more mountainous headwaters which represent the most remote and undeveloped parts of the catchment. These include the Cheviots bounding the South of the catchment, Tweedsmuir and Moorfoots to the West and Lammermuir hills to the North of the catchment.

Tackling habitat loss

There is one dominant ecological problem that has shaped these head water areas into their present state and that is the loss of habitat. This is largely due to agricultural intensification and, in particular, overgrazing. Due to historic clearances, the region has one of the lowest percentages (less than 1%)[2] of ancient woodland in the UK despite having a history of ancient woodlands, such as the Ettrick Forest and Jed Forest. Much of the natural habitat has been cleared or drained to improve the pasture potential and the high stocking densities have meant that the grazing pressure has been intense. In addition to the clearance of trees and shrubs to increase the grazing area, there has been a corresponding loss of heather and herb rich meadows; wetlands have been drained and what vegetation remains is reduced to a short turf of very little ecological value. There are no fallow periods so natural regeneration can never take place. This has led to an upland landscape dominated by bald rolling hills only interrupted by the occasional block of non native commercial forestry.

In the riparian zone the loss of lush marginal vegetation around the watercourse through severe grazing combined with poaching by livestock has led to a decline in the integrity of the banks particularly during high flows. This is largely because healthy marginal vegetation binds the bank substrate together and acts as a cushion against high flows. This increased susceptibility to erosion leads to wide, shallow streams that have little wildlife value due to the complete lack of suitable habitat.

The irony is that it is often perceived by the general public as a wild and starkly beautiful landscape when in fact it is degraded and unnatural.

Rewilding - the objectives and the achievements

Whilst some habitat work was carried out prior to the project, much of it was done in isolation and it is only since the TRHP that efforts have become more integrated and strategic as the bigger picture has been taken into account. A number of organisations have been carrying out similar types of habitat work in the upland areas under the TRHP although each of them have different approaches.

The main players with a riparian focus include Borders Forest Trust, which improves and expands native woodland through sustainable management; Northumberland National Park, with a wide landscape and biodiversity remit; and the Tweed Foundation which is concerned with fishery enhancements (Salmon fishing bringing in £13m a year to the local economy and supports over 500 jobs[3]).

All of these organisations work with farmers and landowners to increase and restore these lost habitats although this is conditioned by the needs of the farmer and loss of grazing area. Many of the land owners are keen to work on a far greater scale, but they are restricted by the majority of the land being under tenancy arrangements.

Despite these differing remits, the nature of the work remains similar with the two main prescriptions being the exclusion of livestock through fencing to allow natural regeneration, and the planting of native trees and shrubs. The effect on aesthetics and biodiversity is easily apparent in such an open landscape and the success can be gauged by the status of Local Biodiversity Action Plan indicator species such as Black Grouse, Ring Ouzel, otters and Atlantic Salmon which rely on the restoration of the whole ecosystem to maintain healthy numbers. The recent return of ospreys to the upper Tweed acts as a prime indicator of wildness and the Forum has actively promoted the tourist potential of such an iconic species.

Once fenced off, the riparian vegetation quickly takes off and streams narrow and become deeper providing better cover for fish. Shade from trees and shrubs guards against high water temperatures in the summer and the organic input from leaf litter increases the invertebrate populations and thus the food supply of fish. The increased vegetation enhances the microclimate and provides food and cover for a far greater variety of insects, birds and mammals.

The main difficulty in getting these projects established is the reluctance of farmers to lose valuable pasture, particularly as the valley floor offers some of the best grazing. To address this the Borders Forest Trust has reintroduced wood pasture up the valley sides. The project uses robust individual box tree guards that do not reduce the grazing area yet will have massive landscape and biodiversity impact in years to come.

River Lilburn - before fencing (Tweed Forum)

River Kilburn - after fencing (Tweed Forum)

River Till - before (Tweed Forum)

River Till - after (Tweed Forum)

The other big player in the uplands is the Forestry Commission with a very large landholding and with objectives much broader than timber production. The Forum has worked closely with the FC on opening up the often ecological barren old style conifer plantations and planting native species along the stream banks. Work to improve conditions for black grouse includes 'feathering' the forest edges to create a glade habitat, creating ponds and scrapes, blocking drainage ditches, scarifying rank heather and planting native trees. All this has additional benefits for the character of the landscape.

There are a host of other Forum members who have complimentary projects under the TRHP banner who are all restoring lost habitats including FWAG (ponds and tress), Scottish Water (native replanting around its upland reservoirs) and Scottish Borders Council (tree grant scheme) and Northumberland Wildlife Trust (restoration of raised mires).

The sum of the parts

The combined actions of many bodies have delivered benefits for biodiversity and the landscape along the Tweed. The accompanying map shows the work of just two organisations (BFT – Borders Forest Trust and TF – Tweed Foundation) involved in the project and how it is beginning to join up with the remnants of ancient woodland. This together with agri-environment and foresty grants such as Rural Stewardship Scheme and Woodland Grant Scheme are beginning to create a robust ecological network. However, efforts are often frustrated by being forced to compromise on scale, and this will only change through measures which encourage lighter stocking densities.

A further frustration is that the economic benefits are often not recognised. These include the more obvious such as fishing, but also the increasingly important nature-based tourism sector to which the success of the osprey and salmon viewing projects on Tweed are a testament. There are also the savings that could be made by reducing the flood risk to downstream areas by slowing the run-off and reducing the 'peak' of flood hydrograph.

Tweed Forum will continue to work with its members to encourage further habitat work on the ground. It will also continue to influence CAP reform and the implementation the Water Framework Directive, so these complement and add value to these efforts, rather than standing in the way as they have done in the past.

References and notes
1.See www.tweedforum.com for more information.
2. Scottish Borders Woodlands Strategy, *Draft Review 2004*. Scottish Borders Council.
3. The Tweed Foundation. (1996) Economic Report – *The Way Forward* .

THE NORTH WEST

Wild Ennerdale – letting nature loose

ECOS 25 (3/4) 34-38 (2006)
The bodies responsible for managing Ennerdale are letting natural forces etch out the future.

GARETH BROWNING & RACHEL YANIK

"As he approaches the vale of Ennerdale, in whose bosom one of the most enchanting of the lakes is seated, he will find the rugged scenery of the country gradually refining, and as he winds round the foot of Pillar, he will discover a vista which cannot fail to strike the most indifferent observer with astonishment and pleasure"

> **Extract from William Wordsworth's *A Guide to the Lakes*, 1789**

A wild valley, a violent river...

Ennerdale has witnessed many changes to its landscape since Wordsworth wrote the above remarks over 200 years ago. During that time, the main influences have been farming practices, water management and the arrival of forestry activities in the 1920s. More recently, a new change is developing, supported by the three main landowners in the valley: the Forestry Commission, National Trust and United Utilities, driven by a range of economic, social and environmental factors.

The Ennerdale valley is located on the north west fringe of the Lake District National Park. The valley extends to around 4,500ha with an altitude range of 770m and valley width ranging from 1.7 to 5.2 kms. The majority of the southern ridge (1498ha) is a Site of Special Scientific Interest (SSSI) and cSAC, designated for being one of the best examples of altitudinal succession in England. This generates some of the most dramatic, awe-inspiring scenery in Cumbria. In the valley bottom flows the River Liza, one of the most wild and

269

geomorphologically natural rivers in England. The Liza is not under direct human influence anywhere along its length and is constantly eroding new courses (moving as much as 100m in a flood event in the late 1990s) and regularly depositing vegetation and trees downstream. The western end of the valley is dominated by Ennerdale Water (338ha), a SSSI designated for its lakeshore habitats and flora and fauna which includes examples of nationally rare and local species, including the Arctic Char. Walking into the valley, the visitor is struck by the spectacular craggy mountains, numerous waterfalls, violent river, green conifer forest, mixed woodland and perhaps most significantly, the sense of remoteness and solitude.

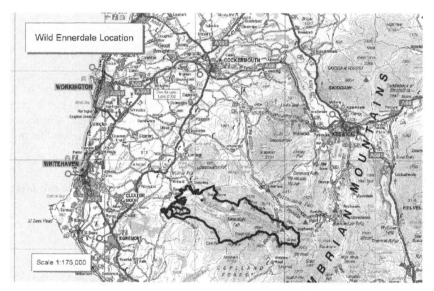

Wild Ennerdale in the western Lakeland

What's wild about Ennerdale?

In the late 1990s the Forestry Commission and National Trust both agreed they needed a shared vision for the valley. Over the next couple of years the two organisations held numerous meetings and consulted with local communities, visitors and a number of landscape ecologists.

In 2002 the original partners were joined by United Utilities (owner of Ennerdale Water) and the 'Wild Ennerdale' partnership was formed, with a philosophy encompassing two key areas:

Biocentric - ecologically based: encouraging the greater involvement of natural forces in the long-term development of the valley in terms of the distribution, extent and variety of habitats and ecosystems that make up the future character of the valley.

Anthropocentric - people based: recognising that wildness is a human experience. Seeking ways to increase the sense of wildness by limiting the visible impact of people in the valley but at the same time encouraging the involvement of people in employment, economy and recreation.

The partners believe Ennerdale has wild characteristics in the context of the English landscape due to:

- the large scale of nature
- a sense of remoteness and solitude
- absence of intrusive man-made built structures
- opportunity for unrestricted and challenging exploration and adventure
- plants and animals of special ecological value
- impressive geological features
- cultural-historical features
- ecological processes freely shaping the landscape

The braided River Liza (Gareth Browning)

Looking forward, not back

'Wild Ennerdale' is not about re-creating a past landscape, but about allowing the character of the valley to develop into the future.

The vision agreed between the partners is to "allow the evolution of Ennerdale as a wild valley for the benefit of people, relying more on natural processes to shape its landscape and ecology". As a result, there is no fixed 'end point' for Wild Ennerdale as natural change often occurs over a long period of time, seldom responding to targets, deadlines and funding criteria.

Since the partnership was formed in 2002, efforts have been focused on gathering together a portfolio of information about the valley. A full vegetation survey was be completed in 2004 (2,649ha has already been surveyed by ecologists, with 34 National Vegetation Classification habitats identified[1]). This will be added to the Historic Landscape Survey[2] completed in 2003 which identified 552 individual archaeological sites. The earliest occupation of the valley dates back to the Bronze Age and the report described Ennerdale as being of "exceptional archaeological importance."

Ennerdale (Gareth Browning)

What detracts from wild character

Much work has been done through discussions with local people and visitors to the valley to identify what they view as wild features in the area, and what features detract from the sense of wildness people experience.

Examples of detracting features people have identified include:

- the network of forest roads & tracks
- vehicle movements

- blocks of closely planted spruce
- stark boundaries between different land use
- areas of recently felled forest
- fences and signs which restrict the sense of openness; and
- the lack of diverse vegetation in some areas.

With help from a newly established 'advisory group' the partnership is drawing up proposals to reduce detracting features, enhance the wild features and give natural processes a greater involvement in the future development of the valley. GIS has been used to show the spatial distribution of 'wild' and 'detracting' features and has helped in understanding and identifying the distribution of the 'sense of wildness' across the valley.

The contradictions of conifers

The partnership is also exploring the future of forests and grazing and how the associated natural process can be given more freedom. Through the past four years of discussion, results show that people have mixed views about the conifer forest, viewing it as both a wild and a detracting factor. Specifically, the large groups of conifer in the central valley, the larch by Ennerdale Water and areas of well thinned conifer woodland is viewed by most to add to the character of the valley as a wild place. On many occasions, people remark that it reminds them of Canada or Scotland and that the combination of conifer, river, scree, crags and mountains within one landscape is very important. In contrast, the dense spruce and regeneration at the eastern end of the valley is seen as a significant detracting factor. This could also be attributed to the narrow width of the valley and the monoculture of the forest. To address this issue, all the remaining mature (seed bearing) spruce at the eastern end of the valley is currently being felled and will, over the next five to eight years, be replaced by the planting of native broadleaves produced from locally collected seed. In addition, there will be less clear-felling and restocking, and the forest will be allowed greater freedom to develop for itself. Levels and distribution of regeneration versus grazing will determine where and what species should regenerate.

The future of natural grazing

The Partnership wishes to see a greater involvement in natural processes influencing grazing patterns, with a move away from grazing that is wholly determined by land ownership, fences and subsidies. One natural process currently missing is a large dynamic disturbance factor which could be provided by introducing cattle. The introduction of cattle is planned to a pilot area of 145ha, with the potential to extend into adjacent sites over a 10 year period, covering an area up to 2000ha. The aim is to reach a point where the herd is able to develop and explore the valley free from intervention and control. This clearly raises many issues, not least of which include public safety and animal welfare, however the partnership is keen to explore these with the appropriate bodies and is not committed to any particular timescales.

The work of Wild Ennerdale will involve setting certain 'trigger levels' for intervention. For example, were the valley to become significantly forested and obscure views of the crags and river, this would trigger intervention as views of these features contribute significantly to the sense of wildness.

Ennerdale: after removal of spruce in the foreground (Gareth Browning)

The next century...

So, what will Ennerdale look like in 100 or more years time? The reality is that we don't really know. The direction in which natural processes shape the valley and the influence of external factors, along with the degree to which we choose to let go or intervene as land managers will all have an effect. What happens beyond the realms of the present partners will be determined by future generations. We hope that the Ennerdale of the future will be a more diverse and robust environment and a major enhancement of what is perhaps its most significant characteristic – the sense of wildness.

References

1.The National Trust (2003) Ennerdale Survey of National Vegetation Classification Communities, Rigby Jerram. National Trust, Cirencester.

2. The National Trust (2003) Historic Landscape Survey, Ennerdale. Oxford Archaeology North, National Trust, Cirencester.

SCOTLAND

Alladale's wilderness – seeing through the fence

ECOS 29 (3/4) 18-24 (2008)
How far does Alladale's concept of fenced-in predators aid the cause of returning former native species to Scotland?

PETER TAYLOR

Following the September 2008 conference on species reintroductions at Findhorn[1], the participants were hosted at three different projects across Scotland: Alladale in Easter Ross; Glen Affric; and Carrifran in the Southern Uplands. Of these, Alladale is pressing ahead with bringing back the wolf, lynx and bear, albeit in restricted enclosures, whilst Glen Affric[2] and Carrifran[3] are pursuing native woodland restoration with landscape-scale management, and only much later envisage the full spectrum of predator-prey relations. The Alladale project may not see itself as integral to the debate on predator reintroductions, but many others believe it has great influence given its tangible goals of having large carnivores in place soon, and its high profile in the media. In this article I discuss the strategic issues presented by the project.

The House and the Glen

As we entered the Alladale estate, our motorcade wound its way up to the big house, via a newly bulldozed tradesman's track to the rear and the barn-cum-workshop where Alladale's project manager Hugh Fullerton-Smith briefed us on the project's progress amid all the paraphernalia of a construction operation. Outside stood a gleaming Japanese truck donated to the project. Overalled men scurried amongst the recycled steel beams, halfway shot-blasted and destined for new-build accommodation. A team of Polish builders would be at work – apparently there were no local takers.

In the briefing we heard the context and history of the Alladale Wilderness project , a story now familiar to the public from the recent TV coverage: the house is family home to Paul Lister and also a high-class hunting, shooting and fishing lodge. One reason he chose the estate when scouting for land in the Highlands was that it contains no Munros, which are a magnet for hill walkers who tick-off these peaks above 3,000 feet. Lister's ultimate aim is to bring back large carnivores to the 25,000 acre estate, and hopefully combine the holding with at least one neighbouring land-owner to double the overall size. This could happen by collaboration with an adjoining estate, or through acquiring one when the opportunity arose. Indeed, there was gossip about the prospective sale of a neighbouring holding during our visit.

A small fleet of new Landrovers – not the flashy models, but the genuine workhorses, took us up the glen to the mobile sawmill and the new hydro-station that will service the estate's electrical needs and export a surplus. Two itinerant Kiwi guys worked the sawmill. Elsewhere on the estate, half a dozen men, including locally skilled Scots have been enlisted on the project to use their traditional land management skills. They also oversee visits from local schoolchildren, stretching their skills as they help explain practical estate work, and fishing and hunting, to eager young minds.

Upper part of Alladale showing regeneration after deer-culling (Peter Taylor)

Coming to terms with the fencing

On the way I looked up at the rising hills either side of the glen – badly scarred by new fences. A large wild-boar enclosure and another for the recently imported pair of Elk (Scandinavian Moose), and then a whole series of rectangular pens along one side of the glen marked the experimental smaller wild-boar enclosures – about half-a-dozen, with varying family groups of boar. An Oxford University wildlife biologist oversaw that part of the project – to test out the boar as 'management tools' in controlling bracken and scarifying the heather-covered slopes for future tree planting. Deer had been culled from the valley in order to aid regeneration, but there was constant ingress from above.

Scars that will heal in time - fencing for deer exclusion zones (Peter Taylor)

The boar pens had smaller holding enclosures of galvanised metal, an assortment of buckets, feeding troughs and shelter for the pigs, which it was admitted, were of dubious parentage and in any case, once the study was complete, were destined for the local sausage parlour. They looked very wild to my untrained eye – quite thrilling on first close-up encounter, but the feeling rapidly wore off as they huddled for warmth, and watched intently to see if any extra food would be forthcoming. Some of the pens were half stripped of vegetation.

Penned wild boar - an experiment in bracken control (Peter Taylor)

Our tour took us next to the larger enclosures. The zoologists were studying a family group of boar that built dens but were as invisible as nature intended. The fences were electrified and pocked with day-glow notices of the danger. It appears that one public body required such a warning not to enter, and another regarded them as illegal under the right to roam laws. We learnt that the wider plan to bring back predators was caught in a similar wrangle – with ramblers objecting to the closed nature of the reserve, and government animal welfare regulations opposing keeping predators and prey in the same enclosure.

Finally, I saw the Elk. The male had his head stuck in a blue bucket of specially constituted moose-mash. I contemplated a photo through the steel mesh. Then I saw the female emerging shyly from a birch copse, and again there was a little thrill, momentary, as this prehistoric mammal stood amid Scotland's trees once more, and I could forget the fencing.

Elk - in Scotland after several thousand years absence (Peter Taylor)

The business ethos

Hugh Fullerton-Smith admits they have made some mistakes. They are doing their best to heal the fencing scars, which were a talking point at a previous visit from Trees for Life, who run the Glen Affric restoration project where much fencing has been installed with minimal landscape impact. Alladale is working hard to employ local artisans and bring much-needed employment through the project's support facilities. They are beginning an outreach to schools and the local community. They will build new bothies in an environmentally friendly way, sourcing local materials. The long term vision is to take away the fences (well, the internal ones – because we are reminded, this is not a re-introduction project *per se*). In reality, it is a safari-park on the South African model. As such, it is emphatically a business. It may offer lessons for others, but that is not its intention. It will provide jobs and an educational experience – but the main business, for now in the early stage, is still rooted in the deer-stalkers and fishermen who stay in the hotel.

We didn't get to meet Paul Lister. But a few days later I caught one of the Alladale programmes from the BBC TV series *the Real Monarch of the Glen*. It was very candid – a reality TV show that laid bare the personal dramas of the project, such as the departure of the hotel manageress under the stresses of advertising and running such a remote business. Paul gave the staff a stern talk-to about business acumen – including cutting the portions on the venison-with-everything menu.

Gaining acceptance?

Outside of the fence, the TV programme interviewed Cameron McNeish, a leading figure in Scotland's outdoor recreation movement. He has taken a defiant stance. In aggrieved tones, his voice represented 500 years of colonial oppression, dispossession and imposed values – even if all he talked of was the right to roam, now enshrined in Scottish law.

I suddenly felt the fragility of this project. If it did not meet the business goals, if the opposition prevented the dream, then how long would Paul Lister persist? Everything depended upon this one very rich man's whim. The whole estate could be sold on with hardly a dent in its traditional virtues. Is this a model for reintroduction projects in the Highlands? There cannot be room for more than two or three such 'Pleistocene Safari Parks' – and clearly, any further large scale fencing projects would encounter even fiercer opposition.

Given the lack of acceptance in some quarters, could the project learn from others' experience. Firstly, there is a spectrum of rewilding, and it might serve to explore the further reaches, as exemplified in Glen Affric and Carrifran. In the former, the land is held in a trust for all time and over 20 years the Trees for Life team has gained the active cooperation of nearby estates, the Forestry Commission and the National Trust - largely because there has been a great deal of giving of energy to those outside projects. Trees for Life worked with others planting trees voluntarily for two decades before being given an estate of their own. They held the dream – not just of a complete ecosystem but of a returning *relationship* to the forest, its animals and plants, and the spirit of wholeness that it exudes. The *wild* has to come from *within* first. Otherwise, people become mere watchers or worse, entrepreneurs and other *takers* where the sense of giving something back is lost. This can apply as much to adrenalin thrills as to high-quality venison-filled lunch-boxes that merely and momentarily make people feel connected to something wilder.

Anyone who has spent time with indigenous peoples notices first and foremost the gratitude and the giving – the *reciprocal* nature of the relationship. But what have we, in our vulnerable humanity and short lives, immersed now in an all-pervading economy, got to give to the land, to the Glen, and the spirit behind it all?

Finding friends

Two days later at Carrifran in the Southern Uplands, the smaller band of visitors was guided through the terrain. We reached an almost invisible turf-roofed bunker with a little stove, where the track faded, and all around, after only eight years, the forest was visibly returning and all trace of human exploitation receding. I realised that although it would not describe itself as such, this whole project was a ritual of a kind – not just a dream of something wilder returning that is beyond species and habitat plans, European directives or lottery grants – but an element of belonging shared by the holders of the land, the many hundreds with their stake in the project's goals. Of course, Carrifran also represents a constituency of people who have thought through the scientific basis, the practical management issues, the communication needs, and created a network of committed and skilled members who undertake tasks to manage and nurture it.

The contrast with Alladale is stark. Paul Lister risks creating opposition that runs deep in the Scottish psyche. It could be viewed as an old-style colonial enterprise where the wilderness becomes playground for a recreational indulgence – a man's world of hunting, shooting and fishing. It is also a businessman's adventure. Everyone works for a single landowner who is finite upon this earth. No one else can be truly committed, and there is no constituency of people who feel emotionally linked to the project and will strive to nurture it, and fight its cause for the long term.

These issues are inherent in the private landlord model. For the project to be successful it needs to find a mutually acceptable solution to the access issue as well as a way through the animal welfare legislation and the ecological dynamics of enclosed herbivores and predators. Then it would be an exemplar - one of a number of different schemes from which lessons can be learnt, across different sectors. Visitors would be able to see a spectrum of ecological relations and it would stand as a major educational project. As a business model for the wider private sector, however, it cannot be repeated without compromising its unique selling point – how many such safari parks would be viable in the Highlands?

Can the project be fine-tuned to tackle some of these issues? The outer fence is a problem, but then without the enclosure it is doubtful that permission would be granted for elk and boar as the project would flag up all the legal problems of re-introductions. On the organisational side, there could be scope for a wider membership and involvement (a Friends of Alladale), perhaps by setting up a charitable organisation or a link with other charitable bodies in a wider group whose membership and grant-aid could equally provide for traditional skills and employment. There are many models – some of which would keep the private landlord status and perhaps provide an example for others to follow, and others which might move closer to the Carrifran example of a dispersed membership.

Ecological integrity

On an ecological level, much headway could be made by pushing the envelope regarding boar, beaver and elk – not in the form of a fenced safari park, but a genuine re-introduction, whilst keeping the goals of wolf, lynx and bear alive for a later time. The idea of even an enlarged 50,000 acres acting as an ecological model for all these species is anyway dubious. This is still a small area and would be highly compromised by future climatic shifts and the inability of herbivores to migrate. The small numbers of wolves and lynx that such an area could support would need to be culled as they increased, and the area is probably too small for a viable brown bear population.

I may be unduly pessimistic but I can't see the project succeeding in its present strategy and it needs some element that will strengthen its position within the Scottish psyche. As it stands, if successful as a business, I am not sure it will advance the cause of reintroductions – indeed, it could work the other way where a future Scottish minister might well take the view that as people could see the animals better in such an enclosed space, Scotland need go no further to embrace genuine reintroductions.

References

1. For a write up of the see 'events' at www.wildland-network.org.uk
2. www.snh.org.uk/nnr-scotland/reserve.asp?NNRId=17
3. www.carrifran.org.uk

Alladale's fenced wilderness
-making a breakthrough?

ECOS 27 (3/4) 30-35 (2006)
Will the vision of a complete Highland ecosystem at Alladale fare any better than previous proposals for reintroductions?

ROGER SIDAWAY

Given the fiasco over the reintroduction of the beaver into Scotland early this year, can wealthy landowners claiming the sanctity of private property rights succeed where more cautious conservation bodies fear to tread? To exponents of change, the tortuous process of developing rational evidence-based policies is daunting. It is tempting to conclude that caution only gets us so far and that it needs the brass neck of a passionate landowner to make large-scale species reintroductions happen.

Predators and fencing

Paul Lister, heir to the MFI retail empire, bought this Sutherland estate in 2003 and has invested heavily in an award-winning tourism enterprise. Alladale House offers luxury accommodation, seclusion and guided excursions into the hills as well as the usual highland opportunities for deer shooting and salmon fishing. Inspired by the safari parks he has visited in Africa, he now plans to re-introduce a range of predators to reduce deer numbers on his 23,000 estate and to persuade neighbouring estates to join in the scheme, thereby doubling its area. So far he has planted large areas with native trees and created a small 1200 electric-fenced enclosure stocked with 22 wild boar. His longer-term plan is to fence the remaining area and stock it with elk, wolf, lynx and brown bear. Lister sees this as a logical extension of his dream to restore a complete Highland ecosystem and the fence as the only way the Scottish Executive will sanction the reintroduction of controversial species like wolves and bears.[1]

Two aspects of the scheme make the proposal particularly controversial: predators and fencing. Although reintroducing the wolf to the Scottish highlands was first proposed in the late 1960s[2], the superstition and mythology surrounding the beast has prompted catchy headlines whenever new proposals are mooted. The Deer Commission for Scotland is unconvinced that predation is an effective means of controlling deer populations [3] while local sheep farmers are concerned about loss of stock from possible wolf escapes. Lynx predation is equally controversial in sporting circles. Hence the comment of Bert Burnett of the Scottish Gamekeepers Association: "I also don't believe for one minute that lynx wouldn't attack stock, and lambs would be especially vulnerable." [4] Lister counters these objections saying the animals will be tagged and compensation paid for loss of farm stock. But as the scheme is without precedent, the legalities are obscure. To release predators to run wild within the fenced area probably requires a licence under the Wildlife and Countryside Act if not a zoo licence. Admitting he needs Scottish Executive permission, Lister claims "It's totally do-able. It's just whether or not we can deal with all the red tape we've managed to swamp ourselves with in this country".[5]

Although there are precedents of sorts for fenced reintroductions in Scotland with 11 wolves already in the Highland Wildlife Park in Kingussie and beaver in a private enclosure in Angus, neither is on the scale of the Alladale proposal. The main opponents to a fenced enclosure on this scale are the Ramblers' Association, as it transgresses both the spirit and the intent of the 'freedom to roam' provisions of the Land Reform (Scotland) Act which gives Scottish walkers arguably the best access rights in Europe. Ian McCall, Ramblers' Scotland campaign and policy coordinator, claims the erection of the 10 foot high 50 mile fence would need special exemption from the Scottish Executive. Claiming to support the reintroduction of wolves ("If we can't reintroduce them without putting a big fence around them then it is not worth doing?" [6]) the Ramblers' are particularly concerned about the precedent such a fence would set in tempting other privacy-minded landowners and pop stars to dream up similar wheezes to preserve their splendid isolation in Scotland.

Another objection to a fenced enclosure is that it isolates the introduced population and its prey from natural patterns of migration with the likely need to curtail numbers by shooting rather than more natural processes of disease and starvation (which are unlikely to appeal to squeamish safari park visitors).[7]

Lessons from the failed beaver scheme

The history of attempts to reintroduce the European beaver to Britain were documented in *ECOS* 27 (1).[8] Prompted by the 1992 European Habitats Directive, SNH began a laborious programme of investigating the effects of introducing beaver into the wild in 1994. Forestry Commission woodland on the Knapdale peninsula was selected as the pilot reintroduction site, and the project gained popular support according to national opinion polls and local consultations. The main opposition came from influential local landowners whose views were often based on suppositions that European beaver, like their North American counterparts, are prodigious dam builders and eat fish.

"The concerns raised about the reintroduction of beaver are mainly based on ignorance, conservative thought and fear of the unknown. ... to an extent the stridency of a minority of the landed class is driven by a legacy of expectation that their views are correct and should be acted upon." [9]

Ironically when drawing up a programme of speakers for a lecture series at Edinburgh University earlier this year, I had no difficulty finding supporters but considerable difficulty in finding a speaker opposed to beaver reintroduction, even from known opponents in farming and angling circles. The 'opponent' from the Scottish Countryside Alliance sceptically questioned the basic premises of the scheme.

The decision by the Scottish Executive to refuse a license for the trial was even more curious. The Executive's permission was certainly required to release beaver into the wild.[10] But the ostensible reason, that reintroduction would have potentially damaging effects on an SPA, does not tally with the obligation on member states under Article 22 of the European Habitats Directive of 1992 to consider species reintroductions. Didn't the right hand know what the left hand was up to? A private complaint that SNH should not have been a proponent of the beaver scheme but as adviser to the Executive should have remained on the sidelines, also lacks credibility. It appears from the infighting that if the project had been promoted by an NGO such as the Scottish Wildlife Trust, it would have been successful.

Perhaps the circumstances surrounding the beaver reintroduction make it a special case. But if a carefully researched pilot scheme promoted by the Executives' conservation advisers is overruled by cautious bureaucrats[11], what chance is there that the Executive will favour the more ambitious Alladale scheme?

Paul Lister has done some basic-level consultation. He held a conference for landowners and land managers in Alladale in November 2004 and reported that they were 'generally positive' towards the scheme.[12] A public meeting in the neighbouring village of Ardgay in September 2005 was more eventful. A picture was circulated of a man who had been mauled by a bear and Lister apparently angered opponents by refusing to allow the proposal to be put to a vote. One less than happy participant said "He was there to put his opinion and that was all" [13], clearly illustrating the limitations of public meetings.

Lack of policy direction – Scary or what?

On the one hand, we have the wildland agenda cautiously tempering enthusiasm for charismatic species with recognising the need for research on predator-prey relationships and for gleaning the most from experience from bird re-introductions. The case for wolf reintroduction would certainly gain from the meticulous approach taken toward the lynx.[14]

On the other hand, as in so many other conservation topics, there is a lack of policy guidance. Witness the Scottish Executive's poor track record of developing policy on conservation topics and reconciling EU directives. The nearest we get is the 'species management' approach contained in SNH's recently completed consultation. This 'Action Framework' for species management includes four mammals: beaver, red squirrel, wildcat and water vole as 'species for conservation action'. Two 'invasive non-native species' species: mink and hedgehog (on islands) are proposed for drastic management, while red deer are categorised as 'species for sustainable use'. The observation that "The management of red deer as a sporting resource and the absence of natural predators, can lead to locally high numbers leading to levels of grazing and trampling on natural habitats" [15] is as near as the document gets to any notion of the wildland agenda. SNH's pronouncements following this consultation are expected soon.

We lack a well-defined and transparent decision making process to get from national policy to local consultation or vice versa. Whilst we dither, precedents could be set by irresponsible clandestine releases of wolf and lynx by groups such as the Wild Beasts Trust.[16] Although many suspect that the Wild Beasts Trust has not implemented its announced releases, lynx sightings across Britain are on the increase, along with consistent stories of unlicensed breeding and of various subcultures using lynx for 'sport'. Both the former native Eurasian lynx and (less often) the American bobcat are seen by witnesses. As *ECOS* goes to the press we learn of a new consultation by the Scottish Executive on invasive non-native species. Although wild boar is recognised as a former native species, it is one of the five mammals on the list of 150 species included in the consultation. The apparent purpose of this inclusion is to ensure that any reintroduction should be conducted responsibly, under licence as part of an official programme or project. See:
 www.scotland.gov.uk/Publications/2006/11/InvasiveSpeciesResponse

Where do we go from here?

Ideally we would chart our progress on reintroductions against broadly agreed species action plans with staged reintroductions over a 10 year period or longer. Even if this is the time to take risks we are left with the challenge of trying to gain more widespread support from within key stakeholder groups, especially from landowning, farming, forestry, and game interests, and indeed within many wildlife groups.

If we pursue ambitious species reintroduction projects beyond fenced experiments such as at Alladale, we will need to develop support, advice and outreach measures for the areas hosting these ventures. Here are some of the issues and measures which would need consideration:

What are the ecosystem consequences of the particular species in mind, and indeed, what are the likely effects of more than one reintroduced species within a habitat and neighbouring forest and farmland? We can never know or predict all the consequences, so how would advice and land-management services be provided to accompany the first tranche of say, beaver and lynx reintroductions?

How can local people, businesses, and landowners gain benefits from the reintroduction, and how can those who experience any disbenefits, be compensated, and/or be given practical advice and support? Grants, visitor income, area branding measures, advice, outreach support, and actual compensation payments may all play a part perhaps.

Species returning to our shores will create new talking points questions, emotions and reactions. No doubt art and literature will help us with this cultural challenge, and indeed playwright Samantha Ellis has already made a start. She has invited ideas for her forthcoming play 'The Stare', on wolves returning to Scotland, and is already getting plenty of advice through her web link at the Ashden Directory: see :
http://www.ashdendirectory.org.uk/featuresView.asp?
pageIdentifier=2006109_74465579&view=

As I look down from my top-floor flat 10 minutes from the centre of Edinburgh on the foxes nestling on the winter warmth of my compost heap, which of us is the 're-introduction'?

References

1 Meiklem, P. J. (2006) 'Landowner feels call of the Wild', *The Big Issue in Scotland*, October 6-12, 6
[2] Wolves and Highlands Foundation
www.wolvesandhumans.org/wolf_reintroduction_scotland.htm
accessed 20/10/06
[3] SCENES June 2005
[4] Quoted in James Reynolds 'Call for lynx to prowl Highlands Again,' *The Scotsman*, 22 January 2005
[5] Adrian Turpin 'Beware of the wolves' *Independent on Sunday*, 25 June 2006
[6] Meiklem, ibid

[7] Peter Taylor personal communication 25/10/06. See also his Knepp article in this issue.

[8] Gow, D. 'Bringing Back the Beaver' *ECOS* 27 (1) 2006, 57-65

[9] Gow ibid

[10] Evans, S. 'The Coming of Wolves' *Daily Telegraph*, 5 September 2006

[11] Watson, J. 'The Call of the Wild' *Scotland on Sunday* 19 February 2006

[12] Gilchrist, J. 'Public opinion is seen as the key to any plans to reintroduce animals like the wolf to Scotland', *The Scotsman*, November 2004

[13] Turpin, ibid

[14] Hetherington, D.(2006) 'The lynx in Britain's past, present and future', *ECOS*, 27,1 66-74

[15] Scottish Natural Heritage (2006) *Making a difference for Scotland's Species: a Framework for Action - Public Consultation*, SNH, Battleby

[16] SCENES, September 2006.

The Carrifran Wildwood project

ECOS 25 (3/4) 11-19 (2004)

The Carrifran Wildwood project has happened through local people wanting to improve their landscape. The way it is being delivered may be as significant as the achievements on the ground, if it convinces people of the value of supporting grass-roots ecological restoration.

PHILIP ASHMOLE & HUGH CHALMERS

The Carrifran Wildwood project is establishing a mosaic of near-natural woodland and heathland vegetation up to 800 m altitude in a whole catchment in the Southern Uplands of Scotland. The initiative came from a local environmental group, and land purchase and much of the restoration work is funded by money donated by the public, with over 800 major stakeholders. Planting is by contractors and volunteers, managed by professional staff and a grass-roots steering group

Getting lost in the woods...

The Tweedsmuir and Moffat Hills in the Southern Uplands of Scotland are perhaps more thoroughly bereft of their natural vegetation than any other part of Britain. The upland habitats now comprise wide expanses of overgrazed sheepwalk, interspersed with hard-edged blocks of Sitka spruce and patchwork areas of heather moorland frequently burnt for management of grouse. Only tiny relict groups of broadleaf trees in steep cleuchs (gullies) provide a glimpse of the native forest that clothed the hills 6,000 years ago.

In some areas woodland contraction may have a partly climatic cause: blanket peat and the associated heather moorland vegetation spread widely in Scotland several millennia ago.[1] In many parts of the Southern Uplands, however, the main cause of forest loss was grazing by domestic stock, together with burning and felling.[2] Sheep were a mainstay of the monastic economy from early medieval times[3] and the denudation occurred so long ago that there is no folk memory of natural forests on the hills.

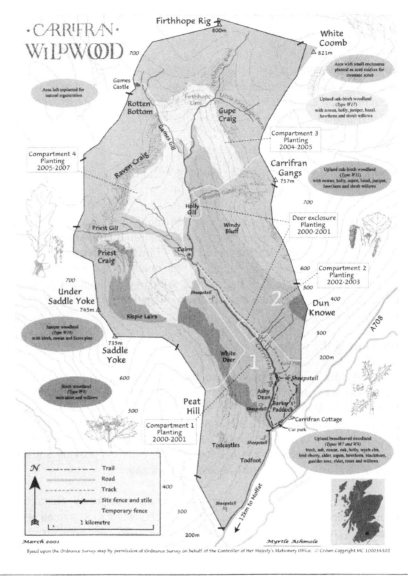

Planting Schematic for Carrifran Wildwood

Carrifran - at the outset

In the early 1990s a group of friends in the Peebles area, saddened at the loss of so much beauty and diversity in the landscape, conceived the bold idea of acquiring an entire valley and transforming it to a relatively natural forest ecosystem. The vision was ambitious and clear, and is embodied in the Mission Statement:

> "The Wildwood project aims to re-create, in the Southern Uplands of Scotland, an extensive tract of mainly forested wilderness with most of the rich diversity of native species present in the area before human activities became dominant. The woodland will not be exploited commercially and the impact of humans will be carefully managed. Access will be open to all, and it is hoped that the Wildwood will be used throughout the next millennium as an inspiration and an educational resource."

The statement reflects the original determination to create a whole range of habitats, from tall forest in a valley bottom to treeline woods and montane scrub near the highest summits, in a valley of at least 1,000 acres. The result would be a relatively natural entity in the landscape where there would be a chance - in years to come - of losing oneself in the woods.

In the context of the challenging debate on rewilding in *ECOS* 25 (1), the vision of the Wildwood project may seem naïve and simplistic. It reflects, however, both understanding of the complexity of the historical and ecological arguments, and impatience with any tendency to substitute endless discussion about issues on which there will always be divergent opinions, for action on the ground. The members of the Wildwood Group were happy to let others continue the argument while they tried to make something happen. They found sufficient justification for their initiative in the contrast between the wholly artificial habitats that now dominate the local countryside and the richer diversity of vegetation structure in past millennia demonstrated by paleoecological evidence from many sites, including Carrifran.[4, 5]

The group is convinced that the lives of local people and visitors will be enhanced by the re-creation of some areas in which agriculture, plantation forestry and intensive game management take a back seat while ecological processes get a chance to flourish. We regret that at the scale of our current project, there will not be room for many species of large herbivores and their co-evolved predators. James Fenton[6], however, can be confident that despite our efforts, there will still be plenty of the sheep-shorn upland habitats that he claims lie within the range of natural vegetation.

Conception rather than conservation
In contrast to a conservation scheme, the Wildwood project was conceived in abstract and thus had to start by finding a suitable site. Initially, the chance of a small community-based group being able to buy a whole valley seemed remote.

The development of the Millennium Forest for Scotland Trust (MFST) funded by the National Lottery gave the group courage to embark on an active search, although in the end none of the money for land purchase came from this source.

A decade on, it is clear that the successful creation of the project stemmed from the grass-roots strength of the Wildwood Group. The origins of the group lay in Peeblesshire Environment Concern (PEC), which was dedicated to raising awareness of global and local green issues. PEC had organised the *Restoring Borders Woodland* conference in 1993 [3], and two years later the Wildwood Group was formed, with around 35 "members" whose diverse talents provided a vibrant mix of idealism, scientific knowledge and practical expertise. Its informal style, flexible structure and consensus approach to decision-making have been key features of the project.

Land and labour - marshalling the resources

It was in negotiations for Carrifran that the calibre and commitment of the group first had an obvious effect. The fact that well respected individuals (for instance in law, land agency and business consultancy) were working for free undoubtedly helped the shift from an opening asking price of £1m for 1,600 acres of hill land to a more realistic figure of £330,000.

However, a third of a million pounds still represented a tough challenge, and the embryonic fund-raising subgroup made a key decision: to ask private individuals to "adopt" nominal half hectares or hectares in the valley by giving £250 or £500 or more (though of course smaller sums were welcomed). The project website www.carrifran.org.uk, designed by a member of the group, played a key role in fundraising from the start. Seven years on, more than 600 Founders (who helped to buy the valley) have been joined by nearly 200 Stewards (who support its restoration) and a large number of regular and one-off contributors. It is clear that the Wildwood project strikes a deep chord in many people, and the existence of this wide network of substantial stakeholders, in Britain and around the world, is one of the remarkable features of the initiative.

The total sum raised from individuals is now over £450,000 (including Gift Aid) and around £150,000 has come from charitable trusts (including a striking commitment by the David Stevenson Trust to pay for all the trees). Crucial support in fundraising came from the John Muir Trust, who viewed the project as complementary to their protection of wild land in Scotland by means of purchase. The upshot was that on 1 January 2000 - after two years of fundraising - Carrifran was purchased and 100 people came to plant the first trees.

Since millennium day it has been possible to access some public funds and increasing professional input has been required for efficient management of a large project. There was a danger that volunteers who had initiated the scheme might feel sidelined. However, this has been largely averted, and those involved have set a high value on the stimulating and forbearing cooperation between the members of the Wildwood Group and the staff of Borders Forest Trust (BFT), the charity that its members helped to establish in winter 1995/96.

The Wildwood Group is now defined as comprising all current members of BFT who are active supporters of the Wildwood project. It functions as a devolved entity within BFT, which has legal responsibility for Carrifran and handles contracts and accounts. Day-to-day management is by the Project Officer advised by a Site Operations Team that also includes the BFT Director and the volunteer Co-ordinator of the Wildwood Project. Policy decisions, however, are made by the Wildwood Steering Group, a self-perpetuating body meeting every two months. It is chaired by turns and comprises about 10 volunteer members, together with the Project Officer and BFT Director; additional BFT staff members and visitors frequently attend. Informal subgroups with wider membership are responsible for ecological planning, fundraising and seed collection. *Wildwood News* is published annually to keep supporters in touch, and BFT members also receive more frequent news in the Trust's newsletters.

Planning and planting

In planning the restoration of Carrifran, strong links with academics and professional foresters have always been fostered, and efforts have been made to learn from experience elsewhere. A senior Forestry Commission staff member was invited to talk to the group about new native woodlands long before the site was found, and study visits have been made to Creag Meagaidh, Ben Lawers, Rum, Mull, the Cairngorms, Deeside, Glen Finglas and elsewhere. In late 1997 the group organised, jointly with Edinburgh University, a conference at the Royal Botanic Garden Edinburgh: *Native woodland establishment in southern Scotland - principles and practice*[5]. This both raised the credibility of the project in the eyes of the professionals whose support was essential, and provided benefits of experience from around Britain on establishment of broadleaf woodland. The latter fed directly into the communal process of developing the Environmental Statement to support the application for Woodland Grant Scheme (WGS) funding.[7] Drafting took place mainly in six long evening meetings in a Peebles pub during 1998, in which the number of participants varied between 12 and 25.

The Wildwood ethos

The wide diversity within the group was evident in these sessions, each of which focused on a different aspect of the project: from detailed discussion of what trees and shrubs were appropriate for establishment at Carrifran, to silvicultural techniques, interpretation, research, herbivore control, and the line to be taken on access. However, a clear thread running through all meetings of the Wildwood Group has been a determination to maximise the role of natural processes, to minimise the use of physical and chemical intervention, and to make the Wildwood feel wild. The overriding aim is to create a functioning ecosystem that will evolve through the centuries and where human influence will decrease gradually as nature takes over.

Within two weeks of gaining access to the site, the WGS contract was signed and a Project Officer funded by Scottish Natural Heritage was in post. Some 30,000 trees were planted in Spring 2000 and by the end of summer the 11 km perimeter stock fence and 3 km of electric fence had been built with funding from MFST. The main planting was planned to take place over eight years, and by arrangement with the previous owner the withdrawal of sheep grazing has been phased. This helped to reduce the purchase price and avoids excessive growth of the sward in areas awaiting planting. It necessitated several internal fences that are dismantled as sheep are withdrawn. Two small compartments centred on tiny groups of surviving trees were deer-fenced, to encourage regeneration and to provide direct evidence about the ongoing effects of deer-browsing on the rest of the site; they will eventually be removed.

Seed collection by group members started in 1996 from local ancient woodland sites. Many trees have been propagated in back gardens, but the bulk are cell-grown from our seed by commercial nurseries. Around a tenth of the trees have been planted by volunteers, but the rest by contractors who had to be taught about sensitive planting in (more or less) random patterns. Tree and shrub species include downy birch, rowan, sessile oak, holly, ash, wych elm, aspen, alder, Scots pine, bird cherry, hazel, hawthorn, blackthorn, juniper, guelder rose and many species of willows. The lower part of the valley should eventually become upland broadleaved and oak-birch woodlands with strong representation of hazel (National Vegetation Classification types W7, W9, W11 and W17), with small areas of birch woodland (W4) as shown in Figure 1 (MAP). At higher levels there will be juniper woodland (W19) with birch, rowan and some pine; above this there will be scrub of juniper and specialist willows, with montane heath near the exposed summits.

Fire, feral goats, and other challenges

This account may make the project sound straightforward. Along the way, however, many tough decisions have been taken, often after tortuous discussion. From the start, the group was determined to maintain control and avoid compromising the principles of the project, even when large-scale funding was at stake. But the authorities do make some reasonable stipulations. Scottish Natural Heritage (SNH) were wonderfully supportive of the plan to alter the entire ecology of a large section of a Site of Special Scientific Interest (now candidate Special Area of Conservation), but botanically rich flushes and areas with rare montane plants have to be treated with discretion. Dumfries & Galloway Council insisted on avoidance of planting around archaeological features, and their comments on landscape issues led to withdrawal of the area near the main road from the WGS contract. The Forestry Commission allowed 20% of open space within our grant-aided woodland, but specified a density of 1,600 trees per hectare in the planted areas and a maximum of 10% of woody shrubs (this limit is now 20% in new native woodlands).

There have been several significant setbacks. First, the feral goats in the valley have been removed to adjacent areas and further afield, but only after prolonged and difficult discussions with some local people. Second, Foot & Mouth Disease hit when we had taken delivery of 30,000 trees for planting in early 2001. These trees had to be retained unplanted through the summer, resulting in significant mortality and large numbers of sickly trees, some of which have still not fully recovered. In spring 2003 a farmer carrying out muirburn on adjacent land lost control of his fire, which spread over the Carrifran boundary and killed 10,000 recently planted trees.

By planting nearly half a million trees we can give Carrifran a vigorous shove towards the goal of a re-created natural ecosystem, but often that goal seems very distant. We find ourselves opposing natural processes as we try to cope with rampant growth of grass and bracken and with voracious deer, voles and hares (not to mention straying sheep and goats). We eventually decided on an initial herbicide treatment around each tree, even though this went against the organic gardening background of key members of the group. An early decision to use vole guards on all trees has saved us many sleepless nights, but we have recently had to intensify control of roe deer and some culling may continue to be necessary so long as their natural predators are absent from the Moffat Hills.

Letting nature take over...

We are continually learning more about our site, trying to relax and modify the pattern of planting when sickly trees tell us that they have been planted in the wrong place, or that we must have patience while they adjust to difficult conditions. In the long run, we want to ensure that natural variations in soil, exposure and drainage are fully reflected in the pattern of the developing habitats, rather than intervening to try to minimise the variation and impose uniformity on a complex system. Similarly, during beating up we sometimes augment tree species that are clearly well adapted to the site and which may have been under-represented in local relict woodlands as a result of modification by human activities long ago.

After five years of ownership by BFT, Carrifran is looking pretty good. The burnt trees have been replaced, internal fences are being removed, three quarters of the trees have been planted and a young woodland is clearly established in the lower part of the valley. Inevitably, there are continuing preoccupations with funding, since the available grant aid (from the FC, SNH and other sources) does not fully cover the cost of planting on such difficult ground, and we also have to make provision for future costs, especially the eventual renewal of the perimeter fence. Donations from the public have so far enabled us to maintain the schedule of planting envisaged at the start. If this inflow of funds can be maintained, the main planting should be complete in two more seasons, along with replacement of missing trees in areas already planted. Then the focus will shift to the more gradual establishment of treeline woodland and montane scrub around the lower fringes of the high surrounding plateaux. Then, in a few years, we can begin to let nature take over most of the management of Carrifran.

References

1. Tipping, R (1994) The form and fate of Scotland's woodlands. *Proceedings of the Society of Antiquaries of Scotland* 124: 1-54.
2. Tipping, R (1997a). Vegetational history of southern Scotland. *Botanical Journal of Scotland* 49(2): 151-162.
3. Badenoch, C (1994) Woodland origins and the loss of native woodland in the Tweed valley. Proceedings of the *Restoring Borders Woodland* conference, 11-26. Peeblesshire Environment Concern.
4. Tipping, R (1997) Rotten Bottom - Holocene upland environments. In R M Tipping (ed.) *The Quaternary of Dumfries & Galloway: Field Guide*, 171-181.
5. Newton, A C & Ashmole, P (eds.) (1998) *Native woodland restoration in southern Scotland: principles and practice.* University of Edinburgh & Borders Forest Trust.
6. Fenton, J (2004) Wild thoughts followed up… *ECOS* 25 (1): 18-20.
7. Newton, A C & Ashmole, P (eds.) (1999) *Carrifran Wildwood Environmental Statement.* Wildwood Group of the Borders Forest Trust.

Ecological restoration without all the pieces: early news from Carrifran

ECOS 28 (3/4) 89-95 (2007)

Conservation groups are addressing the crucial need to manage deer numbers on nature conservation sites – this article discusses the challenge at Carrifran Wildwood when trying to restore natural habitats.

HUGH CHALMERS

Aldo Leopold wrote that "to keep every cog and wheel is the first precaution of intelligent tinkering".[1] The ecology of Britain has long since been dismantled and we have broken that first rule by discarding some essential elements. David Blake's article[2] in the last *ECOS* touched on the critical need to have control of deer numbers when managing nature reserves, but the challenge is greater when trying to restore natural habitats. The cost of doing so is considerable and difficult to estimate, and is the kind of semi-natural woodland habitat we get when we try to mimic predation what we want? The experiment is under way. At Carrifran we are creating a kind of natural woodland by planting trees and mimicking lynx predation (by stalking) and other natural processes until such time as we can arrange to have the real thing.

Planning and planting

At Carrifran Wildwood in the Southern Uplands of Scotland, the Wildwood Group of Borders Forest Trust (BFT) is attempting to restore the natural vegetation cover and associated fauna to an entire upland catchment with an area of 660 hectares and reaching a height of 821m a.s.l.[3] The major commitment of time, energy and money over the last 8 years has been to plant 400,000 native trees of local origin. The valley has been sheepwalk for hundreds of years, and as there were only a few small remnants of woodland and a limited range of species, the decision was made to apply to the Forestry Commission for a planting grant under the Woodland Grant Scheme.

In order to qualify for this grant aid an Environmental Statement was required – a major undertaking for a recently formed group of volunteers. In order to garner the current expertise in native woodland restoration, BFT and the University of Edinburgh organised a one day discussion meeting in late 1997 (see below)[4], and the resulting report formed the basis for a two year communal discussion on how such a valley as Carrifran could be restored to native woodland. After a lot of hard work and deliberation an Environmental Statement was produced resulting in a smooth application process to the FC Woodland

Grant Scheme and approval for our activities from Scottish Natural Heritage (the whole site is a Site of Special Scientific Interest and a Special Area of Conservation, notified for its geomorphological interest and arctic-alpine plants).

Regenerating birch and new plantings - after nine years. (Peter Taylor)

Deer dynamics

During a two year discussion process by an enthusiastic 'Wildwood Ecological Planning Group', there was a feeling that perhaps the biggest threat was from the lack of natural roe deer predators, as emphasised by the Deer Commission Scotland (DCS). In fact, in the ES the following was stated: *"Finally, a cautionary note is necessary. There are few convincing examples of woodland deer being controlled by shooting over periods greater than three or four years, and the ability to maintain populations at the required levels in perpetuity has not been demonstrated. Only in the very long term will it be possible to demonstrate that at Carrifran, deer numbers are being kept low enough for a self-sustaining woodland to be maintained indefinitely".*[5]

So far so good, and with this warning ringing in his ears, the Wildwood Project Officer (funded by Scottish Natural Heritage) organised contractors to fence out domestic stock, set up an adequate deer culling operation and to plant trees, with lots of volunteer backup on the ground and from the Wildwood Steering Group. In the Spring of 2000, an area of 24 hectares was fenced off with temporary electric stock fence, and 12ha of trees planted. The plan was for the previous owner to progressively withdraw his livestock by October 2004 in 4 stages, with Borders Forest Trust constructing lengthy (and porous) internal electric fences, as well as a substantial boundary fence of 11km to keep out sheep and feral goats. A professional deer stalker was employed to visit Carrifran once per fortnight and this was deemed adequate at the time to deal with incursions from neighbouring woodlands.

The advent of Foot and Mouth Disease and consequent access restrictions from January to June 2001 gave us a foretaste of what was to come as we were not allowed to cull deer. It soon became apparent that the ungrazed and untainted (by sheep) rough pasture was very attractive to roe deer, who were also partial to young tree leaves and liked to mark territories by fraying any trees which reached above 40cm in height. At one point six roe deer were seen regularly in the 12ha of new planting, though 3 were dispatched as soon as we were allowed on site.

By June 2004, we had planted around 100ha of trees, protected only by 20cm tall vole guards, and had been carrying out regular monitoring of tree survival, to make sure that we would make the FC Woodland Grant Scheme target of having at least 1,100 trees/ha established within 5 years. The definition of established has since been defined officially by FC as "*trees must be present; to the stocking levels specified; healthy; and in a condition capable of continued growth given no further weeding and subject to normal ongoing maintenance operations such as protection from inappropriate grazing by wild or domestic animals*".[6] Our surveys in June 2004 were showing some worrying statistics. Over 45% 'severely browsed' with some losses also due to bracken smothering, and survival rates in some areas of less than 500 trees per hectare. We considered all the possibilities; poor planting stock, poor weed control, lack of nutrients, browsing from brown hare, stray sheep and goats. We do have areas fenced against deer but not against hares, and high survival in these pointed the finger at deer (saplings cut by hare are easy to distinguish from deer browsing) and this showed us that browsing from something large was the problem. A site visit from a very helpful Deer Commission for Scotland advisor laid the situation on the line: increase deer culling or face the loss of the trees.

Deer culling – the determining factors

The frequency of visits from the stalker at that time was governed partly by the cost (£80 per visit, or around £2,000 per year) and by the policy of the professional stalker, who had also been involved in the initial DCS discussions. Around 10 deer per year were shot during this period. Deer were not shot out of season, and the 'stand-buck theory' was being used. This is the idea that if you retain a roe buck in a 'stand' of trees or territory, he will exclude other males.

So, in practice, we had a very selective deer culling policy in place, which allowed deer to do a lot of damage to small, vulnerable trees, (though of course there was the confusion over the effect of the other browsers – the marauding sheep and goats). In addition, the professional stalker was keen to shoot the valley exclusively as having other people stalking deer would make it more difficult for him to cull deer. On reflection, we had a sound deer control policy in theory, but this differed from what happened on the ground. On other BFT woodland restoration sites, there is a similar reluctance by gamekeepers to control deer effectively, perhaps because of the time and effort it takes to do so. The effort required to control each deer depends on the density of deer present and the type of woodland cover present. At Carrifran there is a low density of deer, and an open landscape which is makes it difficult to stalk roe deer.

It was obvious that something would have to change, and that the cost of deer control would increase substantially, though by how much it was impossible to tell. This was quite an uncomfortable period in the management of the project, the ultimate cost of not controlling deer properly would be the failure of the project, and paying back the FC grant with interest – a figure over £100,000 in 2004 (over £300,000 now after further planting) and one which could not be contemplated. By September 2004, after some awkward decisions, the original deer culling policy was in place with a different professional stalker visiting once per week, with the visit being a good 8 hours, reaching way off the beaten track, and discarding the stand buck theory. The Project Officer, a novice stalker, also visited once per week, and he recruited qualified and experienced volunteers who would also assist in deer culling. The cost of deer control increased to £4,500 per year, with no contribution from the Forestry Commission or government bodies, simply a challenge to the fundraising efforts of the Wildwood Group. A night shooting licence from the DCS was also granted over certain winter months, with DCS Best Practice Guidance adhered to.

Since September 2004, the deer control effort has increased approximately four-fold, with around a doubling of costs - the latter helped by stalking volunteers. Deer shot have increased from an average 10 per year between 2000 and 2004, up to an average 19 per year from 2005 to 2007. The actual cost of adequate deer control at Carrifran at present is around £200 per deer. Most importantly, tree survival monitoring has shown that our trees are growing well, with less that 10% browsed per year, though we don't mind bushy trees. We were also pleased that in June 2007 the FC Woodland Officer classed as 'established' the 50 hectares planted in the 2001 to 2002 planting season which were in poor condition due to browsing in June 2004. Perhaps there was some leniency here, but I am convinced that the change of policy will now allow all 280 hectares to become established. When all the planted trees are classed as 'established', hopefully by 2013, the deer control policy can be reviewed, and in the meantime fundraising can ensure the contractual obligations are met.

Facing the financial costs

Perhaps it would have been possible to restore the lost woodland of Carrifran over a longer time scale, by relying more on natural regeneration of trees and planting small areas of 'seed' trees. Even then, predation on deer would be required to allow trees to grow and to allow subsequent generations of trees to form natural woodland. One of our objectives at Carrifran is to demonstrate to a wider audience the difficulties in restoring woodland to the uplands in the present time. We have already had to find funds for a perimeter fence to keep out domestic stock and feral goats (£90,000) and we will probably need to find £5,000 per year for the next 10 years to replace a missing part of our ecosystem.

The sort of costs outlined above are worrying for individuals and organisations which aim to plant or restore native woodlands. An alternative to deer control may be the use of deer fences though these can have adverse impacts on landscape and wildlife while their effectiveness is of limited duration. Deer fences are also very costly as seen with the Millennium Forest for Scotland initiative where deer fencing was necessary with 26 woodland restoration projects at a cost of £1.82m between 1997 and 2000.[7] Despite their impacts, deer are welcome at Carrifran as part of a natural ecosystem, where at one time deer evolved along with large predators. But with a vital component of that ecosystem missing, our current management approach has to be more interventionist (as well as more costly) than we would have wished.

Aside from the challenge of excessive browsing of native tree saplings at Carrifran, we had to relocate around 50 feral goats which were present in the valley. 21 went to heathland grazing projects in Windsor and Kent in October 2001, and the remainder to the farm next door, in October 2004. There was local opposition to these plans, but Scottish Natural Heritage, with the cooperation of all landowners in the area finally produced a 'Moffat Hills Feral Goat Management Plan' in 2005. Feral goats will continue to thrive within the Moffat Hills SSSI, but not in Carrifran.

Coping with climate change

In 1999, when the restoration plan for Carrifran was finalised, the matter of climate change did not seem so pressing. The main tree and shrub plantings reach to 500m, and in the event of a gradual warming of the climate, there is room for trees to expand to higher, cooler areas. If all vegetation zones move higher, then there would perhaps be some losses of the mossy habitats at 800m. Other issues, such as atmospheric nitrogen deposition, may also threaten these habitats. Tree species at Carrifran follow guidance from the pollen record, but certain species, such as small leaved lime, which seems to have a natural distribution as far north as Carlisle, could be considered for planting. The tolerance to warming of our existing species mix may be sufficient to accommodate small changes in average temperatures in the medium term. With 2,000mm per annum of rain on White Coomb, we are reliant on damp conditions. If climate change means much less rain, then it is difficult to know how we would cope. However, other more obvious changes are happening which may threaten native woodland establishment, such as the spread of Muntjac deer. Sika deer are close too, and we have recently seen our first rabbit...

References

1. Leopold A. (1949) *A Sand County Almanac*. Oxford University Press.
2. Deer in Britain: the challenge for nature conservation. David Blake. *ECOS* 28 (2) 2007
3. The Carrifran Wildwood Project. Philip Ashmole and Hugh Chalmers. *ECOS* 25 (3/4) 2004
4. Newton, A.C. and Ashmole, P (Eds) (1998). Native Woodland restoration in southern Scotland: principles and practice. Occasional paper no. 2, Borders Forest Trust, Ancrum, Jedburgh, Scotland, UK.
5. Newton. A.C and Ashmole. P (Eds). 1999. Carrifran Wildwood Project, Appendices to Environmental Statement. 17. Deer Management.
6. Forestry Commission (2006) Scottish Forestry Grants Scheme Contracts.
7. John F Hunt (2003) Impacts of Wild Deer in Scotland – How fares the Public Interest?

Rewilding in the north-central Highlands – an update

ECOS 25 (3/4) 4-10 (2004)
*Freeing up the ecological processes within a renewed Caledonian forest is a
250 year project. This article describes progress with the first phase.*

ALAN WATSON FEATHERSTONE

Native forest recovery – the vision

It is over seven years since I wrote in *ECOS* about the work of Trees for Life for
the 'Wild Heart of the Highlands' (*ECOS* 18 (2) 48-61). Our vision is to return a
large area in the north-central Highlands west of Inverness to a more wild and
self-willed condition, complete with natural forests, large mammals and their
predators.[1] In my eyes this has always been a vision which would unfold and
fully develop over a period of 250 years – the time it will take a young Scots
pine of today to reach maturity – so we are still very much in the first phase of
implementing it. However, a review of the progress provides an opportunity to
re-evaluate the project's goals, in the light of experience to date.

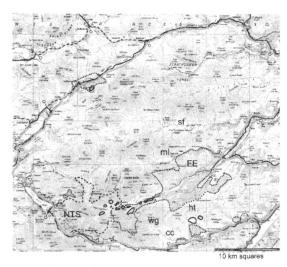

PUBLIC LAND

FE   Forest Enterprise

NTS National Trust Scotland

PRIVATE ESTATES
with planting agreements

sf   Strathfarrer

ml   Mullardoch

cc   Ceannacroc

ht   Hilton

dg   Dundreggan

wg   Wester Guisachan

10 km squares

Solid line: TfL exclosures for planting or regeneration
Broken lines: Forest Enterprise and National Trust
boundaries. Orange line indicates extent of potential
core area proposed by Trees for Life. (Thick grey line)

The map illustrates the locations where we work – a target area of about 918 square miles (2,377 square kilometres), where we aim to return native forest to 600 - 700 square miles. We selected this area because it contains a number of good fragments of the Caledonian Forest, because there is very little economic activity taking place there, and, in terms of landscape, it includes mountains, rivers and lochs, all of which provide a sense of relative wildness. The area also embodies a quality of remoteness, and has minimal human infrastructure (roads, houses etc.) in it. Taken together, these elements form the basis for what is possibly the best opportunity in the UK to assist the recovery of self-willed, healthy ecosystems on a significant scale.

The first phase of restoration

Trees for Life tries to kick-start the natural recovery of native forest to suitable sites, so our first efforts were concentrated mainly in Glen Affric, as it contains the largest remnant of native pinewoods in the area (this is also the largest extent of least-disturbed forest in Scotland). In 1989 we began a series of projects enclosing areas of naturally-regenerating tree seedlings with deer fences, to protect them from overgrazing by deer and sheep. We also plant trees in appropriate sites where regeneration is unlikely to occur because of the lack of a seed source. Planting is done in ways which mimic natural regeneration as closely as possible, utilising irregular and clumped spatial distribution of the trees, and matching the species to soil types and site hydrological conditions.

Upper Glen Affric grazed out by deer (Peter Taylor)

The aim of this is to establish a new generation of native trees growing healthily in key sites throughout our target area. These can then form the nuclei for subsequent further natural regeneration of native forest, once the grazing pressure of both wild and domesticated herbivores has been reduced to a level commensurate with the recovery of the vegetation. From our initial focus on Glen Affric we have now spread out to include other parts of our target area, and have carried out significant forest restoration work at sites in Glen Moriston, at the RSPB's Corrimony Nature Reserve, at Achnashellach and in Grudie Oakwood, amongst others. To date we have planted almost half a million native trees, and have protected over 150,000 naturally occurring tree seedlings.

Some of the trees we've protected or planted are now over 4 metres tall, and are producing seeds each year, thereby adding to the process of forest regeneration. In addition, these young trees are already providing a habitat for insects and other invertebrates such as spiders. Those, in turn, are food for birds, so even after just 15 years (a short period in the life of a tree) some of the fundamental strands in the web of the forest ecosystem have become re-established. The young trees are also providing a restored habitat for shade-loving forest species such as blaeberry (*Vaccinium myrtillus*), while in the first area which we protected the pinewood orchid species, creeping lady's tresses (*Goodyera repens*), has become much more abundant since the area was fenced in 1990.

These early results confirm the experience of similar schemes elsewhere in the Highlands, that the removal of excessive grazing pressure enables the regeneration of both trees and other vegetation - the critical first step towards the recovery of healthy ecosystems. Just how dramatic this recovery can be was graphically illustrated this year when I visited an area on West Affric, the headwaters region of the Affric River, which is owned by the National Trust for Scotland. There are very few trees left on this 4,000 hectare estate, which now consists mostly of open grassland and heath and is heavily grazed by red deer. In 1997 we had installed several small areas of stock fencing alongside the river, to protect some heavily-overgrazed eared willow seedlings as part of a project to restore the riparian vegetation zone. When I checked these exclosures in May 2004, I was astonished to discover bluebells flowering in one of them, under the partial shade of an eared willow bush which was now about a metre in height. The bluebells provided a remarkable contrast with the close-cropped, depleted landscape outside the fence and are probably the first of their species to flower on West Affric for decades, or possibly even centuries.

A key element of our work is the reconnection of some of the isolated fragments of native forest in our target area. At present, these remnants are islands of woodland surrounded by treeless areas and as a result they suffer from some of the classic problems associated with fragmentation [2], such as loss of species like wood ants. The importance of reversing this process has been recognised by Scottish Natural Heritage [3] amongst others, and the new Scottish Forestry Grants Scheme (SFGS) is designed in part to address this issue. Because of the nature of the topography in our target area, the forested parts have always been somewhat isolated by the high ground between the glens, but there are a number of locations where the hills separating adjacent glens are lower than the natural tree line (600 metres). For a number of years we've been working to restore a forest linkage in one of the best of these sites, between Glen Affric and Glen Moriston. Named after one of the streams flowing south into Glen Moriston, the Allt na Muic Forest Corridor project consists of a series of fenced exclosures between the two glens for forest regeneration, and on the higher ground, the restoration of montane scrub.

For ecosystem recovery to be achieved outside of fenced exclosures the critical issue in our target area is a substantial reduction in the grazing pressure from red deer, and to date there has been less progress on this front. As Trees for Life does not own any land itself, we have no direct control over the numbers of grazing animals. Thus, we have to rely on sympathetic landowners and the relevant agencies to bring about a reduction of red deer numbers. While some landowners such as Forest Enterprise have been implementing considerably increased culls on their land, the overall deer population has not significantly changed, and there is virtually no tree regeneration outside the fences.

However, there are some encouraging signs that this situation is about to change. The Deer Commission for Scotland has been given more power to address the problem of overpopulation, and can step in to achieve cull targets in cases where landowners consistently fail to do so themselves. Together with changes in the Deer Management Sub-group for the Affric area, this should ensure that the deer numbers do come down in the years ahead.

Regenerating alder along streamside, with regenerated birch on hillside exclosure, 2009 (Peter Taylor)

*Heavily grazed rowan
(Alan Watson Featherstone)*

Athnamulloch, 1991, left,

and 2002, below
(Alan WatsonFeatherstone)

Deepening the restoration process

In recent years our restoration work in Glen Affric has entered a new phase. Initially we concentrated on expanding the area of native pinewoods, both through fencing for natural regeneration and by planting trees, especially Scots pines. With a new generation of young trees now growing successfully, we've turned our attention to a deepening of the restoration process, to encompass other species and parts of the forest ecosystem. For example, research has shown that broadleaved trees are generally underrepresented in most pinewood remnants, because of being preferentially eaten by deer in the past. Thus, we

309

have a project to restore more broadleaved trees, particularly the scarcer species such as hazel, oak, holly and aspen.

Of these, the aspen project is most developed, and it consists of three main parts - surveying and mapping of existing aspen stands, measures to regenerate aspen and create new aspen stands, and research into the ecology of aspen and its associated species. To date we have identified and surveyed 345 aspen sites throughout our target area, and we've propagated over 10,000 aspens from root cuttings in our specially-designed aspen propagation unit. These have been planted out both to increase the clonal diversity of this dioecious species in its existing stands, and to establish new stands in suitable sites.

Aspen is an important tree for a wide range of organisms, including rare species of moths, lichens and saproxylic flies [4], and we are tailoring our project in part to provide for the habitat requirements for these species. Aspen is also a preferred winter food for the European beaver (*Castor fiber*). In light of the proposed reintroduction of beavers to Scotland, we are working to regenerate and expand the aspen stands around Loch Beinn a'Mheadhoin in Glen Affric, which is a possible future site for beavers. Research we've had carried out on aspen includes work on the clonal diversity of aspen stands [5] and documentation of the galls associated with aspen [6], while an upcoming 3 year project is planned to study the mycorrhizal fungi associated with aspen.

Other elements of our current work include projects to regenerate and restore the tree-line montane scrub community (we've already carried out the most extensive mapping programme in Scotland for dwarf birch, a key component of montane scrub); a woodland ground flora project which involves surveying the forest for key flowering plant species and action to restore those where they are missing; and the riparian forest project, to restore the stream and loch-side zones, where the deciduous trees provide nutrients for the aquatic food web through their fallen leaves.

Another project will involve the translocation of wood ants (*Formica lugubris*) within Glen Affric from an area where they are abundant to an isolated stand of mature pinewood which the ants cannot colonise by themselves because it's too far from any existing ant nests. The intention with this is to use the translocation as an opportunity to develop a protocol for such work, which can be a guide for other similar projects. Many new native pinewoods have been established recently in the Highlands, and these are often isolated from existing ancient forest remnants, so that natural colonisation of those by wood ants is unlikely to occur – hence translocations may become more common in future.

Other work which we're currently involved with includes a project to inventory the biological diversity in Glen Affric. Almost 15,000 hectares of land managed there by Forest Enterprise were declared Scotland's newest National

Nature Reserve in 2002, in recognition of its biological, scenic and conservation importance. However, although some groups of organisms such as dragonflies are well-studied in the glen, there had until recently been no comprehensive studies carried out on the species occurring there. The consequence of that can be seen in the table, which provides a comparison between our knowledge of biological diversity in Glen Affric and that in Abernethy, another large remnant of the Caledonian Forest, which is owned by the RSPB.

Numbers of species recorded in pinewood areas

	Affric	Abernethy
Fungi	225	699
Lichens	178	300
Mosses & liverworts (Bryophytes)	55	293
Flies (*Diptera*)	36	260
Spiders (Arachnids)	76	128
Beetles (*Coleoptera*)	155	904
Moths & butterflies (*Lepidoptera*)	261	264

The differences in numbers between Affric and Abernethy for most groups of organisms do not mean that Affric has a significantly lower level of biological diversity than Abernethy – instead they are a reflection of the fact that much less survey and inventory work has been done in Affric. We've now initiated a series of studies to identify what species are present in Affric; the first of these, in 2003, was for moths, while a similar project for beetles is being carried out in 2004 and 2005.

Underlying principles

Our work is guided by a set of principles of ecological restoration which we've developed, based on the premise that 'Nature knows best'.[1] Our objectives are focussed on getting all the parts of the ecosystem back in place, beginning with the establishment of a new generation of young trees, then ensuring that they and all other vegetation communities can grow successfully without being overgrazed, and ultimately going on to the return of the missing large mammals, including the top predators.

As our project has developed over the years, a critical insight has been the recognition of the importance of restoring ecological processes, such as the balance between herbivory and regeneration, predation, occasional large-scale disturbance and the like. It is the loss of these which has kept the land in its present degraded condition, and it is only with all of them back in place that there will be self-sustaining healthy ecosystems in the Highlands, rather than ones which require ongoing human management. Our goal is not to create some sort of 'planned' new Caledonian Forest, but rather to enable the return of a large contiguous area of land to a self-willed condition – once we've got all the elements of the ecosystem back in place again, we'll let Nature take over fully and will not do any further management, such as tree planting, fencing and the like.

The need for mammal reintroductions

The most challenging and perhaps controversial part of this is the return of the missing mammal species, especially predators such as the wolf, and we are under no illusions about the difficulty of advancing this agenda. The failure so far to implement the proposed reintroduction of European beavers to Knapdale in Argyll provides an indication of the obstacles which have to be overcome in this regard.

Trees for Life continues to be a strong advocate for the return of beavers, as a first step in the recovery of our missing mammal species, and we are currently working in partnership with some local people on a project with wild boar. Initiated by a resident of the village of Tomich, just outside Glen Affric, this three year project will study the effects of wild boar, kept in fenced exclosures in the forest, in assisting tree regeneration through their disturbance of the soil, and their role in controlling bracken. The project will also evaluate the economic return from the sale of wild boar meat to ascertain whether this is compatible with the ecological benefits of wild boar, and thereby providing a potential sustainable livelihood for local people.

In the longer term though, it is the predators which will be most important to return to the Highlands. Research in the USA in particular is increasingly documenting the essential, irreplaceable role which top carnivores play in regulating the healthy functioning of ecosystems, and it has been shown that their absence "appears to lead inexorably to ecosystem simplification accompanied by a rush of extinctions".[7] In our Highland context, the key carnivore is the wolf, although the lynx and brown bear would also have been important in the past.

The role of the wolf would not just be limited to controlling deer numbers by killing individuals (usually the weak, sick, old or very young), but perhaps more importantly, its disturbance effect in moving the deer around would facilitate the recovery and regeneration of trees and other vegetation. This has already been documented in Yellowstone National Park, where wolves were reintroduced in 1995.[8] Given the impossibility of returning wolves to the Highlands in the immediate future, we suggest that large dogs could be used as surrogate disturbance agents. Landowners or land managers could train dogs to chase deer (but not harm them) out of sensitive areas, such as native forest remnants and riparian zones to aid their regeneration.

Cultural prejudices

Interest in the possibility of returning wolves to the Highlands continues to be high, judging by the number of research students who contact us and by regular articles in the mainstream press. However, given the vocal opposition to the wolf from groups such as farmers, some conservationists now consider the lynx to be the predator which could realistically be reintroduced in the near future. Unhindered by the prejudices, media stereotyping and myths which surround the wolf, lynx have already been successfully reintroduced to Switzerland and the Vosges Mountains in France. People coexist with predators such as the wolf and lynx in many other countries in Western Europe, from Spain and Italy to Germany and Sweden, so surely it is time to recognise that it would also be possible to achieve this in the Highlands of Scotland, where the human population density is much lower than most of those other carnivore-inhabited countries. Wilderness advocates, I believe, must do a better job of emphasising the importance of carnivores, and should also initiate a programme of education and information about them, as part of the preparation for their eventual return to the Highlands.

Conclusion

Although it is far too early to evaluate the success of our efforts, the growth of new trees and the consequent benefits for other species are positive signs that it will be possible to restore the forest on a larger scale. Whether the other elements of our vision, such as the return of a large area of land to 'self-willed' status complete with reinstated large mammals and top carnivores, come to fruition, will most likely be decided decades from now. The task for the immediate future is to lay the groundwork for that, to build an irrefutable case for why it should happen, and, by so doing, to play a role in healing the relationship between humanity and the rest of Nature.

References

1. Watson Featherstone, A. (1997)   The Wild Heart of the Highlands   *ECOS* 18 (2) 48-61.
2.   McArthur, R. H. and Wilson E. O.   (1967)   *The Theory of Island Biogeography* Princeton, NJ: Princeton University Press
3.   Peterken, G.F; Baldock, D & Mampson, A.   (1995)   *A Forest Habitat Network for Scotland*, SNH Research, Survey and Monitoring Report no. 44, Scottish Natural Heritage, Perth.
4.   Cosgrove, P. and Amphlett, A. (eds.)   (2002)   *The Biodiversity and Management of Aspen Woodlands* The Cairngorms Local Biodiversity Action Plan 2002

5. Lees, S. (1998) Clonal diversity of aspen (*Populus tremula*) in Glen Affric. Honours Thesis, University of Edinburgh (Unpublished).
6. Hancy, R. (2004) Galls on Aspen - A first look. *Caledonia Wild!* Trees for Life newsletter, Spring 2004
7. Terborgh, J. et al. (1999) The Role of Top Carnivores in Regulating Terrestrial Ecosystems. *Wild Earth* 9 (2)
8. Pickrell J. (2003) Wolves' Leftovers Are Yellowstone's Gain, Study Says *National Geographic News* (online)
 news.nationalgeographic.com/news/2003/12/1204_031204_yellowstonewolves.html
(accessed on 20/9/04)

Scotland's core wild land – the potential of Mar Lodge

ECOS 25 (3/4) 20-23 (2004)
Clear management aims and working to long timescales are helping wild land on the Mar Lodge Estate to reach its potential.

PETER HOLDEN & ALISTER CLUNAS

Mar Lodge and its dowry

At 29,340ha, Mar Lodge Estate is the largest single landholding of the National Trust for Scotland. Situated at the heart of the recently designated Cairngorms National Park, some of Britain's finest mountain scenery is encompassed within its boundary. The Estate was purchased in 1995 with funding from the Easter Charitable Trust and the Heritage Lottery Fund (HLF). The HLF gave a generous endowment of £8.5m to fund the property in future years - a far sighted action to be encouraged should HLF assist in the purchase of other properties which are not able to be self funding. Since its acquisition in 1995, the Trust has undertaken an active programme of work following the production of detailed management plans, which are a condition of the Heritage Lottery Funding and are approved by Scottish Natural Heritage. The first management plan covered 1996-2000 and the current plan covering 2002 –2006 is to be reviewed in 2005.

The Trust's aims for the estate are to achieve a successful integration of conservation of the natural heritage, public access and enjoyment, and traditional sporting activity; and to share with others an appreciation of the issues involved, as a demonstration of integrated land management in the Scottish Highlands.

Wild land – keeping the resource

Since its creation in the 1930s, the NTS has promoted the cause of wild land conservation in Scotland, recognising its value both as a distinctive part of the nation's heritage and identity, and for the opportunities it provides for outdoor recreation. Much of the experience gained at Mar Lodge Estate has influenced the Trust's *Wild Land Policy* issued in 2002. The Trust's working definition is: "Wild land in Scotland is relatively remote and inaccessible not noticeably affected by contemporary human activity, and offers high-quality opportunities to escape from the pressures of everyday living and to find physical and spiritual refreshment."

At Mar Lodge, the principle of management is to avoid any reduction in wild land quality, and where possible to enhance these qualities or extend the area that exhibits them. Natural processes are the favoured means of bringing about a return to a wilder environment, so that the rewilding process takes place on a habitat and landscape scale, which avoids being drawn into 'gardening' for individual species and their requirements. Key species are identified in the management plan (examples include Golden Eagle, Capercaillie, Black Grouse, and the Narrow Headed Wood Ant) and where present, these tend to benefit through habitat improvement. However, a level of intervention may sometimes be required. Most notably, the Trust has been steadily reducing the red deer population to a target of 1650 by the year 2005. The target population of 700 stags for the estate has been achieved and in the regeneration zone, numbers are almost at the target population of 350 deer. The main problem remaining is high hind numbers in the moorland zone.

Woodland management and regeneration

There are 2103 hectares of woodland on the estate consisting of a mixture of core native pinewoods, birchwoods, 19th Century plantings, 1970s plantations and New Native Woodlands dating from the early 1990s, Table 1 summarises the woodland types found on the estate.

315

Table 1   **Woodland types found on the estate**

Woodland Type	Area in Hectares
Core Native Pinewoods	
Glen Derry	246
Glen Lui	118
Glen Quoich	425
Total	789
Allanaquoich Birchwoods	15
C19 plantations (Scots Pine, European Larch and Norway Spruce)	195
1970s plantations (Scots Pine, Sitka Spruce and Lodgepole Pine)	685
New Native Pinewoods (Scots Pine, Birch and Rowan)	85
Area enclosed for regeneration (pre NTS)	334
Total area of woodland	2103

Potential area for regeneration	
<600 metres	3603
>600 metres (montane scrub)	3847

Three core areas of mature, native Caledonian pinewood presently cover a total of 789 hectares.

Most existing plantations have had some form of management, which includes removal of deer fences, creating glades, and re-spacing. A total of 37 kilometres of deer fence has been removed and a further 4.5 kilometres of fence has been marked to reduce the hazard of collisions by woodland grouse. Glen Quoich now has no deer fencing within the glen.

Management goals, for regeneration and for moorland

For management purpose, the estate is divided into two zones – the regeneration zone covering the Glen Quoich, Glen Lui and Glen Derry, and the moorland zone. In the regeneration zone seedling regeneration is slowly taking place, with almost all seedlings below vegetation height except in those areas inaccessible to grazing. This will eventually greatly extend the existing areas of native Caledonian pine and birch. By not relying on fencing, it is hoped to achieve naturally regenerated woodland, of mixed age and species on a landscape scale, the boundaries of which are not dictated or sharply defined.

The reduction in grazing has led to a measurable increase in the amount and quality of montane scrub, a community extensive in Scandinavia, but rarely seen in the Scottish uplands. Dwarf birch *(Betula nana),* willows, and juniper are the major beneficiaries.

Treading lightly...

Perhaps the greatest success has been the Trust's work on the restoration of bulldozed hill tracks. Twenty-five kilometres of track have been restored, either by complete reinstatement of the ground or reduced to a narrow pedestrian footpath width. Much of the early work, carried out to an altitude of over 1,000 metres on Beinn a'Bhuird was pioneering. Individual turves of native vegetation, lifted from the spoil heaps, have been painstakingly handcrafted back into the re-profiled ground surface. Early trials were akin to landscape gardening on a montane scale, and following these early successes, machines became part of the reconstruction technique, a 14 tonne JCB being deployed in the less sensitive, heather dominated swards below altitudes of 850 metres. Confidence in the restoration design has enabled us, through continued SNH and EU funding, to extend the work with JCB to lower altitude tracks in the Cairngorm glens. The predominately grassy vegetation here transplants even more readily as large turves than the deeper rooted heather swards. In the context of rewilding, track restoration has achieved two main objectives: First, the removal of obvious landscape scars in an otherwise 'near-natural' environment; and second, through the cessation of vehicle movements, a significant expansion of a remote area, free from mechanical intrusion.

As an additional consequence of the revegetation methods used (no seeds or fertilisers have been used in any path or track work at Mar Lodge), we have applied these techniques to our high level and remote footpath construction and repair. The Trust's upland path repair programme is designed to combat erosion within a wild land perspective, rather than to facilitate access per se, so that pre-emptive and light touch techniques have been developed in the highest and remote sites. There is a subtlety of construction and route definition, and it demonstrates an empathy with our wildest and most beautiful mountain landscapes, with a much reduced visual impact.

Outwith Scandinavia and Eastern Europe there are few large areas of wild land in Europe. Hence Scotland's wild land is valued both at home and by visitors from the UK and abroad, both as a distinctive part of Scotland's heritage and identity, and for the outstanding opportunity for outdoor recreation and wildlife tourism.

Recognition for core values

For rewilding projects on this scale, where habitat change or enhancement is seen as a desired outcome, a long-term commitment is required. Too often, such a visionary approach may take second place to short-term economic expediency, or simply a desire to 'see things happen' immediately. By owning land in perpetuity, and by setting clear management aims, the National Trust for Scotland is in a strong position to promote rewilding in the uplands, and commit to that. In order for Mar Lodge Estate to reach its potential in terms of of habitat conservation as well as wild land within the Cairngorms National Park it is essential that the park is zoned to give special protection to the mountain core. The enabling legislation for the creation of National Parks in Scotland emphasised the need to cater for and be sensitive to the special qualities of each Park. The special qualities of the Cairngorms National Park are its wild land and montane areas. Such an approach provides a compelling case not only for zoning the park but for a 'core' zone matching the IUCN Category II, i.e. a National Park meeting international criteria. It would be the first National Park in the UK to have such recognition and would reflect on an international scale our responsibility to the Cairngorms.

WALES

Wilder slopes of Snowdon

ECOS 25 (3/4) 39-41 (2004)
Reducing stocking densities and regenerating woodland at Hafod y Llan farm is already rejuvenating habitats and creating a wilder landscape character on the fringes of Snowdon.

RICHARD NEALE

"Gelyn mwyaf dafad yw dafad arall" meaning "a sheep's worst enemy is another sheep" is often quoted by farmers to refer to the strong competition that exists between individuals within a flock. Even the most dyed-in-the-wool commercial sheep farmer will recognise that the prospect of stock reduction for nature conservation has a silver lining: fewer sheep means less competition, which means healthier, fatter stock. This is one of the lessons that are now being learnt – and taught - at Hafod y Llan farm, the National Trust's conservation farming venture on the slopes of Snowdon.

'Save Snowdon'

The 2000 'Save Snowdon' appeal captured the hearts of people world wide. The appeal's president, Anthony Hopkins dipped into his own pocket to the tune of £1m. The high profile nature of the appeal stirred up a debate about how best to care for beautiful places in our countryside. Time and again those of us who were fronting the appeal struggled with the question, what *difference* can the National Trust's protection actually make? So, now that the dust has settled and we have started to get to grips with managing the estate, we would like to think that the difference is starting to show.

The history of Hafod y Llan farm – and thousands of upland farms like it – over the last half-century or so is a familiar story. As stock numbers steadily increased, the biodiversity was insidiously eroded to the point that much of the farm hardly merited the status of National Nature Reserve. Mires and wet heaths that used to support breeding curlews and lapwings turned into expanses of unpalatable purple moor grass.Dry heath, once the domain of red grouse and merlin retreated to a few inaccessible cliffs, leaving a sea of mat grass in its wake. Furthermore, the distinctive Western Atlantic oak woods and upland ash

319

woods that clothe the lower slopes were grazed at levels that excluded any chance of them regenerating.

So, having acquired the estate in November 1998, it was clear to the Trust and the Countryside Council for Wales that here was an opportunity to reverse this decline and to restore the habitats over a large block of the Snowdon NNR. Rather than let the farm on a tenancy in the usual way, the Trust managed the farm itself and employed a farm manager to oversee a grazing regime based on habitat restoration.

The grazing and monitoring regime

For the first two years, under farm manger John Till's management, we tackled the backlog of work on boundaries, buildings and infrastructure to get the farm back into shape. As this was in progress, we drew up a grazing and monitoring regime that now forms the basis of a management agreement with the CCW, which will fund a project to restore the habitats of this 1,112ha block of the Eryri Special Area for Conservation.

The regime itself identifies 14 management compartments at Hafod y Llan and 7 at Gelli Iago, the other farm that was acquired with Snowdon. In each compartment, the area of forage was measured accurately and a stocking figure was allocated according to the desired vision of 'favourable condition' (See Table 1). The statements of 'favourable condition' were agreed and monitoring of general condition in permanent quadrats was set up.

When the prescriptions from all of the compartments were added up, a global stocking figure for the farm was achieved. This resulted in sheep numbers being cut by half from about 3,000 ewes to about 1,500, and 65 head of hardy Welsh Black cattle being reintroduced. Additional land in Llŷn has been taken on to over-winter the sheep and finish the lambs for market. In addition, the farm is in organic conversion and has been entered into the RSPCA Freedom Foods scheme.

Woodland expansion and rewilding

One of our more radical plans is to rewild a 93ha hanging valley known as Cwm Merch. This entails restoring about 1 km of drystone walls and providing sensitively sited fences to allow heath and upland scrub to develop on a large block of open upland, by grazing it seasonally with a few Welsh Black cattle. Monitoring will show if this approach is the best way to restore the wildlife of similar areas that have been heavily sheep-grazed for generations.

Welsh Black cattle replacing sheep to improve the sward (Joe Cornish)

Another element is the expansion and restoration of the farm's woodlands by 50%. This will be achieved by stock exclusion in a few areas, but more experimentally by a pasture woodland regime involving light grazing by sheep, and occasionally cattle, in most woodland areas. The aim is to create a chain of diverse woods with open glades and scrub as well as tall trees. This part of the project has used the Forestry Commission's Woodland Grant Scheme and Partnership Funding grants.

Fitter herds, fitter habitats…

The reduction in sheep numbers have now been completed and we are building up a pedigree herd of Welsh Black cattle. It is too early to gauge whether we have got the initial regime right, but the agreement with CCW will allow for fine-tuning as a result of our monitoring. Already, there are very encouraging signs: heath is recovering sooner than expected in many areas and there is healthy tree regeneration appearing where woodland expansion is the aim.

The other result is that the stock reductions allowed John to select the strongest ewes and rams to breed from and the reduced competition between them has resulted in healthier, fatter lambs – with fewer enemies.

321

Part of the Hafod y Llan estate (Joe Cornish)

HAFOD Y LLAN ESTATE: FACTS AND FIGURES:

- 4,118 acres (1,666 hectares) of mountain land rising to the summit of Yr Wyddfa, Snowdon.
- 3 Farms currently managed by the National Trust as one unit
- 5 lakes.
- 250 acres (100 hectares) of oak and ash woodland
- Watkin path up Snowdon and other low-level walks
- Part of the Snowdon National Nature Reserve
- 2 outdoor pursuits centres
- 4 cottages, 2 chalets and 4 bunkhouses
- Premises for tree-surgery contractor
- Nantgwyant Village Hall
- Important flocks of Welsh Mountain ewes
- Summit of Cnicht and footpath to Croesor

322

Table 1   Example of a compartment grazing regime

Compartment Name: Bylchau Terfyn
Area   71 ha

Current Condition

Whole area dominated by Molinia; apparently a legacy of frequent burning and constant moderate sheep grazing. Some fragments of oak woodland and bracken in east of compartment.

Favourable Condition

Predominantly wet heath with areas of dry heath on rocky areas. Some bracken. A few scattered hawthorns and rowans becoming established in sheltered areas and sparse regeneration of oak adjacent to existing woodland pockets.

Initial Grazing Regime

Graze with 10 suckler cow equivalents from May to July to graze Molinia and otherwise 40 ewe equivalents (30 ewes + 10 ewe lambs) 16 GLUs. No supplementary feeding.

Other management needs

No burning. Compartment needs stockproofing from Dan Wal, Parc Hafod y Llan and Craig Llyn

Manage as separate Craig y Llyn flock (using Craig y Llyn earmark)

{**ed. note:** Richard Neale has updated us:

'The developments are that Arwyn Owen has taken over from John Till as our farm manager and, with the help of our Ranger, Dave Smith,has successfully completed a capital works programme to enable the package of diverse conservation grazing prescriptions to be followed. Our Wildlife officer's monitoring is showing that thanks to a balance of low density grazing by cattle and sheep, most compartments are classed as 'unfavourable recovering', as opposed to 'unfavourable stable' as they were when we took the farm on. Engagement is becoming ever more important to the farm, with many study visits from groups of all ages. We are currently working on a plan of installing hydro turbines to produce renewable energy for the farm'}

HOLLAND

Connectivity of nature in the Dutch landscape

ECOS 27 (3/4) 61-64 (2006)

The Dutch have a saying that "God made the earth, but the Dutch made Holland". Today the saying applies equally well to Dutch nature areas as to land reclaimed from the sea for over 800 years.

STEVE CARVER

This article explores the role of nature within the Dutch landscape and looks at recent developments in enhancing natural areas and connectivity across Holland and beyond.

At only 41,526 square kilometres in area (of which only 33,883 square kilometres is dry land) and with a population of nearly 16.5 million people, the Netherlands is the most densely populated of the principal European countries, with around 395 persons per square kilometre. This creates a need for a highly planned and managed landscape. As a result, few of us would normally associate Holland with wild nature, yet between the fields, houses and factories lies a remarkably dense network of National Parks, nature reserves and wildlife corridors. Many of these have always existed in one form or another, but have recently received protected area status. The Drentsche Aa, for example, was only designated as a National Park in 2002. Indeed, the Dutch nature 'planners' are currently engaged in a bold programme of nature creation, the flagship of which is the Oostvaardersplassen in Flevoland. Here, an area of polder of around 5600 hectares, reclaimed from the Ijsselmeer in 1968, was originally earmarked for agricultural land, housing and an industrial estate. It was later deemed surplus to requirements and has been developed into a natural wetland landscape of open water, reed beds and grasslands populated by a diverse range of bird life including spoonbills, cormorants, purple heron and Savi's warbler. To maintain a healthy ecosystem-mosaic, the reserve managers introduced a population of large herbivores in 1984, including Konik ponies, Heck cattle and Red deer. These are unmanaged and, with the exception of certain animal welfare practices, are essentially wild, self-sustaining populations. There are other such areas within the Biesbosch National Park, and along the Waal, Maas, and Lower Rhine rivers where previously agricultural land is being returned to a natural state by a combination of hands-off management, promotion of natural processes and introduced grazers.

Konik horses at Oostwaadersplassen (Hans Kampf)

Corridors, bridges and ecoducts...

The stated intent of the Dutch nature planners within the Ministry of Agriculture, Nature and Food Quality (LNV) is to create a highly connected network throughout the country and even joins up with similar networks in neighbouring Belgium and Germany. This is the Ecologische Hoofdstructuur (EHS or National Ecological Network), and is itself intended to link to the wider Pan European Ecological Network (PEEN) via core ecological areas, ecological development areas, preservation areas, and buffer zones with strategic ecological connections. The EHS takes its lead from Article 10 of the EU Habitats Directive which states:

> "Member States shall endeavour, where they consider it necessary, in their land-use planning and development policies and, in particular, with a view to improving the ecological coherence of the Natura 2000 network, to encourage the management of features of the landscape which are of major importance for wild fauna and flora. Such features

are those which, by virtue of their linear and continuous structure (such as rivers with their banks or the traditional systems for marking field boundaries) or their function as stepping stones (such as ponds or small woods), are essential for the migration, dispersal and genetic exchange of wild species."

Natura 2000 is the European network of protected nature areas and includes the intention to improve spatial connectivity between the protected areas for the sustainable protection of biodiversity. Connectivity is therefore a key concept of European nature conservation programmes. It is important in allowing for the movement of flora and fauna both as part of species re-introductions (whether planned or spontaneous) and in response to potential latitudinal and altitudinal migrations that might arise out of predicted climate change. Without such a system of connected natural areas and wildlife corridors some species might become isolated and locally extinct as habitats are modified. Because the original Natura 2000 network in the Netherlands contains insufficient connectivity, and the Dutch nature areas are fragmented and often widely separated, the LNV has proposed to link these areas via a series of bridges and corridors (Figure 1).

This is described in the paper on 'Ecological Networks: Experiences in the Netherlands... a joint responsibility for connectivity'.[1] This commitment extends to relocating agricultural production (including whole farms) and bridging physical barriers such as motorways with eco-bridges and eco-ducts (Figure 2).

The factors to connect ...

Many of these Dutch projects are based on the need not just for nature, but also for wash lands for flood protection and storage. Since the near-disastrous floods and mass-evacuations of 1995, the Dutch government has been seeking ways of making the low-lying flood plains and polders that make up a large part of the country more resilient to the effects of flooding and climate change. Reverting large areas of the flood plains which adjoin the major rivers and their distributaries in the Rhine delta area is one way of achieving this goal. Together with a highly informed and 'green' population these plans and the associated resources have met with only limited resistance from some local interests, since they are widely seen as being in the best national interest.

■ Ecological Network (water)

Ecological Network

➡ Indicative robust connection

— Robust connection

Figure 1. Ecological network proposals in Holland

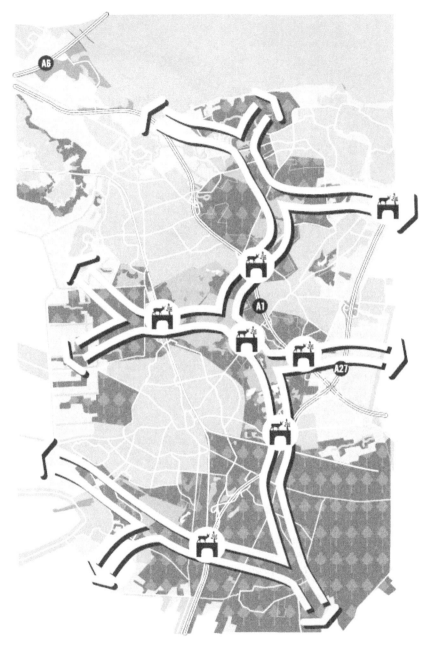

Figure 2. Eco-bridge proposals to counter habitat fragmentation

There are perhaps lessons here for our own implementation of the Nature 2000 network and linking up of existing designated areas within the UK. Efforts should be made towards mapping the potential linkages between our natural areas, improving those that already exist (whether notionally or on paper) and identifying gaps and opportunities for bridging these. Many of the UK's protected areas show remarkably good connectivity, whereas others do not, such as the 'Black Hole' of the Midlands area. A wider overview of the functionality of the UK's natural areas, their connectivity and resilience is needed. This needs to be done at multiple scales from national, through regional to local in order to develop both a broad brush and detailed understanding of the potential to link our nature areas into a network. Of course, good work is being done in this field, but a comprehensive overview and national strategy is perhaps still lacking. A multiple benefits model will help 'sell' this approach to both the general public and decision-making bodies, as well as making it worthy of public funds. The former Countryside Agency's 'Countryside In and Around Towns' initiative (2005) is perhaps a useful starting point in that it provides a framework for looking at green infrastructure for nature and people with a particular focus on functional green spaces at the urban-rural interface.[2] Connectivity is again seen as pivotal in planning a better linkage between these green spaces. One means of achieving this would be the bold use of existing physical networks in the form of floodplain corridors and river restoration schemes to link existing green infrastructure. Figure 3 shows existing Natura 2000 sites and other designations for part of the Greater Ouse catchment centred on the Humber. The flood plain areas show how the existing nature areas could be connected using flood plain nature corridors, given appropriate political will. With the Dutch experience in mind, this might just be the vehicle for promoting Natura 2000 connectivity across the UK over the next 20 years.

References

1. LNV (2004) Ecological Networks: Experiences in the Netherlands…A joint responsibility for connectivity.
http://www9.minlnv.nl/pls/portal30/docs/FOLDER/MINLNV/LNV/STAF/STA
F_DV/DOSSIERS/MLV_NPVN/SOORTEN_GEBIEDSBESCHERMING/MLV
_NPVN_NATUURWETGEVING_DOCUMENTEN/107046.PDF

2. Countryside Agency (2005) The Countryside In and Around Towns: a vision for connecting town and country in the pursuit of sustainable development.
http://www.countryside.gov.uk/Images/CAT_tcm2-22089.pdf

New nature in Holland – attitudes and achievements

ECOS 27 (3/4) 65-69
The Dutch are investing in new spaces for nature and in connecting them up.
Understanding what motivates this approach in Holland might help us make the
case here in Britain.

ALISON PARFITT

Two maps ...

I have two maps on my wall. One is the Character Map of England – Landscape, Wildlife, Natural and Cultural features. It is beautifully coloured, outlining the 159 different Character areas with towns and transport routes to show where you are. This map summarises a vast amount of knowledge about the diversity and character of our landscapes; and should be one of the main building blocks for the new agency Natural England.

Beside this map is one I brought back from the Netherlands. It is a more sketchy, lively bird's eye view of the Veluweroute, part of the Dutch ecological networks (EHS)[1] connecting 'nature' land and waterways across the Netherlands and into neighbouring countries. Drawings of numerous animals and bits of vegetation indicate the species (some are re-introductions) that the networks will support. Then walkers, canoeists and winter skaters illustrate how the human species benefit too. Here is creation and recreation. This map has a different feel - does it indicate a more dynamic aspiration for future land-use planning?

I went to the southern Netherlands with a lot of binocular-toting wildlife enthusiasts and it was wonderfully easy to be completely in the moment seeing beaver, spoonbills, beautiful gutsy Konik horses, Heck cattle and many other charismatic creatures in 'new' habitats. Nonetheless the visit sparked two broad questions:

First: What has changed the attitudes of a whole nation, to embrace this new nature?

Second: How are people persuaded to choose nature and wildlife above all else at a local level?

Here are thoughts on these two questions...

330

Heck bull with red deer in the background (Hans Kampf)

A solitary mustard

It was a Dutch ecologist who reminded me that in living memory, just over 50 years ago after WWII, there were people starving in the Netherlands. It is easy to imagine how that prompted a national commitment to feed the nation at home and the success of intensive agricultural production becoming a source of pride. This is now the most densely populated country in Europe and talking about land use to a Dutch friend prompted her to ask if I had seen any farm cows? "No, don't think I have", I replied. "Because they are all inside these days, it is more economic…" she said. On the last day of our visit, one of the group commented on not having seen wild flowers outside 'nature areas'. Another replied that he had seen one volunteer mustard on a road side.

The EHS will connect up Natura 2000 sites and deliver the EU HabitatsDirective[2] . It is seen mainly as a response to climate change threats and associated flood water management.[3] But perhaps even more significantly, when thinking about people's attitudes, the EHS is seen as a way to meet the increased Dutch demand for countryside. This springs from choices about use of free time, increasing prosperity, urbanisation and an ageing population. The Dutch want to have accessible nature closer to their doorsteps, without barriers or borders. They desire nature, which they can enjoy, walk in and cycle through. Is this why the EHS has struck a chord with local authorities and private enterprise as well as with nature organisations, and at a national policy level?

Pony burgers and seeing storks

The Geldersee Poort is the area between and around the cities of Arnhem, Nijmegen and Emmerich where the great River Rhine branches into the Lower Rhine and Waal. Here regular flooding, controlled by systems of summer and winter dykes, hampered the latest intensive agricultural advances so the lands known as the river forelands have been seen to be 'economically handicapped'. In 1992 WWF Netherlands launched *Living Rivers*. This scheme introduced clay extraction as a new economic driver which could:

- (partly) substitute the declining role of agriculture
- contribute to the ecological restoration of the riparian landscape
- contribute to improved and sustainable flood prevention.

New partnerships between land owners, the clay and sand extractors and brick makers and nature organisations have profited and grown. Surface clay deposits are removed and then nature reclaims the place. At the same time Stichting Ark[4], an NGO partnering WWF Netherlands, delivers a field education programme for primary schools and promotes the opportunities for the local population and for tourists who are discovering this new nature area. As an example they run the Wilderness Café where you can buy local produce and eat the meat from animals in herds of natural grazers. It really is an experience of sampling pony burgers, eating the view and seeing storks.[5]

A new type of flood

All this makes great sense and feels like a win-win. It is even more inspiring when we remember that it is the Dutch who centuries ago taught much of the world about draining wetlands, managing water and stemming the tides. Several times when arriving at a site, amongst the first things we were told is how far below sea level we were. But several people spoke about the great floods of '93 and '95. The power of these floods to overcome all controls came as a shock to a nation of people used to the idea that you move stock from one field to another by boat and live between land and water in harmonious ways. Somehow this shock was converted into realisation that it was time for established practices and cultures of water management to change. Even in this country of tightly managed land, with not a space wasted, the rivers must be given more land to swell and recede. Flood plains will flood. So documents talk of budgets for river flood defence delivering the EHS as well.

Prof Bob Johansen of the Institute for the Future IFTF, talking about another map, the IFTF Map of the Decade which outlines future trends that will shape our world, says that "it takes about 30 years for a major shift to become an 'overnight success'. The shift in the attitudes of consumers towards sustainability being a prime example."[6]   Perhaps some attitudes might be changing faster than that in the Netherlands.

Nature plus

When in nature areas in Holland I was very aware of the rest of the world at the same time. Enormous barges go about their international business on the rivers; giant pylons and wind turbines are obvious and effects of trains and traffic are often close. I saw my first beaver on the other side of the waterway from the hostel I was staying in. It all feels very local, with little feeling of being remote or 'in the wild'. Perhaps more like living different layers of life simultaneously, just like the EHS eco-bridges which carry the green of the landscape and animals of the nature places over multi-lane motorways and railway. But even with this clever layering, some choices have to be made.

The Dutch 'Serengeti' at Oostwaadersplassen (Hans Kampf)

Disappearing act

West of Arnhem and also on the Lower Rhine is the town of Renkum. Here the small Renkum stream flows beside the town, from the Veluwe to the north into the Rhine. On the western edge of the town, straddling the stream was a large industrial site of several hectares. Now it is not there.[7] The complete site was removed, not bridged over, in order to reinstate the valley of the Renkum stream as a green corridor connecting the Veluwe heathland with the Rhine valley. I expect that compensation funds were central to this disappearing act, as they have been elsewhere in acquiring strategic tracts of land for parts of the ecological network. Having a compensation fund to draw upon puts you in a helpful bargaining position, and in this instance a figure of Euro36 million was mentioned.

Fast changes

At a national level there seems to be much support for more nature and the ecological network approach, but how does this work at the intimate local government level, especially when the local economy is involved and jobs disappear? The Dutch have a commitment to complete their ambitious and robust ecological network by 2018. We could learn a lot from knowing how they are making this happen and how and why attitudes are changing.

References and notes

[1] Due to the large changes in land use since the beginning of the 20th century the countryside in the Netherlands has deteriorated a great deal. The area of nature in the countryside has halved from around 900,000 ha in 1900 to 450,000 ha in 1990. The EHS is an extensive national network of nature reserves linked by robust ecological wildlife corridors, covering 750,000 hectares. The Dutch are committed to have all this in place by 2018. Over 250,000 hectares will be developed from scratch to create the EHS. Around 150,000 hectares of agricultural land will be transformed into nature reserve. The 'new nature' is in part entrusted to nature conservation organisations. Increasingly often however, the land stays in private hands. In this case the owner receives a subsidy for private nature development.

[2] Working Paper Ecological Networks: Experiences in the Netherland by Monique Hoostmans & Hans Kampf pub Ministry of Agriculture, Nature & Food Quality Dec 04; Papers at European Nature Conference 2005 hosted by the Dutch in Apeldoorn and the resulting Apeldoorn Appeal http://www.natureconference.org/default.asp?id=173

[3] http://www.snm.nl/pdf/0100_climate_change_and_the_effects_on_nature_september_2005.pdf

[4] http://www.stichtingark.nl/

[5] http://assets.panda.org/downloads/policyguidegeldersepoortdef.pdf

[6] quoted in elements, journals of the Environment Council Issue 30 05/2006 Reviewing the Future

[7] Before and after photographs on page 16. Working Paper Ecological Networks: Experiences in the Netherlands by Monique Hoostmans & Hans Kampf pub Ministry of Agriculture, Nature & Food Quality Dec 04

PART III

Our once and future fauna

ECOS 29 (3/4) 4-17 (2008)
This article looks at progress with reintroducing the beaver in Scotland, and beyond to the ecological and cultural issues surrounding lynx and wolf.

DAN PUPLETT

On a sleety day in late October, some friends, my wife and I were lured to the Highland Wildlife Park in Kincraig, near Aviemore. The new star attractions were two magnificent Amur tigers, which rank among the most splendid and endangered predators on the planet. I was suitably impressed as one of them stretched up to begin devouring the deer haunch which had been dangled from a birch tree. It was snowing more heavily now, but the cat looked unconcerned, tearing at the meat with almost lazy, yet soberingly powerful shakes of its massive head. I later reflected on how we naturally appeal to people in Russia, India, Africa and elsewhere to protect and try to co-exist with large animals, even those that present a potential threat to livelihoods and lives. I then wondered what some of those people might think of our pleas if they knew of our fuss over the return of beaver, a mellow aquatic rodent, to Scotland!

September's reintroductions conference, 'Wild, Free and Coming Back?', held in Findhorn, near Inverness, was to my mind a rich and fruitful event. In hindsight it would have been interesting to have had among the delegates people who live daily alongside leopards, elephants, tigers and the like, to give a different perspective on relatively easy-going neighbours such as the beaver and lynx!

Nevertheless, progress is slowly but surely being made with mammal reintroductions in the UK. What follows is a review of the current situation surrounding three of the most serious candidates for reintroduction, the beaver, lynx and wolf, including some thoughts and ideas arising out of the conference.

Return of the beaver

The granting of the licence for a trial beaver reintroduction in Scotland was a milestone for UK nature conservation, and a cause for celebration. It was also the culmination of a long and convoluted process and a great deal of hard work.

The European beaver *(Castor fiber)* was once widely distributed through Britain, but was hunted to extinction probably by the end of the 16th Century, chiefly for its fur, meat and castoreum.[1] This pattern of exploitation occurred throughout Europe, although it has since been reintroduced to more than 24 European countries. For over a century there have several unsuccessful attempts at restoring the beaver to Britain[2], but in 1994 serious investigations into the possibility of beaver reintroduction began, prompted by the 1992 EU Habitats Directive, which requires Member States to examine the feasibility of reintroducing certain missing species.[3] Although it was ascertained that there was sufficient habitat and public support, a small but powerful lobby opposed it with largely groundless concerns.[2]

Hopes were raised again in 2002 when an application was made to the Scottish Government for a trial reintroduction. However this was turned down in 2005 on the questionable grounds that as a protected species, the beaver could not be controlled by lethal means if the need arose. Also, as the proposed release site, Knapdale, is in a Special Area of Conservation, there were concerns that unacceptable damage would be done to the Atlantic Oakwood habitat. For the most part conservationists refuted the validity of these claims, but the licence was refused nonetheless.

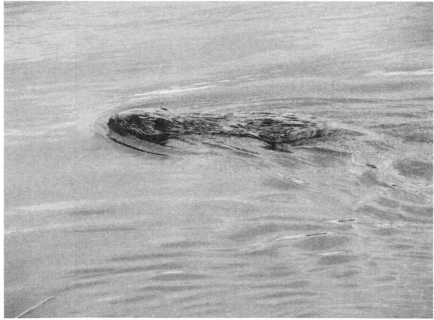

Swimming beaver (Derek Gow Consultancy)

The beaver trial

Encouraging signs appeared with the newest Environment Minister, Michael Russell MSP, clearly expressing his support for a beaver reintroduction. At the reintroductions conference, Iain Valentine of the Royal Zoological Society of Scotland (RZSS) pointed out that the change of government and minister, combined with the European beaver's inclusion in the Scottish Natural Heritage (SNH) Species Action Framework were all key factors in the favourable response to the licence application. The Scottish Wildlife Trust (SWT) and RZSS conducted a consultation in the mid-Argyll area to assess local feeling towards bringing back beavers. Encouragingly, around 72% of the population were in favour and 24% opposed. In the immediate vicinity of Knapdale, opposition was stronger, with 44% for, and 54% against.[4] Nonetheless it was still deemed that this represented sufficient support overall.

SWT and RZSS submitted the licence application to the Scottish Government on Christmas Eve 2007, and approval was given in May 2008. The beavers were trapped in Norway in September and will be held in quarantine before being released in April or May 2009. The release site, Knapdale Forest on the Argyll Peninsula is owned by Forestry Commission Scotland and the trial will be jointly managed by SWT, RZSS and other partners, and guided by the Beaver Steering Group. The site contains a variety of woodland habitats and a substantial amount of lush riparian habitat.

The beavers will not be fenced in, but will be radio-tagged so that they can be retrieved if they go astray. The licence contains specific recommendations, such as mink control to reduce the possibility of predation on beaver kits, and the establishment of a forum to allow the views of the local community to be fed into the decision-making process. Effects on other wildlife, vegetation, hydrology and the local economy will all be closely monitored.[5]

The trial will be evaluated against a range of criteria. To be deemed a success there have to be certain levels of survival along with a stable or increasing population, the reintroduction has to be integrated with habitat management and restoration, and positive contributions to ecosystem function and the economy of the area must be demonstrated. It will be seen as a failure if mortality levels are too high, if there is significant ecological or economic damage, or if overall costs significantly exceed expectations.

SNH will provide independent monitoring and report back to the Scottish Government on the relative success of the project. If at any point during the trial, insurmountable problems arise, then an exit strategy would be implemented. However, if the trial is successful, at the end of the five-year period, another licence application could be made to the Scottish Government, but this time for a full reintroduction.

It is encouraging to see that the arguments in favour of beaver restoration are becoming more widely appreciated, thanks to excellent educational work by the likes of SWT, RZSS, the Aigas Field Centre and others. There is no doubt that the presence of these ecosystem engineers can dramatically enhance biodiversity. Furthermore, worries about the *Giardia* parasite and impacts on salmonid movements appear to be unfounded.[3]

In recent years there have been several projects involving captive beavers that have played a useful role in educating the public and firing imaginations as to how much more complete our freshwater and woodland ecosystems might be with these influential and charismatic rodents back in their rightful place. Although none of these projects are reintroductions, I believe they will continue to have a crucial role to play in the process of restoring this mammal to Britain. It is also heartening that beaver reintroduction is being given serious consideration in England and Wales.

Return of the lynx

The Eurasian lynx *(Lynx lynx)* has been the most seriously discussed candidate for a potential predator reintroduction, much of the work on the feasibility of its return having been carried out by David Hetherington when at Aberdeen University. It is clear that there is sufficient habitat for lynx in Scotland. Lynx aren't overly choosy about the 'nativeness' of woodland, and conifer plantations would be welcome cover, in combination with the expanding area of native woodland.[6]

It has been shown that there is a habitat network in the Highlands capable of supporting around 400 lynx, a viable population which would also be one of Europe's largest.[7] A smaller population of around 60 could live in the Southern Uplands, although this would not be viable as a breeding population and would need supplementing with new genetic stock. Measures to mitigate the barrier effects of busy roads in central Scotland would also be desirable to link the two populations.

There is sufficient prey, roe deer *(Capreolus capreolus)* being its main quarry, and thus the lynx could play a role in encouraging woodland regeneration. It is not a threat to humans, nor is it perceived as one, and the potential for conflicts with farming also seem minimal as the lynx tends to keep to woodland cover, and sheep are usually on open ground. Evidence from Sweden suggests that lynx predation can be a significant factor in limiting fox *(Vulpes vulpes)* populations[8] and therefore could have benefits for ground-nesting birds.[6]

On a visit to the Carpathian Mountains in Romania, my guide informed me that some of the shepherds in the region had been completely unaware that there were any lynx in the area, although they were accustomed to warding off bears and wolves with the aid of their fierce dogs. In a lifetime in the area, over a decade of which had been spent tracking and studying local carnivores, my guide himself had only ever seen a lynx on two occasions – and this was in one of Europe's lynx hotspots! Yet in spite of this elusiveness, there is no doubt that the lynx is a significant boost to tourism in parts of Europe where this charismatic cat is used to symbolise the wildness of places; the same could be the case in Scotland.

Lynx: lower, Iberian Pardel lynx; middle, Central European and upper, Scandinavian subspecies. (Peter Taylor)

Wolves and the ecology of fear

Wolf *(Canis lupus)* reintroduction is a topic guaranteed to get journalists drooling. Clearly it is crucial to communicate the facts regarding any animal, maybe even more so with the wolf considering the amount of misinformation that surrounds it. Perhaps the most relevant piece of research on this issue is a report by researchers at Imperial College and the University of Oslo that used population modelling software to forecast some of the ecological and economic impacts of reintroducing a population of wolves to the Scottish Highlands.[9]

Their predictions were based on the hypothetical release of three wolf packs, each consisting of a breeding pair and two subordinates. The simulation showed that after an initial population expansion, numbers stabilised at 25 wolves per 1,000 square kilometres. After 60 years red deer *(Cervus elaphus)* populations would be reduced to seven per square kilometre. This reduction could represent as much as 50% of the population, and could be more dramatic than has been observed in other countries because of the slow rate of reproduction of Scottish red deer. It is often assumed that given the current high deer populations in Scotland, wolves would have little impact on their numbers. While that may be the case in the shorter term, an important influence on ungulates would be on distribution and feeding patterns. The situation in Yellowstone National Park illustrates this effect, referred to as the 'ecology of fear'.[10] In Yellowstone, where wolves were extirpated in 1926, elk (synonymous with red deer) had been concentrating their browsing in riparian areas, which were sheltered and provided a ready supply of food. Following the reintroduction of wolves however, the elk were much more vulnerable in those areas, and tended to feed more on open hilltops where they had a better prospect of the surrounding area. This resulted in a trophic cascade, with riparian vegetation such as aspen and willow regenerating, encouraging and benefiting song birds, beavers, insects etc.

In economic terms, the Scottish wolf report suggests that the influence of wolves on deer populations would dramatically reduce the need for hind culling.[9] While deer estates usually make a profit from stags killed as trophies, culling hinds actually incurs a loss, and a significant saving might be made if wolves were present. Other knock-on effects resulting from the presence of wolves would be increased woodland regeneration, a possible reduction in Lyme disease (which is carried by deer ticks), and benefits to grouse moors due to a reduction in foxes and other smaller predators.

The authors of the report acknowledge the potential for conflict with sheep farming. Free roaming Scottish sheep would be ready prey for wolves. If predation of sheep did occur, while it may have minimal economic consequences for subsidised farmers, the emotional response should not be underestimated. Wolves' propensity to prey on domestic dogs would be emotive and the authors suggest it would be partly addressed by education of dog owners. Compensation schemes for livestock losses could be employed, and organisations such as the Wolves and Humans Foundation may well have a role to play in administering these.[11] In 2005 subsidies changed so that rather than paying farmers per head of sheep, a Single Farm Payment is now in place. As a result of this and other factors, sheep farming is going into steep decline[12], and with proposals to end subsidies for hill farmers in 2013, the future of hill farming is in question.[13]

It could be that tourism may become a viable alternative to farming for some rural communities. Judging by the situation in Yellowstone, wolves could be a substantial draw for tourists. The Scottish wolf report does not address this aspect, but there seems to be no obvious reason why the presence of wolves would not result in a significant boost for tourism in the Highlands, possibly making a substantial contribution to the Scottish rural economy.

The report also surveyed attitudes of various stakeholders, and found that public opinion was fairly positive, and that while the National Farmers' Union for Scotland as an organisation was strongly opposed, the actual sample of farmers showed much milder opposition, possibly because of the low profitability of sheep farming.

At the conference, Alan Watson Featherstone made a case for the reintroduction of the wolf by 2043. There were comments that this was much too far off, while others believed it to be overly optimistic, and that attitudes would not change in time. In any case, he advocated the use of 'stretch goals' and 'backcasting'. This involves setting targets which may seem overly ambitious viewed from the current paradigm, but can be achieved with bold, creative thinking, strategic planning and a willingness to think outside the box.[14]

Thoughts on strategy

The granting of the licence for the beaver trial was a huge step forward for species reintroductions in the UK. The trial is in good hands, and financial support and continued good publicity are what is now needed. Regarding the predators, several interesting points were raised at the conference. There were strong calls to act soon to promote the reintroduction of the wolf and especially the lynx. Roy Dennis, who has experience in reintroduction projects, notably the sea eagle, felt that the conservation community is often far too cautious, compared to sectors such as business and industry, which are more inclined to make bold moves and to just get things done. There were also notes of caution – handling the issue clumsily, or preaching to the wrong people at the wrong time, could backfire.[15] Bearing in mind the Autumn 2008 protests from crofters on the west coast of Scotland, concerned that their lambs are under threat from sea eagles *(Haliaeetus albicilla)* it is clear that reintroductions can be an extremely sensitive issue and that appropriate timing and effective communication are crucial.

It is essential that the debate is kept as open and inclusive as possible. Roy Dennis pointed out that while it is impossible to get everyone to agree, it is also vital that communities have a sense of ownership for reintroductions, and ultimately it needs to be local people who drive reintroductions forward themselves. People have to *want* these creatures back for it to work.

There was general agreement at the conference that education is key. This would be true of any proposed reintroductions, although carnivores, particularly wolves, present the most significant challenges and suffer the most from a frequently inaccurate negative image. Developing an appropriate educational resource, and funding it, would therefore be critical initial steps, and it was highlighted that a good deal of this work needs to be aimed at tomorrow's decision-makers.

Science or emotion?

Peter Cairns, co-founder of Tooth and Claw, gave a fresh slant on the debate by stating *"the science doesn't matter"*. Some ecologists may have shuffled in their seats, but he was stressing that talk of "trophic cascades" and "keystone species" is unlikely to resonate with Joe Public. As the Tooth and Claw project demonstrated, most people's relationship to charismatic wildlife is to a large extent an emotional one.[16] While I, (and no doubt Peter) believe that the science *is* relevant, as humans we engage the world on many levels, and not only with our intellects. When animals are naturally perceived as sexy, cool, scary, infuriating and more, the science inevitably becomes just one part of the picture. Indeed, a strong case was made for engaging the cultural and aesthetic aspects of reintroductions, and recognising that art, literature and music relating to creatures such as the wolf, can influence people's attitudes.

As well as dramatically enriching our own island, from a global perspective reintroductions may have a role in the conservation of charismatic species overseas.[17] We encourage poorer and sometimes more densely populated countries to conserve animals that are often more dangerous than the proposed Scottish candidates. Might we have more credibility if we allowed a bit more wildness to return to our own back yard?

References

1. Yalden, D. (1999) *The History of British Mammals*. Poyser: London.
2. Gow, D. (2006) Bringing back the beaver. *ECOS*. 27 (1), 57- 65.
3. Gaywood, M, Batty, D. and Galbraith, C. (2008) Reintroducing the European Beaver in Britain. *British Wildlife* 19 (6) 381-391.
4.http://www.swt.org.uk/Uploads/Downloads/BeaverConsultationReport_Dec07.pdf

5. http://www.scottishbeavers.org.uk

6. Hetherington, D. (2006) *The lynx in Britain's past, present and future. ECOS* 27 (1), 66-74.

7. Hetherington, D. A., Miller, D. R., Macleod, C. D. and Gorman, M. L. (2008) A potential habitat network for the Eurasian lynx *Lynx lynx* in Scotland. *Mammal Review,* 38 (4), 285-303.

8. Helldin, J.O., Liberg, O. & Gloersen, G. (2006). Lynx *(Lynx lynx)* killing red foxes *(Vulpes vulpes)* in boreal Sweden – frequency and population effects. *Journal of Zoology,* 270 (4), 657- 663.

9. Nilsen, E.B., Milner-Gulland, E.J., Schofield, L., Mysterud, A., Stenseth, N.C., Coulson, T. (2006). Wolf reintroduction to Scotland: public attitudes and consequences for red deer management. *Proceedings of the Royal Society B.*

10. Ripple, W. J. & Beschta, R. L. (2003) Wolf reintroduction, predation risk, and cottonwood recovery in Yellowstone National Park. *Forest Ecology and Management,* 184, 299–313.

11. Morley, R. (2007) Is the time right for reintroduction? *The Newsletter of the Wolves and Humans Foundation,* 6 (Spring), 1-2.

12. Scottish Agricultural College (2008) *Farming's Retreat from the Hills* SAC, available at: http://www.sac.ac.uk/mainrep/pdfs/retreatreport.pdf

13. McIlwraith, E. (Broadcast: 3 October 2008) Sheep from the Hills. *Landward.* BBC.

14. Manning, A., Lindenmayer, D., Fischer, J. (2006) Stretch goals and backcasting: approaches for overcoming barriers to large-scale ecological restoration. *Restoration Ecology,* 14 (4) 487-492.

15. Breitenmoser, U. and Arx, M.V. (2004) Reintroduced lynx in Europe: their distribution and problems. *ECOS* 3 (4), 64-68.

16. Cairns, P. and Hamblin, M. (2007) *Tooth and Claw: living alongside Britain's predators.* Whittles Publishing: Dunbeath.

17. Taylor, P. (2005) *Beyond Conservation.* Earthscan: London.

BEAVER

Beavers in Britain – laying the foundations

ECOS 23 (2) 23-26 (2002)
Beavers will soon be out of quarantine and part of the Mull of Kintyre landscape. Where else can they go in Britain, and how will they refashion their host habitats?

PETER TAYLOR

The beaver is about to become the first formerly indigenous mammal to be re-introduced to Britain. Scottish Natural Heritage and Forest Enterprise have instigated a project in the forest of Knapdale (Mull of Kintyre) that will act as a pilot scheme. If 'successful', other sites will follow. The first animals are due to be released in Spring 2003. The scheme follows ten years of fact-finding and consultation, since the idea was mooted by, among others, Alan Watson of Trees-for-Life at Findhorn, The beaver was part of a longer term vision for re-establishing the ancient Caledonian Forest as a wild and dynamic ecosystem with its full set of herbivores and carnivores: first the beaver, then the boar, moose, bear, lynx and wolf.

By Brittany's streams...

In 1992 I accompanied Alan Watson and assorted SNH, English Nature, and Wildlife Trust enthusiasts on a visit to the closest European beaver re-introduction sites – just over the water in Britanny's Parc Amorique. We caught little more than a glimpse of the elusive nocturnal rodents, but had ample opportunity to look at habitats and see how the Parc dealt with the potential problems of conflict with agricultural and fishery interests. I was struck by the variety of habitats the beavers occupied – belying conceptions from literature, especially American.

The programme in Britanny had begun in the 1970s following successful introductions elsewhere in France, and the Parc was still expanding the programme by purchasing suitable habitat. Beaver had colonised a variety of sites ranging from small streams in meadowland, reed-fringed lakes (one with a nuclear power station much like Trawsfynnedd in Snowdonia), and most remarkably, some steep boulder-strewn mountain streams reminiscent of Dartmoor. Small dams were evident on the smaller streams, but there were no large beaver ponds and lodges – European beaver do not build large dams, but seem content with small pools, wet meadows and even mountainous terrain, where they engineer at most a series of still reaches and generally wetter meadows. Above all, beaver require luxuriant streamside vegetation for their summer feeding, and ample supplies of usually small trees for winter feed when they strip the bark from twigs.

We could see clearly how the French beaver had coppiced the emergent willow, alder, ash and even oak, creating a bushy habitat. The stereotypical knawed-off stumps of large trees were not in evidence. It took a practised eye to tell that beaver were present – the meadows and intermittent pools of still-water had lots of emergent vegetation with a pattern of small bushes and glades outward of 50m from the streams. In the mountain stream habitat there were few signs, and rather than a lodge, a den was secreted under big boulders on essentially dry land.

Countering officialdom

Everyone on that fact-finding tour to Brittany was impressed and expectations were that re-introducing beaver would be no problem. There was ample experience of beaver co-existing happily with game fisheries in Norway, where they were re-introduced earlier in the century. Forestry interests had little to be concerned about (Finland led the European recovery programme – unfortunately bringing in American beaver to augment the native species at a time when they were thought conspecific) and in any case modern forestry now practices conservation planting for streamsides. Agriculture could prove problematic but given the plethora of EU schemes to pay farmers for conservation value in an area on essentially marginally economic land, that should not be a stumbling block.

However, attempts to interest the Countryside Council for Wales, the National Trust and others, for Snowdonia (and to steal a march on the Scots) demonstrated what lay ahead. Nobody wanted to stick their necks out – "the Scots are leading on that one", and officialdom was glad to keep out of any controversy. SNH persevered, however, and set up the obligatory consultation process that finally found an approving public and a willing participant in Forest Enterprise. Even so, neighbouring landowners in Knapdale campaigned to have the programme stopped on the grounds of potential impact on sport fishing. This despite an extensive educational programme that should have allayed such fears – salmon and trout can benefit from the enhanced riparian habitats.

Beyond quarantine

The Scottish project now has some Norwegian animals in quarantine and it looks as if the first family group will be let lose next spring. However, I was surprised to discover only last year that Kent Wildlife Trust were about to let beaver loose in one of their reserves! No consultation process, no computer models, no messing! Except on closer inspection it is not a 're-introduction' programme – the beaver are 'management tools' in a wider scheme to re-wild Near Natural Areas and use herbivores (Heck and Highland cattle and wild ponies as well as roe deer). The animals will be penned and carefully monitored to assess their effectiveness. The Kent Wildlife Trust now has several animals through the quarantine period. So, England lead by the back door. Perhaps the Countryside Council for Wales will be more open to assessing sites once the trial periods are over.

Beaver were once extensive residents on the major rivers and wetlands of Britain, and well into the Scottish highlands. They were trapped to extinction by the 13th century, for their musk as well as their fur. Derek Yalden gives a detailed account of their history, including place names related to beaver, and the archeological evidence for their general distribution.[1] They were already scarce by Saxon times. The question is to what extent could they re-establish themselves in former habitats such as the Broads, the Somerset Levels and marshes around the Humber? Most of the English wetlands are now a complex of levees, dykes and pumping stations with small nature reserves where water regimes are artificially regulated. In the fens, some reserves such as Wicken stand above the surrounding terrain, and in the Somerset levels newly engineered reed beds are as much as a meter below the water level in the main dykes. In these highly engineered systems, beaver would be rather chaotic management tools. Perhaps the answer lies in a few Near Natural Area schemes such as the Kent experiment, and they could be part of river restoration projects where natural watersheds prevent colonisation of areas where their presence would be more problematic. In the Parc Amorique, the authorities sought out and purchased suitable habitat, and held a land-bank for exchange with farmers.

Exit strategies

If we can cope with the beaver, the precedent will be set for the return of the other animals whose spirits have long been absent. In Native American lore, the beaver symbolises the building of strong foundations (the foundations of its dams are extremely resistant to winter floods), industrious activity, and the maxim of always having more than one exit from any situation. In ecological terms, the lush beaver meadows provide a foundation for richer biodiversity, and especially for moose, which feed in the shallows. Moose are also a major constituent in the diet of wolf. Native Americans would study the habits of animals and become imbued with their spirit, so it is interesting that for those

346

who have worked hard to get the beaver here, there are many caveats and exit points for this re-introduction programme.

Notes and References

1. Yalden, D (1999) *The History of British Mammals* Poyser.

Details of the projects mentioned in this article can be found at:

Scottish Beaver Network: www.scotsbeaver.org
Kent Wildlife Trust: www.kentwildlifetrust.org.uk
Scottish Natural Heritage: www.snh.org.uk

Bringing back the beaver

ECOS 27 (1) 57-65 (2006)
If we cannot restore the beaver as an architect of wetland biodiversity and good water management then any talk of future wild lands and wilderness is meaningless.

DEREK GOW

Beaver trends in Britain and Europe

The fact that the European beaver (*Castor fiber*) was once widely distributed throughout Britain is corroborated by a rich body of archaeological evidence, place name associations and historic references.[1] It was probably more abundant in lower Britain where larger, lusher wetlands with longer growing seasons ensured its prehistoric existence in considerable numbers. Dam remnants and field signs have been identified from a range of locations and an indication that the species excavated bank-side tunnels is supported by the discovery of an adult's skeleton in a burrow on the banks of the river Frome in Somerset.

Beaver were hunted to extinction for their valuable fur, meat, castoreum and body oils. Their slaughter was based purely on their product value and not as in the case of the wolf (*Canis Lupus*) because they were responsible for significant human inconvenience, commercial loss or superstitious fear.

The only written description of this species' natural history in Britain comes from the journal of Giraldus Cambrensis who recorded their presence on the Welsh river Teivi in 1188. In 1526 Hector Boece recorded them as being abundant around Lochness but by 1577 William Harrison the Canon of Windsor stated that:

> "I wortherilie doubt whether that of our beavers or marterns may be thought to be the lesse" "...the tail of this beast is like unto a thin whetstone, as the body unto a monstrous rat; the beast also itself is of such force in the teeth, that it will gnaw an hole through a thick plank, or sheer through a double billet in a night; it loveth also the stillest rivers." [2]

This historic pattern of over exploitation was repeated throughout Europe. By the 16th century European beavers were largely extinct and North American pelts were beginning to enter the British fur market.[3] At their lowest point the European beaver was reduced to 200 on the Elbe, 30 on the Rhone, 100 in Telemark and less than 400 in the Pripet Marshes of Belarus.[4] By the beginning of the 20th century this decline had been reversed with legal protection and European beavers have now been restored to over 24 nations where they were formerly extinct. They are currently estimated to number around 639,000 individuals in mainland Europe.[4]

So why are there still no wild beavers in Britain? It's not for the want of effort as there have been a number of historic releases of both European and Canadian beavers (*Castor canadensis*). In 1870 beavers escaped from Sotterley Park in Suffolk but "their lodges were deemed an eyesore and therefore they were destroyed".[5] Also in 1870 beaver were released into a large enclosure at Leonardslee in Sussex where one family of "five old beavers and their young... converted a narrow brook into a long lake of some 50 yards by 15 or 20 yards broad".[6] In 1874 the Marquess of Bute released one pair of French and one pair of Canadian beavers into an enclosure near Kilchattan bay on the island of Bute.[5] Although these animals fought with each other and none survived long they were replaced with another colony which was still in existence in 1890 when they were visited by the Glasgow Naturalists Society.[7] Around 1880 the photo shown here was taken of a tame beaver in a Scottish stream and in 1902 the Duke of Argyll introduced seven beavers into the grounds of Inverary Castle. Escapes of Canadian beavers have occurred in recent years in Dumbartonshire, Somerset and Kent.

A European beaver photographed in Scotland around 1880.

The most intriguing and forward thinking of all these random efforts was a 'nearly ran' exercise in the Lake District. In 1969 the Forestry Commission's chief forester for the Lake District, Bill Grant returned from a trip to Canada impressed by the habitat creation skills of the beaver. With the support of his boss Jack Chard he started to release beavers in Grizedale forest. Two holding ponds were dug and fenced to acclimatise the beavers, wetland trees were planted and an observation hide built. Although most of the personnel involved with this project are now dead it is believed that the Nature Conservancy Council persuaded the Commission not to proceed with this venture.

In 1977 a campaign to reintroduce the European beaver was instigated by *Wildlife Magazine* under the then editorship of Nigel Sitwell. This advanced all the modern arguments for their restoration but was put down by Sir Christopher Lever who argued that beaver reintroduction would lead to their felling conifers, that valuable farmland would be flooded, that they would consume fruit or cereal crops, that capture would not be easy and that farmers, foresters and fishermen would not support their presence.[8]

Beaver reintroduction - the groundwork and the prejudice

The torturous politics of official beaver reintroduction began in 1994 when, prompted by the 1992 European Union Habitats Directive, Scottish Natural Heritage (SNH) began to consider the prospect of restoring several species of former native mammals. Wolves and wild boar (*Sus scrofa*) were discounted but beaver were considered possible. English Nature (EN) also examined the prospects for their restoration at this time and quietly concluded that it would be feasible before deftly ducking-out of the process in order to avoid the verbal flak of opponents. Consultants examining the feasibility of reintroduction into the Scottish countryside concluded there was widespread suitable habitat. Public consultation exercises on the desirability of reintroduction were undertaken and these suggested a local support of 65% and a national support of 86% in favour. (M. Gaywood. Personal communication).

Despite the transparency of this process a trade-off with opposing interest groups culminated in a virtual stalemate by 1998. This was broached in 1999 when a trial release was proposed for a site offered by the Forestry Commission at Knapdale in Kintyre. A comprehensive assessment of the impact of beavers on their immediate environment costing in excess of £500,000 was designed to prove to a minute but politically powerful opposition that their perceived concerns were groundless. They proved implacable to even this limited option and the Scottish Executive refused a licence for the project to proceed despite receiving a clear public mandate.

The project's few opponents accused SNH of being "economical with the truth" while they laboured to create a facade of malicious cant. Beaver were labelled as "disease ridden rodents" which rendered forests "killed, swamped, drowned". The most absurd of these 'braveheart' cries came from landowner Robin Malcolm who stated that "...these are English creatures. There are no plans to introduce them in England because the English wouldn't have them". These views were neither commonly held nor representative. In 2002 I took two juvenile female beavers to the Scottish Game fair in Perthshire for an information display organised by the Game Conservancy Trust. In talking to a wide range of country people at the event it was evident that most were content with the species restoration providing reasonable management controls were in place. A minority believed beaver reintroduction to be a good thing and a minority believed it to be bad. The only implacable opponent I encountered proved to be a large landowner who repudiated the ecological ability of beavers, raged about seals eating his salmon, raptors eating his pheasants and the fact that in his considered opinion there were too many coloured people in Birmingham. This 'cutting edge' thought process was not historically untypical of the large landowning class which linked strong antipathy to "them bloody useless" wild mammals with equally strong racist sentiment. In 1886 a debate to use public money to assist the extermination of the by then already scarce and economically insignificant Thylacine (Thylacinus cynocephalus) was considered by the Tasmanian parliament. During the proceedings a Mr Hawkes stated that "he might shortly have to ask for a vote to exterminate another animal his constituents were suffering from – the yellow agony - ...the Chinaman".[9] Presumably by this stage there were no Aborigines left to hunt.

If a list of contemporary objections were independently drawn today they would differ little from those advanced by Christopher Lever. In a changing climate of land use they are however largely insignificant and in any case had a fragile grounding in fact.

Beaver grooming (Chris Robbins/ Derek Gow Consultancy)

Beaver benefits

In a time of changing political priorities the Forestry Commission is now moving from a timber production to an ecological ethos. We know that European beaver have no appetite for conifers other than the introduced North American hemlocks (*Tsuga spp*) and that although their dams do drown trees these now constitute a more valuable resource for woodpeckers, beetles and bats than they do for the treasury coffers.

Beavers have a positive effect on coarse fish populations and a neutral relationship with game fish. It has been suggested that beaver dams in the head waters of Scottish salmon rivers would destroy spawning beds. Although this is a debatable contention it is true that beavers can build dams from rocks. However they have not yet developed the ability to consume them and in the treeless uplands scalped by historic overgrazing this myth is discountable. Experience from Norway where a healthy, wild salmon population exists demonstrates that they can readily leap beaver dams to spawn in the waters above (Halley. Personal communication).

351

Flooding of farmland is a relatively easy issue to resolve by the drainage of dams, their removal, the translocation of beavers or their humane culling when this is no longer possible. From ample European evidence in landscapes similar to Britain we know that beaver populations spread very slowly and are extremely easy to effectively control (Halley. Personal communication).

As the use of the countryside changes, more persuasive political arguments to restore this natural engineer are beginning to emerge. On 31 January 2006 the *Daily Express* ran a head line "Britain Runs Out Of Water". The article explained that both underground and surface water supplies were at their lowest level since 1904 and that water conservation measures would have to be introduced within weeks. Although this is being blamed on a second successive winter of lower than normal rainfall there is little doubt in the medium term that increasing water use coupled with extensive house building programmes in the South east of England will exacerbate this issue further. Politicians and policy makers now recognise that the over-engineering of our countryside has proved disastrous for water retention. An ever increasing number of communities are now faced with a hazardous cycle of 'boom and bust' typified by torrents pouring through their houses, villages or towns in the winter followed by a hose-pipe ban two months later. No matter how many reservoirs we build this will not prove sustainable if we do not address the vital need to retain more water in the uplands. Sponge complexes of bogs, pools, lakes and wet meadows are all common features of beaver generated landscapes. They slow and retain water allowing it to percolate at leisure down to the lowlands below. Recent studies in Keriou, France conservatively suggest that the retention of water in a single channel of 1025 meters in length rose from a capacity of 515.5 meters cubed to 3230.85 when it was dammed continuously by beavers. It is highly likely that the activity of this species in the uplands of Britain would give us water management services we badly need. As the value of upland agricultural production declines there would be a good case for landowners being paid to manage beavers.

Beaver are an incredibly well studied species in both continental Europe and North America. In Indian folklore they fulfilled the function of the "earths kidneys" and there can be little credible dispute about their pivotal ecological role as the generators of healthy wetlands. On 1 February 2006 the Royal Society for Protection of Birds, The Environment Agency and English Nature launched a Wetland Biodiversity Strategy for Britain. The importance of wetlands for wildlife and aquifers was highlighted in their press release which reeled out bitterns, water voles and otters as likely beneficiaries. No mention was made of the architect of just such an environment - the beaver. If we fail to return this creature then our own efforts to restore sustainable wetlands will be forever plagued by loss of open water, a requirement to create artificial barriers and scrub encroachment, all of which are transitory features of beaver habitats. There are unarguably greater densities of bacterial, plant, insect, fish, amphibian, bird and mammal life in the habitats created by beavers than in those where they are absent.[10]

Obstacles to change

Why has there been so much fuss over a species that we know from both historic and contemporary European experience is easy to control, extremely ecologically important and could be such a powerful tool for our own ultimate benefit? In many other European countries where reintroduction has occurred it has done so in the face of stiff opposition from other land-use lobbies only to culminate in complete anticlimax when beavers proved to have a negligible commercial impact. Beaver damage in the whole of Bavaria is currently estimated to amount to a couple of hundred thousand euros per year and is easily managed. The counter value of their ecological activities has never been assessed. In stark contrast car insurance companies pay at least 35,000,000 euros annually for collisions with game species. This figure does not include uninsured damage due to game bird collisions, death and injury claims, forest damage, crop damage, deer fence subsidies, deer damage prevention schemes, agricultural subsidies or un-harvested agricultural waste. Even if this is calculated on a conservative basis the annual bill for beaver damage equates to significantly less than the average daily cost to the public purse for all the above combined. (G. Schwab. Personal communication).

The concerns raised about the reintroduction of beaver are mainly based on ignorance, conservative thought, and fear of the unknown. This conservatism is a natural characteristic of tight knit communities used to facing natural hazards and is commonly reinforced by the precepts of tradition. In a time of changing land-use priorities and economics this does not negate the necessity for change. To an extent the stridency of a minority of the landed class is driven by a legacy of expectation that their views are correct and should be acted upon. Our modern wildlife compliment is a diffuse legacy of their historic whim and savage slaughter. They have a threadbare soapbox from which to lecture others on environmental responsibility.

A recent conference in Wales reported that of the national Gross Domestic Product agriculture contributed 1% which was falling whilst tourism contributed over 20% and was rising. Ecotourism developed by rural communities can allow them to reap the rewards and retain much of the income locally. This is something that we should all be concerned to develop. It is highly likely that the growing market in the watchers of sea eagles, red kites or ospreys would prove highly amenable to the addition of beavers.

Recent action and results

The refusal of the Scottish Executive to grant a licence to the beaver reintroduction in Knapdale poses a challenge. What should we do now? There have been two well publicised projects to employ beavers as habitat mangers in England. The first of these in 2001 at Kent Wildlife Trust's Ham Fen Nature Reserve with the sanction of EN encountered considerable opposition from the senior civil servants of Global Wildlife Division of DEFRA. Their political chicanery had no good reason and no legal mandate and extended the quarantine period from a statutory six months to thirteen. The personal intervention of Michael Meecher broke this deadlock which resulted in the needless deaths of several beavers and produced a weak release population.

The second attempt in 2005 at the Lower Mill estate in the Cotswold Water Park clarified the law in that no licence is required to contain European beaver in securely fenced areas. Six beavers – two family groups of three males and three females – are now enclosed on the Lower Mill estate in a 15ha gravel pit lined with an abundance of willow (*Salix spp*) and semi emergent plants. The whole site is on private land which is securely fenced to prevent escape and is being monitored by ecologists from the Cotswold Water Park. The beavers' interaction with other wildlife is positive and their wood debris is soon expected to help the fortunes of the greater stag beetle. In the near future the fence will be extended to incorporate 500 acres of the estate leaving the beaver population free to breed and expand. Both the public and the popular press support for this project has been significant. This exercise should now be repeated wherever possible, and related eco-tourism revenue should be explored.

Action or inaction?

The hollow excuse touted for years by both EN and the Countryside Council for Wales that they would wait for a Scottish result on beaver prior to acting should be immediately discounted and exploration should begin of the potential for restoration in both these regions. The paper thin excuses for the rejection of the Knapdale trial should be exposed. Most of the reasons given were site specific and projects elsewhere should now be developed by NGOs and private individuals to keep the issue of reintroduction on the agenda. The Scottish Wildlife Trust has played a creditable role in raising the profile of beaver and other groups should press for further political and public support for its reintroduction. The release of beaver into the wider countryside is still only permissible with a licence from the Secretary of State and it is overcoming this challenge which now needs to be addressed. If the organisations and individuals who support the restoration of the beaver work together with determination on this issue there is little doubt that it can be guided to a successful conclusion now. Nothing will happen if we remain supine.

References

1. Yalden D. (1999) *The History of British Mammals*. Poyser Natural History.
2. Parker E. (1935) *Game birds, beasts and fishes*. Lonsdale library.
3. Kitchener A. (2001) *Beavers*. Whittet books.
4. Halley D.J & Rosell F (2002) *Mammal Review* 32. 2002
5. Fitter R.S.R. (1959) *The Ark in our Midst*. Collins.
6. Various authors (1880) *Living Animals of the World*. Hutchinson and Co.
7. Gibson J.A. (1980) The Bute Beavers. Buteshire Natural History Society.
8. Lever Sir C (1980) No to the Beaver. *ECOS* 1(2).
9. Owen D. Thylacine (2003) The Tragic Tale of the Tasmanian Tiger. Allen and Unwin.
10. Coles B (2001) *Journal of Wetland Ecology*. Volume 1. Oxbow Books.

Tayside beavers – rights in the watershed?

ECOS 32 (in press, 2011)
Proposals to remove beavers on the River Tay have met with critical reactions. Many nature conservationists will regard the action as ill considered and profoundly wrong. The River Tay beavers provide an opportunity to learn lessons about beaver behaviour and effects outside the official trials.

DEREK GOW

Watch and learn or shoot and stress?

Although little is known about the distribution of the beaver population on the Tay they are known to be breeding - juveniles have been filmed playing outside their lodges - and are probably of mixed European origin - Polish, German and Scandinavian. The source population is thought to have escaped from a wildlife park in Perthshire in 2001.From that small beginning they have migrated up into Angus and other parts of east Perthshire. Estimates of the established population vary between about 30 and 100. Scottish Natural Heritage has asked the Scottish Agricultural Sciences Agency to to trap the Tayside beavers and relocate them to captive situations in Britain or wild ones in relevant parts of Europe.

Beavers do not hibernate and rely instead for over-winter survival on their autumn body fat reserves coupled with 'feeding caches' of branches which they collect and submerge in the bottom of water courses. While these strategies assist the survival of healthy adults they are less effective for juveniles in their

355

first year of life. These small individuals cannot retain significant fat and are therefore reliant on the strong adults retrieving food from the caches. They are a social species and depend on the close contact of their parents and older siblings for warmth. Beavers live in families based around a central monogamous pair. The splitting of these bonded units through a regime of random capture will result in significant distress. The random removal of adults by trapping in winter could easily result in the death of one year olds from starvation or hypothermia. There is no sentient animal welfare case to be made for this casual action.

I have a beaver family on my farm in Devon and have been involved with the species for many years. I know most of the centres who maintain this species in Britain. A hidden detail in the Tay agenda is the ultimate fate of the captured individuals. If they are not to be sterilised and released then there is currently no zoological facility in Britain or Europe which has the capacity to keep around 50 beavers. Even if they could be exported to Europe there is little wild space for them there as a result of either natural re-colonisations or past reintroductions. If there is therefore no space in captivity for captured individuals and no prospect of their release elsewhere then they will have to be killed in significant numbers by rifle shots to their heads or lethal injections. It is inconceivable that SNH, the Scottish Executive and their partner organisations are not perfectly well aware of this.

An official study undertaken by Natural England (NE) suggests that once established in the wild that European beavers would be protected by EU law. This situation is however complex. Normally it would be an offence to "release or allow to escape into the wild any animal" which "is not normally resident.......to Great Britain". European beavers undoubtedly were a former resident and may have survived as a wild species until the 16th century. No definition of what is ordinary resident has ever been recorded in UK law and if the Tay beavers are established then no licence may be required from any nature conservation body in Britain for further releases.

Genetic nit-picking

The Tay beavers in the opinion of SNH are not the 'right beavers'. To understand this position it must be considered that by the beginning of the 20th century the beaver population in Western Europe had been reduced by human hunting to less than 400 individuals. These were confined to small populations in France, Germany and Norway. A study undertaken for SNH of the semi-fossil remains of beavers in Britain suggested that those in Scotland were more closely allied to the French population than any other. On the basis however that the English sample were closer in type to modern Scandinavian beavers a decision was made to use these for Knapdale. The genetic difference between these populations is insignificant and physical abnormalities have been widely recorded in Europe where reintroduced populations have been formed from these single source stocks alone. In Eastern Europe a population of perhaps 2000 beavers survived. These are much more genetically variable than those in the west and will readily interbreed. Both subspecies are already mixed throughout their current wild range as a result of natural re-colonisation and past reintroductions. As far as the wider ecology of the beaver is concerned the otters that hunt in the pools they create, the frogs that spawn in their wetlands and the woodpeckers which bore holes in the dead wood they provide will be un-influenced by what type of beaver created the habitat. If the restoration of the beaver in Britain is based on the significant ecological benefit they bring to wetland environments for other species then this dogma makes little sense.

Tayside – what we can study

It is to the credit of SNH and their partner organisations that they persevered with the return of the beaver for so long and were ultimately successful with a licence grant for the Knapdale Trial. Those involved with the project however recognise its limits. It will not answer many of its critic's queries regarding game-fish interaction with beavers or the impact of beavers in intensively developed agricultural environments. The Tay beavers are living in a landscape which affords these study opportunities in abundance.

Knapdale is an unusual site in respect of its ownership being largely held by the Forestry Commission. Throughout most of mainland Britain the opportunity to replicate projects of this type will be negligible. The single largest consummate challenge for those who wish to restore the beaver will be the development of a process which works in landscapes with multiple landownership. This is a social rather than scientific exercise. European beavers are a well studied species. We know the benefits they bring to riparian habitats and the challenges which arise from their presence in the contemporary countryside. There are effective blue-prints in Europe which show that the presence of beavers in developed landscapes is quite possible and that where issues do arise these can be managed. These projects rely absolutely on 'whole-community' engagement. The fact that beavers have survived on the Tay for some time now with no recorded conflict suggests either a degree of tolerance from private landowners or their pragmatic resolution of any arising issues.

Another perspective on the learning opportunity provided by the River Tay beavers has been summarised by naturalist and beaver expert Roy Dennis:

"It seems to me that nature is trying to tell us something with its Tayside beaver colony. We spend so much of our time and energy and resources trying to persuade nature to do our bidding, to operate within conditions we impose on it. Here is an all too rare opportunity to bear witness as nature unfolds the direct opposite of that process, as nature imposes new conditions on us. We should

watch and learn and delight in the possibilities that will flow whenever we are willing to give nature its head."

The beaver population on the Tay is of considerable importance. Although its creation is unconventional its existence offers significant opportunity. All that is required to develop this resource is an informed, unbiased appraisal of its worth coupled with a flexible approach to its development. If Scottish Natural Heritage decides to remove the Tayside beavers, the decision will have nothing to do with welfare and little with legality.

BOAR

A wallowing good time – wild boar in the woods

ECOS 23 (2) 14-22 (2002)

The wild boar's return to parts of southern England impacts on farm land, and creates challenges for woodland managers. Is the wild boar a pest or an asset in the countryside?

DEREK GOW

Jumping the fence

In the last decade free-living wild boar have returned to Britain. Although anecdotal reports of escapees have been widely recorded the only two 'large' populations would appear to be in Dorset and on the border of Kent and East Sussex.[1] Purged from the British Isles in the late middle ages due to a combination of over hunting and habitat loss, they are a lost large mammal staging a return.

The founding fathers of the current population were audacious escapees from 'boar farms' where they were bred for their meat. Further odd truants from farm parks, hobbyists and zoos may well have subsequently added themselves to the melt. It would appear that the original farm stock, were largely derived from surplus zoo animals of predominantly French origin,[2] but both German and Polish animals are purported to be kept on some farms.

The medieval greenwood

Wild boar featured prominently in British folklore, heraldry and art. Roman legions carried their emblem on banners, Picts carved their whorlled caricatures in stone and the Celts cast the image of a charging boar in bronze to create head crests for their war helms. In Norman time's wild boar were protected by draconian forest laws as a beast of the chase, for the sport of the powerful. Penalties for poaching boar were severe, eyes of offenders could be put out and in extreme cases a tortured death could be ordered. When William the Conqueror died it was recorded in one obituary that he thought more of his stags and boar than of his own people, but rooted in this statement of haughty disdain were the seeds of the species' destruction.

Although wild boar were sought after for food and for feasts they were more highly valued by the nobility as trainers of men. The ritualised medieval boar hunt with its relays of chain mailed hounds and elaborate horn calls was believed to develop the qualities of stamina, courage and leadership most prized in a medieval war lord. This religious conviction led to a dramatic conflict of interest between the nobility who wished to retain this creature for its martial qualities, and peasant farmers who could not tolerate the destruction that wild boar sounders inflicted on their pitiful crops. Famine years as a result of crop failure, and human or livestock disease, would have exacerbated this struggle and despite severe penalties both wild boar and deer would have been eagerly slaughtered and consumed.

By the late Middle Ages the boar that survived were enclosed in hunting parks like that surrounding Falkland palace in Fife where they were difficult to contain. Despite this difficulty wild boar were maintained in enclosures in Windsor Great Park until the reign of Queen Victoria and wild boar wood is still identified on ordinance survey maps of the park today. As wild populations buckled and disappeared the genes of the species struggled to survive in corners of Britain carrying populations of hairy, wiry black pigs with large tusks. In the late 1800s one of these swine was described by a Welsh chronicler as more akin to an alligator than a pig, with bristles instead of scales. Eventually these semi-wild creatures proved so destructive to the emerging farming systems that they were eaten to extinction.

Given this dramatic historic tussle it is perhaps not so surprising that the return of the wild boar has prompted a ready nostalgia for the medieval Greenwood. In the past the simple biological activities of large wild mammals have always been viewed through narrow agricultural blinkers and their presence refused. In 21st century Britain the return of free living wild boar presents us with an opportunity to re-evaluate this relationship in a more balanced light at a time when the calls for major agricultural and countryside change are strident. Wild boar could be a potent ecological resource, with profound effects on woodland habitats. Properly managed they could also constitute an important economic resource for   hunting and for game meat. Should we therefore welcome the return of the wild boar and celebrate the success of this former native species in its bid to reclaim its ancestral throne? Or should it be hounded again to a second national extinction as a result of its reputation as a fearsome fighter and agricultural pest?

Effects on farm land

In several European countries wild boar are classed as a pest species as a result of their feeding on agricultural crops. In Poland, Italy, France and Luxembourg compensation schemes operate to re-imburse farmers for their economic losses, and research has been conducted into the appeal of different crop cultivars[3] to try to reduce the scale of the damage. In southern England, farmers were the first to detect the presence of wild boar, with reports of damage to agricultural crops being reported to the then Ministry of Agriculture Fisheries and Food in the early 1990s.[1]

Boar rooting and creating wallowing areas (Chris Robbins/Derek Gow Consultancy)

Wild boar are mainly nocturnal and only venture from the security of woodland during the hours of darkness, so their original night time forays were rarely witnessed. Damage to pasture land was on occasion quite spectacular and immediately obvious where boar had ripped up large sods of turf with their snouts in search of roots, grubs and worms.

Studies on continental populations have shown that the severity of wild boar crop damage is related to the availability of acorns, beech mast and other tree fruits in the autumn. In years when natural foods abound, less agricultural damage results so the level of damage attributable to wild boar in southern England is likely to differ from year to year.[4] Similarly, should the wild boar population in Britain increase, then an increase in the level of agricultural damage could be expected. In north-east Switzerland where wild boar numbers increased considerably in the early 1990s there was a concurrent rise in the number of complaints from farmers, and wild boar became a political issue.[5] To-date, in southern England, the amount of agricultural damage attributable to the wild boar is not significant but is currently being investigated by DEFRA, which may ultimately decide whether wild boar is to be classified as an agricultural pest species or not.

The foot and mouth outbreak of 2001 demonstrated how a larger threat to agricultural production might well stem from wildlife spreading transmissible disease to domestic livestock, with massive economic consequences. Wild boar can carry diseases such as Foot and Mouth, Rinderpest, African and Classic Swine Fever and Aujeszky's disease to domestic livestock. In Britain, should such a disease become established in the free-living wild boar population, domestic stock could be continually infected. Incidents of free-living male wild boar breaking into domestic pig enclosures, inadvertently lured by oestrus sows, have been recorded[1] and even filmed during the TV cookery series *Return to River Cottage*.

The risk of free-living wild boar becoming vectors of the foot and mouth virus was considered by DEFRA and its findings published in a Veterinary Risk Assessment.[6] The assessment noted that "if Foot and Mouth disease were to be confirmed in an area where feral wild boar herds are known to be present, cage trapping and serological sampling of the boar could be considered as part of the procedure leading to removal of the Infected Area restrictions". It also stated that "shooting is likely to increase dispersal (and so spread the risk), and should be avoided if possible". English Nature has issued a statement on the impact of Foot and Mouth disease on wildlife, and expressed concern about inadvertently promoting the dispersal of wildlife.[7] The statement acknowledged that deer, grey squirrels and hedgehogs also can carry the disease but suggested that control measures "should be targeted at key species known to be susceptible to disease or are likely to carry it significant distances (*eg*. wild boar)". Fortunately the Foot and Mouth outbreak has been eradicated and wildlife, particularly wild boar, can for the time being breathe a collective sigh of relief.

Part of the woodland ecosystem...

The effect of wild boar on woodland ecology is mixed. Rooting through the surface layers causes a disturbance regime that will favour some species but not others, although the intensity of rooting will vary from year to year due to fluctuating boar numbers and the abundance of natural food supply. Wild boar are a former native species and therefore the woodland ecology of the British Isles would have evolved in conjunction with their activity. For this reason they could be expected to directly benefit woodlands where they exist. Alternatively their absence for at least 700 years coupled with historic woodland loss, fragmentation and the replacement of rich, seed bearing broadleaf with conifer might compromise the likely benefits of their re-appearance.[8]

One question often asked is how will wild boar affect bluebell woods, which are one of Britain's great wild flower spectacles in the Spring.[9] Bluebells are a global conservation issue and the UK is credited with holding up to 30% of the European/World population.[10] Bluebells abound in the woodlands which wild boar frequent in Kent and East Sussex and are occasionally uprooted.[1] Commonly when this occurs many bulbs are not eaten and are even redistributed and recovered by the boar's truffling action. It is not yet clear whether wild boar rooting will bring about a further reduction in bluebell numbers, which have already declined by 25-49% in the last 25 years[10] and there has to date been no research on how rooting affects other important plants such as wood anemones.

Wood anemones also occur in continental woodland where the effect of wild boar rooting has actually been studied. One study determined that the feeding of wild boar on the plant's rhizomes greatly reduced their growth[12] but this contradicted earlier research which stated that the wood anemone benefited from rooting due to regeneration of the fragmented rhizomes.[13] Of more concern are plant species, which are already in serious decline, for example wild daffodils, which are now rare throughout most of England. Wild daffodils do grow in woodlands where wild boar currently exist and these too have been up rooted. Due to their scarcity this species may be much more vulnerable to local extinction.

The short and long term effects of rooting on a woodlands floral ecology are unknown. One possible clue may come from Sweden, which like Britain has a recently established wild boar population that originated from captive escapees. A recent study there suggested that in the areas where wild boar exist floral diversity had increased due to the re-colonization of disturbed patches of rooted soil.[14] In Britain anecdotal evidence supports this view which is demonstrated dramatically in coniferous forest clearings where boar activity has destroyed mature bramble and bracken dominance, allowing many other plant species to proliferate. Significant holes dug by wild boar at the base of sweet chestnut stools in Kent last summer may have been connected to individual animals seeking edible fungi, but this benevolent aspect of their presence remains wide open for effective study.

Effects on woodland fauna

It is difficult to predict what effect the presence of wild boar will have on woodland fauna. Although their diet is predominantly vegetarian they will consume insects, larvae, birds eggs, nestlings, small mammals and carrion.

363

These vertebrate food items are only taken opportunistically and significant direct predation on a single species is therefore unlikely. The wild boars main influence is likely to be as a food competitor, particularly with species such as jays, wood pigeons, squirrels and small rodents which rely on acorns. It has been suggested that wild boar will deliberately seek out wood mouse burrows, in order to purloin their acorn stash[15] and the relationship between wild boar and badgers would also be worthy of study. Their diets are very similar, both root through leaf litter, are opportunistic, omnivorous and nocturnal.

Wild boar's behaviour may well provide opportunities for other species. For example, does wild boar wallowing in the heavy clay soils of woodland rides provide suitable ephemeral pools for aquatic invertebrates or their larvae? Do their tusk marking habits which open up tree bark provide insect feeding opportunities? And might their ivomectin free dung provide a suitable dormitory facility for the larvae of decomposing beetles? These aspects of their activities remain to be studied

Who likes them? Who doesn't?

The prevailing attitude to a wild boar or feral pig population differs from one country to another. In certain countries they are viewed as a pest to be controlled or eradicated, while in others the animals are regarded as an economic resource generating considerable revenue from either trophy hunting fees or from the sale of meat.[16] Attitudes within a country can be equally varied: in Sweden, hunting associations want to keep the accidentally re-introduced wild boar whereas the National Board of Agriculture does not.[16] In France, prior to 1970, the wild boar was considered an agricultural pest to be eradicated. This attitude changed after the 1970s when they were declared a game species and a compensation scheme was established funded through hunting fees, to indemnify farmers suffering crop damage.[17]

The presence of wild boar in Britain has provoked conflict between organisations that are in favour of their presence and those who are opposed. The RSPCA is against eradicating wild boar as "They are still very rare now and it's hard to see how the slaughter can be justified"[18] while the National Trust favours their managed presence.[19] Conversely, the Pig Veterinary Society, the National Farmers Union (NFU) and the British Association for Shooting and Conservation (BASC) support eradication of the animals.[20,21,22,23] The Game Conservancy Trust, a charity whose objectives are to "promote for the public benefit the conservation and study of game species" has also called for the eradication of wild boar deeming it "better to err on the side of caution",[24] but to date there has been no comment from the Mammal Society - "the voice for British Mammals" which is apparently still clearing its throat. The official attitude of English Nature has been ambivalent and the Forestry Commission, which has supported the program of DEFRA research in its forest holdings has apparently no official opinion as this animal does not officially exist.

The role of the press in informing the general public of wildlife issues has become an important consideration for wildlife management programmes, particularly those involving re-introductions or population control. A review of press articles which referred to free-living wild boar showed a predominantly negative although improvingly positive media coverage.[25] Perhaps not surprisingly, the most commonly reported concern was the potential threat the animals posed to public safety.

Hazards to humans?

Captive wild boar are covered by the *Dangerous Wild Animals Act* 1976, as amended in 1984. Along with wildcats (*Felis silvestris*) they are the only free-living species in UK to have this classification apply to their captive brethren. Is it therefore still safe to walk in the woods which wild boar frequent? Kent County Council thinks it is. A notice at the entrance to its woodlands inhabited by wild boar includes: " They are not regarded as a danger to the public; however, injured or distressed animals should not be approached." Similarly, East Sussex County Council display the notice "Caution. Wild boar in Woods. Please take care and keep to the path" in the presumable hope that the boar would not!. In these litigious times it obviously pays to show 'due-diligence'.

Wild boar are by nature shy and retiring animals whose daylight hours are spent hidden in thick vegetation. Even glimpsing an animal is unusual and although they will avoid human contact whenever possible their nonsensically fearsome reputation, acquired during the pig-sticking era, precedes them. Very few instances of wild boar attacking humans are recorded throughout their extensive European range and those that do generally revolve around hunting accidents or poorly trained domestic dogs chasing piglets which are then attacked by the wild boar sow in defence of her young. Occasionally the owners attempting to retrieve their canine companions are also attacked but this set of circumstance is just as applicable to domestic cows and calves as it is to wild boar. To date the press have reported no instance of personal injury resulting from a wild boar attack in this country[25] and if European experience is anything to go by human injury from boar is much more likely to result from collision with a motor vehicle.

The prospect of wild boar causing a threat to human safety is officially the concern of the Home Office. DEFRA recommends that "cases involving wild boar where there is a risk to human safety should be reported to the police". Sightings of free-living wild boar "where there is no risk to public safety should be reported to the relevant local authority, as they are responsible for ensuring that wild boar are kept in secure conditions".[27]

Prospects for boar in Britain

The Government has pledged to consider the re-introduction of native species that have been lost in historical times through human activity (Article 22, EC Habitats and Species Directive, EC 92/43). Examples of such species are listed in Annex 4 of the directive and include the wolf, beaver and lynx. Wild boar are also such a species but are not listed possibly because wild boar numbers on the continent are on the increase. The biological feasibility of re-introducing wild boar into Scottish woodlands has recently been researched but as the authors state "a feasibility study must also consider the desirability of re-introduction of a species within the wider ecological, social, and economic aspects of ecosystem and protection".[26] Scottish Natural Heritage, officially responsible for wildlife re-introductions in Scotland, has no current plans to re-introduce wild boar.[26]

The wild boar in southern England established themselves in a clandestine manner without bothering about a feasibility study, but it is not clear whether DEFRA will allow them to remain. Doubts exist about the animals' genetic purity because some wild boar farmers in Britain cross purebred male boar with domestic pig sows to give larger litters and increased piglet growth rates. If the free-living wild boar in southern England escaped from an establishment containing pure bred and hybrid animals, the escapees may have been pure wild boar, hybrids, or a mixture of both. Some white or cream animals do occur in the Kent and East Sussex population but these colour variants also occur in some German and French populations - along with spotted individuals - and may well be indicative of nothing other than a small start up gene base which has a predilection for this trait. The bulk of the free living animals all look very like wild boar without any other notable characteristics of hybridisation.[1]

Stand up and be counted

For a 'new' mammal species to reach Britain, considerable stretches of water have to be crossed which are only realistically negotiable with the assistance of human activity. All the mammal species naturalised since the last ice age have either been deliberately released, have accidentally escaped from captivity or have relied on human activity.[28] Wild boar arrived again in this island as a bi-product of agricultural diversification. Unlike the North American mink and Coypu which followed the same route, they emphatically deserve to be here. They have skipped the process of population modelling, feasibility study and weary consultation which has bedevilled the restoration of the European beaver, and come off their marks running. For far too long British re-introductions have focused on cuddly or non-contentious species such as Pasque flowers, sand lizards or dormice rather than concentrating on bigger mammals which through their behaviour provide many other species with living opportunities. If conservation bodies are ever to raise their horizons then the return of the wild boar must be ringingly endorsed.

References

1. Central Science Laboratory (1998) *Current status and potential impact of Wild Boar (Sus scrofa) in the English countryside: A risk assessment*. Ministry of Agriculture, Fisheries and Food. London.
2. Booth, W D (1995): Wild boar farming in the United Kingdom. *Ibex Journal of Mountain Ecology*. 3, 245-248.
3. Stopar, J & Zgajnar, J (1995) Palatability of the five most frequently grown potato cultivars in Slovenia to wild boars. ZB. *Biotehnike fak. Univ v Ljubljani, Kmetijstvo (Zootechnika)* 66, 151-160.
4. Genov, P (1981) Food composition of wild boar in North Eastern and Western Poland. *Acta Theriologica* 26 (10) 185-205.
5. Geisser, H (1998) The wild boar (*Sus scrofa*) in the Thurgau (Northeastern Switzerland): population status, damages and the influence of supplementary feeding on damage frequency. *Gibier Faune Sauvage*, 15, 547-554.
6. DEFRA (2001) *What is the risk of feral wild boar becoming infected with FMD and subsequently causing new incidents of FMD in domestic livestock*. DEFRA Veterinary risk
assessment No. 7, 11 June 2001.
7. EN (2001) *Foot and Mouth disease - impact on wildlife*. English Nature press release EN/01/08, 02 March 2001.
8. Yalden, D W (1999) *The history of British Mammals*. T & A D Poyser, London.
9. Mabey, R (1996) *Flora Britannica*. Sinclair-Stevenson, London, England.
10. HMSO (1994) *Biodiversity. The UK Action plan*. HMSO, London.
11. Anon 1995
12. Bialy, K (1996) The effect of boar (*Sus scrofa*) rooting on the distribution of organic matter in soil profiles and the development of wood anemone (*Anemone nemorosa* L.) in the oak-hornbeam stand (*Tilio-carpinetum*) in the Bialowieza primeval forest. *Folia Forestalia Polonica Series A - Forestry* 38, 77-88.
13. Falinski, J B (1984) *Vegetation dynamics at temperate lowland primeval forest. Ecological studies in Bialowieza forest*. Dr. W. Junk Publishers. Dordrecht.
14. Welander, J (2000) Spatial and Temporal Dynamics of a Disturbance Regime: Wild boar (Sus scrofa L.) rooting and its effects on plant species diversity. PhD Thesis, Swedish University of Agricultural Sciences, Utgivningsort.
15. Focardi S, Capizzi, D & Monetti, D (2000) Competition for acorns among wild boar (Sus scrofa) and small mammals in a Mediterranean woodland. *Journal of Zoology, London* 250, 329-334.
16. Tisdell, C A (1982) *Wild Pigs: environmental pest or economic Resource*. Pergamon Press.
17. Vassant, J (1999) Management of Wild Boar populations in mountain environments using management units. Abstracts of the European Wild Boar Research Group, 4-5 Dec 1998, Zaragoza, Spain.

18. Anon (1994) End boar culls. *Daily Express* 17 March 1994.

19. Coy, S & Bullock, D (1999) The potential impact of wild boar on National Trust properties. *Views* 30, 41-43).

20. Anon (1997) Swine fever boar cull 'impractical'. *Kentish Express,* 19 June 19

21. Anon (1997) Call for cull of free-ranging wild boar. *The Times,* 20 June 1997.

22. Downing, G (1999) Wild boar to be eradicated. *Shooting Times and Country Magazine,* 18 April 1999.

23. Prestage, M (1999) Wild boars face extinction - for the second time. *Daily Telegraph,* 18 April 1998.

24. GCC (1999) *Wildlife group calls for wild boar eradication.* Game Conservancy Trust press release, 23 January 2001.

25. Goulding M J & Roper, T J (In Press) Press response to the free-living wild boar in southern England. *Mammal Review.*

26. Leaper, R, Massei, G, Gorman, M L & Aspinall, R (1999) The feasibility of re-introducing wild boar (*Sus scrofa*) to Scotland. *Mammal Review* 29 (4) 239-259.

27. MAFF (1998) *MAFF study confirms wild boar in the countryside.* MAFF press release, 21 October 1998.

28. Baker, S J (1990) Escaped exotic mammals in Britain. *Mammal Review,* 20, 75-96.

Book review:

ECOS 24.2 (2003) Peter Taylor

WILD BOAR IN BRITAIN
MARTIN GOULDING
Whittet Books, Stowmarket. 2003.
112 pages
Hardback £14.99   ISBN 1 873580 58

This is a decidedly useful booklet dealing with the cultural and biological history of the boar in Britain as well as its reappearance in the woods of Kent, Sussex and Dorset, and the controversy that has followed. I found the cultural elements particularly interesting, including the Celtic mythology. The final days of this keystone species of woodland ecology are accounted from detailed historical records with the last dating from the mid 1500s.

The first re-introduction of a British mammal may have taken place at Windsor Park in 1608 by James I importing stock from France. Further attempts followed at various times in the 17th and 18th Centuries, only to founder on the unpopularity of crop-raiding boar with local farmers. The current successful populations in Kent are escapees from farmed wild stock and are thought now to number over 200 animals. Goulding describes them with some fondness, as escapologists and masters of evasion! They are equally unpopular in agricultural circles, but modern farming, at least in these wooded regions of Britain, is probably less intensive, with fewer people working the land, and hunting down wild boar, is a labour intensive operation.

Goulding's account of the initial refusal of officialdom to recognise the reality of wild boar parallels the 'big cat' phenomenon. However, he does provide ample evidence in the form of photographs, even of family parties, from his six years of close study of these feral populations. DEFRA is now considering policy. Sadly, farmers, as well as, curiously, the Game Conservancy, have been calling for eradication. Lovers of bluebell woods would likely form an effective pressure group, as wild boar can 'damage' large (and obviously 'unnatural') expanses of edible bulbs.

Goulding makes a case for 'boar watching' as well as hunting, and in addition to providing a useful chapter on biology, gives an account of their status as a game animal on the continent. There is also a discussion of the genetics of wild and domestic animals – the new British wild boar are a mixture of the French sub-species, taken to be closest to the former indigenous populations, and the Eastern European, as well as some domestic genes. The evidence suggests there are no actual 'hybrid' animals and all those so far observed look like wild type animals. Some wild populations on the Continent are similarly 'impure' and Goulding, rightly in my view, questions the importance of genetic purity and provenance as against the value of this once native animal being an accepted member of our woodland fauna.

Wild Boar: what should DEFRA do?

ECOS 25 (1) 34-38 (2004)

Many wild boar farmed in Britain have broken the bounds of captivity for a more stimulating life on the outside. It is unprecedented in Britain for a former native species to take matters into their own hands and re-introduce themselves. There are now breeding populations of free-living wild boar in at least four counties. DEFRA has the task of deciding the fate of these escapees and their freeborn descendants. It is not an easy decision…

MARTIN GOULDING

Just rooting around…

Rarely has any one animal species put DEFRA's Policy Division in such a quandary, and that includes even the most TB ridden badgers. Step forward the wild boar Sus scrofa. Guilty as charged, wild boar will trample and consume cereal crops, rip up pasture, transmit disease to livestock (including TB) and slaughter as potential love rivals domestic boars, before servicing any receptive sows who are putty in the hands of this wild, carefree, shaggy haired Romeo. The resulting piglets take after their father and soon become uncontrollable delinquents, hell bent on escape. However, away from the farmyard the wild boar, a former native species, is one our keystone woodland species.

A missing piece of the ecological jigsaw, found again after being lost for hundreds of years, wild boar are mother nature's farmers. Rooting for food their strong snouts plough the surface layers mixing and redistributing nutrients and minerals essential for life. The bare earth left from rooting among, for example, monocultures of grasses or bluebells acts as a seed bed, enticing long dormant seeds to germinate or accommodating dispersed seeds from annual plants swift to take advantage.[1] Local biodiversity increases, temporarily at least, before the dominant grasses or bluebells return, but by then another seedbed has been prepared, and the cycle repeats. The wild boars' will even sow a few seeds themselves, collected in their hairy coat as they bulldoze through the undergrowth, and displaced after wallowing or whilst rubbing against a tree. An odd piece of fertiliser is also deposited for good measure. Pest control is broad spectrum and relentless, as grubs and larvae form part of their natural diet.

Their effect on a woodland ecology can quickly become apparent. For example, a patch of Fleabane *Pulicaria dysenterica* flowering in the corner of a wood I regularly frequent was, last summer, alive with butterflies. I recognised Common Blues *Polyommatus ivarus*, Red Admirals *Vanessa atalanta* and Speckled Woods *Pararge aegeria*, but many others amongst an impressive display of colour were unfamiliar. A myriad of insects also competed for a place on the bright yellow flower heads. This riot of life in the corner of the wood was there for one reason only; there were wild boar in the wood. The previous winter, when the ground was wet and easy to work, the wild boar rooted up an area of perennial grasses to feed on the edible rhizomes. I watched the exposed soil being re-colonised by the Fleabane, which then flowered and became soaked in insects and butterflies. Unfortunately, that same winter there was not enough food in the woodland to sustain the wild boar and nocturnal forays into an adjacent field brought them into conflict with the farmer. The yield from his maize crop was seriously reduced and the wild boar made another enemy.

Welcome to the neighbourhood

Three free-living populations of wild boar are recognised to exist: in Kent/East Sussex, Dorset and Herefordshire.[2] Furthermore, animals are still haemorrhaging out of the captive enclosures where they are held and sometimes a main artery is severed; recently it was reported that 30 wild boar escaped in a mass break out from a farm near Bridport, Dorset, to supplement the free-living animals already present.[3] In-breeding depression is not likely to be an issue. Contrary to popular belief, wild boar are shy and retiring preferring to spend daylight hours hidden in the thickest vegetation available. Sightings by the public are therefore quite rare. However, a person walking through the wood with a dog off its lead scampering into the undergrowth may tell a different story. Dogs have disturbed sleeping boar, which once rudely awoken, may chase the dog.

This becomes a problem if the owner positions themselves between the boar and the dog. There are no reports to-date from already over stretched NHS casualty departments but time will tell. DEFRA side steps all responsibility and advises: "Public safety is primarily the concern of the Police rather than DEFRA. If you are concerned that wild boar are present and a safety hazard in a particular area you should inform the local Police".[4]

For DEFRA, life is not easy. For example, the thought of an outbreak of swine fever or foot and mouth disease becoming entrenched in the free-living wild boar populations gives the Pig Veterinary Society nightmares. "We would urge the Ministry of Agriculture [now DEFRA] to waste no time in taking steps to control the current wild boar population now", jointly wrote the society's president and a past-president way back in 1998.[5] History suggests that future outbreaks will occur. Wild boars' are great travellers and sub-dominants can wander over 20km in search of a better life, potentially coughing up infectious bacillus all the way. Conversely, scientists have already muted the feasibility of their re-introduction, on the grounds of replacing a native animal lost in historical times through human activities.[6] Furthermore, and of potential embarrassment for DEFRA, Margaret Beckett, Secretary of State for Environment, Food and Rural Affairs, launched amongst much trumpeting a Biodiversity Strategy for England in October 2002 at the London Wetland

Centre. One aim of which is to 'manage and extend woodland so as to promote enhanced biodiversity'.[7] The strategy had in mind red squirrels Sciurus vulgaris, bullfinches Pyrrhula pyrrhula, delicate flowers and gossamer winged butterflies, certainly not powerfully built wild boar complete with their own tusked armaments. Governments are not that bold. To now eradicate the boar, a former native species and prime contender for re-introduction, would make a mockery of DEFRA's promise to enhance biodiversity.

DEFRA in the Greenwood – the choices

What policy decision can DEFRA therefore come up with in the face of such a controversial animal? It has tree options: eradicate, do nothing, or manage the population. It wil be difficult because wild boar are shy, nocturnal and rest during the day in thick woodland vegetation. Thus the practicality of targeting every animal in a population could be difficult. It may also be prohibitively expensive. For example, the last mammal deliberately eradicated in Britain was the unlovable and (crucially) non-native Coypu Myocastor coypus, at a cost of £2.75m in 1989 (but even this figure is cheap when compared to the bill for cleaning up after a Notifiable Disease outbreak).[8] Furthermore some members of the existing boar population are located on the estates of influential people who are known strongly to oppose the killing of animals. These estates could act as refuges. Eradication would also be unpopular with certain groups interested in animal welfare issues or who favour the species' re-introduction. On the other hand, to do nothing would mean that we are likely to be overrun with wild boar as they have no natural predators, now the lynx and wolf have been forcibly moved on. As a former native species, climate, habitat and food supplies are all to the wild boars' liking and an increasing number of sightings of characteristically striped piglets trotting through the Greenwood is testament to their breeding success.

Population management is the one option left. Should DEFRA now recognise the boar to be a re-introduced native species and designate it as a game animal? Disgruntled farmers and land owners could then 'exterminate' any boar caught marauding crops and fraternising with domestic livestock. Revenue from hunting rights and carcass sales would benefit the farmer and local economy alike. An annual closed season during the spring breeding period would protect pregnant or lactating sows. The health status of the animals could be periodically monitored by live trapping, while a contingency plan would be necessary, should the frightful scenario of transmissible livestock diseases such as foot and mouth or swine fever again raise its fearful head. Regarding public safety, recreational woodland containing boar, for example Forestry Commission land, should have notices posted advising the public that boar are in the area. People can then make up their own minds whether to venture forth or not.

The only certainty regarding Britain's resurgent wild boar population is that a management plan completely acceptable to all interested parties is unlikely. Has anyone any better ideas?

References

1. Welander, J. (2000) *Spatial and temporal dynamics of a disturbance regime: Wild boar (Sus scrofa L.) rooting and its effects on plant species diversity.* PhD Thesis, Swedish University of Agricultural Sciences, Utgivningsort.
2. DEFRA, Wildlife and Countryside. Current Status. http://www.defra.gov.uk/wildlife-countryside/vertebrates/wild-boar.htm
3. 'Wild boar herd escapes'. BBC on-line news. Thursday, 5 February, 2004 http://news.bbc.co.uk/1/hi/england/hampshire/dorset/3461207.stm
4. DEFRA, Wildlife and Countryside. What should I do if I see a wild boar? http://www.defra.gov.uk/wildlife-countryside/vertebrates/wild-boar.htm
5. Williams, Gareth & Wilkinson, John. *Free-living wild boar in south-east England.* The Veterinary Record, Letters page. November 14, 1998.
6. Leaper, R., Massei, G., Gorman, M.L. & Aspinall, R. (1999) The feasibility of re-introducing wild boar (*Sus scrofa*) to Scotland. *Mammal Review,* 29, 239-259.
7. DEFRA: Working with the grain of nature: a biodiversity strategy for England. http://www.defra.gov.uk/wildlife-countryside/ewd/biostrat/
8. Gosling, L.M.. (1989) Extinction to Order. *New Scientist,* 121, 44-49

Decision time for the wild boar?

ECOS 27 (1) 49-56 (2006)

Defra has consulted on what to do about the free-living wild boar populations present across southern England. Opinion on the merits of wild boar varies amongst conservation, game, farming, and other groups, so what do we know about the return of this prodigal pig?

MARTIN GOULDING

Ten years ago farm-bred wild boar in Britain crossed the rubicon of freedom to establish free-living populations. From initial sightings in 1996 Defra subsequently confirmed that wild boar, after an absence of several hundred years, had re-colonised the counties of East Sussex, Kent and Dorset.[1] What have we learnt about the species in that time and are Defra any closer to deciding what to do next - can wild boar stay or should they now go?

Increasing populations and recent escapes

Not surprisingly, there are now considerably more wild boar on the outside than in the previous 10 years. A former native species with no natural predators (the wolf and lynx are long gone), the founding populations are holding their own despite considerable hunting pressure, and sightings in new areas continue to occur.[2] Furthermore, there have been some spectacular additions. In 2004 approximately 40 wild boar suddenly appeared in the Forest of Dean, Gloucestershire. These animals were relatively tame implying they were farm-bred animals deliberately dumped by a disillusioned farmer, or an impatient re-introductionist. More recently, in December 2005, Animal Rights Activists cut through swathes of wire fencing to liberate over 100 wild boar from a farm in North Devon. Mass breakouts such as these are the perfect seed for founding new populations as the animals are already in family groups of mature sows, dominant males and juveniles of both sexes.

Should the government have acted sooner and nipped the fledgling populations in the bud with a swift, no warnings given, desert storm eradication strike? No, their hands were tied because the Government had agreed in the European Community Habitats Directive 1992 (92/43/EEC) to consider the re-introduction of former native species, lost in historical times, through human activity. Although the wild boar was not listed by name, it has been suggested as a candidate for reintroduction on several occasions.[3,4] If Defra had acted as judge, jury and executioner, without a proper trial and with no defence witnesses called, it would have made a mockery of future commitments concerning species re-introduction. Better to have a considered response to an unprecedented situation than a knee jerk reaction.

However, it is not as if the Government wasn't warned. Back in 1990 *Mammal Review* published a paper, actually authored by a Defra (then MAFF) employee, which foretold if legislation to prevent escapes of captive stock was not effective "we will almost certainly see new species of exotic mammals established in Britain...and wild boar will probably be amongst the first".[5]

Public safety

What are the issues surrounding wild boar that have caused Defra to spend £433,305 of public money conducting a six year investigation?[6] Biodiversity Minister Jim Knight, in a recent News Release,[7] noted several issues surrounding feral wild boar. They included disease risk, potential for damage to crops and property, effects on animal exports, animal welfare, conservation and biodiversity, game and shooting interests, and human safety.

Personal safety is most peoples first thought when escaped wild boar are mentioned, and this subject gained most attention in a survey of press coverage of the free-living wild boar.[8] I am frequently e-mailed by concerned members of the public with comments such as this:

> *"Whilst cycling around the High Peak area in Derbyshire, I rode off the main footpath and came across three boar resting in the afternoon sun. One male (with very large tusks) and two females which I almost ran over. I am all for the introduction of extinct species back into the wild, but this fellow was rather aggressive - as this is an area used by mountain bikers and walkers; is this really safe?"*

Defra states that the only incidents where actual physical contact between a wild boar and the public appears to have been made involved two people knocked over by an animal that had just escaped from an abattoir.[2] However, Defra still issue general guidance on what the public should do to avoid dangerous encounters with wild boar whilst out in the countryside. This includes keeping dogs on leads, avoiding dense undergrowth and walking away from any animals that are encountered.[2] Defra add the caveat that people concerned that wild boar present a safety hazard in an area should inform local Police.

An accident waiting to happen? (Chris Robbins/Derek Gow Consultancy)

Road traffic accidents

> "A large sow boar last night did some damage to my car. She ran off
> with a headache and I was left with a bashed car and having the fun of
> explaining it to my insurance company this morning! Very shocked that
> such a beast is running freely in my village"

- wrote Deborah from Beckley in East Sussex, an area with more
than its fair share of free-living wild boar.

Road traffic accidents have claimed the lives of several wild boar in Britain
to date. Wild boar that I radio-tracked in East Sussex criss-crossed roads
throughout the night, particularly where roads bisect areas of woodland. To
make matters worse, they often rooted on roadside verges, or loitered on the
edge of the tarmac. In the dead of night, on a pitch black country road, breaking
distances are likely to be woefully inadequate. No human injuries have been
recorded, but the situation is a loaded gun with a hair trigger. Defra calculate,
using data from continental populations, that the UK can expect about six wild
boar road traffic accidents annually.[2]

Agricultural damage and disease

Emerging at night from the security of the woodland for a nocturnal nibble, wild boar can cause havoc in an agricultural environment by rooting up pasture, consuming cereal crops and breaching stock fences. Indeed, wild boar are considered an important pest of agriculture in much of Europe. Defra note the most evident form of damage so far with the English feral populations is rooting of grassland, although other crop damage recorded includes rooting in recently sown cereal fields, damage to ripening maize, trampling in wheat crops and rooting and trampling in turnip fields. Agricultural damage is only minor and localised at present. Fields bordering woodland are particularly vulnerable. However, an expanding wild boar population would equate to an increase in agricultural damage.[9]

Crop losses attributed to wild boar are substantial enough for some countries, for example Poland, Italy and France to adopt compensation schemes to reimburse farmers for their economic losses. Revenue generated from the sale of hunting licenses forms a compensation kitty from which farmers are compensated, at no cost to the tax payer. Could such a scheme work in Britain should wild boar become an agricultural liability? In principle, I believe yes. Although a compensation scheme would be open to abuse and require considerable administration, it may also benefit the species. For example, in France prior to the 1970s, the wild boar was considered an agricultural pest to be exterminated. Attitudes changed when they were declared a game species and a compensation scheme was established funded through hunting fees, to indemnify farmers suffering crop damage.[10]

A more insidious threat to farming interests is that wild boar can carry transmissible livestock diseases such as foot-and-mouth, swine fever and bovine TB. There is a real danger that domestic livestock will infect the free-living wild boar with some economically unpleasant disease which will become endemic within the wild boar, who would return the favour by re-infecting the domestic livestock at every opportunistic meeting. The Veterinary Risk Assessment at the time of the UK epidemic recommended that emphasis is placed on rapid diagnosis and destruction of infected stock and exclusion of feral boar, rather than on control of the boar population. This is a sensible option considering wild boar can wander several kilometres in a single night, and occasionally move much longer distances. One animal I radio-tracked died in a road traffic accident 20km from where it was originally trapped and tagged. The thought of a poorly pig coughing up foot-and-mouth bacillus over such a distance would make a mockery of any contingency plans involving culling all susceptible wildlife, and domestic stock, within a designated area. Don't even mention contiguous culling.

The list of uncertainties about a resurgent wild boar population go on and on. For example, will the public refuse to visit nature reserves containing free-living boar? Should the Home Office be concerned about the increase in fire-power from the larger rifles that would-be boar hunters are quietly accruing? If the pro-advocates are wrong in 50 years time, who clears up the mess? (R.Trout *pers comm.*). Answers do not come easily, but perhaps we should look to fellow European countries where wild boar are widespread and these concerns are lived with and are rarely an issue .

Serendipity

Enough of the problems. Should we not rejoice that a species lost to these shores has honoured us, albeit accidentally, with its presence once again? Why should a former native species have to justify its presence in the first place? Defra, under the heading 'Potential Benefits of Wild Boar', and with one-eye on the piggy bank, suggests that the presence of a large and novel wild animal may provide economic opportunities for areas with feral wild boar to benefit from 'wildlife tourism'. The establishment of feral wild boar is also seen by some as presenting an opportunity for a highly valued form of hunting not previously available in this country. Revenue could be generated from the sale of sporting rights and carcasses.[2]

Defra make no mention of the wild boar's reputation as 'nature's plough'. Wild boar are adapted to search for food among the surface layers of the woodland floor. Their strong snouts root through the leaf litter and vegetation ripping up the earth, creating bare patches of soil. The disturbance this causes has noticeable effects on plant and animal communities. For example, on one grassy woodland ride in an East Sussex woodland I noticed the bare earth was first recolonised by the annual plants Scarlet Pimpernel *Anagallis arvensis* and Common Centaury *Centaurium erythraea*. Later followed perennials such as Dog Violet *Viola ariviniana* and Creeping Buttercup *Ranunculus repens*. A monoculture of grasses had become interspersed with flowering plants and the biodiversity of that particular woodland ride had increased. Ultimately, perennial grasses will again crowd out the recolonising flowering plants but by then other areas would have been rooted and the cycle repeats. And it is not just the flora that benefits, all the associated invertebrate life that depend on these species of flower for a stage in their life cycle may also benefit.

The impact of wild boar on woodland ecology is complex and has still to be fully understood. Rooting through the surface layers causes a disturbance regime that favours some species but not others. The intensity of rooting is likely to vary from year to year due to fluctuating boar numbers and natural food supply.

Silviculture and bracken control

Wild boar could also have use as a silviculture tool. Rooting and feeding behaviour by wild boar in commercial woodland has reduced populations of three harmful moth species at larval stage.[2] Pioneering work using wild boar to clear bracken is currently underway at Glen Affric National Nature Reserve, near Cannich, Scotland. Begun in 2005, under the direction of ecologist Liz Balharry, the four year project aims to reduce the spread and dominance of bracken, to increase the number of regenerating tree seedlings needed to regenerate the forest and provide an income from farming boar. Early results are fascinating.[11] On the upside, test plots indicate that the boar rapidly impact on the vegetation and create bare patches of well-dug ground suitable for seedling regeneration. The boar happily feasted on the al-fresco bracken, consuming both the rhizomes and fronds, mature and young. On the down size boar in test plots which contained little or no bracken-rich areas caused damage to existing trees by bark scraping, root stripping and root exposure. Also wet areas became heavily impacted by the boar, whereas drier areas recovered quickly. The delicate balance between boar density and movement within the test plots is being fine-tuned to encourage the boar to spend more time in the bracken-rich areas and less time in more vulnerable boggy areas. Final results are eagerly awaited.

Defra's consultation

The public have been invited a say on what to do about the free-living wild boar and to submit opinions on the way wild boar are to be managed. Submissions closed on 6 January 2006. The Government's stated aim was "to create an acceptable balance between wild boar and the interests of farming, conservation, woodland management and human safety."

Five options were proffered for consideration ranging from 'no direct Government management on all current and future populations' to 'eradicate all existing feral populations and cull all new escapees'. Intermediate options were more ambitious and include treating feral pigs/hybrids and feral boar separately, eradicating all feral pig populations and culling all escaped feral pigs and hybrids but allowing the continued, managed existence of feral wild boar populations. Also on the table was managing existing wild boar populations on a regional basis by limiting the spread of existing populations and preventing establishment of wild boar in some areas, particularly those with extensive populations of domestic pigs in outdoor units. Finally, no direct government management of the existing established populations but prevention of new populations becoming established. A government announcement is due in summer 2006.

Defra has therefore nearly decided on how to manage the free-living wild boar. Meanwhile, reports of sightings still drift in:

> "Seen today (5 Jan 06) at Aldington in Kent (circa 5pm) four boar running from one field to another across country lane and seemingly heading towards a wooded area. Appeared to be a parent and three near-grown young, seemed to be healthy and enjoying themselves. Regards Councillor Woods."

Lessons from the recent escape in Devon

This damaged fence at a wild boar farm in West Anstey, Devon, was the work of animal rights activists. The herd of 100 wild boar escaped on 22 December, with 40 of the animals retrieved straight away, while 60 remained on the loose. Activists struck again at the farm in February.

And what about the hundred or so released in December in Devon? They could be anywhere by now. A much publicised 'boat hunt' to round-up the escapees using fox hounds and armed personnel on quad bikes was, thankfully for animal and public welfare reasons, a failure. During the hunt no boar or bystanders were scented, sighted, attacked or shot. The only boar to make an appearance was an individual wandering back to the pens on its own accord just prior to nightfall, much to the delight of a small army of assembled media reporters.

The exercise was always a non-starter as wild boar will not let themselves be herded like sheep, and they do not appreciate being disturbed by dogs, which they are more likely to attack rather than run from. Plus the alarming noises emitted from a quartet of quad bike engines would inform any beast that it would be wise to lay low for a while, or to quickly move to pastures new. Exmoor is just around the corner, quiet and peaceful - that will do nicely. The hunt was a desperate attempt from a desperate farmer trying to get his livelihood back before it was too late. Actively seeking help and advice from the authorities, he found none was forthcoming. It was too late from day one, the boar were out a day before Christmas and Defra, who do have experience in trapping free-living wild boar in Britain, had no-one available.

And that is where the gaping hole lies. Not in the sabotaged fences of a wild boar farm, but in our knowledge of this fascinating and formidable beast. Ten years on and we still don't know what to do when this species breaks loose.

References and notes

1. Goulding, M J, Smith, G. & Baker, S J, 1998, *Current status and potential impact of Wild Boar (Sus scrofa) in the English countryside: A risk assessment.* Central Science Laboratory report to the Ministry of Agriculture, Fisheries and Food.

2. Moore, N P & Wilson, C J, 2005, *Feral wild boar in England: Implications of future management options.* A report on behalf of Defra European Wildlife Division.

3. Howells, O & Edwards-Jones, G, 1997, A feasibility Study of reintroducing wild boar (*Sus scrofa*) to Scotland: are existing Woodlands large enough to Support a Minimum Viable population *Biological Conservation* 81 77-89.

4. Leaper, R, Massei, G, Gorman, Ml.. & Aspinall, R ,1999, The feasibility of re-introducing wild boar (*Sus scrofa*) to Scotland. *Mammal Review* 29 (4) 239-259.

5. Baker, SJ,1990, Escaped exotic mammals in Britain. *Mammal Review.* 20 75-96.

6. *The Ecology and Management of Wild boar in southern England. Defra Final Project Report (VC0325).* On-line,
http://www2.defra.gov.uk/research/project_data/projects.asp?
M=KWS&V=wild+boar&SUBMIT1. Accessed 25/01/06

7. Defra News Release: *Last chance to have a say on wild boar.* 30 December 2005.
On-line, http://www.defra.gov.uk/news/2005/051230a.htm. Accessed 25/01/06

8. Goulding, M J & Roper, T J, 2002, Press responses to the presence of free-living wild boar (*Sus scrofa*) in southern England. *Mammal Review,* 32, 272 - 282.

9. Goulding, M J, 2003, *Investigation of free-living wild boar (Sus scrofa) in southern England.* DPhil thesis, University of Sussex, 2003.

10. Vassant, J, 1999, *Management of Wild Boar populations in mountain environments using management units.* Abstracts of the European Wild Boar Research Group, 4-5 Dec 1998, Zaragoza, Spain.

11. Trees for Life: *Restoring the Caledonian Forest.* 30 January 2006
http://www.treesforlife.org.uk/newsletter/winter05.html#boar.   Accessed 02/02/06

Living with wild boar in middle England – lessons from abroad

ECOS 29 (3/4) 39-44 (2008)

In various countries wild boar have become habituated to residential areas, but scavenging in dustbins and rooting up gardens has made the species unpopular with the locals and authorities alike. To stop our wild boar from becoming habituated to residential neighbourhoods across Middle England, do we need to be cruel to be kind?

MARTIN GOULDING

Boris from the Forest

'Boris' is a wild boar who to the delight of children but consternation of parents, frequently meanders out of the Forest of Dean and into an adjacent housing estate. Boris' appearance is rewarded with treats of apples, M&Ms, and anything to hand that the residents believe is palatable to a pig, which does not rule out much. Not surprisingly, Boris has become accustomed to these sugary delights, a notable change from his normal fayre of vegetation with occasional carrion. Boris is becoming habitualised to people. He represents a species that has throughout history been associated with bravery, ferocity and derring do, whose accidental re-introduction into Britain sent fear throughout the nation.[1] But has he sold his soul for handouts on easy street? More importantly, will this interaction between people and unpredictable beast be allowed to continue by a Forestry Commission ever fearful that this unlikely alliance may turn nasty with Boris biting the hand that feeds him?

Boris may be just one step away from the great woodland in the sky, where it rains truffles and bullets are banned, because one of his compatriots has already been dispatched there. A widely, and wildly, reported incident of a wild boar being shot dead in the playground of a primary school on the edge of the Forest of Dean recently made headline news.[2] Wild boar should not be in a school playground, and the boar's end was as sudden as predictable. I sympathise with the Forestry Commission ranger who had to act as judge, jury and executioner – I have primary aged school children, I would have done the same. When I wave my children off in the morning, I check they have remembered their dinner money, Power Ranger pencil case, and tennis ball for a playground kick-about. I don't check they are aware of what to do if confronted by a feisty wild boar as they change ends at half-time. However, the truth will always out and once the media hysteria died down it transpired that the playground was actually part of the school's nature trail at the edge of the forest, and the boar didn't want a kick-about, it was minding its own business eating wind-fall crab apples. Once spotted, the attention from onlookers unnerved the beast, its body language changed to threatening, and it began to advance towards the assembled throng doing the school-run. The Forestry Commission's local marksman was called to despatch it.

Pointing the finger of blame would not be a fruitful exercise, but there are lessons that must be learnt as to how this situation can be avoided, because for certain another wild boar will one day fancy a crab apple or two. A child's safety is absolutely paramount, but playing fields should not be killing fields. I suggest now is the time for the school to fence off the nature trail to exclude wild boar, to post notices highlighting that wild boar are present, to devise interpretation boards explaining wild boar behaviour, and to add wild boar to the school's curriculum. Education, children and wild boar form a wonderful trinity, and I have been trying to marry the three together for some time. Following the principles that we fear what we don't know, and the pen is mightier than the sword, I had written a short book specifically for an audience of 5-15 year olds explaining about Britain's reintroduced wild boar populations, which included personal safety advice.[3] With more than a hint of embarrassment that I may be pouring petrol onto flames, I sent a copy to the schools' headmaster. I was relieved to receive a heart-warming reply thanking me, and with an unsolicited assurance the book would have a prominent place in the school's library "once I have been able to retrieve it from the staff". As *ECOS* went to press, there was news of more marauding wild boar in the Forest of Dean, when a freshly re-laid football pitch at Soudley was roughed-up by the rooting of wild boar. Team members and their friends were not happy, and this is the sort of incident which certainly does influence people's attitudes.

From Japan to Berlin – the boar's urban refuge

Other countries are home to wild boar populations far older and greater in number than our own emerging population. We should therefore look to these countries to see if they have an issue with wild boar fraternising with the locals and becoming habitualised, and if so, learn how they deal with the issue. Unfortunately, a glance around the world shows the wild boar appear to have the upper hand and lesson-plans are still being drawn up. In the Far East, for example, the land of the rising sun also has a rising wild boar population that is becoming habitualised to urban areas. In Kobe, a city in Japan famous for its Kobe beef, wild boar in search of food are reportedly breaking down front gates and garden fencing before ransacking vegetable patches and tulip bulbs.[4] Residents have also complained about rubbish bins being raided, wild boar droppings littering the ground, and frightening encounters at night. Some Kobe wild boar have taken so fondly to urban life they no longer return to sleep in the relative safety of the woodland, preferring to dream the day away in urban thickets or backyards. The reason for the troubles is partly blamed on those residents who have been putting out feed for the boar. Kobe officials have now introduced laws banning the feeding of wild boar and ensuring that household rubbish is only put out on the actual day of collection. The laws are designed to create an environment that will not attract wild boar, and are communicated by leaflets, signs, community newspapers and even loudspeaker cars. The odds are currently stacked in the wild boars' favour since the use of firearms inside Kobe is banned, and to even capture a wild boar a special license is required. The authorities state that they cannot trap a boar simply because it has ruined a garden, but they can act if "people are being bitten, chased and gored"![4] Captured wild boar are recommended to be put down because if returned to the woods, the animal is likely to wander back. It seems that once the bright lights and forbidden fruits of the city have been tasted, there is just no going back.

In Berlin, Germany, where east once met west, a similar situation has occurred as wild boar 'overspill' from burgeoning boar populations in the Grunewald Park have relocated to the city's suburbs. Wild boar have reportedly been found sleeping on garden compost heaps, caught red-handed devastating flowerbeds and prized lawns, and in the ultimate lack of respect, desecrated a graveyard by covering hundreds of memorial stones with overturned soil.[5] However, pro-wild boar groups have not appreciated forestry rangers sending the wild boar to graves of their own and have made their feelings known.[6] Shooting wild boar in urban Berlin is outlawed unless the animal, on a par with Kobe and common sense, is becoming dangerous. Ironically it is thought that heavy hunting pressure in forests close to Berlin, in itself a response to the growing wild boar populations, drove the wild boar into their urban sanctuary. Wild boar are intelligent creatures and quickly learn that they are less likely to be shot at in urban areas. Berlin's boars have reportedly not killed anyone to-date, although some domestic dogs that sows thought were threatening their piglets, have not been so fortunate.[6] A ranger has lamented that several old ladies have been feeding the wild boar causing them to become even less fearful of people, thus increasing the habituation problem.

International tales of boar as new neighbours

Similar tales of wild boar habituating to urban areas are reported in several other areas of the world. In France, a press report notes that numerous wild boar are spending their days hiding in the brush around coastal town of the Côte d'Azur.[7] During the night they descend into built up areas and make a bee-line for the lush watered private lawns and local golf courses where the worm content of the soil is irresistibly high. Local laws here too forbid the shooting of animals in built up areas and the wild boar have learnt they are safe as long as they stick to a residential environment. In Israel, a British expat and former wild boar farmer tells me there are small groups of wild boar active in a number of Israeli towns, including Haifa. The wild boar, safe from being hunted because of Muslim aversion to all things piggy, have lost their fear of man and are guilty of raiding dustbins and rooting up gardens. This former farmer has heard of no credible story of a member of the public being hurt by a wild boar, although he points out he always hesitates to tell the public that wild boar are not dangerous 'because people are prone to do the stupidest things". Herds of boar are reported to be running amok in the Polish city of Swinoujscie. The town's mayor is said to be "at the end of his tether" trying to deal with the problem and recently had to pay out from the town's coffers compensation to a tourist bitten by one of the wild boars as he was trying to pet it.[8] People really are prone to do the stupidest things.[7] It is happening in parts of Romania too - a neighbourhood in the city of Constanta is having wild boar visitations, reportedly because an area of their natural habitat was cleared for construction work.[9]

In comparison to the Forest of Dean, wild boar in Collserola Park, Barcelona, Spain, were thin on the ground until quite recently, but a recent surge in wild boar numbers has led to a sharp rise in contact between wild boar and people. Like the Forest of Dean, Collserola Park attracts visitors who come to walk, jog or cycle in scenic surrounds. It bodes well for people visiting, or living near the Forest of Dean, that a colleague of mine who studies wild boar in Collserola Park has recorded no attacks by wild boar on visiting people.[10] However, general complaints from the visitors highlight the fear people have of these beasts, regarding their personal safety and especially that of accompanying children. As has happened with Boris in the Dean, some of Collserola's wild boar have become habituated to people and urban life, either by people feeding them (some boar apparently will even feed out of your hand), or by rummaging through lawned gardens and rubbish bins, often during broad daylight. No Collserola wild boar has yet turned ugly and had a go at a resident, but their nuisance factor (from digging up lawns, jay-walking across roads, and scattering rubbish) is high, and the boar are poorly tolerated by the majority of residents. In response, park rangers capture habituated wild boar using a dart gun and removed them to a discreet place away from public eyes, where they are sent away, permanently, to be rained on by truffles. However, prevention is determined the key management tool and Collserola Park maintains a public awareness campaign that informs visitors and locals alike to the negative implications of feeding the wild boar. Advice is also given on garden fencing and the disposal of rubbish inside specific containers to reduce the attraction to wild boar.

Back in Britain – meddling with fertility

In Britain, is the Forestry Commission learning these lessons? Yes it is beginning to, and credit where credit is due, notices have begun to appear in strategic locations in the Dean, such as camp sites and picnic areas, where visitors or locals are most likely to come into contact with a wandering wild boar. The notices advise that wild boar are not to be fed and dogs should be kept on a lead, it is a start at least. Defra on the other hand, and in cahoots with the Forestry Commission, has gone one giant step further and is conducting ground breaking research trialling chemical contraception as a method of reducing boar numbers in the Forest of Dean. This form of population control will also negate the need for shooting, which could have driven some of the wild boar out of the woodlands and into residential areas. The research, involving the gonadotropin releasing hormone (GnRH) under the trade name GonaConTM has been underway for three years. The hormone has been shown to be effective in preventing sows in captive enclosures from becoming pregnant, and also in trapped, jabbed, and then released free-living wild boar in the Forest of Dean.[11] In fact, Defra reports that all six females vaccinated in 2004, and five of the six females vaccinated in 2006 were still infertile in 2008[12], which to me is more akin to sterilization than contraception. However, it is early days yet and I must not be as negative as the sows' next pregnancy tests are likely to be. Flushed with success, Defra has just extended the research for a further three years, with an aim to "develop and evaluate species-specific systems to deliver oral vaccines to key target species". Sadly the research is, at this point, completely dead in the water as far as being of any practical use to humane wild boar management. Trapping wild boar is very labour intensive and not cost-effective, and for the vaccine to be of any value the sows need to eat a bait laced with the vaccine to achieve 'oral delivery'. However, no method has been devised or is ever likely to be, whereby a hormone-laced bait system can accurately deliver the correct dosage to the correct target wild boar, without the rest of the group also getting inadvertently dosed-up.

Defra has come up with the BOS (Boar Operated System), said to be "an effective, relatively inexpensive and species-specific device to deliver contraceptives and other pharmaceuticals to wild boar".[13] The BOS is described "as consisting of a metal pole onto which a round mesh base is attached. A metal cone with a wide brim slides up and down the pole and fully encloses the base onto which the baits are placed". However, such a system does not discriminate between sex, size or appetite, and individuals who eat like a pig are in danger of getting dosed-up to the eyeballs. If the preliminary results are anything to go by, the sows' eggs will be addled for a lifetime, and the boars will be grunting in soprano.

More sinisterly, wild boar are messy eaters and even if only wild boar, through intelligence or brute force, are the only species able to open a dedicated feeding device, they will spill part of what they eat onto the forest floor making it available to non-target species. When observing wild boar at bait stations, I was always amused to see kamikaze mice dash between stomping trotters to grab a morsel of grain before rapidly retreating. Mice of course are eaten by a host of other species and so on up the food chain. I also watched chaffinches, blackbirds, pheasants, and rabbits all dine out on the scraps from the wild boars' table. The effect of GnRH on small non-target species through direct consumption or environmental contamination from rain-induced run-off, for example, is as far I can ascertain through literature searches, completely unknown. Furthermore, having watched wild boar toss logs of wood the size of railway sleepers about as if they were match sticks, to get at grain I had strategically placed underneath, I strongly doubt the longevity or biosecurity of such a feeding device. I suspect that under field conditions BOS will soon be BUST, spilling its guts of drug-ridden grain to all and sundry. Let us hope that Defra has done its homework and it has been marked correct by a higher authority. Introducing strong biologically active chemicals into an ecosystem must be done very carefully. And if I was a frog, and wanted to hang on to all my limbs, I would certainly be fearful.[14] Unless Defra has a cunning plan it is keeping to itself, this research is likely to be a waste of so much public money that Baldrick himself would be embarrassed.

Older, wilder and wiser?

Interestingly, Britain's other main wild boar populations, in the south east, are considerably more wild than the boar in the Dean. In Kent and East Sussex, where the wild boar are totally nocturnal, even to observe the animals poses a considerable challenge, and there is no chance of hand feeding any, even with pockets full of M&Ms. When I needed to observe these wild boar for research purposes, the animals were so afraid of people I found it necessary to occupy my favourite vantage point well before nightfall, never daring to move for fear of betraying my presence. I measured time from a solitary distant streetlight that became increasingly brighter as the sky darkened, until it was the only light visible from the pitch-black woodland. At times it felt like being in another world and I would not have been surprised if Narnia's Mr Tumnus himself had appeared by the glowing light. By contrast, in the Forest of Dean the wardrobe door appears permanently open as the wild boar can often be seen in broad daylight. The reticence shown by the Kent and East Sussex wild boar to be gazed upon by curious eyes is understandable when hunting pressures are considered: 7 out of 10 animals I identity tagged were all shot dead within a few months of tagging. However, sanctuary for these boar lay in large blocks of woodlands owned by a celebrity musician with a strong aversion to shooting, as opposed to bullet-free zones in nearby suburbs.

Although the wild boar in privately owned satellite woodlands around the Forest of Dean are being hunted, the wild boar in the 'main block', where the Forestry Commission reigns supreme, have so far been reprieved. However, with the advent of Defra's Wild Boar Action Plan permitting local control with a rifle, and an increasingly nervous Forestry Commission management fearful of possible lawsuits for boar-damaged crops, dogs, cars or people, the writing is on the wall. Current Forestry Commission policy is that boar are only culled on an individual basis where they have directly caused problems relating to health and safety.[15] This policy relies on good intelligence and identification skills as all wild boar look alike. The possibility for mistaken identity will add further to the boars' growing uncertainty about their new two-footed friends.

I suspect that if Boris wants to live a long life, and avoid the truffle rains, he will have to forsake the M&Ms and return to a more mundane diet of roots, berries, and dead things. And if we want our wild boar to be truly wild, we must play our part too.

References and notes
1. Goulding, M.J. & Roper, T.J. (2002) Press responses to the presence of free-living wild boar (Sus scrofa) in southern England. *Mammal Review*, 32, 272 - 282.
2. BBC (2008). Wild boar shot on school grounds, 31 January 2008. http://news.bbc.co.uk/1/hi/england/gloucestershire/7220272.stm (accessed 7 October 2008).
3. Goulding, M.J. (2007) *Wild Boar - our new neighbours*. Wild Boar Trading, Cheshire. ISBN 9780955787904.
4 Kobe-city Higashinada Ward Office (undated). Wild Boars. http://www.city.kobe.jp/cityoffice/81/e/wildboars/index.html (accessed 7 October 2008).
5. Anon. (2008). Wild boar wreck one of Europe's biggest cemeteries. http://www.spiegel.de/international/zeitgeist/0,1518,509138,00.html (accessed 7 October 2008).
6. Ridgley H. (2006) The Boar Wars. *National Wildlife Magazine* 44;3.
7. Jeffries S. (2001) Wild boar eat path through French riviera. http://www.guardian.co.uk/world/2001/sep/09/stuartjeffries.theobserver.
8. Sibirsky M. (1999). Boars cause chaos in Poland. http://news.bbc.co.uk/1/hi/world/europe/493656.stm (accessed 7 October 2008).
9. Anon. (2002). Police bullet end wild boar rampage. http://news.bbc.co.uk/1/hi/world/europe/2236497.stm (accessed 7 October 2008).
10. Cahill S, Llimona F and Gràcia J. (2003) Spacing and nocturnal activity of wild boar *Sus scrofa* in a mediterranean metropolitan park. *Wildlife Biology* 9:3-13.
11. Defra (2008). Towards practical application of emerging fertility control technologies for wildlife management - WM0408 http://randd.defra.gov.uk/Default.aspx?Menu=Menu&Module=More&Location=None&Completed=2&ProjectID=16127 (accessed 7 October 2008).
12. Massei G. Effectiveness and Potential Side Effects of the Immunocontraceptive Vaccine ConaConTM on The Wild Boar. 2008 National Conference On Feral Hogs, Louis, Missouri. April 13–15, 2008 (Abstract).

13. Massei G. The BOS (Boar-Operated-System): a novel method to deliver baits to wild boar. 2008 National Conference n Feral Hogs, Louis, Missouri. April 13–15, 2008 (Abstract).
14. Sower SA, Reed KL, Babbitt KJ. (2000) Limb Malformations and Abnormal Sex Hormone Concentrations in Frogs Environ Health Perspect. 108:1085–1090.
15. British Wild Boar. Defra and wild boar. www.britishwildboar.org.uk\defra.html (accessed 7 October 2008).

The wild boar action plan - shooting in the dark?

ECOS 29 (1) 98-100 (2008)
Defra's new action plan for wild boar simply offers a comfort break before assembling guidance and coordinating the action that has long been obvious and necessary.

MARTIN GOULDING

In Februray Defra released its policy document on the management of wild boar in England.[1] After reading it, the saying 'it is better to travel hopefully than to arrive', sprang immediately to mind. Furthermore, the journey was long - over 10 years, and the ticket expensive: well over one million pounds of tax payers money spent on research alone.[2] Regrettably, Defra has not delivered the first class service we expected.

A list of eight action points frames the plan, with each action delegated to one or more of the various government partners, for example, Natural England (NE), Deer Initiative (DI), Food Standards Agency (FSA) and Lacor - see list below.

Main action to be co-ordinated by Defra for advice on feral wild boar

- Guidance for land managers on the impacts of wild boar and their management. (DI & NE)

- Guidance on welfare such as minimum recommended firearm calibers. (DI & NE)

- Guidance on best practice and safe shooting (DI)

- Guidance on carcass handling including meat for human consumption and waste disposal (DI & FSA)
- Advice to aid hunters, gamekeepers and stalkers in disease identification (DI, FSA & Defra)
- Public awareness of wild boar including safety advice (DI & NE)
- Advice on dealing with wounded wild boar (DI)
- Advice for keepers of wild boar and local authorities to minimise the risk of further escapes (DI, NE, Local Authorities Coordinators Of Regulatory Services)

These action points will eventually deliver useful information, but not today. The journey still continues. This is just a comfort break. We have waited over 10 years and spent a small fortune just to be presented with a list of action points that were obvious from day one, when the first wild boar set down a liberated trotter on the outside of the fence.

Action and management needed now

What is desperately needed today, and what should have been delivered, is advice that is essential to enable the boar to be managed, borrowing a quote from the Deer Initiative themselves, with "a humane, responsible and sensitive approach".[3] For example, advice on a close season to reduce the number of lactating sows with dependant piglets from being shot. Advice on which age class of animal to shoot, and how many, and how often, and of which sex, and at what time of the year? Also, advice on how to shoot cleanly and safely without just maiming the pig or person - an injured wild boar is a very dangerous animal, an injured person very litageous. Furthermore, where is the awareness that wild boar groups are matriarchal and if the alpha female is shot, bang also goes group cohesion. More wild boars are therefore likely to turn up, in an excitable and unpredictable state, in unsuitable places as school playgrounds.

And that is where the truth behind the release of the action plan lies. Despite the considerable wait for the action plan, in the end it was hurriedly written and rushed out to placate parochial unrest in the Forest of Dean stemming from a wild boar straying onto a school playing field adjacent to the forest. And to silence a disgruntled Conservative MP who was using the wild boar to score political points.

As a result of the action plan stating *"regional management to be most appropriate"*, the Forestry Commission, particularly in the Forest of Dean, now has permission to start culling wild boar. Unfortunately it will be doing so with no idea as to what an acceptable or sustainable boar population level is. The wild boar reintroduced themselves into Britain through the back door, but they are now in danger of being eradicated by a government action plan using the same entrance.

However, the boar train does not recognise national boundaries. The action plan concerns only England, and there are feral wild boar populations in Wales and Scotland. I wonder if Defra has plans for a border patrol?

References

1. Feral wild boar in England: An action plan.
http://www.defra.gov.uk/wildlife-countryside/vertebrates/pdf/feralwildboar.pdf.
Accessed on-line 21 Feb 2008
2. Defra and Wild boar. http://www.britishwildboar.org.uk/defra.html. Accessed on-line 21 Feb 2008
3. The Deer Initiative Accord.
   http://www.thedeerinitiative.co.uk/pdf/deeracc.pdf. Accessed on-line 21 Feb 2008

Hindsight in the management of Britain's wild boar

ECOS 31 (2) 36-41 (2010)
The reality of co-existing with wild boar has hit home with the first known dog casualty. Dogs need to be controlled in the presence of boar and the various messages on public information signs need careful thought. Meanwhile, perhaps the Forestry Commission should adopt a consistent line on management of wild boar...

MARTIN GOULDING

Cara the Greyhound has the unfortunate distinction of being the first known domestic dog to be killed in Britain by a free-living wild boar.[1] With a shoulder shattered beyond repair *"the damage was just unbelievable – it looked as if a sledgehammer had gone into her"*, the local vet had no choice but to put Cara to sleep.[1] Circumstances that stopped Cara's owner from intervening *"she was just screaming and screaming, it was this awful noise but I had the other two dogs so I did not dare go in after her"* [2] were a blessing in disguise, otherwise there may have been a human casualty too.

Cara was being exercised on Forestry Commission land in the Forest of Dean, Gloucestershire, and her owner was reported to say "*If I had thought the boars were a danger, I would never have taken her to the Forest in the first place*".[2] This I find the most disturbing aspect of this very regrettable, but completely preventable incident. Wild boar are a potential threat to domestic dogs, and this has been known since 1998 when the Food and Environment Research Agency (FERA), in their past life as part of MAFF (one life before DEFRA, two lives before FERA) first confirmed the presence of free-living wild boar in England "*...the question of safety can also be extended to domestic animals as wild boar are recognised as a potential danger to domestic dogs*".[3] So is this information not being delivered where it matters? Ominously, the vet that treated Cara had just patched up a Golden Retriever attacked in the Forest of Dean just days earlier.[1]

Warning notices

The Forestry Commission does post warning notices around the Forest of Dean advising the public of the presence of wild boar, and the need for dog-owners to keep their dogs on a lead. I visit the Forest of Dean frequently and see the notices, and see the dogs, but rarely do I see the dogs on leads. The notices are not being noted. The message has become diluted or lost amongst the myriad of other notices around the forest advising on parking charges, penalty parking tickets, the need not to leave valuables in your car, gate-locking times, things to do and see in the Forest, your opinion of the forest, the latest open-air concert, the new Go-Ape climbing experience, cycle hire, etc, etc. Perhaps it is time the Forestry Commission had a policy rethink on how best to communicate important messages about the wild boar, such as those they recently quoted to the press: "*There's a need for dog owners to understand that when they're in areas where there might be wild boar, particularly at this time of year, that they're going to have to keep their dogs under quite close control*".[1] The message is correct, but the Forestry Commission need to find the correct mediums to deliver it – and it would be wise to assume that in *every* area of the forest there might be wild boar.

Road Traffic Accidents

Cara's fait begs the question 'Are there other issues concerning Britain's wild boar where forewarned is forearmed?' Where, if we act now, future injuries, tragedy, hassles or unpleasantness can be avoided? Yes there are, and the potential of wild boar to cause a road traffic accident (RTA) immediately springs to mind. Warning shots have been sounded; wild boar RTAs have occurred on Britain's roads "*friends of mine, with whom we had just had a meal that evening, were first on the scene of this accident, and comforted the driver who was dazed and had struggled from his car to the gutter, until the ambulance arrived"* (pers comm.). It is now only a matter of time before a person is seriously injured or worse in a wild boar-related RTA. The clock is ticking.

A German automobile association recently carried out crash-tests by ploughing a Volkswagen hatchback into life-size models of wild boar at 80 km/h.[4] Emerging from the wreckage was the reassurance (for VW drivers at least) that although the front of the vehicle was damaged, the passenger cell remained stable. The association's practical conclusions to tackle jay-walking wild boar were:

- Don't swerve to avoid animals - trying to spare the animal's life by moving into the opposite lane carries a far greater risk of smashing into an oncoming car;

- Dip headlights to give animals a chance to run away - they get fixated by a strong light beam;

- If a wild boar appears suddenly apply the brakes as hard as possible, keep a tight grip on the steering wheel and stay in the lane - in the worst case scenario, a collision with the animal has to be accepted;

- Drive slowly to minimize the risks.

This advice is also relevant to Britain, and if it can save just one person from serious injury or loss of life, then we should be shouting it from the rooftops, or at least the Highways Agency should be. This government agency is responsible for 'managing traffic, tackling congestion, informing road users, improving safety, minimising adverse impact on the environment and more'.[5] The Forestry Commission's current advice to drivers around the Forest of Dean to "*drive at a reasonable speed in the Forest at night - boar can cause great damage to vehicles if hit*" [6] can now be usefully embellished, supported by the German research. Vorsprung durch Technik.

Urbanisation

Wild boar venturing into urban areas always causes a fuss, even in countries such as Germany, where the general public and local authorities are far more familiar with the species than we are in Britain. Wild boar have a propensity to become urbanised. They quickly twig they are less likely to be shot at by the houses than in the woodlands, and they find abundant food in vegetable patches and rubbish bins - some residents even deliberately put food out for them. However, not everyone is pleased and urban wild boar are accused of being a traffic hazard, attacking dogs, rooting up prized lawns, frightening residents, and

393

bizarrely, office staff seated at their desks - just the kind of story the press delight in: "*Armed police had to gun down a wild boar that broke into offices in Hamburg when a herd of the animals went on the rampage in the city's centre. Officers armed with sub-machine guns were called to the consultancy in Hamburg on Friday night after one of 12 boars smashed through a window to enter the building. Stunned staff were evacuated as it crashed through open-plan office causing thousands of pounds of damage. It was shot dead next to the office photocopier*".[7]

Here in Britain our wild boar are now venturing into urban areas. The rural Gloucestershire town where wild boar were recently photographed scavenging amongst bin bags awaiting collection at the end of someone's driveway[8] doesn't quite equate to the bright lights of Hamburg, but it is the first step on the road to urbanisation. Are we paying heed to the advice that we should not be feeding these wild boar that are boldly going where none have gone before? It appears not. The local vet who euthanased Cara lamented "*It is becoming more evident that people are feeding the wild boar, encouraging human contact*".[9] The Forestry Commission stresses: "*Do not feed the boar - feeding encourages them into closer contact with humans where the scope for less desirable activity increases*". [6] Regrettably, this advice is often ignored, as people indulge in the novelty of feeding the wild boar anything from fruit to confectionary.

Livestock disease

The Forestry Commission have a difficult time trying to manage the wild boar on their turf. Some people and organisations want the Forestry Commission to shoot all wild boar, some a few, and some none at all. Sightings of wild boar have recently been reported from Thetford Forest, Norfolk, which is managed by the Forestry Commission, and boy are they are up-in-arms about it. Interviewed on Radio 4's Farming Today programme, the Forestry Commission's Head Ranger for the area described with gusto their zero tolerance policy towards wild boar in Thetford Forest:[10,11]

"*We will resist a wild boar population establishing on a public forest estate in any way we can, be it with shooting, trapping or any legal method to stop them establishing a population here. We have men on the ground all times of the day and night who are trained for wildlife duties, controlling deer, rabbits, hares, that sort of thing. They are out at night as well. So there are eyes on the ground all the time. My men have instructions to shoot wild boar on sight, if safe to do so. If wild boar got into the forest they would be detrimental to the Breckland ecology.*

Where is the mandate for the Forestry Commission to take such sweeping action, and what is the justification for this unilateral voice of hostility from the

Thetford Head Ranger? The accusation that wild boar are a threat to the area's ecology is puzzling. Wild boar are a former native species, and our woodlands would have grown up with wild boar rooting amongst them. However, the forestry tracts of Thetford Forest stem from post first world war timber production, so perhaps this particular woodland's ecology is so far removed from a natural state there is no place for wild boar. Although, as Thetford Forest Park is a public forest estate, were the public asked what they thought before the Forestry Commission declared themselves judge, jury and executioner?

The Forestry Commission's wild boar management policy at Thetford Forest does have support from the National Pig Association (NPA),[10] a group that represents domestic pig farmers. The NPAs concerns are for the several large-scale outdoor domestic pig units within wild boar-commuting distance from Thetford Forest. Wild boar will freely mate with domestic pigs producing hybrid offspring that will throw any unit's economic forecasts to the dogs. More sinisterly, contact between free-living wild boar and domestic pigs could provide a transmission route for the spread of diseases. A transmissible disease becoming endemic in the wild boar population could continually re-infect the domestic pig stock, with considerable economic consequences.

To-date in Britain, most interference between wild boar and domestic pigs has occurred in small-holdings or petting zoos. Male wild boar are not choosy, and the breeds of domestic pigs receiving unexpected nocturnal visits from an amorous suitor have included Kune Kune, Oxford and Sandy and Black, and Berkshires.[12] Again, we have been forewarned that the day will come when a testosterone-loaded male wild boar will break into a large free-ranging domestic pig unit, and then the fun will really begin. I doubt whether shooting all wild boar on-sight is a feasible preventative measure. The ranger's men may well be out at night, but the wild boar will have the greater staying power, night after night, and especially on those long, cold, windswept, pitch-black nights.

As well as being a disease liability regarding domestic pigs, a wild boar in Britain has recently been confirmed as being infected with the zoonotic disease *Mycobacterium bovis* (*M. bovis*),[13] the causative agent of tuberculosis (TB) in cattle. *M.bovis* had previously been diagnosed on two captive wild boar farms in the Southwest of England, in 2000 and 2006 respectively,[14] and it was only a matter of time before a free-living wild boar was identified as infected too. Wild boar now join an eclectic mix of mammals susceptible to bovine TB infection including deer, pigs, sheep, llamas, camels, alpacas, and domestic cats and dogs. The epidemiology of bovine TB is not completely understood, but badgers are of course the most infamous animal regarding the transmission of bovine TB to cattle, but on the continent wild boar are also implicated as a potential reservoir for, and transmitter of, bovine TB.[15,16] I suspect this will not be the last we hear about bovine TB and Britain's wild boar.

Eco-tourism

A more 'desirable activity' of wild boar is their potential to generate income for local people through, for example, the sale of shooting rights, meat, and eco-tourism. The first eco-tourism holiday to focus on Britain's wild boar is now being advertised.[17] A farmer near Rye, East Sussex, is the first to tap into the potentially lucrative market of wild boar watching holiday-breaks by renting out their holiday cottages to 'the serious wildlife lover'. On offer are day and night guided trips to view wild boar in their natural habitat, a visit to local woodland to view boar signs, dinner at a local inn, and back to the farm to experience the nightly visits of the boar in safety. It will be fascinating to see if this enterprise is a success - I wonder if the Forestry Commission would ever contemplate something similar to increase awareness and understanding of the species.

Hindsight

In Britain we have the fortunate opportunity to manage our fledgling wild boar populations with the benefit of hindsight gained from how continental Europe manage their populations. Potential areas of conflict involving domestic animals, people, or livestock can be foreseen, and the necessary corrective action or contingency plans put in place, ready to be actioned. However, this opportunity will be lost if appropriate advice is not being heeded.

The death of Cara the greyhound exemplifies how advice from the Forestry Commission is not getting through to people who need it the most. All of us who have an involvement with Britain's wild boar, such as the Forestry Commission, government agencies, local authorities, private organisations, hunting enthusiasts, and interested individuals, need to ensure that these messages do get through.

References

1. BBC News (2010). Warning to Forest of Dean dog owners after boar attacks
   http://news.bbc.co.uk/1/hi/england/gloucestershire/8711014.stm
   Accessed 29 May 2010.
2. This is Gloucestershire (2010). Warning after wild boar savages rescue greyhound http://www.thisis gloucestershire.co.uk/news/Warning-wild-boar-gore-dogs/article-2218148-detail/article.html accessed 29 May 2010.
3. Goulding, M.J., Smith, G. & Baker, S.J. (1998) Current status and potential impact of Wild Boar (Sus scrofa) in the English countryside: A risk assessment. Central Science Laboratory report to the Ministry of Food, Fisheries and Agriculture.4. Spiegel Online International (2010). Wild Boar Crash Test Highlights Growing Accident Risk

5.Spiegel -Accessed 29 May 2010.
http://www.spiegel.de/international/zeitgeist/0,1518,690156,00.html#ref=nlint
6. Highways Agency (2010) http://www.highways.gov.uk/aboutus/about.aspx
Accessed 29 May 2010.
7. Forest of Dean Tourism (2010) Wild Boar Information.
http://www.visitforestofdean.co.uk/outdoors/wildboreforestofdean.aspx
Accessed 29 May 2010
8. Mail Online (2010) The ultimate office boar: How herd of wild pigs went on
rampage in Hamburg.
9. http://www.dailymail.co.uk/news/worldnews/article-1259772/Releieving-
office-boar-dome-The-wild-pigs-rampaged-Hamburg.html#ixzz0qOszSg4
accessed 7 June 2010
10. Telegraph.co.uk (2010) Wild boar ransacking rubbish bins.
http://www.telegraph.co.uk/news/uknews/6973152/Wild-boar-ransacking-
rubbish-bins.html. Accessed 07 June 2010
11. This is Gloucestershire (2010). Don't feed wild boar, warns dog attack vet.
http://www.thisisgloucestershire.co.uk/news/Don-t-feed-wild-boar-warns-dog-
attack-vet/article-2258963-detail/article.html Accessed 29 May 2010
12. NFU (2010). Feral wild boar in East Anglia? It would be A catastrophe
http://www.npa-uk.org.uk/Pages/newsNPA.html Accessed 29 May 2010
13. Farming Today. Radio 4. BBC iplayer
http://www.bbc.co.uk/iplayer/episode/b00nd1c8/Farming_Today_27_10_2009/
Accessed 29 October 2009.
14. BWBO (2010). Domestic Livestock and Wild Boar Confrontations.
http://www.britishwildboar.org.uk/index.htm?Livestock.html Accessed 8 June
2010.
15. Foyle KL, Delahay RJ and Massei G. (2010). Isolation of Mycobacterium
bovis from a feral wild boar (Sus scrofa) in the UK. Vet Rec. 166(21): 663 -
664.
16. DEFRA (2010) Bovine TB: TB in other species.
http://www.defra.gov.uk/foodfarm/farmanimal/diseases/atoz/tb/abouttb/otherspe
cies.htm Accessed 8 June 2010.
17. Serraino A, Marchetti G, Sanguinetti V, et al. (1999) Monitoring of
Transmission of Tuberculosis between Wild Boars and Cattle: Genotypical
Analysis of Strains by Molecular Epidemiology Techniques. J. Clin.
Microbiology. 37 (9): 2766-2771
18. Vicentea J, Höflea U, Garridob JM, et al. (2006) Wild boar and red deer
display high prevalences of tuberculosis-like lesions in Spain. Vet. Res. 37: 1–
11
19. BWBO (2010). http://www.britishwildboar.org.uk/ Accessed 8 June 2010.

WOLF

Wolves are returning

ECOS 23 (2) 2-8 (2002)
Wolves are making a come-back in Europe and the US as opinions aboutthem change. The last British wolves were exterminated in the ScottishHighlands, where we should now focus our efforts to reintroduce them.
ROGER PANAMAN

Changing attitudes

People's perceptions of wolves before the 1960s derived mainly from folklore. Because wolves were thought to be menacing, by threatening human life, livestock and game, people made a concerted effort to destroy them. By the early twentieth century the only wolves left in western Europe amounted to a few hundred in Spain and Italy. They had been wiped out from almost all the US, and were extinct or severely reduced in many other countries.

Since the 1960s, research on wolves has grown apace and today they are among the most studied of mammals. Knowledge changes attitudes and has brought wolves a measure of legal protection in western Europe and the US. As a result, since the 1990s, wolves from remnant populations have started to recolonise Iberia, settle in France (from Italy), and migrate to Germany from eastern Europe. Atabout the same time, the US set a precedent by reintroducing wolves toa number of states.

The Scottish Highlands

In Britain, the last wolf population was exterminate in the ScottishHighland region because of its rugged and remote terrain, which makes it a good place to reintroduce them. More importantly there is plenty of natural food for wolves in Scotland: about 350,000 red deer, 350,000 of the smallerroe deer, and over 100,000 fallow deer and sika deer. In comparison,England is deer-poor and Wales is almost deer-less.[2] With the lowhuman density of the Highlands (one of the last large semi-wildernessareas in western Europe) wolves will come into less conflict there withhuman activity.

There is a myth that wolves need forest or wilderness to live in. In truth, wolves live in all types of terrain, from deserts to the Arctic.[3] Wolves even live on the outskirts of villages and towns. A wolf pack was even studied living on the outskirts of an east European city. At night the wolves went into town foraging for food. People did not kill them because they thought they were stray dogs.[4] Therefore, wolves are highly adaptable and the Highland landscape does not need reforesting or changing to accommodate them.

How many wolves?

How may wolves could the Highlands support? Wolf density is largely related to food supply: where food is scarce, wolves must search further to find it. Thus a pack's territory (from which it repels other wolves) may be as small as 100 km^2 where prey are plentiful or can exceed 2,000 km^2 where prey is scarce, as in the Arctic.

The Highlands (25,000 km^2) are awash with deer, therefore territories will probably be small. A wolf pack usually consists of fewer than ten individuals. So, as a rough generalisation, say each pack occupies a 500 km^2 territory and consists of five wolves, then there could be 250 wolves. Of course numbers would fluctuate, but they would be in the hundreds, not the thousands.

Wolves and people

Will Highland residents and hill walkers be safe among wolves? The first detailed study of attacks by wild wolves on humans in Eurasia and North America has been recently published by 18 researchers from several countries.[5] They reviewed the most reliable records they could find, dating from the 16th century to the present, and identified three kinds of wolf attack: rabid - by wolves who have gone mad because the rabies virus infected their brains; predatory - where wolves appear to regard humans as prey; and defensive - where wolves are provoked by people to attack, such as when trapped or cornered.

The researchers found that several hundred people have been killed, with the majority of fatal attacks by rabid wolves (rabies does not exist in Britain). There were relatively few predatory attacks and none in North America, and wolves did not kill anyone when acting in self-defence. Predatory attacks were mainly on small children and characterised by lack of natural prey, habituation to people, and wolves living very close to large numbers of children left unattended by impoverished families - the kind of situation still found in the poorest parts of India today, but not in Europe or North America. The authors of the report found that most fatalities in Europe and Russia were before the 20th century. In the last 50 years, despite better recording and better access to reports, they could only find records of 17 people killed in Europe and Russia and none in North America.

Thus, averaged over centuries and large geographical regions, being killed by a wolf is a very rare event. In comparison, an average of three people die in Britain every year from the rarity of a lightning strike.[6]

Wolves and deer

Deer in Britain have had no predator other than humans since wolves were exterminated. It is thought that this situation has contributed to a decline in the overall health of deer populations. What impression would a few hundred wolves make on the Highland's massive deer population? This is a question predator-prey specialists will argue over, with few, if any, firm answers.

For example, first, by preying on calves and the very young, wolves might have a disproportionate influence on the number and health of deer in the population which reach adulthood. However, about 50 per cent of red deer and roe deer fawns die young anyway, so if wolves kill only the sick calves they may have little influence on the population. Second, a wolf might kill up to 20 adult deer a year.[7] So 250 wolves, say, might kill around 5,000 adult deer annually. This compares with the 60,000 red deer shot every year. What impact the loss of 5,000 deer may have on the food and sport shooting markets remains to be seen.

However, whichever way wolves influence deer numbers, at least their reintroduction will help the deer population to begin to evolve in the presence of their natural predator once more.

Wolves and farmers

Depredation (predators killing domestic animals) is the main problem for any reintroduction of large predators anywhere in the world and the number one problem for the wolf reintroduction in the Highlands. Farmers fear wolves will ignore fleet-footed deer and go for their slower sheep. So to what extent will depredation occur?

Most wolf research comes from North America, where about 40 percent of the world's (roughly 150,000) wolves live. The research shows that where wolves and livestock share the same range, wolves generally take few livestock (usually less than 0.1 percent per year on average over large regions).[8] The research also shows that wolves have a minimal affect on livestock ranches (usually less than 1 per cent per year),[8, 9] and depredation is negligible to the livestock industry.[8,10] This shows that wolves do not necessarily slaughter livestock. Why they do not is a question that has yet to be fully answered.

Spain and Italy were the only countries with surviving wolf populations in western Europe. Their wolf populations rose when given legal protection and Spain now has over 2,000 and Italy about 1,000. Researchers conclude that the main factor influencing sheep depredation in both countries is the style of sheep management.[11,12] Sheep in Spain wander the mountain region largely un-shepherded and depredation is 10 times higher than in the lowlands, where sheep traditionally are watched through the day by shepherds and enclosed at night; 20 per cent of wolves live in the Spanish mountains but cause 80 per cent of losses.[11] Similarly, in the Tuscany region of central Italy, most sheep depredation involves flocks unattended by shepherds.[12]

As depredation is increasingly researched, it is becoming clear that wolf depredation is not catastrophic (nor an easy problem to solve). Therefore, it is unlikely that the worst fears of farmers in the Scottish Highlands will be realised, but depredation can be expected to be a lot higher than if the sheep were guarded by shepherds. Shepherds work in the Highlands but presently they are too few and flocks are too big to guard the sheep effectively.

Farmers and subsidies

Most sheep farms in the Highlands are not economically viable because of the unproductive soil, inclement weather and remoteness of their markets.[13] They and other farms on poor agricultural land in Scotland (about 85 per cent of the country) depend on subsidies averaging £481m per year to stay in business.[14] Without the subsidies most farms would collapse. This raises an interesting question: given that most Highland sheep farmers are completely dependent on taxpayers' money, can they reasonably object if the public (the taxpayer) want a wolf reintroduction?

The subsidy system appears about to change as the momentum to revise it gathers pace. If the system changes to favour only farms competing successfully in the free market, then most Highland sheep farms could disappear. A new subsidy system should only give payments to farmers if they adequately care for their sheep (up to 4 million lambs die in Britain annually because of poor husbandry),[15] which could stimulate a move to more traditional shepherding. The balance of argument might then shift in favour of a wolf reintroduction.

Helping farmers

One way to help farmers is to manage the wolf population. A humane method is by fertility control which does not disrupt normal hormonal activity. Usually only a single male and female breed per wolf pack.In North America they have found that by vasectomising the breeding male and tying the fallopian tubes of the breeding female the birthrate of packs of wild wolves drops off without disturbing the wolves' behaviour.[16] In this way the size of a small wolf population can be reduced, and fewer wolves mean less potential for depredation. At the same time, because the population is not expanding, this control by contraception also limits the radiation of wolves looking for new areas to occupy, such as the Lowlands.

Researchers also find that wolf depredation tends to recur on the same flocks and farms.[9] Focusing on these hot spots would be better than a widespread indiscriminate cull of wolves. Individual wolves, therefore, who become habitual depredators would have to be shot(caging wild wolves as an alternative is cruel). Shooting wolves is unfortunate, and unacceptable to many people, but it does allow the greater number of wolves who do not kill livestock to continue to live without persecution. Research is ongoing to find non-lethal means to control de predation, but presently there is no single method that works all the time.

SNH remains evasive

According to Recommendation 17 of the Council of Europe's Bern Convention, Britain should promote public awareness about wolves and study reintroduction possibilities.[17] And under the European Union's Habitats Directive, Britain must "study the desirability, of reintroducing species in Annex IV".[18] Annex IV species include the wolf.   Scottish Natural Heritage (SNH), is the government conservation body responsible for considering and overseeing the reintroduction of wolves in the Highlands. It erroneously believes that 'Recommendation 17' has been superseded by 'The Action Plan for the Conservation of Wolves (Canis lupus) in Europe' which, SNH says, excludes the UK Government from having to take any action at all regarding wolves.[19] SNH also believes that by reintroducing the beaver (another species on Annex IV) it is fulfilling the 'Habitats Directive' and therefore claims it does not need to consider wolves as well. SNH is probably happy to bury talk of wolves for fear of a backlash from landowners and farmers, who control the land, and therefore SNH's conservation work. However, the very least SNH can do is just to allude to the recovery of wolves when an opportunity occurs, especially in its publications.

Wolves earn income

Wolves in the Highlands would present an opportunity to increase employment and income in the region through wolf ecotourism. Wolves are large charismatic animals, like elephants, tigers and whales. People pay to experience and learn about these animals in the wild and the income could benefit local communities, wildlife and the environment.

Ecotourism involving large carnivores (bear, lynx, wolf and wolverine) is developing in Europe. An example is the Carpathian Large Carnivore Project in the Romanian Carpathians.[18] Wolf ecotourism is well established in the US, with a number of wolf centres; the International Wolf Center,[20] in Minnesota, dedicated to wolf conservation through public education and wolf ecotourism, grosses over a million dollars annually.

Local control of wolves

If wolf ecotourism in the Scottish Highlands is managed carefully, a fund drawn from it could compensate farmers for livestock depredation - an example of private enterprise helping conservation. Taking part in the implementation of wolf ecotourism and controlling a board to manage and distribute compensation funds are two clear areas in which the Highland community can take part in and help manage the recovery of wolves. In general, local people must be given every opportunity to manage wolves when they are reintroduced. When residents feel they have influence over the wolf recovery, they may be more willing to accept wolves.

Highland Wolf Centre

Public education is a necessary preliminary for any successful reintroduction of large mammals. This is especially true of wolves because a recovery will not succeed without good public knowledge and understanding of them. Therefore, a wolf centre in the Highlands would achieve a great deal. Like other wolf centres, it could have tame wolves for visitors to experience, and to go on outreach to schools and events for people to discover first hand what wolves are really like.

Given the lack of lupine ardour by Scottish Natural Heritage, the centre will have to be funded by donations and develop from wolf ecotourism income. After all, conservation need not, and should not, be entirely dependent on governments. The wolf centre is a great opportunity for private enterprise to show what it can do for conservation.

References

1. Harting J E (1880) *British Animals Extinct Within Historic Times*. Trubner, London.

2. Harris S, Morris P, Wray S & Yalden D (1995) *A Review of British Mammals.* JNCC, Peterborough.

3. Mech L D (1970) *The Wolf.* Natural History Press, Garden City, New York. 4. Promberger C & Schroder W (eds) (1993) *Wolves in Europe.* Munich Wildlife Society, Germany.

5. Linnell J D C, *et al* (2002) *The Fear of Wolves: a review of wolf attacks on humans.*
Norsk Instituttfor Naturforskning. Oppdragsmelding, 731, 1-65.

6. Elsom D M (2001) *Atmospheric Research.* 56, 325-334

7. Mech L D (1991) *The Way of the Wolf.* Swan Hill Press, Shrewsbury. 8. US Fish and Wildlife Service (1993) *The reintroduction of gray wolves to Yellowstone National Park and Central Idaho: environmental impact statement.* Gray Wolf Environmental Impact Study, Helena, Montana. 1993, 407p.

9. Fritts S H, Paul W J, Mech L D, and Scott D P (1992) *Trends and management of wolf-livestock conflicts in Minnesota.* US Department of the Interior, Fish and Wildlife Service, Resource Publications 181. 10. Bednarz J C (1988) *The Mexican wolf: biology history, and prospects for re-establishment in New Mexico.* US Fish and Wildlife Service, New Mexico. Endangered Species Report 18.

11. Blanco J C (2000) Large carnivore damage in Spain. *Carnivore Damage Prevention News,* 1.
http://www.kora.unibe.ch/pdf/cdpnews/cdpnews001.pdf

12. Ciucci P & Boitani L (1998) Wolf and dog depredation on livestock in central Italy. *Wildlife-Society-Bulletin.* 26 (3) 504-514.

13. The Scottish Office (1998) *Agriculture In Scotland.* Agriculture, Environment and Fisheries Department, Edinburgh.

14. . Scottish Executive Environment and Rural Affairs Department (2001) *Agriculture Facts and Figures.* Scottish Office Publications, Edinburg. 15. MAFF (1995) *Improving Lamb Survival.* http://www.defra.gov.uk. (Input 'lamb survival' in the search box.)

16. Spence, C (1998) *Wolf Fertility Control Study in Aishihik, Yukon*: http://aurora.ak.blm.gov/fmcaribou/trail2/news4.html

17. Council of Europe (1989) Recommendation 17 of the Bern Convention: http://www.nature.coe.int/english/main/Bern/texts/rec8917.htm.

18. European Union (1992) Habitats Directive:
http://europa.eu.int/eur-lex/en/lif/dat/1992/en_392L0043.html.

19. Boitani L (2000) *Action Plan for the Conservation of Wolves (Canis lupus) in Europe.*
http://www.nature.coe.int/cp20/tpvs23e.htm.

20. Carpathian Large Carnivore Project: http://www.clcp.ro.

21. International Wolf Center: http://www.wolf.org.

Wolf territory in Germany

ECOS 25 (3/4) 73-77 (2004)

Lessons from current wolf management in Germany show that action is crucial at the local level and across the countries across which wolf populations roam.

ILKA REINHARDT & GESA KLUTH

New wolf countries

After centuries of persecution wolves (*Canis lupus*) are on their way back in some areas in Europe. Eradicated in most of central and northern Europe by the middle of the last century, small but healthy populations survived in Eastern and Southern Europe. Due to an improved protection status some of these populations were expanding in the last two decades. But it was a slow process till the remaining populations could recover. Granting of closed hunting seasons (e.g. Poland in 1975),[1] the prohibition of poison (e.g. in Spain 1984)[2] and the abandonment of bounties gave these populations a break. Sometimes, for example, in Sweden, full protection status was given after the last wolf disappeared.[3]

Distribution of the wolf in Europe

Today the wolf is strictly protected in many European Countries. It is listed in Appendix II (strictly protected species) of the Bern Convention and Appendix II (needs habitat conservation) of the EC Habitats Directive - with the exception of the populations in Spain north of the river Duero; the population in Greece north of the 39° longitude and the populations in Finland. The new EU member states - unless giving full protection - have had to present management plans for wolf, bear *(Ursus arctos)* and lynx *(Lynx lynx)* to ensure hunting will be on a sustainable basis. This is the measure which makes it more likely that wolves will reappear in countries where they were eradicated a long time ago. France, Switzerland, Germany and the Czech Republic are such new wolf countries.

Making space in the German landscape

In Germany the very last wolf was eradicated in 1904. However, for the past 60 years, single wolves have wandered from Poland into Germany. Until recently they all were shot (first legally, later illegally) or run over by cars. The hunting law of former East Germany required the shooting of any wolf sighted. GDR authorities claimed there was no space for a big predator in its cultivated landscape – a view still widespread. The number of wolf immigrants reflected the situation on the Polish side.[4] When wolf numbers in Poland were growing more wolves made it into Germany, where they didn't survive for long.

Wolf tracks near Blomberg (Lupus)

Times are changing, for people and wildlife. Since the reunification of Germany in 1990 wolves are strictly protected in the whole country. However, even after becoming a protected species by law at least eight wolves were shot. Obviously it will take some time to welcome a once outlawed species as an enrichment of nature. In 1995 a single wolf made the right choice and established a territory in the Muskau Heath, an active military training area in Upper Lusatia, in Northern Saxony close to the Polish border. Military training areas are federal land. Hunting and forestry are managed under the jurisdiction of the federal forest agency. By 1998 the single wolf was joined by a mate and in 2000 the first reproduction of wild wolves for a century was documented.

Understanding wolf behaviour

During the first years of their appearance the presence of the new neighbours was kept almost secret. Some people think the best way to protect wolves is not to mention their presence, but this tactic turns out to be fatal in the long run. Nobody is going to miss a wolf that is not known. More over, wolves can draw attention to themselves in pretty spectacular ways, when killing large numbers of livestock. It is much easier to deal with these situations if the public has been well aware of the presence of wolves beforehand.

In 2002 a sheep flock in Saxony was attacked twice by wolves, resulting in a loss of 33 sheep, and great shock to the public and the sheep farmers in the area. Many media reports presented the wolf as a blood-thirsty beast, ignoring the fact that at least one wolf had been in the area for seven years without causing trouble. Previously the wolves roamed mostly on the military training area and there had been no need for public relations work. When the first generation of young wolves dispersed from their natal pack and attacked the sheep flock, the lack of previous public education and public relations work became obvious. Wolf management is only to a minor extent about managing the wolves themselves. It is mostly about helping people to understand and to live with wolves. However, Saxonian authorities were quick to react to the incident, compensating the shepherd and engaging wildlife biologists to monitor the wolf population. They also provided advice to shepherds in livestock prevention measures and carried out public relations work, (Since 2002 this work has been done by LUPUS wildlife consulting).

Upper Lusatia is the only area in Germany with permanent wolf presence and wolf reproduction. It is certainly not a wild area, but wolves have shown they can live anywhere where they find enough food and where they are not killed by humans[5] Besides the military training area of about 168 km², active and disused opencast coalmines are shaping the landscape. Though several federal roads are dividing the area, the density of 128 human inhabitants per km² is low compared to other parts of Germany. The forest consists mostly of intensively managed pine plantations. Five ungulate species, red deer (*Cervus elaphus*), roe deer (*Capreolus capreolus*), wild boar (*Sus scrofa*), fallow deer (*Cervus dama*) and mouflon (*Ovis ammon musimon*) can be found here. The latter two are not native but introduced for trophy hunting. The area currently used by wolves covers about 600km^2.

Sheep strategies

Compared to countries like France, Switzerland or Norway where wolves can cause immense damage by killing free ranging sheep[6] the situation in Eastern Germany is quite favourable. Ungulate densities are very high in many parts of the country and the majority of the potentially vulnerable sheep and goat flocks are kept behind electric fences.

The areas' sheep farmers cooperated very well after realising that they were not left alone and that wolf-livestock conflicts can be kept at a low level with appropriate prevention. Two strategies are currently focused on: first, electric fences traditionally used in sheep herding have been upgraded to improve their protection value and second, livestock-guarding dogs have been introduced by some shepherds. The fact that Saxony does have a compensation system surely helps to keep tensions at bay. However, this regulation only applies if a professional shepherd is affected. For private sheep owners there is no such system. In the few cases occurring so far the German Society for the Protection of Wolves has paid for the damage. A more appropriate damage compensation regulation that is valid across state borders is nevertheless needed.

During the last two years a huge effort has been made to raise public awareness of wolf presence. This work is targeted on the wolf area, and informs inhabitants about wolves in general and 'their' wolves in particular. It replaces the old prejudices with facts. The unbroken interest of the media has led to a high level of recognition of wolf presence in Upper Lusatia all over Germany. With very few exceptions the reports are usually based on facts and communicate a tolerant attitude towards wolves.

Wild genes?

The year 2003 seemed to be a further step forward in wolf conservation in Germany. Two wolves had established a territory adjacent to the Muskau Heath pack and pups were born in both territories. The euphoria about this sign of stabilisation was over when the pups were filmed. They didn't look like wolf pups but like wolf-dog hybrids. International wolf experts reaffirmed this suspicion, and it was later confirmed by genetic analysis. Obviously the female wolf had mated with a dog. This may happen when maturing wolves do not find

409

non-relatives as mates, a situation arising above all in small, scattered populations. With the development of new genetic methods, wolf-dog hybridisation has been proven in several countries, such as Norway[7], Italy[8] or Latvia[9]. When occurring in large healthy wolf populations these hybridisation events are of less concern. However, in small fragmented populations hybridisation may threaten the entire wolf population by swamping it with dog genes, thus counteracting any wolf conservation effort.

In Germany, the possible solution to shoot the putative hybrids as was done in Norway in 1999,[10] was considered to be socially unacceptable. In a long discussion about how to deal with these animals the decision was made to live-capture the pups. Early in 2004 two of the surviving four hybrids were successfully captured and transferred into an enclosure, the other two vanished before they could be captured. So far, the female wolf has remained alone. Although she tried to mate with a dog in Spring 2004 she luckily produced no pups, giving conservationists a break. However, the problem of possible wolf-dog hybridisation remains as long as the wolf population stays this small and isolated.

Local action in a big context

The German wolf story reflects the challenge that the return of wolves may provide. German wolves are Polish wolves and depend on immigrants from the Polish population. In Western Poland wolves are very scattered and decreasing in numbers[11] - they all are on the drip of dispersers from the Eastern Polish population, several hundred kilometres away. This illustrates the crucial wider context when dealing with wolf conservation. Wolves don't care about human territories. They ignore state borders and they don't know that wildlife management in Germany is under the jurisdiction of the states. Clearly management of large predators must be adapted to and focussed on local situations. On the other hand, the huge areas that wolf populations are roaming make a large scale co-ordination across national and international borders necessary. Bringing both issues together is one of the main challenges in wolf conservation. In Germany we are just at the beginning. Since their appearance, a handful of wolves have managed to keep wildlife managers in suspense, teaching us the essentials in wolf conservation. We are willing to learn these lessons. However, the German wolves are living a fragile existence and we have to learn quickly.

References and notes

Okarma, H. (1997) Der Wolf. *Ökologie*, Verhalten, Schutz. Parey Buchverlag Berlin.

[2] Blanco, J.C. , S. Reig and L. Cuesta (1992) Distribution, status and conservation problems of the wolf Canis lupus in Spain. *Biological Conservation*, 60: 73-80.

[3] Kaczensky, P. (1996) *Large carnivore – livestock conflicts in Europe*. Report. NINA, Norway. 106 pp.

[4] Promberger, C. & D. Hofer (1994) *Ein Managementplan für Wölfe in Brandenburg*. Report.

[5] Boitani, L. (2000) Action plan for the conservation of wolves in Europe (Canis lupus). *Nature and Environment No. 113*, Council of Europe Publishing. 86pp.

[6] Kaczensky, P. (1996) *Large carnivore – livestock conflicts in Europe*

[7] Vila, C., Walker, C., Sundqvist, A.-K., Flagstad, Ó., Andersone, Ž., Casulli, A., Kojola, I., Valdmann, H., Halveson, J. & H. Ellegren (2003) Combined use of maternal, paternal and bi-parental genetic markers for the identification of wolf-dog hybrids. *Heredity* 90: 17-24.

[8] Randi, E. & V. Lucchini (2002) Detecting rare introgression of domestic dog genes into wild wolf (Canis lupus) populations by Bayesian admixture analysis of microsatellite variation. *Conservation Genetics* 3: 31-45.

[9] Andersone, Ž., Lucchini, V., Randi, E. & J. Ozoliņš (2002). Hybridization between wolves and dogs in Latvia as documented using mitochondrial and microsatellite DNA markers. *Mammalian biology* 67: 79-90.

[10] Vila, C., Walker, C., Sundqvist, A.-K., Flagstad, Ó., Andersone, Ž., Casulli, A., Kojola, I., Valdmann, H., Halveson, J. & H. Ellegren (2003) Combined use of maternal, paternal and bi-parental genetic markers for the identification of wolf-dog hybrids. *Heredity* 90: 17-24.

[11] Sabina Novak, pers. communication

Wolves in the French Alps – lessons in acceptance

ECOS 27 (3/4) 23-29 (2006)
This article describes an example of farming alongside wolves in the French Alps, where the stock management has been adapted and the predator has been respected.

TROY BENNETT

Wolves are expanding their territories in several parts of Europe, including Spain, Portugal, Poland, Germany and Austria. In 1990 there were no known wolves in France. Today there are an estimated 100, covering the Alps from the Mediterranean in the south, up into Switzerland where there are now around 20 wolves. This article discusses what has happened as wolves have returned to part of the French Alps.

The Massif Du Monge in France rises to 2115 meters close to the border with Italy. There is a mixture of oak, beech and various pines, interspersed with open grasslands and scrublands. Hunting has been restricted for over 100 years, which makes for a high diversity of species. Large populations of wild boar and roe deer are present, and there is a high diversity of mustilids (the weasel family), and a great variety of birds. We also have lynx, and mouflon longhorn sheep were introduced 20 years ago. Baudinard, the village where my story comes from is situated on the western arm of the mountain, at 1100 metres. Just two people live here all year round and four of the houses are holiday homes. The rest are ruins.

The first tracks

In 1992 12 wolves were found to be living in the Mercantor National Park on the borders of France and Italy. Six promptly disappeared. National Park officials claim they found their way there from the Abruzzi Mountains further south. This is plausible as wolves have been documented to disperse for up to 600 miles to find a new mate, or a new territory. But 12 wolves all dispersing to the same place? And from the same origin? Legends could be founded on that.

It was in 1992 that I first came across the signs of wolves on the massif du Monge where I was at the time working as a goat herder. I was out tracking with my 12 year old daughter when she came across a print that measured around 13cm by 10 cm. When she asked me what it was I told her that it was probably some kind of monster.. At that time I didn't know how close I had been.

The reality of the kill

In the summer of 1998 the shepherd who guarded sheep for our co-operative lost half the flocks in one night. 280 sheep were herded over a cliff - no one knew by what. In farming you accept that you will lose stock from disease and hard winters, from predators and occasionally thieves, but this seemed unnatural and disturbing, 280 sheep went over the cliff but many more hit the ground. Some hung on the cliff and in the trees below. Some were still wounded and bleeding.

You are not allowed to kill your wounded animals. A vet, the police and experts have to examine them to determine the culprit and cause of death, like a murder scene. But I could not watch sheep that I had bottle fed and nursed suffer in such a pitiful state. With great regret I killed them then and there, and I was then subjected to lectures from the vets, the police and the experts on why I should have waited before despatching them.

Despite being hardened by mountain life, no-one felt able to clear up the carnage from that attack. Instead we let scavengers do it, watched by forest guards who were also looking to see if the culprits returned. They didn't. The guards counted the species instead: eagles and vultures, corvids (the crow family,) mustilids, badgers and foxes. Feral dogs appeared, and these were dispatched and examined. The birds got so fat that they could not fly, and if you could stand the smell, the flies or the view, you could watch normally nocturnal animals in the daylight and walk within metres of golden eagles.

We were asked to help find and gather the lost sheep that were still wandering the mountains in small bewildered groups. With 10 volunteers working in shifts, this took around a week and a half. Every day we found fresh kills. On the Thursday morning of that second week my younger brother and I set out at 5.30am and began our long walk up to and along the crest. We found two lambs, one paralysed by a bite to the spine, the other who would not leave its side. We carried them on our shoulders for three hours until we recovered more sheep for the active lamb to run with. We carried the wounded one between us for seven hours and recovered 18 more sheep. With the light fading we descended. Then, on the lower slopes we stopped, and for no apparent reason both turned to look into the trees. There, about five metres away a wolf was looking back.

Connecting with the predator

People talk about the way wolves stare: how it holds you, and how it holds its prey. When a wild wolf fixes your eyes it looks deep, and you cannot look away. I did not feel fear, but I was held. And in that look I felt an exchange of

413

information. I don't know what the wolf took from it, but something primeval in me was awakened that day.

When I was herding on the mountain the wildlife grew used to me: deer ignored me, mouflon came and fed with the goats, sometimes even trying to herd them into their own harems. I had watched the eagles outwitting marmots, and I had become the ravens friend and plaything. I knew where the foxes and martins kept their winter stashes. But from that experience with the wolf, I suddenly began to see things differently.

I began to look at things with a predator's eye. I now look at mountain features as likely places to catch unwary animals, or as lines along which to herd them into traps. And with this insight as I am tracking in the forest examining signs, I see where the prey will pass, and where it hides and where it will fall, and in knowing the prey you can work out the predators. This leads me to find their tracks, their scats and their kills, and occasionally to glimpse the wolves. I hear them howling, and find myself strangely drawn to howl back.

From that first chance encounter my life was changed, wolves have become a passion for me, and I have followed the life of that wolf and her family ever since.

First reactions to the wolves

It was three months later that the wolf was officially recognised as being in the massif du Monge and subsequently in France. I suspect that the foresters and officials already knew that they were there, but had kept it quiet, perhaps not to panic people or perhaps to hold off on compensation payments for as long as possible. The local papers were soon full of headlines like "shepherd sights wolves" and "300 sheep slaughtered". We lost around 700 animals that year: sheep, goats and even young donkeys. The farmers were not prepared for wolves and the wolves took full advantage. These wolves had come from Italy where natural prey was scarce and they existed mainly on domestic animals and refuse. Now in France they were amidst surrounded by game and hundreds of unguarded farm stock. That winter was even harder for us. The only stock left on the mountain was ours, and the wolves had followed the game down into our valley. Every morning we found fresh prints around our barn and every night the dogs went wild. We took it in shifts to sleep in with the sheep, waking constantly to the dogs barking or sheep's nightmares. My boss's wife left as the stress for her was too much.

With the coming of spring the pressure eased and we decided to find a solution. I signed up for the Large Carnivore Project in Romania, where I learnt livestock guarding methods from local shepherds. I discovered that by chance we were already doing most of the right things, such as 24hour guarding and locking the sheep away at night. This explained why we were losing so few animals compared to our neighbours.

I also learnt about wolves and soon realised that they had not read the textbooks. So much was unknown, and so many myths and stories sprang up around them. The wolf has been around for millennia, it is said to be the most successful canid ever to stalk the earth. Its range once covered almost the entire northern hemisphere. It is found from the frozen tundra just south of the North Pole, down to the deserts of Arabia and India. In forests and on open plains. It is an ultimate survivor, and adapts readily. They have been persecuted to extinction across the world, but they are still found in many parts of the world. They are a mythical beast both revered and hated.

Keeping our heads and keeping our sheep

When I arrived back in France we built a protection area so that the sheep would not have to be crammed into the barn every night. This consisted of a two metre high fence with an additional metre buried into the ground to prevent tunnelling. We surrounded this with an electric fence. We were then able to sleep soundly at night. But our nearest neighbour was still experiencing problems - being only a summer resident he had no barn for his sheep. He used flexible electric fencing to pen the sheep at night. But the wolves learnt that by running alongside it they could panic the sheep and stampede them into breaking down the fence. They could then pick off the sheep as they fled into the forest.

They did this six times. We advised other shepherds to change their methods, but some refused and have subsequently given up keeping sheep after suffering too many losses and too much stress. Taking stock will always be viewed as a crime, especially with what appears to be wanton killing. Even if it is the fault of farmers, too slow, or too poor to guard properly. But the issue is not what it used to be: the average number of sheep lost during an attack in 1998 was 22. Today the figure is one or two. In addition, the wolves are helping control feral dogs, which are another predator - The wolves are either scaring them off or preying on them.

Compensation is a big stress issue. Firstly it depends on proof, and proof is hard to determine even if you can find your missing sheep while there is still enough carcass left to identify, or before other scavengers have covered all the signs. Most shepherds would rather kill their wounded animals, and not just because they attract predators. Farmers are hardened but they are rarely heartless.

Fear and prejudice

Some people will not respect the wolf for the wild predator that it is. Propaganda by newspapers or farmers blaming wolves in order to claim compensation money will never help. Folk tales like Little Red Riding Hood that have spooked our minds for centuries will not disappear. Sadly some of the stories are true: wolves do occasionally attack and kill humans. In Utah Pradesh in India wolves killed nine children in four years - this was a single pack that had attacked children whilst they were playing on the forest edge. Most of these wolves were destroyed but two are thought to remain. They might pass on this trait when drought or food shortage puts their supply of prey under stress. We have had one reported attack in France: an old shepherd was mauled by a female wolf and her two cubs. How this happened is unclear.

The summers for us are still problematic as all the sheep flocks are brought together and ascend to the summer pastures where there are too many to guard efficiently and they are vulnerable. We don't lose many sheep and some sheep often die naturally. Is it not natural that wolves take the occasional sheep? Wild sheep do form part of their prey. The wolves have every right to be there – perhaps we just have to adapt.

The wolves have adapted to our guarding methods: In 1998, 85% of the attacks were at night. Now, as we guard at night and lock away our flocks, the attacks are 70% by day when the sheep are out amongst the trees, or drinking at the river.

By sightings and scat analysis we found we had six wolves living in our area in 1999. An Alpha male and female, two yearlings and two pups. DNA analysis also proved them to be Abruzzi wolves that had indeed found their way from Italy. The yearlings and pups accounted for the surplus killings found amongst the sheep. Young predators have to learn to hunt and to kill, and with the unguarded stock they could have all the practice that they needed.

The deadly bait

In 1999 the pack split. Four remained and two passed the crest to start a new pack further north. I continued tracking these two packs until 2001 when they suddenly disappeared.

They stopped howling. I searched but found nothing. Then one day I came across a deer skeleton, badger and fox skulls, two dead badger cubs, rat skeletons and a dead feral cat. This was not a natural find and I soon realised that the deer carcass had been poisoned. Two local dogs died confirming this. From my observations, the following fauna feed on a carcass: first come flies and butterflies whilst the blood is still warm. Beetles, tits and corvids then arrive, and vultures, eagles and mustilids follow. As night falls along come cats, rats, foxes and badgers, and wild boar clean up. Wolves, if not protecting the kill, come last, especially if the scent of humans is around. So, how many animals are you willing to kill with a poisoned carcass? I have even fed from fresh kills myself, if I have been tracking for days living off the forest.

Poison is documented to be the easiest and most efficient way of killing wolves, and I fear it was. In a few months of tracking I came across the tracks of only one wolf, the large male. Maybe he had arrived late at the carcass as he was often on his own, or maybe he was just too big for it to work properly? But had he had to watch his mate die? His pups? He began to be hard to track. I would think that he had gone and then find a deer carcass or a single track in the bed of a river.

Back on the trail

In the autumn of 2003 I began to find two sets of prints and more kills. Then in the winter of 2004 the forest guards found blood in the sets of tracks they had been following.
DNA tests showed this to be menstrual blood; the wolves were back and hopefully breeding. They began to howl once more, filling the nights with their haunting songs.

In autumn 2004 forest guards howled from different points on the mountain to elicit a response, but these tests proved inconclusive, probably due to the inflexible way in which they were conducted. During those surveys we came across two sheep wandering lost in the forest. Closer examination of these sheep showed that they had cyanide capsules glued to their necks and rumps. We had to shoot them, and we used them to try to bring a case against the farmer who owned them. This is still under investigation.

In winter 2005-6 we tracked to see if the wolves had bred, but we only found traces of a single wolf. DNA will show us whether it is the male or the female, but it is evident that our pair has gone, perhaps poisoned by a sheep we failed to find. Or perhaps the male has succumbed to old age. We hope that the remaining wolf will attract another and once again build our hopes of wolves breeding in our mountains.

417

LYNX

Reintroduced lynx in Europe: their distribution and problems

ECOS 25 (3/4) 64-68 (2004)

Experience of reintroducing lynx in Europe shows what is needed to make future reintroduction programmes a success – the biological, organisational, and commincation factors all need rigorous attention.

MANUELA VON ARX & URS BREITENMOSER

Reversing the downward trend

The Eurasian lynx (*Lynx lynx*), once widespread across Europe, reached the minimum of its historic distribution during the first decades of the 20th century. Due to human persecution, habitat destruction and loss of prey, the species only survived in the large continuous forests of Scandinavia, where it was almost extinct, and mainly in Russia, the Carpathian Mountains and in the western Balkans. Around 1950, the general downward trend came to a halt and the autochthonous populations started to recover. Not only the ecological conditions had improved, but also the general attitude of people towards large carnivores had changed and they were granted legal protection or at least some form of controlled hunting.[1] A natural re-colonisation of the former habitats in central, southern and western Europe from the remaining populations was however no longer possible – the lowlands between the forested mountain ranges were too heavily altered. Therefore, several lynx reintroductions into suitable areas were implemented from the 1970s (Table 1).

Lynx in the Harz Mountains National Park (www.luchsprojekt-harz.de)

Population / Occurrence	Location of the re-introduction	Years	Number of animals	Origin of animals	Fate *
Bohemian-Bavarian	Bavarian Forest (DE)	1970-75	5-9	mix	failed
	Sumava Mts. (CZ)	1982-89	18	wild	(success)
Dinaric	Kocevje (SI)**	1973	6	wild	(success)
Alpine	Swiss Alps	1971-80	14-18	wild	(success)
	Kocevje (SI)**	1973	6	wild	(success)
	Gran Paradiso NP (IT)	1975	2	wild	failed
	Austrian Alps	1977-79	9	wild	failed
Alpine/Jura	Swiss Plateau	1989	3	unknown	unknown
Jura	Swiss Jura Mts.	1971-80	10	wild	(success)
Vosges-Palatinian	Vosges Mts. (FR)	1983-93	21	mix	uncertain
Kampinos occ.	Kampinos NP (PL)	1993-95	30	captive	uncertain
Harz occ.	Harz Mts. (DE)	since 2000	at least 19	captive	uncertain

Table 1: Lynx (*Lynx lynx*) reintroductions in central and western Europe. Data compiled from Breitenmoser et al. 2001 [2] and von Arx et al. 2004. [5]

* Fate: "Success" in brackets as these populations have up to now been surviving for 20-30 years with reasonable numbers of animals, however their long-term survival is not yet secured (see Table 2)
** Animals expanded as well south (Dinaric Mts.) as north (Alps)

At the outset of the reintroduction programmes, nobody was aware of the various and long-lasting problems when reintroducing carnivores: first, the return of large predators can provoke massive opposition from people who regard them as competitors. Further, large carnivores need extended living space to establish viable populations, and nowhere in Europe can protected areas alone offer such space. Finally, the realisation and monitoring of a reintroduction programme is a difficult, expensive and long-lasting task due to the slow turnover and elusiveness of the animals. It needs long-term commitments of all partners.[2] To make reintroductions a success, many additional factors, listed in the guidelines of the IUCN Re-introduction Specialist Group, are important, such as the number, age, sex ratio and origin of the animals released, the time scale, and the quality and number of release sites.[3, 4] Finally, a sound knowledge on the species' ecology, behaviour, and genetics is required, and the ultimate scientific surveillance of the programme helps to inform the optimal strategy.

The effects of reintroductions

Table 1 summarises the lynx reintroductions in Europe. Many of these reintroductions were poorly prepared and documented, and the public badly informed. Furthermore, unofficial releases caused public mistrust.[2] Normally, fewer than 20 lynx, often much less, have been released at a few sites. Where wild caught animals were used, they were taken from the Slovak Carpathian Mountains, the geographically nearest autochthonous population. Apart from the Vosges reintroduction, the fate of the released animals was nowhere monitored. In Switzerland, a scientific follow-up was only established in 1980. In spite of these shortcomings, in around half of the reintroduction attempts the released animals established well, reproduced and expanded their distribution range. The remaining projects, however, failed (Table 1).

Lynx released in eastern Switzerland (Fridolin Zimmermann/KORA)

At present, we distinguish between the Bohemian-Bavarian, Dinaric, Alpine, Jura, and Vosges-Palatinian populations that were founded through reintroductions (Table 2, Figure 1).[5] A recent inquiry for the Eurasian Lynx Online Information System (ELOIS) for Europe[5] revealed that, some 30 years after the reintroductions, all populations are still considered to be "Endangered" to "Critically Endangered" according to the IUCN/SSC Red List criteria.[6] The population sizes range from 20-37 (Vosges-Palatinian) to 130 (Dinaric). To be upgraded to "Vulnerable", an effective population size of at least 250 mature individuals would be necessary. Many reintroduced populations however showed rather a negative than a positive trend during the past few years (Table 2), thus indicating that it will still require a long time and continued support before they can actually be considered as not threatened.

Table 2: Status of the reintroduced Eurasian lynx (*Lynx lynx*) populations in Europe in 2001 (von Arx et al. 2004 [5]). Area: cont. = range continuous, frag. = range fragmented. Trend: → = stable, ↗ = increasing, ↘ = decreasing, exp = expanding. Judgement: EN = Endangered, CR = Critically Endangered. Threats: il = illegal killing, rc = road constructions, tr = traffic accidents, pb = limited prey base, ld = limited dispersal.

Population	Coun-tries	Area (km²)	Size 2001	Trend 96-01	Judge-ment 2001 ***	Legal Status	Livestock Depred-ation	Main Threat
Bohemian-Bavarian	CZ, DE, AT	14'200 (± cont.)	~75	↘	(EN)	fully prot.	occasionally, no problem	il, (rc)
Dinaric	BA, HR, SI	24'400 (cont.)	~130	→ to ↘	(EN)	mainly hunted	occasionally, no problem	il, tr, pb
Alpine	CH, SI, IT, AT, FR	18'100 (frag.)	~120	→, exp	(EN)	fully prot.	yes, potential source of conflict	il, rc, tr, ld
Jura	FR, CH	11'500 (cont.)	~80	exp, ↗	(EN)	fully prot.	yes, potential source of conflict	il, tr, (rc), (ld)
Vosges-Palatinian	FR, DE	6'400 (± cont.)	~20	exp/↘	(CR)	fully prot.	occasionally, no problem	il

*** Judgement according to the *Guidelines for Application of IUCN Red List Criteria at Regional Levels* (IUCN 2003 [6]). Judgement in brackets as 30 years of existence are obviously not enough to fulfil the criteria for the not threatened categories.

Most people in favour of large carnivores live in urban areas, where these species actually do not (yet) exist. Amongst the rural population, many people are more sceptical about predators, and may regard them as a pest and a threat to livestock and wildlife.[1] The last survey on the Eurasian lynx in Europe [5] revealed illegal killing to be the main threat for the species, although there is not much hard data to support this belief. This is especially true for the reintroduced populations (Table 2). Between 1996 and 2001, the yearly number of illegally killed lynx in the Bohemian-Bavarian population – where the topic was thoroughly studied – was seven. In other reintroduced populations, cases discovered per year ranged from one to four.[5] Considering that the majority of illegal acts never become public, we can assume that this is only the tip of the iceberg.

Opposition and illegal killing

The interest groups least in favour of the return of lynx are the hunters and sheep breeders. Hunters consider the lynx as competitor for roe deer and chamois, the cat's main prey in the range of the reintroduced populations. Hunting may indeed become more difficult in the presence of a natural predator. Although the long-term development of the roe deer hunting bag and the lynx numbers both in autochthonous and in reintroduced populations indicate that there is enough prey for the human and the feline hunter, lynx predation can locally have a considerable impact on roe deer. Livestock depredation, mainly on sheep, occurs in all reintroduced lynx populations (Table 2), but to date has only been notable in the French Jura Mountains and the western Swiss Alps. Between 1996 and 2001, lynx killed 775 sheep in Switzerland and 980 in France, and this triggered a major conflict. Depredation in these two countries was only exceeded by Norway, where the numbers are high: more than 50,000 sheep were considered to be killed during this same period.[5] In all three countries, sheep breeders are financially compensated for livestock being killed by large carnivores. Furthermore, lynx causing too much damage are legally removed according to criteria defined in management plans approved by the respective governments. In spite of all these measures, lynx are still illegally killed. The problem goes far beyond financial and rational reasons (see reference[1]), and to mitigate the conflict, both public education and collaboration with key interest groups is crucial.

Influences on population dispersal

There are also some objective obstacles for the reintroduction of lynx. In central and western Europe, the human density, fragmentation of the landscape, and a biologically low dispersal potential of the species, hinders the expansion into new areas. Only the Dinaric and Alpine populations are potentially big enough to be genetically viable in the long-term. However, the gap between the western and eastern Alpine subpopulations (Figure 1) has first to be filled, and this might not be possible without further translocations. The other populations in western and central Europe must be considered under a meta-population concept: improving the connectivity and hence the exchange between isolated and small occurrences is essential. As none of these meta-populations is limited to a single country, cross-border collaboration has to be improved, and coherent strategies developed.

Given the unprofessional approach in most of the reintroduction projects in the 1970s and 1980s, the development of the populations was surprising. However, the assessment of the reintroductions depends on the definition of success and the time frame applied. All populations are still small in size and extension, which makes them not only vulnerable to human induced mortality, but also to genetic and stochastic processes. Obviously, 20 to 30 years are not enough to assure the long-term persistence of the lynx in central and western Europe, and further active support is needed. If the early attempts were not all successful, they have at least allowed us to learn about the reintroduction of controversial animals such as the lynx, and to develop better schemes. Unfortunately, there have recently been two rather counterproductive projects: the reintroductions in the Kampinos National Park in Poland and in the Harz Mountains, Germany (Table 1, Figure 1).[5] Both projects neglected important recommendations from the IUCN guidelines and other professional institutions, and based their justification on false assumptions about the status and biology of the species. The most important shortcomings are:

- a mixture of zoo-born animals of unknown subspecies and unclear genetic status were used,
- release sites are small islands within unsuitable habitat,
- no objective control of the project,
- poor information to the public;
- poor documentation of the project,
- lack of governmental responsibility, and
- no regional co-operation.

Why worry? The tactic of activity groups is "to do something" in favour of the lynx, to try and make progress, regardless of all objections. Such an approach will ultimately backfire. Reintroducing carnivores is a serious business implying a long-term commitment of all partners involved, especially from government bodies. All these projects are controversial, and so diverging interests need to be enabled to negotiate on a clear and long-term goal of reintroducing and managing a lynx population.[5]

References

1. Breitenmoser, U. (1998) Large predators in the Alps: The fall and rise of man's competitors. Biological Conservation, 83 (3): 279-289.

2. Breitenmoser, U., Breitenmoser-Würsten, Ch., Carbyn, L.N. & Funk, S.M. (2001) Assessment of carnivore reintroduction. In: J.L. Gittleman, S.M. Funk, D. Macdonald & R.K. Wayne. *Carnivore Conservation – Conservation Biology* 5, Cambridge University Press, Cambridge. Pages 241-281.

3. IUCN (1998) Guidelines for Re-introductions. Prepared by the IUCN/SSC Re-introduction Specialist Group. IUCN, Gland, Switzerland and Cambridge, UK: 1-10.

   (which is the follow-up of the Position Statement on the Translocation of Living Organisms from 1987

   http://www.iucn.org/themes/ssc/pubs/policy/reinte.htm)

4. Nowell, K. & Jackson, P. 1996: *Wild Cats: Status Survey and Conservation Action Plan.* IUCN/SSC Cat Spezialist Group. IUCN Gland, Switzerland. Pages 263-270 (see also: http://www.catsg.org)

5. von Arx M., Breitenmoser-Würsten Ch., Zimmermann F. & Breitenmoser U. (eds) (2004) Status and conservation of the Eurasian lynx (*Lynx lynx*) in Europe in 2001. *KORA Bericht* No. 19: 1-330. Also published online as Eurasian Lynx Online Information System (ELOIS) for Europe at: http://www.lcie.org or http://www.kora.unibe.ch/en/proj/elois/online

6. IUCN (2003) Guidelines for Application of IUCN Red List Criteria at Regional Levels. Version 3.0. IUCN Species Survival Commission. IUCN, Gland, Switzerland and Cambridge, UK: 1-27.

   (http://www.iucn.org/themes/ssc/redlists/regionalguidelines.htm)

{Editor's note: Since this article was written, the Harz project reports 10-16 wild-born lynx per year. The National Park now uses the lynx as an emblem of rewilding the forest with a special exhibition announced on 20.5.2011: see www.luchspojeckt-harz.de and www.http://www.nationalpark-harz.de/de/aktuelles/2011/05/luchssonderprogramm/#intNavBreadcrumb}.

Figure 1: Current distribution of the Eurasian lynx (*Lynx lynx*) in Europe (von Arx et al. 2004 [5]). Constantly occupied area and single observations (brighter shade) . Reintroduced populations: B = Bohemian-Bavarian, D = Dinaric, A = Alpine (with a western (1) and eastern (2) subpopulation), J = Jura, V = Vosges-Palatinian, K = Kampinos occurrence, H = Harz occurrence.

The lynx in Britain's past, present and future

ECOS 27 (1) 66-74 (2006)

Experience from other European countries shows that a well-planned lynx reintroduction could bring both ecological and economic benefits to the human-modified landscapes of Scotland.

DAVID HETHERINGTON

The calls to reintroduce Britain's extinct mammals have been born of an eagerness to repair the damage done by our ancestors and to restore the missing ecological functions these species performed. Scientific and public discussion of species restoration in Britain has continued to intensify, but until very recently, the Eurasian lynx *Lynx lynx* was often overlooked in favour of other species, especially the wolf *Canis lupus*, largely because of the lynx's rather obscure history in Britain. However, developments in palaeontology, in particular the use of radiocarbon dating, are beginning to paint a much clearer picture of the species' historical occurrence and extinction in Britain. This, along with environmental and societal changes that have occurred in the British countryside, means that a stronger case for lynx reintroduction can now be built.

The history of the British lynx

We know from bone evidence recovered from limestone caves that the Eurasian lynx once roamed Britain from the south coast to the north coast. These bones now tell us that the species survived in North Yorkshire until at least the 6th century AD.[1] Cultural and linguistic evidence further suggest that the species was being hunted in the Lake District during the 7th century AD, and that the Gaelic inhabitants of the Scottish Highlands were still observing its movements into later medieval times. These faint traces of Britain's lost cat are significant in that they point the finger of blame for the species' extinction, not at natural climatic processes which occurred millennia before, but instead at the activities of humans. Under these circumstances, there is an ethical argument for considering reintroduction.

The lynx is a solitary ambush hunter requiring large areas of cover from which to launch a surprise attack on small ungulate prey, such as roe deer *Capreolus capreolus*. It cannot tirelessly run down its prey in open habitats in the same manner that a pack of wolves can. The very severe deforestation carried out over the centuries by Britain's human inhabitants, not only removed the cover that the lynx required, but also led to the depletion of the woodland deer that formed the lynx's prey. Remnant forests were grazed with high densities of domestic livestock by subsistence farmers, thus placing enormous pressure on dwindling woodland deer populations. Lynx would have had little choice but to prey on sheep and goats, and that transgression would have been the final nail in its coffin. The eastern Grampians are likely to have been the last area of Britain to support lynx, as this landscape was last to relinquish its tracts of forest and never entirely lost its roe and red deer *Cervus elaphus*.

Why consider reintroducing lynx?

Lynx release in Eastern Switzerland (Fridolin Zimmermann/KORA)

International treaties, such as the Bern Convention (1979) and the Rio Convention (1992), oblige the UK to encourage the restoration of populations of native species, while the EC Habitats Directive (1992) obliges the UK to consider the desirability of reintroducing such former British natives as the beaver *Castor fiber*, bear *Ursus arctos*, wolf and Eurasian lynx. Guidelines on reintroductions drawn up by the IUCN state that the factors responsible for a species' extinction should no longer be operating, if it is to be considered for reintroduction.[2] Britain, and in particular Scotland, witnessed a sudden and large-scale process of reafforestation during the twentieth century, as well as the problematic growth and spread of woodland deer populations, both native and exotic. Research I carried out for my PhD suggests that environmental conditions over much of Scotland today are suitable for lynx.[3] Forest cover is now sufficiently extensive, well connected and stocked with suitable prey populations that a viable population of lynx could survive in mainland Scotland north of the Central Belt. A smaller, less viable population could exist in the Southern Uplands and extend across the border into the English portion of Kielder Forest.

The lynx as a hunter of deer

The obvious ecological function of most large carnivores is to kill and eat large herbivores. Lynx focus on the smallest species within an ungulate community and right across its huge range from Western Europe and Siberia, the roe deer is the single most important prey species for the lynx. They are, however, capable of taking larger ungulates, and regularly do so, especially in areas where roe deer are scarce or absent. In Finland, lynx hunt introduced white-tailed deer *Odocoileus virginianus*, while right across northern Scandinavia they prey on semi-domesticated reindeer *Rangifer tarandu*s. In the forests of Eastern Europe, lynx often take red deer hinds and calves, while in the Jura Mountains and in the Alps, they frequently take chamois *Rupicapra rupicapra*. In Scotland, roe deer are especially well distributed, occurring in every 10 km square on the mainland, usually at higher densities than those found in lynx-inhabited regions of Europe. Red deer and sika deer *Cervus nippon* are both widespread and numerous in forest habitats in the Highlands, as well as in parts of the Southern Uplands. Given that Polish red deer are considerably larger than Scottish woodland red deer, and that chamois are around the same size as introduced sika deer, then a lynx population in Scotland would certainly encounter an abundance of prey throughout the habitat available to them. Scotland's deer populations are controversial and their browsing and grazing causes problems and can inflict costly damage on forestry, agricultural and natural heritage interests. It has been argued that Britain's deer populations have recovered too well from their historical suppression and that they are out of balance with their environments. It has also been suggested that the return of Britain's native top predators could bring about a reduction in deer populations, thus instilling a more harmonic balance. In some parts of Europe, such as in Norway and eastern Poland, lynx do exert a control on roe deer populations, but densities of roe are much lower there than those encountered in most of Scotland. It is likely that Scottish deer populations have grown too far to be controlled by a reintroduced lynx population. However, experience from areas where lynx occur in forests with high ungulate densities, such as in the Swiss Alps, shows that lynx can have a significant impact by changing the behaviour of its prey.[4,5]

Large carnivores had been absent in Switzerland for around a century before lynx were reintroduced in the 1970s. Prior to the lynx population expanding into new areas, both chamois and roe deer occurred at especially high densities at favourable sites, usually where food was abundant. Colonising lynx would exploit these clusters by repeatedly targeting the naïve prey time and time again. The home ranges of colonising lynx were far smaller than those of lynx in the more established core of the population, because all their prey requirements were being met in a much more concentrated area. After a while, sustained lynx predation brought about considerable local decreases in both chamois and roe densities. After about five years, the remaining chamois and roe had developed stronger anti-predator behaviour and had become much more evenly distributed through the landscape. The lynx responded by greatly expanding their home ranges. If, as in Switzerland, lynx in Scotland focus their predation on those areas that support the highest concentrations of deer, they could bring about a substantial reduction in localised deer densities by changing deer behaviour. Young conifer plantations and areas of naturally regenerating woodland often attract high densities of roe deer and are vulnerable to browsing damage, while thicket stage plantations often harbour high densities of sika deer which can have dire economic consequences for forestry. It is quite feasible that lynx could focus their feeding on areas as compact as a young conifer plantation. One female lynx with kittens in the Swiss Jura Mountains, spent several months in one area of windfall woodland, killing roe deer after roe deer, while a male lynx spent almost a year in 4 km² of woodland on the edge of Zürich, where it killed 40-50 roe deer.[6]

So by restoring lynx, we would be restoring predation on our deer populations, something that, for centuries, has only been achieved by humans with rifles or opportunistically by the odd fox *Vulpes vulpes* or eagle. By killing a deer a week all year round, and leaving what it doesn't eat on the forest floor, including meat, bones and rumen, the lynx also regularly provides food for other species in a way that humans and the opportunistic predators tend not to do. A study in a Norwegian forest found a greater abundance and richer diversity of beetles around a roe deer carcass than elsewhere in the forest.[7]

The function of deer predator could also be performed by our other two missing large carnivores, the wolf and the brown bear. The lynx, however, has several advantages over these two other species, which I believe make it a more realistic candidate for reintroduction. The first of these, and perhaps the most fundamental, is that it is easier for human populations to live alongside it. At around 20kg, the lynx is not a threat to human safety and is not perceived as such. Its relatively small size and its extreme wariness of humans have resulted in no recorded attacks by lynx on people in Europe. Bears are much larger and wolves hunt in packs so that humans tend to perceive these species as a much greater threat to their own safety than lynx. Furthermore, the evidence from Europe shows that lynx cause far fewer problems with livestock than wolves and bears do. In areas such as the Slovakian and Romanian Carpathians where all three species occur in good numbers, the shepherds are most concerned about the depredations of wolves and bears. The measures the shepherds employ to protect their sheep from wolves and bears are extremely effective at limiting losses to lynx, which are negligible.

Another advantage of lynx reintroduction is the greater level of technical experience and advice to call upon. Other than one project in Georgia on the very fringes of Europe, the wolf has not been subject to a European reintroduction project. It has instead relied on its impressive dispersal ability to return to some of its former haunts in Scandinavia, Germany, France and Switzerland. The bear has been the subject of restocking projects in France, Italy and Austria, but always to areas where they already occurred, albeit in very low numbers. On the other hand, a series of lynx reintroduction projects has taken place since the early 1970s in areas of Switzerland, France, Germany, Italy, Austria, Slovenia, Poland and the Czech Republic from where the species had been totally extirpated. Not all of these projects have been successful, but useful lessons can be learnt from the failures as well as the successes. The successful projects have seen the return of the lynx to several human-modified landscapes of western and central Europe, most of which have far higher human population densities than are encountered in either the Scottish Highlands or the Southern Uplands.

The human dimension

Perhaps understandably, a human population unused to living alongside large carnivores will have concerns about their return to the countryside. It is essential for the success of a reintroduction that all sectors of the rural community are involved and allowed to contribute to discussions about the project. A lack of public involvement in the governmental project to reintroduce lynx in Switzerland in the 1970s led to a sense of disenfranchisement, particularly among sheep farmers and hunters. As a result, the illegal killing of lynx in Switzerland still regularly occurs and is a significant source of mortality for the lynx population there.

Those people who are most unfamiliar with lynx may be unclear about their size and habits, and assume that lynx pose a physical threat to them. The dissemination of good quality information on the species is essential to prevent the formation of myths and public concerns about safety should be straightforward to allay.

The interactions of lynx with wildlife and livestock

Gamekeepers and conservationists alike may be concerned about potential impacts on wildlife. Their reluctance to stray far from cover means that lynx are most unlikely to make a nuisance of themselves on the open expanses of the grouse moors. There are, however, likely to be concerns expressed about the effect that lynx would have on threatened populations of the forest-dwelling capercaillie *Tetrao urogallus*. It is true that in the boreal landscapes of Scandinavia and Russia where deer densities are very low, and where woodland grouse are abundant, lynx supplement their diet with capercaillie. However, in western and central Europe where deer are much more abundant and where capercaillie densities are typically much lower, capercaillie is a very rare feature of lynx diet. An intensive 10-year study of the diet of 29 lynx in the Swiss Jura Mountains, where capercaillie are more abundant than in the Scottish Highlands, recovered the remains of 617 individual prey animals using snow- and radio-tracking.[8] As expected, roe deer and chamois represented the bulk of the remains, but in the 10 years of the study, only one capercaillie was found to have fallen prey to the local lynx population. Interestingly, 37 foxes also fell prey to the lynx in the study. Aside from killing large herbivores, large carnivores also frequently kill smaller carnivores. I suspect that 37 foxes would have a greater negative impact on the local capercaillie population than the loss of the one bird attributable to the lynx. Lynx very occasionally kill wildcats *Felis sylvestris*, and one was recorded in the Swiss study. It could be argued that feral cats *Felis catus*, which pose the most serious threat to wildcat populations through interbreeding, are at a relatively greater risk of predation by keen-eyed lynx, because domestication has dulled their anti-predator behaviour and robbed most of them of the camouflaged pelage of their wild cousins.

A central aim of discussions of reintroducing lynx to Scotland should be to allay the fears of farmers that lynx will ignore the ample deer in favour of even more ample livestock. Lynx don't kill calves, but attacks on sheep, particularly lambs, are known from several European countries. It is important, however, to put this in perspective. As already mentioned, levels of lynx depredation on sheep in the Carpathians, where livestock-guarding dogs and intensive shepherding are employed, are negligible in number. The opposite end of the scale is the rather unique situation encountered in Norway, where no protective measures are taken, but where 2.5 million sheep are grazed free-range and unshepherded during the summer in forested habitats, where the lynx occur.[9] Densities of roe deer are very low, and sheep are many times more abundant and even replicate roe deer behaviour by occurring singly or in small groups, and not in flocks. This scenario results in the loss to lynx of round 6000 sheep, mostly lambs, each year, and nearly every lynx is killing sheep. Despite their relative scarcity compared to sheep, however, the most common lynx prey species is still the roe deer. Unlike Norway, the vast majority of forest in Scotland contains no sheep, and the vast majority of sheep are grazed in open habitats. A far more likely scenario for Scotland is the one that occurs in the Jura Mountains and Alps of France and Switzerland. Just as in Norway, very few anti-predator measures are adopted, but the major difference is that the sheep are grazed in open pasture. Here, only a small number of lynx within the population kill sheep, and only at very specific locations or 'hotspots'.

Numbers of sheep killed or wounded by lynx in the French Jura vary from around 100-400 each year, but studies have shown that more than 70% of attacks occurred in nine small hotspots representing 1.5% of the area affected by lynx attacks.[10,11] The majority of affected sheep flocks in the French Jura experience only a very low level of depredation, i.e. 1-2 attacks per year. In the Swiss North-western Alps, 350 of the 456 (77%) sheep pastures experienced no incidences of depredation by lynx in 20 years.[12] A further 15% experienced only one incidence of depredation during this time. The distance of the pasture from woodland or scrub has a strong bearing on levels of depredation. In the Swiss Alps, 88% of lynx kills occurred within 200m of the forest edge, and 95% within 360m. Sheep less than one year old are more susceptible than older sheep, with 78% of those killed falling into this age group. Of those sheep owners who lost livestock in the Swiss Alps from 1979-1999, 80% lost three or fewer sheep during this period. In the French Jura, it was discovered that shooting a nuisance lynx would often solve the problem for a few months, but that ultimately a new lynx would take over the home range of the dead lynx and sheep depredation would commence once again. In these circumstances it is clear that site-specific, environmental factors are determining the likelihood and extent of depredation.

In this last scenario, most lynx depredation occurs to a geographical pattern and to an extent is predictable in its location, allowing steps to be taken to manage the problem. The grazing of sheep, particularly lambs, away from the forest edge reduces the risk considerably. The pattern of hotspots and problem individuals, which affects only a small number of sheep flocks, also allows a targeted response. Problem lynx repeatedly taking sheep can be shot under licence, while those hotspots that appear to be predisposed to depredation by a succession of lynx, justify the use of more costly protection measures. The use of shepherds, or guarding animals such as livestock-guarding dogs, donkeys and llamas are all recommended for reducing lynx depredation of sheep, and are most cost effective where there is an acute problem such as at hotspots. Recently in Switzerland government funds have been used to reduce conflict between lynx and sheep farmers by encouraging changes in animal husbandry, subsidising protection measures and compensating for losses. This has been effective, with the annual number of lynx-killed livestock in Switzerland dropping year by year from a high of 219 kills in 2000 to just 36 in 2005.[13]

The economic opportunities

The tourism economy is especially important in Scotland's remote, rural areas. The wildlife tourism sector in particular is expanding quickly and is likely to continue to do so, with over 3000 people now directly employed within the sector.[14] Large carnivores have the potential to bring economic benefits to rural areas through visitors and tourists, either directly, as people seek opportunities to catch a glimpse of such charismatic species, or indirectly, by acting as a powerful icon of wilderness. Large-carnivore tourism is being developed in several areas of Europe, and since the reintroduction of the lynx to the Harz National Park in Germany in 2000, authorities and businesses have moved quickly to utilise the lynx as a marketing tool. On the German tourism agency's web-site, potential visitors to the Harz Mountains are invited to experience "Incredible wilderness in the Kingdom of the Lynx".[15] Images of lynx are also used extensively on brochures, posters, t-shirts, books and signs promoting the park, and visitors are lured by the possibility of glimpsing a lynx and by an increased perception of the area's wildness. By being similarly marketed in Scotland, especially to UK visitors who represent the leading market for Scottish tourism, reintroduced lynx could bring real economic benefits to remote rural areas. The chairman of the national tourism agency, VisitScotland, recently stated that he felt that discussion of the reintroduction of large carnivores to Scotland was a "hugely positive development".[16] Another advantage of the human fascination with charismatic large carnivores is that there exists a much greater potential to attract sponsorship from private sources. If marketed prudently, a lynx reintroduction project could attract considerable funding which would otherwise not be available to nature conservation, thus considerably reducing the need to divert limited funds away from extant conservation priorities.

Lessons from the sea eagle

Encouragingly, we already have a template in this country for the successful assimilation of a reintroduced and iconic large predator into the rural economy. Persecuted to extinction as vermin, the white-tailed eagle *Haliaeetus albacilla* is now highly valued and jealously protected by the islanders of Mull despite the odd lamb being taken now and then. These losses to the local economy are more than offset by the considerable revenue brought to the island by wildlife tourists who come to see the thriving eagle population. The Mull Eagle Scheme recently launched by Scottish Natural Heritage offers financial support to hill sheep farmers who manage their lambs in a way that reduces the likelihood of predation by the eagles.[17] Furthermore, the scheme rewards farmers who improve habitat and help safeguard the eagles by monitoring their nests. It is this kind of positive agri-environmental funding which could permit the painless absorption of lynx into the human-modified landscapes of modern Scotland.

Conclusion

Extrapolating current trends in afforestation, deer abundance, agri-environmental spending, and public attitudes towards wildlife and the environment, would seem to indicate that conditions are likely to become more and more favourable for lynx reintroduction in Scotland. Indeed it is possible that the reintroduction of Eurasian lynx to Scotland, in addition to restoring natural processes in the forest ecosystem, may actually bring economic opportunities in rural areas. Despite the suitable ecological conditions, reintroduction of lynx in Scotland will only succeed in the long-term if the human population is closely involved and is willing to co-exist with lynx.

References

1. Hetherington, D.A, Lord, T.C., & Jacobi, R.M. (2006) New evidence for the occurrence of Eurasian lynx (*Lynx lynx*) in medieval Britain. *Journal of Quaternary Science.* 21: 3-8.

2. IUCN (1998) *Guidelines for Re-introductions.* Prepared by the IUCN/SSC Re-introduction Specialist Group. IUCN, Gland, Switzerland and Cambridge, UK.

3. Hetherington, D.A. (2005) *The feasibility of reintroducing the Eurasian lynx (*Lynx lynx*) to Scotland.* PhD thesis. University of Aberdeen.

4. Haller, H. (1992) Zur ökologie des Luchses (*Lynx lynx*) im Verlauf seiner Wiederansiedlung in den Walliser Alpen. *Mammalia depicta*, 15, 1-62.

5. Breitenmoser, U. & Haller, H. (1993). Patterns of predation by reintroduced European lynx in the Swiss Alps. *Journal of Wildlife Management*, 57, 135-144.

6. U. Breitenmoser, personal communication.

7. Melis, C., Teurlings, I., Linnell, J.D.C., Andersen, R. & Bordoni, A. (2004) Influence of a deer carcass on Coleopteran diversity in a Scandinavian boreal forest: a preliminary study. *European Journal of Wildlife Research* 50:146-149.

8. Jobin, A., Molinari, P. & Breitenmoser, U. (2000). Prey spectrum, prey preference and consumption rates of Eurasian lynx in the Swiss Jura Mountains. *Acta Theriologica*, 45, 243-252

9. Odden, J., Linnell, J.D.C., Moa, P.F., Herfindal, I., Kvam, T. & Andersen, R. (2002) Lynx depredation on domestic sheep in Norway. *Journal of Wildlife Management*, 66, 98-105.

10. Stahl, P., Vandel, J. M., Herrenschmidt, V. & Migot, P. (2001) The effect of removing lynx in reducing attacks on sheep in the French Jura Mountains. *Biological Conservation*, 101, 15-22.

11. Stahl, P., Vandel, J.M., Ruette, S., Coat, L., Coat, Y. & Balestra, L. (2002) Factors affecting lynx predation on sheep in the French Jura. *Journal of Applied Ecology*, **39**, 204-216.

12. Angst, C., Olsson, P. & Breitenmoser, U. (2000) *Übergriffe von Luchsen auf Kleinvieh und Gehegetiere in der Schweiz - Teil I: Entwicklung und Verteilung der Schäden*. Bericht 5. KORA, Muri.

13. KORA web-site. Lynx and livestock damage statistics for Switzerland. http://www.kora.unibe.ch/en/proj/damage/damagemain.html

14. A & M [Training & Development] (2002) *Review of Wildlife Tourism in Scotland: main report*. The Tourism and Environment Forum, Inverness.

15. http://www.germany-tourism.de/e/6293.html

16. Lederer, P. (2002) Living dangerously will whet tourists' appetite. *Scotland on Sunday*, 30th June 2002.

17. Scottish Natural Heritage (2004) *Mull Eagle Scheme*. SNH, Battleby.

BEAR

Re-introduced bears in Austria

ECOS 25 (3/4) 69-72 (2004)
Austria has a detailed management plan for nurturing its small brown bear population. Commitment from government, foresters and hunters is needed to make it work.

GEORG RAUER

In Austria brown bear populations became extinct in the 19th century.[1,2] The main reasons for the final decline were habitat loss and direct persecution. Due to damages to crops and livestock people tried to eliminate bears for centuries. Authorities encouraged the killing of bears through a system of bounties and by obliging land owners to organize hunts and forcing local people to participate as beaters.[3,4]

Advocates for bears

After their extinction bears occasionally occurred in Austria as migrants from populations in neighbouring countries, but they usually left Austria again or were shot.[5,6] In the 1970s bears became protected by being listed in the provincial hunting laws as game species without open season.[7] At the same time provincial hunting organisations started to compensate for damages caused by bears. In 1989 World Wide Fund for Nature (WWF) Austria started a restocking project in central Austria in an area where a migrant from Slovenia had settled in 1972. One male and two female bears were released until 1993. Further augmentations were stopped due to the occurrence of two problem bears in Austria that caused a lot of negative publicity. [1,8,9]

Austria's management plan for bears

In 1995-1997 brown bear management was put on a new basis, through an EU LIFE project. It was carried out by the Munich Wildlife Society, the University of Natural Resources and Applied Life Sciences in Vienna, and WWF Austria, and it covered the following steps:

1. **A management plan was developed** in collaboration with stakeholders and provincial and federal authorities;

2. **Public education** materials were produced in the form of brochures, videos, and school material, and by offering courses to hunters and schools;

3. **Over 100 electric fences were distributed to beekeepers** in bear areas;

4. **"Bear advocates" were appointed** as contact persons for the local people living in bear areas; in addition "bear advocates" were responsible for population monitoring, damage inspection and the propagation of information about damage prevention;

5. **An "emergency team" was formed for trapping, radio-tracking and aversive conditioning of problem bears.**

Population recovery

Legal protection of bears in the provincial hunting laws was the basic prerequisite for the recovery of brown bears in Austria. The restocking project was successful in terms of reproduction: at least 26 cubs have been born since 1991. However, monitoring of population development by signs of bears, and through observations, and damages as well as genetic population monitoring do not support the estimate of 15-20 bears in central Austria derived from expected mortality rates but rather a population size of 7-10 bears. It is an open question if this difference in population estimates is due to methodological problems with monitoring or due to higher mortality rates than expected. At any rate there are indications that several bears were killed illegally.

WWF has to face a specific difficulty because of raising bear numbers by restocking: even 10 years after the last release of a bear many people believe that the bears somehow belonged to WWF and WWF was responsible for them like a cattle breeder. Yet, even people who accept that bears are wild animals are convinced that damage compensation is indispensable. The management plan was adopted by the provincial authorities but only partly implemented. For example the co-ordination board of provincial representatives for hunting and nature conservation has not played the active role it was designed for, the involvement of interest groups has not happened, and the emergency team has never been officially requested.

Public education

The effect of public education programs on bear conservation is not easy to judge. It is generally assumed that better knowledge means higher acceptance, but this may not be the case. Nevertheless, in the information campaign carried out from 1995-1997 a great demand for public information became evident and information offers were greatly appreciated. However, local opponents could not be convinced. The distribution of electric fences to beekeepers with endangered bee yards proved effective (1989 – 1996: 19.3 bee yards were depredated per year, 1997 – 2002: 1.5 bee yards per year). The installation of bear advocates was a success. Their role is today broadly accepted by both the authorities and the public, whereas many forest managers and hunters are still reluctant to cooperate.

Political commitment

At present lack of funding is not a central problem in bear management. A second LIFE project is funding new information material (brochure, webpage, newsletter, and school material), more intensive monitoring (a third bear advocate for western Austria, DNA analysis of hair and scat samples), the revision of the management plan, and the investigation of habitat fragmentation and migration corridors.

A major obstacle to the recovery of the Austrian brown bear population is the lack of political commitment. The responsible authorities' main interest in bear management is to suppress immediate troubles, not to achieve a viable population size. Management options are quite limited and are complicated due to hunting law regulations. For example the permission to capture a bear can only be given to the owner of the hunting right of a certain area and not to the emergency team. There is no prospect of hunting rights being adapted in the near future because of problems arising by the presence of bears. Illegal killings may happen to an extent that they have a major impact on population development. Living together with bears is still a relatively new and very emotional topic for the public in Austria which makes it difficult to properly balance management decisions and actions when bear problems arise. It seems like bears are still viewed as an exotic species and not seen as an integral part of the natural fauna. In a case of a lethal attack the majority will presumably demand the removal of all bears.

A successful development of the brown bear population in Austria will need the full implementation of the revised management plan, the revision of the legal basis of bear management and an increase in the commitment of provincial and federal authorities to bear conservation.

Bear management is carried out to a large extent by WWF Austria. This means continuity is not guaranteed because of possible future financial constraints. In addition, the willingness of many forest managers and hunters to cooperate is low because WWF sometimes confront them on other nature conservation issues.

The development of the Slovenian bear population and its management is of vital importance for the Austrian bear population. Contacts to Slovenian management authorities have been sought mainly by WWF. The Slovenian government is willing to maintain a migration corridor from the core area of the bear population in the Dinaric mountains into the Alps, but only if the Austrian government is signalling commitment to bear conservation. The commitment of the Austrian authorities must be achieved soon and a major goal of the current LIFE project is to achieve a memorandum of understanding concerning future bear population development and management between the Slovenian and Austrian government.

Damage prevention and compensation

Damage compensation is through a voluntary contribution of provincial hunting organisations to bear conservation, but only as long as damage levels are not too high. With rising bear numbers the number of claims for damage compensation might increase and additional governmental funds will be necessary to ensure indemnification. Damage prevention has to be further propagated as most people are not yet willing to take measures to prevent bear damages, because methods are new and often linked to additional labour and costs. Bears must be able to roam in their fragmented habitat to thrive as a population and regional planning will have to consider migration corridors that are still to be defined.

Collaborating with foresters and hunters

The integration of forest owners and hunters into bear management has to be improved as any management action that takes place on their land needs their approval. The problem of possible illegal killings of bears has to be addressed more vigorously by involving hunting organisations and district authorities. Research on population development has to be continued. Population growth by reproduction and migration is more easily accepted by people than the augmentation by the release of transferred individuals. Therefore WWF will not resume the restocking project. Nevertheless augmentation can be the last option in case the migration from Slovenia should stop and bear numbers should be low and decreasing.

References

1. RAUER, G., AND B. GUTLEB. (1997). *Der Braunbär in Österreich*. Federal Environment Agency–Austria, Monograph Series No. 88. Vienna, Austria. (In German.)

2. SPITZENBERGER, F. (2001). *Die Säugetierfauna Österreichs*. Grüne Reihe des Bundesministeriums für Land- und Forstwirtschaft, Umwelt und Wasserwirtschaft, Bd. 13, Vienna, Austria. (In German)

3. BACHOFEN VON ECHT, R. & W. HOFFER (1931). Jagdgeschichte Steiermarks. IV. Band, *Geschichte des Jagdrechtes und der Jagdausübung*. Leykam-Verlag, Graz, Austria. (In German)

4. LEEDER, K. (1924). Bär, Luchs und Wolf in Niederösterreich. *Blätter für Naturkunde und Naturschutz* 11: 125-131 and 141-147. (In German)

5. REBEL, H. (1933): *Die freilebenden Säugetiere Österreichs*. Österreichischer Bundesverlag für Unterricht, Wissenschaft und Kunst, Wien und Leipzig. 117 Seiten.

6. KNAUS, W. (1972): Der Kärnter Bär. *Der Anblick* 27: 237-239 and 283-285. (In German)

7. ADNDERLUH G. (1987). Der Braunbär in Kärnten. Atti del Convegno, *L´orso bruno nelle zone di confine del Friuli-Venezia Giulia*: 35-39. (In German)

8. RAUER, G. (1997). First experiences with the release of 2 female brown bears in the Alps of eastern Austria. International Conference on Bear Research and Management 9(2):91–95.

9. ZEDROSSER, A., N. GERSTL, AND G. RAUER. (1999). *Brown bears in Austria.* Federal Environment Agency–Austria, Monograph Series No. 117. Vienna, Austria.

The Apennine brown bear and the problem of large mammals in small populations

ECOS 27 (1) 75-79 (2006)
Despite the availability of suitable habitat the relict brown bear population in the Italian Apennines appears to be in decline, partly as a result of direct human-caused mortality. The inherent vulnerability of small populations, which this highlights, needs to be taken into account when considering species for reintroduction in human-dominated landscapes.

CHARLES J. WILSON & CIRO CASTELLUCCI

The reintroduction of large mammals that were once part of the British fauna is being taken increasingly seriously.[1,2,3,4,5] Given the right circumstances, it has even been suggested that this could include the European brown bear *Ursus arctos*.[4,6] However, some existing relict bear populations are already in trouble and before we even get to the stage of considering if this 'ultimate' mammal reintroduction could meet IUCN guidelines[7] perhaps we ought to ask ourselves, in any case, "what's in it for the bears?"

The case of the Apennine bears

Like many large mammals the brown bear is a '*K*-selected' species; slow to reach sexual maturity and with a low reproductive rate when it gets there. So small populations, which any reintroduced population is likely to be, will always be vulnerable. The relict bear population in the Italian Apennines, until recently thought to be the largest in western Europe south of Scandinavia,[8] appears to be showing worrying evidence of this. A recent study identified more than 12,000 km² of suitable bear habitat in the Apennines and suggested a population density in the core area of 1 bear/50-80 km².[9] This implies sufficient habitat for at least 150-240 bears. However, the current core bear range is in good quality habitat, with extensive ancient beech forest blanketing the slopes of limestone mountains, and earlier studies have indicated that this rich environment could probably support even more than this. The first scientific census of the population, at the beginning of the 1970s, using sightings and other signs to estimate population density, gave a figure of 70-101 bears in only 520 km² of the main bear habitat, in and around the Abruzzo National Park.[10] This was almost certainly an over-estimate as it was assumed that the bears were relatively sedentary and did not have ranges extending beyond the study area.[11] However, the study did not encompass the entire bear range and figures of between 70 and 100, for the population as a whole, continued to be cited until quite recently.[8,12,13]

Since the mid-1980s population estimates have become increasingly pessimistic (Fig.1). Some local experts now believe there may be as few as 30-40 animals[14] and even this could be an over-estimate. A recent genetic study involving sampling from hair traps and faeces, although not designed as a census, only identified 26 bears in a study area of over 1500 km² encompassing most of the bear range.[15] So, although the precise figure remains unknown, the population is almost certainly below some estimated minimum viable population sizes for bears of about 100-250.[16,17,18] Nevertheless, there appears to be little evidence of inbreeding[19] and it might have been expected that the population should have a good chance of recovery as long as the bears are given effective protection.

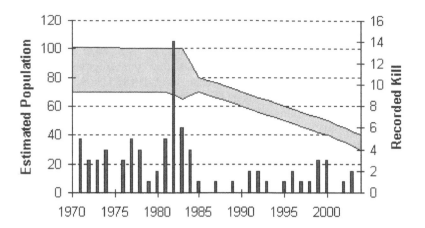

Fig.1. Maximum/minimum range of estimated size of the Apennine bear population (shaded) extrapolated from published estimates for 1970/71[10,] 1981[20], 1983[21] (with 20 added to allow for animals outside the authors' study area), 1985[8] and 2000[33], and for 2004, from L. Boitani.[14] Kill data (bars) from 1970 to 2000 from Castellucci (2004).[22]

Causes of decline

So why does the Apennine bear population appear to be in steady decline? A number of factors may be responsible, including increased tourist pressure[20], greatly increased numbers of wild boar *Sus scrofa* competing with the bears for food[21] and perhaps the decline of traditional farming, which used to provide additional food for the bears. However, in recent years, direct human caused mortality has been the single most important factor. From 1970 to 2000, 78 bears are reported to have been killed, with the majority of deaths caused directly by man.[22] Almost 75% of these were killed within the Abruzzo National Park itself or its External Protection Zone. According to WWF, Italy[23], 36% of the bears killed since 1980 are known to have been shot or snared, 13% were killed in road accidents and 4% were poisoned. Since these figures were compiled, an adult female was shot in the Mainarde, to the south of the National Park, in October 2002, and in September 2003 another female and her male cub were poisoned near Pescosolido in the Park's External Protection Zone.

The vulnerability of small populations

Although the worst death toll in the Apennine bear population occurred in 1982 (Fig.1), and it is possible that this tipped the balance, even the more modest losses suffered since then could have an effect on such a small population. To illustrate this we simulated the possible effects of comparable losses on a starting population of 50 bears using the VORTEX population model.[24] We used population parameters estimated from the literature and carrying capacity set at K=250 (Table 1). This is a reasonable maximum, not only for the Apennines, but for any reintroduced population that might be established in a crowded country like the UK.[18] Because VORTEX requires the same age/sex composition of animals to be removed at set intervals, and the numbers being removed are small, we assumed that animals would be removed every two years. Each simulation was re-ran with maximum breeding age increased to 18 years, or age of first breeding increased to 5 years to allow for variation in the lifetime productivity of adults and to bracket the results with figures for what might be considered high productivity and low productivity populations. All simulations were ran 100 times, with and without in-breeding effects, and without including effects of environmental stochasticity.

The results show that, without any losses, the population has a reasonable chance of survival, particularly in the absence of in-breeding depression (Table 2). However, losing as few as one bear per year has a marked impact on long-term viability. Risk of extinction is increased if in-breeding effects are present, but even without them it is above acceptable levels.[25] The loss of adult females greatly increases the population's vulnerability and, if they are included in losses of three or more animals every two years, extinction is highly likely. So every single individual lost reduces the survival chances of the population, especially if the victims include adult females.[16]

445

Table 1. Parameters used in VORTEX simulation model estimated from published data[10,34,35,36]. Standard deviations (SD) estimated as 0.4 x the mean. Other values used were defaults provided in the model. LP and HP = 'low' and 'high' productivity populations, respectively.

Parameter	Values used in model
Mating system	Polygamous
Age of first breeding	4 years (5 years for LP population)
Maximum breeding age	15 years (18 years for HP population)
Sex ratio at birth	1:1
Percent females breeding	30 (12.0 SD)
Percent litters of: one offspring	20
two offspring	55
three offspring	25
Percent mortality: 0-1 years	20 (8.0 SD)
1-2 years	12 (4.8 SD)
> 2 years	10 (4.0 SD)
Percent adult males in breeding population	50

Parameter	Values used in model
Mating system	Polygamous
Age of first breeding	4 years (5 years for LP population)
Maximum breeding age	15 years (18 years for HP population)
Sex ratio at birth	1:1
Percent females breeding	30 (12.0 SD)
Percent litters of: one offspring	20
two offspring	55
three offspring	25
Percent mortality: 0-1 years	20 (8.0 SD)
1-2 years	12 (4.8 SD)
> 2 years	10 (4.0 SD)
Percent adult males in breeding population	50

446

Table 2. Probability of extinction (%) predicted by VORTEX population simulations for brown bear populations subject to different kill levels and with and without the effects of in-breeding. Start population = 50; K = 250. Each simulation ran 100 times for 100years. LP and HP as for Table 1.

Number & age/sex class killed every 2 years	With In-breeding (HP; LP populations)	Without In-breeding (HP; LP populations)
None	6 (4; 25)	3 (0; 9)
2; 3 yr old male and female	45 (15; 82)	20 (11; 66)
3; as above plus adult male	59 (30; 89)	30 (12; 74)
3; as above but adult female, not male	85 (76; 97)	83 (55; 99)
4; as above plus adult male	91 (79; 100)	78 (52; 99)*
6; as above plus male & female cub	96 (88; 100)	93 (77; 100)

Lower figures than for kill of three animals reflect inherent variability in model.

In the Apennines there are a number of causes behind the killings but it is not usually deliberate persecution. In the past, bears were sometimes killed because of depredation on sheep or perhaps in illegal trophy hunting.[8] However, the main problems now appear to be accidental shooting during wild boar hunts, accidental snaring or poisoning with illegal baits set for dogs *Canis familiaris*, wolves *C. lupus* or foxes *Vulpes vulpes* and animals being killed in road accidents.[8,19,23,26] Some of these might not be relevant in the UK but there are other factors that are; adult females, the most important part of any population, may be disturbed by human activity and development[27]; roads open to vehicular traffic tend to be avoided[27,28,29], effectively restricting available habitat, and access provided by roads almost inevitably increases the risk of mortality.[30] Disturbance of females at winter dens can also lead to increased cub mortality[31] and limit denning to only the most inaccessible refuges.[32]

A reintroduction too far?

So whilst smaller more resilient species may be feasible candidates for reintroduction in the UK, realistically, talk of brown bears is probably a reintroduction too far. Not simply because of potential human opposition or lack of suitable habitat, but because it would be a disservice to the animals themselves, which would probably be doomed to extinction in any case. There is more than enough conservation effort still required to save the existing relict populations elsewhere in Europe, such as that in the Italian Apennines, and it is these that should provide the focus for those concerned with the conservation of Europe's bears. Franco Zunino, former Park Naturalist at the Abruzzo National Park, wrote of the Abruzzo bears in 1981: "nobody, not even a child, is particularly afraid to meet one in the wild".[20] Sadly, the bears have a lot more to fear when living cheek by jowl with humans.

European brown bear (Peter Cairns/Northshots)

References

1. Kitchener, A. C. & Conroy, J. (1996) The history of the beaver in Scotland and the case for its reintroduction. *British Wildlife,* **7**, 156-161.
2. Leaper, R., Massei, G., Gorman, M. L. & Aspinall, R. (1999) The feasibility of reintroducing wild boar to Scotland. *Mammal Review*, 29, 239-259.
3. Macdonald, D. W., Tattersall, F. H., Brown, E. D. & Balharry, D. (1995) Reintroducing the beaver: nostalgic meddling or restoring biodiversity. *Mammal Review*, 25, 161-200.
4. Yalden, D. W. (1986) Opportunities for reintroducing British mammals. *Mammal Review*, 16, 53-63.
5. Yalden, D. (1999) *The History of British Mammals.* Poyser, London.

6. Taylor, P. (2005) *Beyond Conservation; A Wildland Strategy.* Earthscan, London & Sterling VA.

7. IUCN (1998) *IUCN Guidelines for Re-introductions.* IUCN, Gland, Switzerland.

8. Boscagli, G. (1999) Status and management of the brown bear in central Italy (Abruzzo). In *Bears: Status Survey and Conservation Action Plan* (eds. C. Servheen, S. Herrero and B. Peyton), pp. 81-84. IUCN/SSC Bear and Polar Bear Specialists Groups, Gland, Switzerland.

9. Posillico, M., Meriggi, A., Pagnin, E., Lovari, S. & Russo, L. (2004) A habitat model for brown bear conservation and land use planning in the central Apennines. *Biological Conservation*, 118, 141-150.

10. Zunino, F. & Herrero, S. (1972) The status of the brown bear in Abruzzo National Park, Italy, 1971. *Biological Conservation*, 4, 263-272.

11. Stephen Herrero, pers. comm.

12. Tassi, F. (1990) *Orso Vivrai!* Editoriale Giorgio Mondadori, Milano.

13. Randi, E. (1993) Effects of fragmentation and isolation on genetic variability of the Italian populations of wolf and brown bear. *Acta Theriologica*, 38, Suppl. 2, 113-120.

14. Luigi Boitani, pers. comm.

15. Randi, E., Pierpaoli, M., Potena, G., Sammarone, L., Filippone, I., Petrella, A. & Posillico, M. (2004) *Relazione Finale sul Conteggio della Populazione, sullo Status Genetico e Demografia/Dinamica della Populazione.* LIFE Project Report, Corpo Forestale dello Stato, Sangro, Italy.

16. Wiegand, T., Naves, J., Stephan, T. & Fernandez, A. (1998) Assessing the risk of extinction for the brown bear in the Cordillera Cantabrica, Spain. *Ecological Monographs*, 68, 539-570.

17. Wieglus, R. B. (2002) Minimum viable population and reserve sizes for naturally regulated grizzly bears in British Columbia. *Biological Conservation*, 106, 381-388.

18. Wilson, C. J. (2004) Could we live with reintroduced large carnivores in the UK? *Mammal Review*, 34, 211-232.

19. Lorenzini, R., Posillico, M., Lovari, S. & Petrella, A. (2004) Non-invasive genotyping of the endangered Apennine brown bear: a case study not to let one's hair down. *Animal Conservation*, 7, 199-209.

20. Zunino, F. (1981) Dilemma of the Abruzzo bears. *Oryx*, 16, 153-156.

21. Fabbri, M., Boscagli, G. & Lovari, S. (1983) The brown bear population of the Abruzzo. *Acta Zoologica Fennica*, 174, 163-164.

22. Castellucci, C. (2004) *Tata Urze, L'Orso Bruno dell'Appennino Centrale.* Gruppo Ecologico Appennino Centrale, Edizioni Grafitalia, Sora, Italy.

23. WWF, Italy (2003) Orsi uccisi dai bracconieri nel Parco Nazionale d'Abruzzo. *Environment & Nature News, www.wwf.it/news*

24. Lacy, R. C. (2001) *VORTEX: Simulation Model of Population Dynamics and Viability; Version 8.42.* Chicago Zoological Society, Brookfield, IL.

25. Soulé, M. E. (1987) Introduction. In *Viable Populations for Conservation* (ed. M. E. Soulé), pp. 1-10. Cambridge University Press, Cambridge, UK.

26. Castellucci, C., La Pietra, B. & Zunino, F. (1985) *Orso Bruno Marsicano; Proposte di Conservazione.* Gruppo Ecologico Appennino Centrale, Sora, Italy.

27. Gibeau, M. L., Clevenger, A. P., Herrero, S. & Wierzchowski, J. (2002) Grizzly bear response to human development and activities in the Bow River Watershed, Alberta, Canada. *Biological Conservation*, 103, 227-236.

28. Mace, R. D., Waller, J. S., Manley, T. L., Lyon, L. J. & Zuuring, H. (1996) Relationships among grizzly bears, roads and habitat in the Swan Mountains, Montana. *Journal of Applied Ecology*, 33, 1395-1404.

29. Wieglus, R. B., Vernier, P. & Schivatcheva, T. (2002) Grizzly bear use of open, closed and restricted forestry roads. *Canadian Journal of Forest Research*, 32, 1597-1606.

30. Nielsen, S. E., Herrero, S., Boyce, M. S., Mace, R. D., Benn, B., Gibeau, M. L. & Jevons, S. (2004) Modelling the spatial distribution of human-caused grizzly bear mortalities in the Central Rockies ecosystem of Canada. *Biological Conservation*, 120, 101-113.

31. Linnell, J. D. C., Swenson, J. E., Andersen, R. & Barnes, B. (2000) How vulnerable are denning bears to disturbance? *Wildlife Society Bulletin*, 28, 400-413.

32. Petram, W., Knauer, F. & Kaczensky, P. (2004) Human influence on the choice of winter dens by European brown bears in Slovenia. *Biological Conservation*, 119, 129-136.

33. Swenson, J. E., Gerstl, N., Dahle, B. & Zedrosser, A. (2000) *Action Plan for the Conservation of the Brown Bear in Europe.* Council of Europe, Strasbourg.

34. Swenson, J. E., Sandegren, F., Bjärvall, A., Söderberg, A., Wabakken, P. & Franzén, R. (1994) Size, trend, distribution and conservation of the brown bear population in Sweden. *Biological Conservation*, 70, 9-17.

35. Wieglus, R. B. & Bunnell, F. L. (1994) Dynamics of a small, hunted brown bear population in southwestern Alberta, Canada. *Biological Conservation*, 67, 161-166.

36. Craighead, J. J., Sumner, J. S. & Mitchell, J. A. (1995) *The Grizzly Bears of Yellowstone: Their Ecology in the Yellowstone Ecosystem, 1959-1992.* Island Press, Washington, USA.

FERAL BIG CATS

Big Cats in Britain: restoration ecology or imaginations run wild?

ECOS 23 (3/4) 30-64 (2002)

For some, reports of panthers stalking not just the wilds of Bodmin or Exmoor, but the suburbs of Cheltenham and Gloucester, are to be classed along with crop circles and UFOs. However, the big cat phenomenon can no longer be ignored: there is much convincing evidence of an expanding population of black leopard and puma in Britain. Conservationists need to consider how we live with these predators and manage places accordingly.

PETER TAYLOR

Facing up to the issues

Big cat sightings are widespread in Britain, but were absent from the last issue of *ECOS*, which featured reports of lynx and at least one animal shot and photographed. The 'big' cats remain the subject of eye-witness accounts and tell-tale corpses of their prey, with a certain amount of circumspection from scientists who fear the potential ridicule that the profession traditionally reserves for paranormal phenomena. However, it is now accepted by a growing number of experienced field naturalists and zoologists, as well as many local police forces, that large pantherine cats are present in Britain. There are now websites logging the sightings, and plans are afoot for a trip-photography campaign to capture final proof. I present here a brief review of the evidence thus far, together with my own experience. The issue raises a number of challenging questions for conservation groups, ranging from 'alien' invaders *versus* naturalised escapes, to the very real issues of public safety.

Public safety is an issue because these are *big* cats – that is, members of the genus *Panthera (*and *Puma)* quite capable of killing a human. Thus far, they have predated sheep, cattle (calves), foals, rabbits and other small game, and several instances are known of potentially dangerous human contact. The evidence suggests that numbers are growing and the animals are not always shy of contact.

A catalogue of sightings involves two 'types': a black panther three to four feet long with a two or three foot curled tail, often described as slinky and muscular and somewhat larger than a Labrador; the other a fawn, grey or brown panther but sometimes black, longer in the leg, smaller in the head and similar in size. On zoological grounds, this would suggest melanistic leopard *Panthera pardus,* or jaguar *Panthera onca*, and puma *Puma concolor.*[1]

The beasts of Bodmin and Exmoor

Sightings of black panther seemed to begin on Bodmin and Exmoor and reached a peak there in the early 1980s, when I recall the press interest generated by the Government calling out specialist army squads on Exmoor in order to control sheep losses. Army marksmen reported seeing a large black panther, but were unable to get a clear shot. The naturalist Trevor Beer spent six weeks tracking the animal from carcasses of deer, and finally was rewarded with a close up sighting described in his small book, *The Beast of Exmoor.*[2] His drawing is reproduced here – to my eye, it has the look of a puma, rather than a leopard – a smallish head, longer legs, and quite a distinct pale muzzle. In certain parts of North America, black puma are regularly seen, but are very rare in South America. The running pattern, reminiscent to Beer of a greyhound, looks more like a cheetah than the usual ground-hugging stealth of the relatively shorter-limbed leopard. Indeed, zoologists now place the puma close to the cheetah, and there are great similarities in skeletal structure with the small head and longer limbs. Beer's animal, however, had markedly clear green eyes like a leopard. Since the publication in 1984, the author has had a number of sightings and is convinced both black leopard and puma are breeding in the South West of England.

Field drawing of the 'Beast of Exmoor' (Trevor Beer)

The Mendip panther

After the Exmoor incidents seemed to die down, I took little more interest until moving to Somerset in the summer of 1997. The local papers were reporting irate farmers so convinced their sheep were being killed by a large cat, one near Cheddar had employed an ex-SAS marksman to guard his flocks. In the spring of 1998 a close friend saw a black panther in an open field at nearby Priddy in the Mendips. Shortly thereafter things went quiet around Somerset. A year later, the *Daily Mirror* carried a front-page story of a young boy who had grabbed the tail of what he thought was a pussy-cat in bushes, only to have a large black cat rear-up, covered in blood and smelling of rabbit, swipe his face and depart leaving three widely separated but superficial scratches – which the *Mirror* called "mauling". This incident occurred at Trelleck in Gwent, and although such superficial marks are hardly convincing – the local police scrambled a helicopter and firearms team.

An efficient sheep-killer

Despite this coverage, and a sighting in Cumbria by *ECOS*'s managing editor, I took little further interest until last year when close to our holiday campsite in Carmarthenshire, seven sheep were killed in one afternoon, in the very next field to us. Police called at our camp asking had we dogs, and I walked with the officer to the scene. Six of the sheep had been dragged and stashed under the riverbank, the seventh had been partially eaten. Despite the wet conditions I could find no tracks. Dogs usually bring sheep down by snapping at the legs as well as the neck.

Sheep kill in West Wales showing claw marks on back and canine punctures to the throat.(Peter Taylor)

Each of these animals had been killed cleanly by a single bite to the neck – in most instances the canine indentations could be clearly seen, and this is how powerful cats clamp the air-pipe and suffocate their prey. The eyes show characteristic bulging (see photo). One sheep had been dragged down from the rear and had claw marks on the back so deep that they had ripped through to the intestinal wall – each claw mark clearly defined. The canine holes seemed to suggest two animals – one five cms between the teeth, the other about one cm less. The policeman conceded it did not look like the work of dogs, and said there had been reports of a large black panther-sized cat.

The Forest of Dean hotspot

However, it was at our last summer camp that I decided it was time to take the matter more seriously. Two of my children among a group of others were severely traumatised by a night-time encounter in the Forest of Dean woods. They had been out playing with torches and had panicked when they saw a black panther apparently stalking them. In their rush to get out of the woods, one became impaled on barbed wire and their terrified screams brought us to the scene. My 13-year old son, a veteran of tiger stalking in India, related how he could see the animal in his torch-light close by as he hung helpless on the wire. It made no attempt to harm the children. I resolved that the time had come to investigate the subject of big cats more systematically.

USA mountain lion areas

I had just returned from spending several weeks in a wilderness zone in North America where mountain lion were frequent (and black ones at that!), and the children had been instructed that any encounter was to be met by careful behaviour – not to run, not to stare at the animal, and if it approached to stand tall, wave arms and make a lot of noise. There were warning notices on the trails advising members of the public to take precautions. However, North American mountain lions are wary of human contact and generally keep to the wilder mountain areas. Here we are dealing with a population of cats that has never been hunted and has no reason to shun human contact.

Indeed, given how hard it is to see truly wild leopard or mountain lion overseas, the number of broad daylight sightings in Britain, especially on farmland and around cities, is extra-ordinary. If such sightings were due entirely to over-active imagination on the part of the lay public (including postmen, police and farmers), then one might expect the occasional spotted leopard, striped tiger, or maned lion – but there have been no such sightings. Several footprints have been plaster-casted and sent to zoos, and recently the *Independent* newspaper reported that London Zoo experts had identified casts taken in Lincolnshire as being those of a puma. *The Times* (29 January 2000) interviewed an animal trainer, Leslie Martin, who admitted releasing a black leopard and a puma on the moors near Sheffield in 1974 prior to the introduction of restrictive legislation. He said that several trainers he knew had done the same, rather than put the animals down.

After the Forest of Dean encounter, and still believing that active imagination could be playing a part, I checked out the websites of the Big Cat followers – somewhat expecting a mix of crop-circle and UFO mentality. I was surprised to find a well-mapped incident site run by David Walker and very detailed scientific coverage by Scottish observers, as well as lots of useful press reports on the more popularised British Big Cat Society's pages. The Forest of Dean proved a hot-spot. I realised Trelleck, where the young boy was scratched, was no more than four miles from our campsite across the Wye. Police had also issued warnings around Monmouth, six miles further north, after a black panther was seen close to the town. Sightings in the Gloucester and Cheltenham suburbs were frequent. Two weeks later the Independent carried reports of a police team called to a farm on the Gwent levels – the police reported seeing one adult black panther and one smaller animal. The helicopter and tranquilliser team were called out but failed to locate the animals. This incident was less than 20 miles from our campsite.

Checking the website data – and sifting out the problematic 'large moggy' possibilities, leaves several areas as hotspots – starting from Devon in the south, the Forest of Dean for regular sightings of black panther, with north Dorset, the

Somerset Levels and Mendips, Malverns and Worcester for periodic sightings, and finally, Fife as the epicentre of black panther sightings in Scotland. In the last instance the website shows a photo taken of a deer carcass after a driver had surprised a black panther dragging it across a road near Cupar. The characteristic clean white bones of the half-eaten animal are caused by the rasping action of the big cat's tongue. Pumas are sighted regularly in the Surrey woods and Hampshire, Northumberland and Durham (where the police have a special liaison officer), but there are also reports coming from such unlikely un-forested areas as the fens around Kings Lynn and Lincolnshire. My brother, an experienced naturalists' tour leader, saw a puma charge into and take a pheasant from a group in a rearing area in Hampshire.

At the time of writing (October 2002) it was reported in my local press that the Animal Rescue Centre on the hills overlooking the Somerset Levels had a sheep attacked and killed. What was so surprising was that this 'farm' had a series of paddocks by the visitor centre. The attack happened within hearing of the centre, but nothing actually was heard. The vets called to the scene were convinced that the unfortunate animal had been killed by a large cat. A few days later a local farmer at Yetminster had a sheep killed, and he warned in the local press that he had seen the panther and other farmers should guard their stock.

Origins: deliberate releases, or are some indigenous?

What then are we to make of all this? I personally have three friends who have seen large panthers or pumas, and the kills I have examined certainly appear to have been the work of a very powerful cat (try dragging a sheep for 50 yards, or rather, six of them one after another – I know of no dog that can do that).

It appears most likely that these animals are the consequences of releases in the 70s following new legislation: the *Dangerous Wild Animals Act* brought in a licensing system which prompted some private owners to relinquish their big cats. It has been reported that black panthers were popular in the gangster's world as frightening caged pets – but they must have been difficult to procure in such numbers. Puma were apparently easy to buy and keep, and one animal was recaptured near Inverness in 1980 after it had been released. There is the possibility that a small population of inbred puma could produce a large proportion of black animals. It has been suggested that many of these animals result from escapees from the travelling menageries popular in Victorian times – but then why only black leopard?

Some laypeople have suggested the black cats are indigenous – either survivors of an earlier age, or the product of feral cat and wildcat interbreeding. Taking the latter first: wildcat and feral inter-breeding is common in Scotland and thought to have produced the Kellas Cat, a black form larger than an average feral cat (*Felis sivestris* ranges from 3-7 kg). But we are talking of cats that must weigh between 50 and 100 Kg. We know that dog breeders have managed to produce animals of one species that range across these sizes and colours, but it would appear most unlikely that feral cats, with or without wildcat genes, could be worked on by natural processes of selection over such a short time. Indeed, domestic cat genes are derived solely from the African subspecies of *F.silvestris,* and feral crosses between these domestic forms and the European race (*e.g.* the Scottish wildcat) would have begun in Roman times. There appears little possibility of great plasticity in size, although the potential of wolf genes to produce such great plasticity in the domestic dog, and the absence of competition for a large predator niche, should make us wary of generalisations.

What of an indigenous large feline? This is not as outlandish a suggestion by laypeople as might first appear. There are fossil antecedents. European temperate forest fauna evolved to its present assemblage about one million years ago as adaptations to periodic ice ages, and was relatively stable over the last three inter-glacials. Only after the last ice age, a mere 13,000 years ago, did those returning forests lack a large panther (as well as elephant and rhino) typical of their Indo-European connections.[3] The English fossil fauna of the late Pleistocene is replete with leopard, as is a line from mid-England to Hungary. Post-glacial fossils are recorded as near as Italy. Going back to the mid-Pleistocene, produces ancestral forms of a stocky European Jaguar, known as Owen's Panther after the Victorian paleontologist who found its jaw in the Mendip cave deposits. Furthermore, the British form was cold-adapted and persisted even at the glacial maxima and the American jaguar extended to the boreal forest zone before the major extinction event of 13,000 years ago.

What happened to the British leopard?

Why then did leopard fail to return along with their favoured woodland prey of roe deer, wild boar, and the young of aurochsen? Remnant and very secretive populations of leopard still exist in the mountains of Turkey, Palestine, Arabia, Persia and the temperate forest of the Amur in eastern Russia. They have only recently been studied by professional zoologists – most of whom never see the animals in the wild, but rely on trapping and trip-photography. I can see no ecological reason why leopard could not have accompanied the temperate forest herbivores on their return. Most of the other missing elements of the Pleistocene fauna can be explained by habitat change or human hunting pressure. The horse and steppe-bison were grassland dependent, and so probably was the large European lion. The mega-herbivores such as straight-tusked elephant and forest rhino were probably hunted out in the glacial forest refuges in Spain and SE Europe before they could move north as in all previous millennia, and with them went the sabre-toothed cat that specialised on the large pachyderms. Of the other forest predators, wolves, lynx and bear made it here and were present at the time the Romans invaded, and the last Scottish wolf was shot about 300 hundred years ago.

Leopard are a lot less obvious than wolves, but it seems inconceivable that a large cat could have been missed – and why only in Britain? I think the argument deserves a considered response. The latter question first – Britain, as a far-western mountainous outpost, does appear to have refuge potential. Kurten, the great vertebrate paleontologist noted that there existed a remnant population of sabre-tooths in Britain until much later than elsewhere. Some naturalists consider the wild white 'park' cattle as indigenous remnants, and I have seen photos of white cattle, with characteristic neck spotting, in cave drawings of 20,000 years ago. Exmoor ponies are regarded as particularly ancient and may be direct descendents of the forest 'tarpan'. Curiously, Exmoor was the only place in England and Wales that did not lose its free roaming red deer herds. By 1800, most of England and Wales had virtually no deer at all, and of course no wild boar either. The current over-population of roe deer and muntjac is a post-war phenomenon, and they have yet to re-populate Wales to any significant extent.

The legendary Black Dog

Surely, though, the intrepid English game-keepers and amateur naturalists of the Victorian period would not have missed even a small population of big cats (prior to that, almost anything bar a rhino or elephant could have been missed in the remote parts of Devon!). Disconcertingly, these parts of England, and indeed, many parts, have folk legends of large black 'dogs' that haunted the moors. Many people might have readily assumed that what they saw were large 'dogs'. And for those who were a little more advanced in field technique, such as keepers, there would be adequate disincentive to suggest a large cat – just as there has been today in the modern police force and among the farming community who have 'known' about large cats for at least three decades.

Remnants and relics in small areas

Such small areas and small populations are not however that unusual. Currently, the remnant Asian lion numbers 200 animals in an area equivalent to the size of Dartmoor National Park, but fortunately populated only by wild ungulates. The Amur leopard is confined to reserves in areas of a few tens of thousands of hectares. Geneticists reckon the current widely dispersed and endangered population of cheetah must have been reduced to only one family at some time in prehistory. It is not impossible that a relic population of small leopard (the

458

Palestinian form averages only 30 kg), inbred and throwing up regular melanism (the genes of which may confer other advantages in a cold damp clime), could have survived in Britain, but, of course, unlikely.

Deliberate release of caged animals

The likeliest origin is the release of caged animals. We have admissions that some *were* released. Unlikely as it may seem, black leopard were a fashion item for British gangsters. It seems that to account for the population, some dozen or so animals must have been released and subsequently bred in the wild. Escapes of smaller cats are regular occurrences – in addition to lynx (8-30 kg) of unknown origin, such as the one shot in Norfolk (*ECOS*, 21(2) page 11), leopard cat *Prionailurus bengalensis* (3-7 kg) and jungle cat *Felis chaus* (7-13 kg) are known from road kills and farmers shooting them (see the websites for details). Also, one of two escaped clouded leopard *Neofelis nebulosa* (11-20 kg), was at large for several months before being trapped in a London suburb.[4] There is an apocryphal story of a leopard that escaped in transit to a game reserve whilst in the suburbs of Johhanesburg, much to the consternation of the authorities who immediately set up traps. They caught six leopards in one night!

Living with big predators, accepting aliens

Do we, as the community of conservationists, have anything specific to say about all of this? It fits rather squarely into current debates about alien species, assuming they *are* alien, as well as the obvious absence of functional large predators for an over-abundant deer population (and maybe, soon, wild boar as well!). But these are dangerous animals – and therefore, even if we were to get over the alien concept, and turn to a functional approach to species, we would need to look at the potential for human fatalities. We might also look into the psychological differences between having your throat clamped and bones stripped by a big cat, or getting your tongue stung while eating an ice-cream (wasps regularly kill in this way!).

Let us take the alien concept first. Where leopard are concerned, they were a regular native prior to the present human-dominated interglacial, and their absence is not readily explained, as is their demise in the wilder parts of Europe that still hold wolf, bear and lynx. Zoological purists might want to draw a time-line at the Mesolithic and the closure of the English Channel – but that is entirely arbitrary and not representative of the functional ecosystems that existed in all prior inter-glacials. The IUCN rules on re-introductions have the same near-time focus.

There is also a present and future problem with aliens. As Paul Green argued in *ECOS* 23 (2), the whole 'alien' concept requires scrutiny in the light of a globalised wild ecology.[5] In Britain, the main food web for our pitifully reduced diversity of carnivores – top predator being the fox, consists of rabbits, brown hare, brown rat, red-legged partridge and pheasant - all aliens. Our biggest 'forests' consist of alien monocultures of Sitka spruce, Japanese larch and Norway fir. In deeper time – the previous inter-glacial, Britain had Douglas fir, hemlock spruce, and rhododendron.

All of evolutionary history is about invasion, competition and replacement, as land bridges open and close like revolving doors. Since the very recent human invasions of Britain, the larger herbivores have no predators and thus over-grazing has seriously impacted upon biological diversity throughout Scotland (red deer) and the uplands of England and Wales (domestic free-range sheep). We could find cogent ecological arguments for a small population of mountain lion and black leopards, but it is the political argument that will decide. As for that – the risks are obvious, though perhaps likely to be overstated – cars in rural lanes are a far greater threat to free-roaming children, as is pneumonia and rogue collies to hill sheep. But such matters are not rational – and Britain has what can only be described as 'beast' consciousness, reflecting our over-tame national psyche.

However, if we are to have any influence upon Indians to conserve tigers in areas ever more greatly encroached upon by humans, and where fatalities are annual, then we could hardly use 'danger' as a sufficient excuse. We could look to the USA for a modern approach to big cat parallels. Except, much as I would personally welcome it, I cannot see the British public accepting new billboards in the Forest of Dean's country parks, warning children not to stray alone, and to stand tall and make a lot of noise if approached by a black panther! Unless, perhaps, as has happened in the US in modern times, people come to welcome elements of vulnerability, real risk and fear as essential to conserve wild places in the countryside and the wildness in themselves.

If the presence of these big cats is finally proven by trapping or photography, I would hope that we will have anticipated the arguments, and that some conservationists of the re-wilding orientation will stand up for what would be a frisson of risk in the wilds of British nature.

Notes and References

1. Macdonald, D (2001) *The New Encyclopedia of Mammals*, Oxford University Press.
2. Beer, T (1984) *The Beast of Exmoor*, Countryside Productions, Barnstable, Devon.

3. Turner, A (1997) *The Big Cats and their Fossil Relatives*, Columbia University Press.
4. Yalden, D (1999) *A History of British Mammals*, Poyser.
5. Green, P (2002) Riparian alien plants. Towards ecological acceptance, *ECOS* 23 (2) 34-42.

Big cats in Dorset:
the evidence and the implications

ECOS 28 (1) 73-78 (2007)

New alpha predators have melted into the Dorset landscape...

JONATHAN MCGOWAN

In the autumn of 2006 I gave a presentation on large cats in Dorset to a national gathering of the Police force's Wildlife Liaison Officers. They needed no convincing on the evidence for these cats and their comments revealed the respect they pay to the subject. Indeed, they are aware of past and current trends in the exotic pet trade, which is believed to be responsible, in part, for large cats living wild in Britain's great outdoors. There were also some Defra staff members among the delegates, and despite their organisation's uncommitted stance on the subject, they too showed a keen interest, which extended to reporting the location of some scratch marks they were aware of. When I discussed the issue of large cats at a BANC workshop, also last autumn (see report at www.banc.org.uk), people's main concern was to know more about the species 'out there' so that discussions on possible lynx reintroduction could be more informed about the real context of free-living cats across Britain.

'Coming out' on big cats

Dorset is the area where I have done most of my research on free-living large cats (referred to as 'big cats' in the rest of this article for convenient shorthand). It is the area from where I have had most of my sightings, starting in 1984 when I witnessed a puma at close quarters stalking a badger. I then saw what I believe to be the same puma on two more occasions. At first I kept my sightings to myself, having been used to people's sceptical nature. Through my tracking and my nocturnal and crepuscular wanderings I have had several more sightings since: not just of puma, but of leopard and leopard-like animals, and of lynx. On two occasions I have seen puma cubs (each of a different litter) and I have once seen cubs of leopard. Dorset seems to be a hotspot like the rest of the West country, with many sightings a year by credible witnesses, including naturalists, biologists, police officers, foresters, ecologists doing field survey work, and by other people who are regularly outside such as dog walkers, horse riders, car drivers at night, and not to mention lampers and poachers. Often, I ask farmers on the off-chance, and I frequently get a matter-of-fact reply: "Yes, we have them", "No we don't, but the next farm does", "My wife sees them" and so on. It seems that more people see cats than badgers in some areas. That's not because the cats have eaten them all, although some have, as we will see later.

The three main suspects

Big cats are not much of a news story in Dorset any more, as sightings are so regular. The amount of sightings in different areas often on the same day means that there are more than just one or two individuals around, even though they can cover many miles, especially at night when they are more active. Many researchers believe there are several hundred large cats living wild in the UK. The black panther (melanistic leopard, and possibly some melanistic jaguar) is the most commonly seen cat. Sightings of spotted cats are rare, save for small cats like the leopard cat, of which there have been several road kills in the past two decades. Leopard are in the genus of *Panthera* like the tiger and the lion, while puma (or mountain lion) is the second most often seen species, and belongs to the genus of *Felis*, along with most other species of 'small' cats, but physically they can be as large or larger than a leopard. The official term 'big cat' has nothing to do with size, but is based on whether or not the species can roar, due to a fixed hyoid bone in the throat. The lynx is the third most commonly seen species. This gracile cat is of much interest to many conservationists because as a once native species, its unofficial appearance in Britain is welcomed by many, and its official reintroduction is on many people's wish list.

There is much misidentification of all three large species, but generally it is the consistency of witness reports which makes the evidence more robust, coupled with the field evidence, and the occasional amateur video footage, as seen last year on Sky TV's Big Cat Tracks. For my own observations, chances of photographing the cats have been thwarted by lack of time, lack of light and even the lack of a camera – I am not sitting in a hide with an array of photographic and infra red equipment, but on the move, tracking in the field. There are reports of smaller non-indigenous cats but as I have had no evidence in the county, I will not include them in my consideration here. Their impact on the ecosystem is minimal, and their numbers are far fewer than feral domestic cats, which would be feeding on the same sorts of food. I will also exclude jungle cats from my analysis here, of which there are believed to be small numbers across Britain, and possibly some ocelot, perhaps especially in their melanistic form. To back up the sightings of small-medium cats like ocelot and jungle cat, I have found cat spoor larger than domestic, but smaller than lynx, along with smaller droppings in typical habitat such as reed beds in harbours and estuaries.

Understanding the territories

To try and map the large species, I first looked at all the alleged sightings in Dorset and the borders of neighbouring counties. I marked them on a map along with all areas of woodland, rivers, roads, herd deer, rabbit colonies, game rearing, badger sets and any other features relevant to a cat's territory. I then searched these areas for evidence, and found signs in all locations at some time over a period of six years. Some of the signs were old but most were fresh, mainly consisting of paw prints, tree scratches, spraying areas and remains of kills. Particularly helpful are deer remains that have the characteristics of being eaten by large cats as opposed to dogs or other scavengers. A leopard may kill one deer every four or five days, depending on whether it can keep it from other scavengers. It will not kill in the same location twice a week, in order to keep the prey less alert, or so it seems. I have found many field signs scattered throughout the county, but certain hotspots seemed to have emerged. Signs would prevail every week or two in certain areas, in the form of footprints and scats.

Sometimes it took up to three years before these signs ceased, so one can conclude that the animal had a territory. I looked at possible natural boundaries such as main roads, wide rivers, expanses of arable land without much cover, or large tracts of conifer plantations. To judge other parameters of the territories, I have used people's sightings, and speculation as to how far a large cat would travel for food, water, cover and other members of the same species. On the whole, the UK has concentrated amounts of natural prey, especially deer and rabbits. Indeed, these conditions are better than many areas of native country of leopard and puma. Males can encompass several female territories within their own range, but recent research suggests that both leopards and puma may often have smaller territories than was previously first thought.

Proof that these cats are stealthy and elusive comes from a well reported incident when six leopards were once caught in traps left out one night in Johannesburg, SA, meant for one known problem animal. This demonstrated that leopards can live amidst urban settlements but go unnoticed by people.

I first concluded that in Dorset there had to be at least eight leopards since the year 2000 because of the number of cubs seen by myself and others during that time; and taking into account that two is the average litter, and they can remain as juveniles with their mother for up to two years. These are the ones seen or at least known about. It is estimated that for every reported sighting, there are at least 10 unreported. As at Summer 2006, the police estimate in Dorset was of around six big cats.[1]

Looking at the availability of food in these areas and at how many cats they could support along with all the other info, I concluded that there were possibly 20 to 30 leopards, a few less puma, and at least 6 lynx in the county. There are rumours of a lynx liberation group, and even a huge holding compound with many animals caged, has been seen, allegedly, and the police and RSPCA have uncovered unlicensed lynx in captivity. Something is undoubtedly going on in relation to lynx, as cat investigators elsewhere in Britain also conclude from their intelligence. So the facts point to lynx now being introduced to the UK, and I am finding possible signs of their habits in Dorset, backed up by people's regular sightings.

The abundant food supply

I have found that the leopards in my five study areas tend to keep to the large forested tracts and the assumed territories may be up to around 70 per cent woodland. This is mixed woodland with areas of carr in between marshy areas or heathland, and woodland of willow, pine and mainly oak often with an under storey of rhododendron.

These areas are the ideal habitat for sika deer, and in all but one of my study areas there are herd deer, with one herd being fallow. The area with no herd deer has many roe, but I think this territory is larger because of the lesser availability of deer. I believe these forested areas of heathland are the best areas for cats, with lots of cover, water and food. Perhaps the leopard has the upper hand over puma in these areas because from my own sightings there is a marked size difference between the two species here: the leopard seems to be larger than most puma, or the leopards in these areas seem to grow very large. The warm heaths seem to be more suitable for leopards reflecting scrubland or open jungle habitats with very thick cover in the way of bracken, gorse and rhododendron, as these are the areas where I tend to find a lot of signs. Most hunting areas tend to be near water, and several sites are drinking areas for deer among purple more grass which forms dense, high tussocks - the perfect ambush site. The puma also uses this area and in two of my study areas I believe there are at least two species of cats coexisting. These areas are the richest ecosystems and are centred on estuaries and heath bordered by high chalk downs. There is a plentiful supply of prey: thousands of migratory birds such as sandpipers, godwits, curlew, brent geese, shellduck, pintail, teal, and mallard, and large amounts of egrets and herons, of which the later have been predated on quite extensively. Also swans have been taken and dragged a few hundred yards from the waters edge to be consumed under cover of bracken. In these areas are large colonies of rabbits, badger sets and lots of foxes. Amongst the flocks of Canada geese I have found signs of predation by both foxes and cats. There are also large colonies of black headed gulls, where I have also found signs of predation. Within the area are high sea cliffs holding breeding colonies of kittywakes, guillemot and razorbills. The cliffs themselves have natural, but mainly man-made quarrying caves for Purbeck stone, providing the most secure of breeding dens. The chalk downland surrounding the heath and harbour bays hold plenty of hares, roe deer, many badgers and rabbits, and game bird rearing. In addition there are numerous amounts of rats, mice and voles.

The mix of territories

Thus one area which could be a 'small' leopard territory of just five square miles has a concentrated amount of every food source required by the cat. In addition, there may be one or two females of the same species overlapping, or totally within his boundaries, and another species of large cat coexisting alongside with no problems. There is enough food here for that to happen without any part of the ecosystem being changed to any degree, and the way in which cats rotate there hunting areas prevents that. The leopard I believe to be a male mainly concentrates on sika deer, and mainly animals under two years of age. I have noticed that many deer taken have had previous injuries or were sick, and some road kills are scavenged by the cats. From my field work it appears that puma in Dorset tend to keep to the farmland or hills with a small overlap into the valley heathlands, which may suggest mainly rabbit, hare and roe predation. Most lynx sightings are in similar areas but with large tracts of woodland, especially if there is dense cover. I have seen puma cubs on heathland only two miles away from active leopard areas. I am unsure whether they meet, but it seems that each species finds its own niche. This is the case in Africa and Asia where you have areas hosting multiple cat species.

Deer kill - showing typical snipped ribs and stripped flesh (J.McGowan)

The predator in the ecosystem

In my areas I have found a slight reduction in the numbers of deer especially young animals. This may suggest that older wiser animals tend to spread their genes which will make for a more healthy herd. I also observe a slight reduction in the number of foxes mainly cubs, and I have found cat scats containing the whiskers of fox cubs. Badgers are taken too, and in my northern study area where there are no sika deer but a small herd of fallow and many badger sets. Of a whole colony of badgers, most of the approximately 20 animals were taken out, with only 6 remaining in one year - the large boars and elderly sows. These individuals even took to foraging in the daytime. There are numerous amounts of hares and game rearing, so I wonder if the cat could have been injured and unable to catch such well sighted quick animals. The large cat species tend to be doing exactly what nature intended them to do, and in some instances they do a better job than deer stalkers, but I am sure there is room for them both! There may be other benefits, with some species of invertebrates evolved to use the dung of carnivores, albeit that those species are extinct or rare in the UK, while other insects rely on carrion, or bones. Top predators allow this important niche to be filled. As these top predators breed and spread in Dorset I detect a slight change in other animals' behaviour, such as roe resting in the open, foxes and badgers becoming more diurnal, and deer taking less notice of people, and concentrating on the real threat that confronts them.

There is little potential risk to people from large wild cats in comparison to certain dogs, and not to mention wasps, which kill many people across Europe each year, including through throat stings when they get into fizzy drink cans. Many people welcome the prospect of predators and feisty beats such as wild boar back in our countryside, making us more observant, alert, and attuned to risks and responsibilities. Britain and its wildlife can only benefit from having large cats back in the ecosystem.

References

1. *Big Cat Tracks,* Animal Planet, Sky TV 2006

2. Minter, R (2007) 'Big Cats – So What?' *British Big Cats Yearbook 2007.* Big Cats in Britain Research Group/CFZ Press.

WATER VOLE

Water vole reintroduction projects – the lessons and the success factors

ECOS 28 (1) 98-103 (2007)
This article summarises lessons from a sample of water vole reintroduction projects. A longer version of the article is at ECOS *28 (1) on www.banc.org.uk*

DEREK GOW

The endemic subspecies of the Northern water vole (Arvicola terrestris amphibius) was once such a familiar aspect of riparian Britain that Kenneth Grahame based his Wind in the Willows character Ratty on this species. Although widely referred to in modern times as water-rats they were once accorded a variety of other titles such as Crabers, Water dogs, British beavers and Campagnols.[1]

Field signs of water vole

The water vole is the largest of the three vole species native to mainland Britain. Although mature adults in lowland England can weigh up to 350 grams fully grown, Scottish specimens are commonly much lighter in weight with a large individual weighing 265 grams. Unlike its European counter-part (*Arvicola terrestris Sherman*) British water voles normally inhabit riparian fringe habitat and are seldom found in substantial landlocked populations. Water voles can mate on land or in water and females in England can produce between 3-5 litters averaging around 20 offspring per annum in captivity. This figure is in stark contrast to the reproductive capacity of upland Scottish populations which have been recorded as producing only two litters of two offspring per annum.[2] Early litter females are capable of reproduction in their year of birth.

Field signs of water vole presence such as stems of plant material cut at a distinctive 45-degree angle, excavated or gnawed tubers, latrines, feeding platforms, tracks, runs and burrows are easy to observe where they are common. Water vole feeding activity may play a role in the dispersal of some food plant species such as yellow flag iris (*Iris pseudacorus*) whose naturally gnarled root systems are easily separated by gnawing.

Stephanie Ryder writing in 1962 stated that " wherever there is good water contained in firm banks...you may be sure to find signs of water vole habitation" and until comparatively recently this was still widely perceived to be the case. In 1990 a series of national surveys funded by the Vincent Wildlife Trust[3], identified a serious constriction in the national range of the water vole and subsequent repeat surveys[4] now suggest that this species may have disappeared from over 90% of its former range.

Water vole (Chris Robbins/Derek Gow Consultancy)

Impacts on water vole and its population decline

This steep decline is linked directly to the intensification of agricultural practice over the course of the last century. Extensive wetland drainage, overgrazing of riparian vegetation by domestic livestock and arable cultivation to the edge of watercourses have been coupled with substantial river, stream or ditch canalisation programmes and unsympathetic annual dredging regimes. The impact of these processes has been compounded by bank side reinforcement programmes employing concrete or metal pilling, the successful colonisation of introduced North American mink (*Mustela vison*) – a predator against which they have no developed defence - and an associated range of further incidental factors such as accidental poisoning or sporadic human persecution.

469

As a result of the above water voles are now legally protected under Schedule 5 of the Wildlife and Countryside Act but this legal protection although preventing their reckless destruction can do little to halt their continued decline. The national distribution of this species is highly fragmented and in many counties they are already extinct. Current predictions are that this situation will worsen leading to further countywide extinctions by 2010. Where extensive populations of water voles still occur, species recovery incentives are generally focused on improving and extending tracts of suitable habitat coupled with the co-ordinated destruction of mink. Where significant vole populations are no longer extant a more active process of restoration to support, restore and rejoin relict populations will be essential if this species is to recover.

It is against this back-ground that water vole restoration utilising either translocated animals or captive bred offspring has become an identified component of the national Biodiversity Action Plan (BAP) for this species.[5] Water vole translocations (the direct movement of wild caught animals from one site to another) – which have commonly been practised as a component of human development projects - are problematic[6] due to the low number of animals frequently involved, their high territorial fidelity[7] and their short reproductive lifespan. The sourcing of sufficient offspring from healthy donor populations (harvesting) might be a mechanism for providing future release stocks but this - as yet un-quantified - process can only be employed if the security of donor populations can be guaranteed. Water voles are known to be predated by a range of 'native' predators such as red foxes (Vulpes vulpes), otters (Lutra lutra) stoats (Mustela erminea), pike (Esox lucius), grey herons (Ardea cinerea), brown rats (rattus norvegicus) and domestic cats.[8] In a population study on the river Itchen – where no mink were present - the average seasonal mortality of a robust water vole population was estimated to exceed 70%.

Steps towards recovery

The first large scale water vole breeding project began in 1994 at the New Forest Nature Quest with the express aim of developing a sustainable methodology for reproducing this species consistently. Although breeding attempts had been successful in a study population at Queen Mary and Westfield College[9] no effort had been made to reproduce this short-lived species in sufficient numbers to render reintroductions possible. Even though this was not a conservation priority action at that time it is a fundamental error in any recovery process for an endangered species to leave the development of a captive breeding component until individual founders are in short supply. Genetic diversity will by this stage be extremely low and if husbandry protocols have to be developed from scratch any resultant human errors can be critical to the survival of the species.[10] For this reason captive breeding as a component of an overall conservation package is best refined when an initial threat is perceived as part of any process of general biological research.

The first monitored reintroduction of water voles was trialled at the Barn Elms Wetlands Centre in 2001. Although a few older animals were utilised for this project the bulk of the released population of 147 were captive bred juveniles in their year of birth. These animals were all fitted with individual microchips and were selected to ensure an average release weight of around 108 grams. Animals released at Barn Elms in July and recaptured in late summer had more than doubled their body weight and one female released weighing 90 grams produced a litter in a trap when captured in October (Strachan.R. Pers comm). Under a suite of good habitat conditions water voles can obtain a weight gain of 1.2grams per day attaining breeding condition in a single season.

Juvenile water voles were released on both a hard (straight into areas of tall vegetation with no subsequent support) and soft (from release pens dug into the ground with food support for a time) release basis. Preliminary results from this and subsequent projects suggest strongly that the latter option is more effective. (Strachan.R. Pers comm). If maintained together juveniles can be released in sibling groups of up to four animals. Various different styles of release pens have been trialled successfully but they all operate on the principal that the voles dig to freedom through an open earth floor whilst providing temporary cover from predators. Release cages must be supplied with abundant bedding and chopped apples for both food and moisture. They should be dug well into the ground immediately adjacent to the waters edge and screened from the sun with dense vegetation. Water voles are a physically robust species but in common with most riparian mammals they have an extremely dense fur coat and if subjected to stress during periods of extreme heat they can die rapidly. Chopped apple – a quarter per animal – must always be included for consumption to provide moisture during transport and release. Water voles will commonly continue to utilise well-sited release pens as latrine and feeding areas for some time following release.

The timing of release for juveniles should coincide with late spring/early summer vegetative food and cover abundance. Care should be taken that water level stability is guaranteed in potential release sites as severe fluctuations either way can be a critical factor in the success or failure of a colony (Strachan.C. Pers comm).   Failure to achieve this threshold in their year of birth is best remedied by holding over winter and releasing as breeding adults in spring. Releases of both juveniles (in their year of birth) and breeding adults (late litter offspring over-wintered and released in the spring) have been trialled and worked well. The release of small populations of individuals exceeding these age groups produces poor breeding results (Gow and Holder. In preparation).

At the time of writing the authors have participated in the production of over 3000 animals for over 20 translocation/reintroduction/supplementation projects in England. To date one release has failed due to a variety of external factors, seven have successfully established vigorous populations some of which are expanding rapidly, two are indeterminate and ten are too recent to adequately assess. Animals provided historically from this captive breeding programme have established an additional two low-level populations (R.Strachan. Personal communication) which are still extant and a similar captive breed and release project run by Bristol Zoo on a site near the Royal Portbury docks (Eyre. Pers comm) has been highly successful. The best of these projects in large wetland complexes – Pagham harbour and Barn Elms - have within a few years seen released populations of captive bred animals expand rapidly to colonise the entire available reintroduction zone.

Requirements for successful restoration

In conclusion it must be clearly stressed that this captive breeding and release process is currently an effort in the refinement of technique. The two keys to successful water vole restoration are the availability of large-scale mosaics of sustainable wetland habitat and the effective long-term control of North American mink.[11] Both these criteria are obviously reliant on significant cooperative partnerships and until recently is was difficult to envisage how these could be effectively secured. The development of the Chichester Costal Plain sustainable farming partnership provides a tantalisingly, intelligent example of how this can actually be achieved.[12] This remarkable venture has seen a consortium of organisations combine to create through agri-environment schemes a 8,400ha project site within which the availability of water vole habitat has trebled in a very few years. This has been accomplished by the restriction of livestock in riparian corridors by fencing, the creation of field margin junction ponds and the restoration of existing farm ponds. This project has employed a simple but highly effective "mink raft" system designed by the Game Conservancy Trust to target, eliminate and the re-monitor for the presence of this alien predator. Water voles from our captive breeding project released into this site in May 2002 have now combined with few relict populations to colonise most of the available habitat within the project area.

The fact that the once common and widespread water vole has suffered in excess of a 90% range decline in the British Isles is a damning indictment of many previous damaging land-use practices. It is however a robust species capable of incredible regeneration where the circumstances are suitable. There are grounds for considerable optimism that even at this late stage, the water vole's declining fortunes can still be reversed by coordinated action.

References

1. Ryder. S (1962). Water Voles. *The Sunday Times*.

2.. Capreolus Wildlife Consultancy (2005). The ecology and conservation of water voles in upland habitats. Scottish Natural Heritage Commissioned Report No. 099 (ROAME No. F99AC320)

3. Strachan. R. & Jeffries. D.J (1993). The water vole (*Arvicola terrestris*) in Britain 1989-90: its distribution and changing status. The Vincent Wildlife Trust. London.

4. Strachan. C, Strachan. R & Jeffries. D.J. (2000). Preliminary report on the changes in the water vole population of Britain as shown by the national surveys of 1989-90 and 1996-98. The Vincent Wildlife Trust. London.

5. Biodiversity: The UK Steering Group Report – Volume II: Action Plans. HMSO 1995 Tranche: 1 Volume: 2 Page: 82

6. Gow. D, Holder.K and Jeffrey. C (2004). Journal of the IEEM. *In Practice* 44 (14 – 17)

7. Dean. M. (April 2003). Journal of IEEM. *In Practice* No. 39.

8. Strachan. R. (1997). *Water voles* Whittet Books. London.

9. Blake. B. (1982). Reproduction in captive water voles. *Journal of Zoology* 1982. Mammal Society.

10. Durrell. G. (1994). *The Aye Aye and I*. Harper Collins. Pages 159-163.

11. Strachan. R. (1998). Water Vole Conservation Handbook. Wildlife Conservation and Research Unit. Oxford University.

12. Strachan. R. and Holmes-ling. P (2003). Restoring water Voles and Other Biodiversity to the Wider Countryside. Wildlife Conservation and Research Unit. Oxford University

BIG BIRDS

Big Birds in the UK: the reintroduction of iconic species

ECOS 32 (1) 74-80 (2011)

There has been over three decades of success with reintroduction of large birds, some with fierce reputations among farmers and game keepers, some demanding of habitat restoration and undisturbed nesting grounds – are there lessons here for mammalian reintroduction programmes?

PETER TAYLOR

The reintroduction of bird species formerly eradicated from Britain contrasts markedly with the mammalian equivalents. Whereas it took almost twenty years from the first fact-finding trip of Britain's conservationists to see a beaver reintroduction site in Brittany in 1991 before masses of red tape and consultations brought this harmless and iconic mammal to a small remote site in Scotland, big bird enthusiasts began reintroducing sea eagles to Scotland in 1975 and red kites to England in 1989. Programmes of releases continue, with sea eagles now on the Scottish east coast and potentially in East Anglia, golden eagles already breeding again in Ireland, and the red kite programme on its ninth release project in the north-west of England, following the first project in the Home Counties. Great bustards and cranes are currently subject to captive breeding and release programmes in Wiltshire and Somerset. Apart from the cranes and bustards, the avian success story involves large predators that could be expected to engender opposition from farming and game interests unless handled with full involvement of these interests, yet these programmes have had striking success. Are there lessons here for future mammal projects?

The sea eagle

This magnificent eagle – also called the white-tailed sea eagle, is a close relative of the iconic American bald eagle, and despite being a predator and scavenger mainly of fish and wildfowl, had an undeserved reputation as a lamb-killer. It was systematically eradicated in Britain and Ireland where it was confined to coastal wilderness areas, probably numbering about 100 pairs in Britain and fifty in Ireland at end of the 18th century – by 1916, the last pair on Skye had been exterminated.

Sea eagle (Mark Hamblin,/ Northshots)

The reintroduction programme began in 1975 – with Roy Dennis being a key champion of the project. Over a ten year period, 82 birds were released, first in the Hebrides, and in 1985 the first chicks were reared. In the 1990s the programme was extended to Wester Ross, and by 2010, there were 50 breeding pairs raising 46 young with a 10% increase over the previous year. Young birds disperse and one is currently wintering in Hampshire! The RSPB has begun a 5-year project in eastern Scotland, with more young birds being brought over from Norway.

A recent project to begin releases in East Anglia, initially along the Norfolk coast near Brancaster, has been halted, officially due to shortage of funds, but perhaps partly due to bad press and local resistance from farming interests.
Overall, the sea eagle programme has been a resounding success. The eagles released on the Isle of Mull in Scotland have proved a major tourist draw for the island, which receives around 350,000 visitors every year, of whom two-thirds spend their holidays in Mull and 33 per cent are day-trippers spending £38

million in total. Of this, between £1.4-1.6 million per year is attracted by the presence of sea eagles.

The project illustrates the nature of a necessary long term commitment and continued releases over a decade to reach the critical threshold for a slow-breeding top predator.

The golden eagle

Scotland has a relatively stable population of golden eagles – and a significant proportion of the European population of this holarctic species. It would appear another iconic candidate for re-introduction to England, but no attempts have been made. A single pair has attempted breeding several times in the Lake District with a few years of successes and many failures. It may well be the case that prey species and carrion are not abundant enough in the English fells. In contrast, golden eagles were returned to Ireland by taking young birds from Scotland to Glenveigh in Donegal in 2001 and by 2007, there were eight territories and two chicks. This programme was supported by the EU Life fund and many Irish charities and agencies. The Glenveigh National Park has a healthy population of Irish hare and the eagles also feed on fox and badger cubs.

The red kite

Although this species had a recovering population of Welsh birds that had hovered on the brink of extinction and were nursed back by diligent nest-protection under the auspices of the RSPB, the birds had yet to colonise their former haunts in England or Scotland. Reintroductions began in 1989 in the Chilterns, bringing chicks from Spain and Sweden and by 2002 there were 140 pairs in the hills of the Home Counties. Another eight release sites from Devon to Northumberland have seen the English population rise to over 300 pairs, with 200 pairs now breeding in Wales. Scottish releases centred in Inverness and Galloway have been very successful, with the Scottish population at 160 pairs raising nearly 300 young birds in 2010 – a rise of about 10% on the previous year. In 2011, a release programme began in Northern Ireland.

The osprey

Ospreys had been similarly eradicated by Victorian obsessives but recolonised Scotland from Scandinavia in the early 1950s. A diligent programme of nest protection (from egg thieves) by the RSPB saw the Scottish population steadily rise to over 200 pairs by 2010. As this raptor is migratory, young birds began long stays on Welsh estuaries, in the Lake District and Rutland and Kielder reservoirs and this prompted the erection of artificial nest sites leading to the first rearing of English and Welsh chicks.

The great bustard

This large game bird – perhaps the heaviest flying bird, died out on the central plains of England toward the end of the 19th century, and a brief attempt at reintroduction failed. A ten year programme began in 2003, spearheaded by a consortium of interests – the Great Bustard Group, consisting of the RSPB, Natural England and Bath University. In cooperation with the Russian Academy of Sciences, eggs taken from nests endangered by farming in the Trans Volga steppe region of Saratova are first hatched and the chicks transferred to rearing facilities at the Salisbury Plain reintroduction site. The object was to release about 100 birds and to have a breeding population by 2015 – and the first British-born chicks arrived in 2010. The target is 20 breeding pairs by 2030. The project has just been awarded £2.2m of EU Life funding over three years (ed. note: see Alistair Dawes article that dates from 2006).

Great bustard display (Great Bustard Project)

Prospects for this programme are better than might be expected as the source population have adapted to cropland in their home range and seem to prefer it to remnants of the original grassy steppe vegetation. The main threat will be high predation pressure on vulnerable chicks from Britain's high density of foxes.

The species is very shy and it remains to be seen whether it could extend further than the relatively unpopulated land used for military training.

The crane

Another ancient denizen of Britain, well-featured in folklore, has received the helping hand of restoration. It had already begun a slow process of natural colonisation in the fens of East Anglia over the last two decades, but the population remained at about 6 breeding pairs, with about 40 over-wintering adults. The Great Crane Project was set up to establish another population in England, with the Somerset Levels the chosen site. This project is a joint initiative of the RSPB, the WWT and the Pensthorpe Conservation Trust together with interest and funding from the Viridor landfill credits scheme.

Young cranes on the Somerset Levels (Great Crane Project)

Eggs were taken to the Wildfowl and Wetlands Trust at Slimbridge and hatched with the chicks then reared by humans in baggy non-human costumes with dummy crane beaks for delivering food! The first young birds were released in the autumn of 2010 at a site on the Levels. The source population of 350 pairs is in the 130,000ha Schorfheide-Chorin biosphere reserve in eastern Germany.

The goshawk and eagle owl

I bracket these two raptors together as they are classic examples of inadvertent, surreptitious, quasi-legal and accidental re-introductions. The goshawk suffered

478

extermination at the hands of Victorian game-keepers, as it is a powerful predator of reared game birds such as pheasant. The eagle owl existed only in the post-glacial fossil record and if it did survive into medieval times, as we now know the lynx did, as with that animal, it did not impinge upon the national folklore.

The goshawk began breeding in central England sometime after the war and doubtless as a result of falconry escapes. Some of these may have been deliberate, but inadvertent losses of hunting birds are common and this hawk is a favourite of the dedicated falconer. There are now over 400 pairs in England. Scotland and Wales and all of various origins with a mix of sub-species from North America, Scandinavia and Central Europe.

The eagle owl has been observed on numerous occasions since the mid 1800s, but all birds have been assumed escapees, as it is a popular zoo animal and is held in private collections. It breeds well in captivity and is readily sold on to devotees who may not have appropriate training or facilities. The RSPB has data showing that in the ten years to 2007, 123 birds were recorded as escapees, with 73 not recovered; there were 440 voluntarily registered in captivity and over 3000 sold on (a certificate of origin is required by law, but there are no other requirements of ownership). That is not to say that some of the sightings may have been of birds crossing from Scandinavia – another owl species, the long-eared, may be able to make this crossing during winter dispersal, as this forest-dweller is regularly encountered on the headlands of the NE coast.

Whatever their origins, at some time during the last decade, several pairs of eagle owls established a breeding population in a remote upland area of Northumberland. This was not welcome news to the RSPB who were concerned for their small breeding population of English hen harriers – a ground nesting raptor, as eagle owls are known to prey upon other raptors up to the size of buzzard. . A pair of owls that established themselves in the Forest of Bowland were recently seen to take a hen harrier on its nest. There were initial questions of capturing and returning the birds to captivity, despite the outside chance they were indeed colonisers from Scandinavia! However, a government sponsored consultation process came to a view that they should be monitored and action taken only if they became a problem for other conservation priorities and this view was endorsed by the RSPB late in 2010.

Eagle owl (Peter Cairns/ Northshots)

This species has been imported and kept in captivity in Britain for over a hundred years and birds have come from many parts of its range in Eurasia and even North Africa. Sub-species vary in size, from small pale desert races to larger dark-plumaged Siberian forms. It is a bird of wild forests, deserts and crags and highly susceptible to disturbance.

I did once have the pleasure of watching an escaped bird that haunted the local churchyard and rooftops of Glastonbury High Street. It was a magnificent sight and much loved by the more switched-on members of the community. However, others were concerned for their small pet dogs and cats – not that there was any evidence the owl was a danger and it must have found adequate rats and mice, and it was eventually trapped and sent back to prison. In contrast, an incident reported in the Forester and on local TV in a Coleford quarry concerned a very tame eagle owl that apparently brought presents of mice and sundry furry animals to the quarry workers' tea hut - it was seen to be shot by vandals with an air-rifle nd thought to have died, after which the workers left flowers at its favourite perch, only to be later found alive and is now recuperating at a local birds of prey centre.

Issues and lessons

This rather successful history of re-instating large birds, including predators that engender some opposition, is an object lesson for mammalian projects. Firstly, the projects encompass not only exterminated species, but also those re-colonising of their own accord but deemed in need of a helping hand. If we consider the history of mammals, then this would include not just wolves, bears, lynx, moose, beaver, boar and reconstituted wild cattle, but also extending a hand to pine marten, polecat, and wildcat as well as the less problematic water vole.

The example of goshawk is of note from a provenance point of view: the population is made up of genetically diverse races, some quite distinct in appearance – North American birds are large and pale grey, where their European cousins are smaller and browner. From a genetic point of view, the larger the gene-pool, the more resilient and adaptable the population is likely to be. In the case of the legal introduction of red kites, again, birds were of mixed origin and it is seldom noted that the Welsh population, having been isolated from its European cousins, had begun to evolve a distinctive whiter head. Much is made of genetic sub-specific status in mammals – for example, the Amur leopard pedigree is jealously guarded in zoological collections to maintain the sub-species, despite that population being on the verge of extinction compared to the relative success of other more adaptable leopard populations. Likewise, much has been made about the origin of the Tayside beavers (with SNH branding it the 'wrong' subspecies - see Derek Gow's article in ECOS 31 (3/4), and of the genetic purity of wild boar, remnant Scottish wildcat and the Exmoor wild horse.

The issue of aliens has arisen with the eagle owl – despite the presence here of its tiny family member – the little owl, never native and introduced by the Victorians. There is an argument for pragmatism. The natural environment of Britain is far from original, even in its wildest examples in the glens of Scotland. Who is to say what constitutes the best genetic mix for an adaptable and successful repopulation, especially as the climate is changing (natural and otherwise)?

The success of the early 'suck it and see' programmes is also an argument against 'red tape' and the inevitable high cost of official project infrastructure, particularly the propensity for high-tech monitoring with GPS-satellite, and radio aerials in addition to the obligatory wing-tags and leg-rings. These iconic species are symbols of the wild, but I cannot help feel something is lost when birds are encumbered with radio aerials and wing tags. I understand that these are a feature only of the beginning of a programme and a valuable research tool with regard to dispersal. But it can be overdone and despite Ospreys becoming well-established, they continue to be tracked.

In Wales, kites have become a branding emblem and tourist draw, but not as remote dwellers of the fells, rather with many hundreds congregating at public kite-watching facilities, where they are fed offal and religiously watched for their ring colours and origins. The RSPB has osprey and eagle nests wired with video links to the watchers hides which are a powerful tourist draw. In Galloway they estimate over £20 million has been brought to the local economy from kite-watching since 2004 and the sea eagles have equivalent benefits on the economy of Mull.

Conservationists have long argued for the economic benefits of rewilding to be considered in strategies that involve future lynx, beaver and possibly wolf, but without care, wildlife conservation organisations can morph into tour operators and merchandisers with visitor centres, increased car-based tourism and interpretation facilities that are far removed from a wild experience and contact with real nature.

When I saw my first red kite gliding over the M4 near High Wycombe, it brought little excitement – not like my first encounter as a boy on the high moors above Llandovery, in the days when the red kite was a symbol of wildness. I am excited by eagle owls in a remote corner of Northumberland and the mystery of their origins – legal or otherwise, less so by the fledgling cranes just down the road, with their numbered wing tags and radio antennae – not because I do not welcome them back, but because I had been awaiting the first really wild unaided arrivals from Norfolk.

In this part of the world conservation priorities have focussed upon habitat recreation – rewilding the hydrologically challenged Levels with artificial reedbeds aimed squarely at one species – the BAP priority bittern, and yet this has brought six great white egrets to overwinter, cattle egrets have bred, and last year, little bitterns arrived to breed unexpectedly – having bred only once before in Britain. The habitat has increased diversity in the heron and egret family and who knows what might be next? But overall, the feeling remains that the helping hand removes an element of chance and mystery. And my ever present eye on conservation's corporate interest notes the large funds to be had for giving nature that helping hand. It is just a cautionary note – to make the research and monitoring phase as short as necessary and the watcher facilities as small and unobtrusive as possible, lest the object of iconic true wildness be lost.

Details of many of these programmes can be found at www.rspb.org.uk and for the bustard project; damonbridges@rspb.org.uk; see also www.the greatcraneproject.org.uk

Good news from the Plain - the reintroduction of Great Bustards to the UK

ECOS 27 (1) 41-48 (2006)

Reintroducing Great Bustards on Salisbury Plain is helping a globally threatened bird and enriching the chalk grassland habitat.

ALASDAIR DAWES

The Great Bustard *Otis tarda* is the world's heaviest flying bird with old male birds regularly reported weighing as much as 20 kg. However, it is only the males that attain such huge proportions outgrowing females by up to 50 %, to stand over a metre tall with a wing-span of 260 cm. They are highly gregarious birds that form social units termed 'droves' although males and females will often group into separate droves. Their great difference in size (sexual dimorphism) means that females are easily bullied, especially when feeding. As a result, males and females tend to live very independently only coming together at breeding time. The incubation and rearing of chicks is carried out by the female alone and the young birds will stay with the females for at least the first winter.

The Great Bustard is recognised as being a Globally Threatened Bird[1] and is consequently listed as Vulnerable by IUCN.[2] Formerly widespread throughout Europe, many populations of Great Bustards have become fragmented and disappeared since they hit their all-time low in the 19th and 20th centuries. In the past most English counties supported Great Bustards but the last confirmed breeding in the UK was 1832, in Suffolk. Although Great Bustards were certainly caught for food in historical times, their demise in most countries was due to relentless persecution in the form of hunting. The current global population of Great Bustards is thought to be fairly stable with some populations possibly even increasing. What is cause for concern is the continual loss of suitable habitat due to change of land use, general human disturbance and agricultural intensification. Globally, there is still a gradual but noticeable contraction in their range so that in many regions the populations are becoming denser in an ever smaller area. There are obvious problems that lie ahead for seriously fragmented populations and great potential for catastrophe if all your Bustards are 'kept in one basket'. Consequently, several conservation projects have been set up throughout Europe working to secure and manage protected areas and revert areas to natural grasslands. There are projects in Germany and Hungary releasing captive-reared birds to reinforce existing, small and previously declining populations. The UK project is unique because it is the first and only project to expand the global range of the species by reintroducing them to an area from which they have become extinct.

Great bustard ready to transmit (Great Bustard Project)

The reintroduction project – its planning and delivery

The formation of a Great Bustard Group was proposed in 1997 under 'any other business' at the final meeting of the Great Bustard Trust, a registered charity that had been set up by the Honourable Aylmer Tryon in 1970. The Trust was largely concerned with captive breeding Great Bustards at Porton Down in Wiltshire, with an aim of one day releasing captive-bred chicks. Unfortunately, no-one has ever managed to get Great Bustards to breed successfully in captivity and the Trust proved no exception to this trend. The original stock that had been captured in Portugal for the project eventually lived out their days in the care of Whipsnade Zoo. This project is often misinterpreted and cited as being an unsuccessful attempt to reintroduce Great Bustards to the UK when in actual fact no Bustards were ever released into the wild.

The Great Bustard Group became a registered charity in 2002 with David Waters appointed as Director. The Group is dedicated to the interests of the Great Bustard and aims to establish a self-sustaining population of Great

484

Bustards in the UK by carrying out a series of yearly releases of young birds for 10 years in the same location.

The Group had been made aware that in Saratov, an area in the south of the Russian Federation, hundreds of Great Bustard nests in arable fields were being abandoned or destroyed as a result of intensive agricultural activity. The Russian government had been collecting the eggs from doomed nests to supply stock for what ultimately proved unsuccessful captive breeding projects across the Former Soviet Union. The Group proposed that the eggs from these nests should be collected, incubated and reared in captivity in Russia and the chicks released back into the wild. The releases would help boost the existing donor population which is actually considered stable or possibly increasing whilst a more sustainable agricultural program was developed. It was considered that enough eggs would be collected to also support an introduction of Great Bustards to an entirely new location. In 2003, the Group were successful in application to Defra for a trial licence to release up to 40 Great Bustards a year for ten consecutive years on Salisbury Plain. The Plain is the largest known expanse of unimproved chalk downland in north-west Europe, and represents 41% of Britain's remaining area of this rich wildlife habitat. It can almost be thought of as the British steppes[3] and has the potential to provide ideal habitat for Great Bustards.

The successful application was based on a feasibility study that took several years to compile. The study was comprehensive and included cultural aspects as well as ecological and considerable academic investigations. The scientist given the contract to write the study and application demonstrated that the project would not be detrimental to the donor population or to the existing ecosystem that was to receive the Great Bustards.

The birds arrive

August 2004 saw the first batch of Great Bustards arrive from Russia. They were brought to Salisbury Plain aged approximately 6 weeks old and spent 30 days in quarantine. During quarantine they were given all the necessary health checks and on the day of release were fitted with numbered wing-tags that display a unique number and are colour coded according to the year of release (yellow = 2004, orange = 2005, green will be 2006). Unsightly as they may be, the tags are essential for the project. They enable each Bustard to be identified individually. This enables the Group to keep accurate records of the movements and behaviour of each Bustard released. About three quarters of the birds are also fitted with radio transmitters which aid their tracking after release. A common method of attachment for radio and GPS satellite transmitters was used which utilises straps around the body so that they are worn like a back-pack.

The first Bustards were finally ready for release in early September and were taken from quarantine and put into a larger, fully enclosed compound. The purpose of this pen was to give the Bustards more space than quarantine allowed, where they could exercise and acclimatise to the wider environment free from the potential dangers of predation. In reality the pens proved to be a problem with many of the birds exercising so well that they were taking off and hitting the roof netting which catapulted the birds back to the ground. Several birds suffered injuries and it was decided to let the birds go directly into the final 'release pen'.

The release

Twenty-two Great Bustards were let loose in the release pen. The pen had been sown with various crops that are known favourites of Great Bustards and once in this pen the Bustards ceased to be fed and had no more human contact. There is no roof on the pen, although it is fox-proof, so it is up to the Bustards how long they wish to stay in it. Sadly, the Bustards suffered further problems flying out and around the release pen with some of them colliding with the very fence that had been erected to protect them. The wind picked up soon after release and the birds seemed to be suffering with the harnesses used to attach the radio transmitters. The harnesses were restricting the Bustards ability to fly so they were removed from all injured birds that had been taken in. Several birds suffered mortal injuries whilst others were left permanently disabled. Two birds dislocated beaks and sprained limbs so had their flight feathers clipped to enable them to recover in the safety of the pen. They remained in the pen until October 2005, when their flight feathers had grown back and they were finally able to fly free. Although they made a full physical recovery they were not terribly wise to the world and tragically succumbed to foxes about a month later.

The attachment and type of radio transmitters were therefore changed in the second year. The new transmitters are much smaller and are glued to the tail feathers rather than tied around the body. They obviously only stay on the bird as long as the tail feather does, which in Great Bustards is about 12 months. This gives the project long enough to track the birds and follow their movements through their first year and also recover any of those that die for post mortem. The release procedure also changed in the second year and in September 2005, 32 new Bustards went straight from quarantine to the release pen. The behaviour of these birds was noticeably different to those of the previous year. The new birds soon left the pen and formed a single flock that lived on the hills surrounding the release site. The flock regularly interacted with the previous year's birds that were still around the site. They were flying spectacularly well and regularly flew around the Plain, thrilling visitors to the site. Thankfully, they were so capable at flying that there were no collisions with the pen fence.

Predation, mortality and disturbance

The natural mortality of Great Bustards in the wild is high at around 80 % dying within their first year. Great Bustards are ground-dwelling birds, lacking the ability to perch, making them particularly susceptible to predation when feeding, nesting and roosting. The most critical time for young birds is when they are still in the eggs. The chicks are nidifugous, meaning they are capable of looking after themselves soon after hatching and able to leave the nest site. Upon hatching their long muscular legs are well developed and enable them to run quickly. This affords some protection from predation but this is nonetheless a treacherous time. The lucky 20 % to make it through the first year usually live on for another 15 or 20 years. They grow incredibly quickly and by six months are approximately three-quarters full size. Predators of the eggs and small chicks are numerous but as the birds grow, the number of predators reduces to typically include foxes and where they occur, wolves and large raptors such as White-Tailed Eagle. Full grown adults, especially those in groups, are normally capable of either seeing off, or fleeing safely from these predators. In the UK, the only predator of the released Bustards is foxes, and the smaller females are particularly vulnerable. However, the project notices a sudden reduction in the number of Bustards predated after the age of about six months.

A large, healthy population of Great Bustards in the UK should withstand normal levels of predation and the odd collision but in the early days of the project each death is a significant loss. Although the birds tend to stay as one flock, individuals and smaller groups do splinter off making them much more susceptible to predation. To reduce the risk of flocks separating the Great Bustard Group discourages the general public from looking for these very wary and shy birds. Instead, visitors are welcome to view the Bustards at the release site but only on guided tours at certain times of the year. The release site is on private property and adjoins the Ministry of Defence's (MoD) Salisbury Plain Training Area's Danger Area. The lack of public right of ways is also beneficial as the Bustards suffer little disturbance from ramblers or dog-walkers. Bustards will tolerate a certain amount of disturbance but whilst the project has such small numbers of birds, it cannot afford for the small flocks to be flushed and fragment especially if it results in singled birds.

Dispersal

Released Great Bustards can be very capable at living on their own. This has been demonstrated by several birds from the first year of releases but perhaps most dramatically by birds from the second year. In October 2005, a female that had not been seen since the day of release turned up spectacularly almost 100 km from the release site. Despite complete astonishment, the Warden of the Portland Bill Bird Observatory managed to photograph a Great Bustard flying around the Bill. It was only later, when the photos were enlarged on the computer, that the wing tag was clearly visible and it was realised the bird was from the project. This bird demonstrated that not only can Great Bustards find a place to live in the UK countryside without being noticed or disturbed but also that captive-reared birds can learn to feed and fend for themselves, managing to attain sufficient condition to fly considerable distances.

Dispersal from the release site was always anticipated. Most populations of Great Bustards undergo predictable movements between summer and wintering grounds and show high site fidelity. They are not generally thought of as migratory because the distances that different populations move vary enormously from 30 km up to 1,000 km. The population of Great Bustards in Saratov are known to fly to the Ukraine in winter but depend on severe winter conditions in Saratov to prompt their departure. If conditions remain mild then most Bustards stay around Saratov rather than fly the 1,000 km.

There were three noticeable departures from the Project site in December 2005 and the distances flown fit well within the known dispersal range of Great Bustards. The furthest that we know a Bustard from the project to have flown is over 900 km to south of Toulouse. Females are known to disperse further than males and all three birds that made it to France were female. A more typical distance seemed to be about 80 km south-west with several groups wintering in Dorset. Some Bustards moved very little and remained around the Plain but the larger dispersal distances threw up problems with keeping track of the birds. The VHF radio transmitters in use by the project only give a line-of-sight range, which on the ground typically equates to around 5 km. Thankfully sightings by the general public were numerous and enthusiastically reported. There has been some discussion as to whether the Group should use satellite transmitters to relay exact locations of the birds. However, the Group have major concerns not just about the price but also the method of attachment. Trials are currently underway which already suggest it might be more economically sensible to fund aerial surveys from light aircraft using the existing transmitters because the line-of-site reception increases to about 40 km.

Is the reintroduction a success?

The true measure of success of the project will be a self sustaining population of Great Bustards that requires no human intervention and minimal management but in order to reach this point there are many fences to cross. Bustards are notoriously difficult to observe, especially when incubating and rearing chicks. So locating and monitoring nesting females will bring with it a new suite of problems. Male Great Bustards are typically about five years old before they start to breed which would mean that the first breeding in the UK released birds in not to be expected before summer 2009. It is thought that 20-30 birds will be enough to start a population.

The first year of release saw major problems with the transmitter straps causing the birds to collide. The Group often wonder how many birds there would be now if those transmitters had not been used. Having acted on the lessons learned in year one, the project has been encouraged by the behaviour of the birds released in the second year. A significant milestone for the project was the recent return of two birds to the release site that had spent 10 weeks wintering 80 km away on a farm in Dorset. Spring 2006 is an anxious time and all fingers are crossed that other Bustards find their way back.

Great Bustards and the benefits to other wildlife

Habitat management undertaken directly for the Great Bustard is mainly confined to the release pen. Approximately one third of the pen was sown with a feed mix for the Bustards and another sown with an alfalfa (Lucerne *Medicago sativa*) and pollen and nectar mix. Lucerne is a known favourite of Great Bustards on the continent and the mix attracts insects in the spring and summer. The remainder of the pen is grass that has been left to grow rank, providing good cover for the Bustards and is ideal habitat for small mammals. Outside the pen, several game strips have also been planted nearby and there are numerous fields in the vicinity with crops favoured by Bustards. In winter, Great Bustards will often seek out winter arable crops, in particular Oil Seed Rape *Brassica napus* moving onto set-aside and natural grasslands in the summer. Great Bustards are mainly vegetarian, eating young shoots, leaves and seeds year round but also take invertebrates and small vertebrates in the summer months. The management of the pen for the Bustards has helped to increase the number of birds locally and benefited several species in particular. Some 11 species (7 with Biodiversity Action Plan status) of farmland birds of Red List Conservation Concern[4] are highly associated with the pen when breeding, foraging or wintering. These include Corn Bunting *Miliaria calandra*, Grey Partridge *Perdix perdix*, Hen Harrier *Circus cyanus*, Linnet *Carduelis cannabina*, Skylark *Alauda arvensis* and Yellowhammer *Emberiza citrinella*.

Although management of Salisbury Plain for nature conservation has lapsed and occasionally been in conflict with military training in the past it is now being managed sympathetically by Defence Estates (an agency of the MoD), with the help of the recent EU-Life project, restoring and maintaining this internationally important grassland.

A successful regional agri-environment scheme boosted by the Life project targets Stone Curlews *Burhinus oedicnemus* and also appears to benefit Great Bustards. Stone Curlew Plots are ploughed each year before March and remain bare for the arrival of this migratory species. The Curlews lay their eggs on the bare ground and the plot grows weedy throughout the summer providing cover and food for the chicks. When the Curlews have fledged the plots find a new role providing ideal cover and food for the newly released Bustards. Several nearby plots are regularly used by the Bustards in the autumn and consequently it is hoped that the Group can develop an agri-environment scheme with similar prescriptions to the Curlew plots that will no doubt benefit both species.

Funding and support

Funding the project has proved the biggest challenge for the Group. A major obstacle is the fact that the Great Bustard is considered an alien species by the Wildlife and Countryside Act 1981 (as amended). This means a complicated licence procedure is required to release the Bustardsa and the Great Bustard is not eligible for Biodiversity Action Plan (BAP) status because it is an alien species. Most conservation funding organisations have adopted the BAP status as their criteria for eligibility which means that most avenues of funding the reintroduction are not open to the Group. So far the project has relied heavily on an EU and Defra rural grant programme called Sustain the Plain and various Landfill Tax Credit grants. The Great Bustard Group is a membership organisation that generates some of its own income by charging a membership fee and charging visitors who come to see the project and the birds. It has developed a wide range of high quality merchandise which is ever expanding and the sale of these items also provides a valuable and sustainable income.

The Great Bustard reintroduction project is proving to be hugely popular on a local, national and international level. Media interest helps raise awareness of the many global issues that are affecting Great Bustards. It also acts as free advertising for any organisation or individual that supports the project which in turn helps to attract further funding. The project enjoys a uniquely high media profile amongst UK single-species conservation projects. To date, the project has been the subject of over 150 newspaper and magazine articles and is regularly featured on national and regional TV and radio.

Education, interest and pride

The immense charisma of the Great Bustard and the story of its demise combine to produce a powerful educational tool. Each year, over 2,000 people from all over the country visit the release site on guided tours and about 200 presentations are made to organisations ranging from schools and youth groups to conservation groups and pensioner clubs. Groups that come to the project vary from dedicated ornithologists to local residents curious about the project. Salisbury Plain was formerly a major stronghold of Great Bustards in the UK and it has a left a large imprint on the local culture. Support for the project has been enormous from local residents and farmers who all want to see their county bird make a comeback. There also is a sense of pride in having a high profile international conservation project working with a globally threatened species on their doorstep.

References

1. BirdLife International (2005) – BirdLife's online World Bird Database: the site for bird conservation. Version 2.0. Cambridge, UK: BirdLife International. www.birdlife.org

2. BirdLife International (2004). Otis tarda. In: IUCN 2004. 2004 IUCN Red List of Threatened Species. www.iucnredlist.org. Downloaded February 2006

3. Toynton, P., Ash, D. (2002) – Salisbury Plain Training Area – the British steppes? British Wildlife 13:5 p335-343

4. Gregory, R.D. et al (2002) – The population status of birds in the United Kingdom, Channel Islands and Isle of Man: an analysis of conservation concern 2002-2007. British Birds 95 410-450

Lightning Source UK Ltd.
Milton Keynes UK
UKOW06n0558250515

252225UK00009B/116/P